MERCURY READER

a custom publication

College Reading and Writing
Boston University
CAS Writing Program

Pearson Custom Publishing

New York   Boston   San Francisco
London   Toronto   Sydney   Tokyo   Singapore   Madrid
Mexico City   Munich   Paris   Cape Town   Hong Kong   Montreal

Senior Vice President, Editorial and Marketing: Patrick F. Boles
Senior Sponsoring Editor: Natalie Danner
Development Editors: Mary Kate Paris and Katherine R. Gehan
Editorial Assistant: Jill Johnson
Operations Manager: Eric M. Kenney
Database Product Manager: Jennifer Berry
Rights Manager: Katie Huha
Art Director: Renée Sartell
Cover Designers: Renée Sartell and Sharon Treacy

Cover Art: "Gigantia Mountains & Sea of Cortes," by R.G.K. Photography, Copyright © Tony Stone Images; "Dime," courtesy of the Shaw Collection.

Please visit our websites at *www.pearsoncustom.com* and *www.mercuryreader.com.*

Attention bookstores: For permission to return any unsold stock, contact us at *pe-uscustomreturns@pearson.com.*

**Pearson
Custom Publishing**
is a division of

www.pearsonhighered.com

ISBN 10: 0-558-06167-2
ISBN 13: 978-0-558-06167-8

Contents

Critical Reading and Critique

Critical Reading

When writing papers in college, you are often called on to respond critically to source materials. Critical reading requires the abilities to both summarize and evaluate a presentation. A *summary* is a brief restatement in your own words of the content of a passage. An *evaluation,* however, is a more difficult matter.

In your college work, you read to gain and *use* new information; but as sources are not equally valid or equally useful, you must learn to distinguish critically among them by evaluating them.

There is no ready-made formula for determining validity. Critical reading and its written equivalent—the *critique*—require discernment, sensitivity, imagination, knowledge of the subject, and above all, willingness to become involved in what you read. These skills cannot be taken for granted and are developed only through repeated practice. You must begin somewhere, though, and we recommend that you start by posing two broad categories of questions about passages, articles, and books that you read: (1) What is the author's purpose in writing? Does he or she succeed in this purpose? (2) To what extent do you agree with the author?

Question Category 1: What Is the Author's Purpose in Writing? Does the Author Succeed in This Purpose?

All critical reading *begins with an accurate summary.* Thus before attempting an evaluation, you must be able to locate an author's thesis and identify the selection's content and structure. You must understand the author's *purpose.* Authors write to inform, to persuade, and to entertain. A given piece may be primarily *informative* (a summary of the research on cloning), primarily *persuasive* (an argument on why the government must do something to alleviate homelessness), or primarily *entertaining* (a play about the frustrations of young lovers). Or it may be all three (as in John Steinbeck's novel

Reprinted from *Writing and Reading Across the Curriculum* (2007), by permission of Pearson Education.

The Grapes of Wrath, which revolves around migrant workers during the Great Depression). Sometimes, authors are not fully conscious of their purpose. Sometimes their purpose changes as they write. Also, more than one purpose can overlap: An essay may need to inform the reader about an issue in order to make a persuasive point. But if the finished piece is coherent, it will have a primary reason for having been written, and it should be apparent that the author is attempting primarily to inform, persuade, or entertain a particular audience. To identify this primary reason—this purpose—is your first job as a critical reader. Your next job is to determine how successful the author has been. As a critical reader, you bring different criteria, or standards of judgment, to bear when you read pieces intended to inform, persuade, or entertain.

WHERE DO WE FIND WRITTEN CRITIQUES?

Here are a few types of writing that involve critique:

Academic Writing

- **Research papers.** Critique sources in order to establish their usefulness.
- **Position papers.** Stake out a position by critiquing other positions.
- **Book reviews.** Combine summary with critique.
- **Essay exams.** Demonstrate understanding of course material by critiquing it.

Workplace Writing

- **Legal briefs and legal arguments.** Critique previous rulings or arguments made by opposing counsel.
- **Business plans and proposals.** Critique other, less cost-effective approaches.
- **Policy briefs.** Communicate failings of policies and legislation through critique.

Writing to Inform

5   A piece intended to inform will provide definitions, describe or report on a process, recount a story, give historical background, and/or pro-   5

vide facts and figures. An informational piece responds to questions such as the following:

What (or who) is _____?
How does _____ work?
What is the controversy or problem about?
What happened?
How and why did it happen?
What were the results?
What are the arguments for and against_____?

To the extent that an author answers these and related questions and the answers are a matter of verifiable record (you could check for accuracy if you had the time and inclination), the selection is intended to inform. Having determined this, you can organize your response by considering three other criteria: accuracy, significance, and fair interpretation of information.

Evaluating Informative Writing

Accuracy of Information. If you are going to use any of the information presented, you must be satisfied that it is trustworthy. One of your responsibilities as a critical reader, then, is to find out if it is accurate. This means you should check facts against other sources. Government publications are often good resources for verifying facts about political legislation, population data, crime statistics, and the like. You can also search key terms in library databases and on the Web. Since material on the Web is essentially "self-published," however, you must be especially vigilant in assessing its legitimacy. A wealth of useful information is now available on the Internet—but there is also a tremendous amount of misinformation, distorted "facts," and unsupported opinion.

Significance of Information. One useful question that you can ask about a reading is "So what?" In the case of selections that attempt to inform, you may reasonably wonder whether the information makes a difference. What can the person who is reading gain from this information? How is knowledge advanced by the publication of this material? Is the information of importance to you or to others in a particular audience? Why or why not?

Fair Interpretation of Information. At times you will read reports, the sole function of which is to relate raw data or information. In these cases, you will build your response on two questions: "What is the author's purpose in writing? Does she or he succeed in this purpose?" More frequently, once an author has presented information, he or she will attempt to evaluate or interpret it—which is only reasonable, since information that has not been evaluated or interpreted is of little use. One of your tasks as a critical reader is to make a distinction between the author's presentation of facts and figures and his or her attempts to evaluate them. Watch for shifts from straightforward descriptions of factual information ("20 percent of the population") to assertions about what this information means ("*a mere* 20 percent of the population"), what its implications are, and so on. Pay attention to whether the logic with which the author connects interpretation with facts is sound. You may find that the information is valuable but the interpretation is not. Perhaps the author's conclusions are not justified. Could you offer a contrary explanation for the same facts? Does more information need to be gathered before firm conclusions can be drawn? Why?

Writing to Persuade

10 Writing is frequently intended to persuade—that is, to influence the 10 reader's thinking. To make a persuasive case, the writer must begin with an assertion that is arguable, some statement about which reasonable people could disagree. Such an assertion, when it serves as the essential organizing principle of the article or book, is called a *thesis*. Here are two examples:

> Because they do not speak English, many children in this affluent land are being denied their fundamental right to equal educational opportunity.

> Bilingual education, which has been stridently promoted by a small group of activists with their own agenda, is detrimental to the very students it is supposed to serve.

Thesis statements such as these—and the subsequent assertions used to help support them—represent conclusions that authors have drawn as a result of researching and thinking about an issue. You go through the same process yourself when you write persuasive papers or critiques. And just as you are entitled to critically evaluate the assertions of authors you read, so your professors—and other students—are entitled to evaluate *your* assertions, whether they be encountered as written arguments or as comments made in class discussion.

Keep in mind that writers organize arguments by arranging evidence to support one conclusion and oppose (or dismiss) another. You can assess the validity of the argument and the conclusion by determining whether the author has (1) clearly defined key terms, (2) used information fairly, (3) argued logically and not fallaciously.

Summary

What Is a Summary?

The best way to demonstrate that you understand the information and the ideas in any piece of writing is to compose an accurate and clearly written summary of that piece. By a *summary* we mean a *brief restatement, in your own words, of the content of a passage* (a group of paragraphs, a chapter, an article, a book). This restatement should focus on the *central idea* of the passage. The briefest of all summaries (one or two sentences) will do no more than this. A longer, more complete summary will indicate, in condensed form, the main points in the passage that support or explain the central idea. It will reflect the order in which these points are presented and the emphasis given to them. It may even include some important examples from the passage. But it will not include minor details. It will not repeat points simply for the purpose of emphasis. And it will not contain any of your own opinions or conclusions. A good summary, therefore, has three central qualities: *brevity, completeness,* and *objectivity.*

Can a Summary be Objective?

Of course, the last quality mentioned above, objectivity, might be difficult to achieve in a summary. By definition, writing a summary requires you to select some aspects of the original and leave out others. Since deciding what to select and what to leave out calls for your personal judgment, your summary really is a work of interpretation. And, certainly, your interpretation of a passage may differ from another person's. One factor affecting the nature and quality of your interpretation is your *prior knowledge* of the subject. For example, if you're attempting to summarize an anthropological article and you're a novice in that field, then your summary of the article will likely differ from that of your professor, who has spent twenty years studying this particular area and whose judgment about what is more or less significant is

Reprinted from *Writing and Reading Across the Curriculum* (2007), by permission of Pearson Education.

undoubtedly more reliable than your own. By the same token, your personal or professional *frame of reference* may also affect your interpretation. A union representative and a management representative attempting to summarize the latest management offer would probably come up with two very different accounts. Still, we believe that in most cases it's possible to produce a reasonably objective summary of a passage if you make a conscious, good-faith effort to be unbiased and to prevent your own feelings on the subject from distorting your account of the text.

Using the Summary

In some quarters, the summary has a bad reputation—and with reason. Summaries often are provided by writers as substitutes for analyses. As students, many of us have summarized books that we were supposed to *review critically*. All the same, the summary does have a place in respectable college work. First, writing a summary is an excellent way to understand what you read. This in itself is an important goal of academic study. If you don't understand your source material, chances are you won't be able to refer to it usefully in an essay or research paper. Summaries help you understand what you read because they force you to put the text into your own words. Practice with writing summaries also develops your general writing habits, since a good summary, like any other piece of good writing, is clear, coherent, and accurate.

Second, summaries are useful to your readers. Let's say you're writing a paper about the McCarthy era in the United States, and in part of that paper you want to discuss Arthur Miller's *The Crucible* as a dramatic treatment of the subject. A summary of the plot would be helpful to a reader who hasn't seen or read—or who doesn't remember—the play. Or perhaps you're writing a paper about the politics of recent humanitarian aid missions. If your reader isn't likely to be familiar with such groups as Doctors Without Borders, it would be a good idea to summarize the objectives and activities of such organizations at some early point in the paper. In many cases (an exam, for instance), you can use a summary to demonstrate your knowledge of what your professor already knows; when writing a paper, you can use a summary to inform your professor about some relatively unfamiliar source.

5   Third, summaries are required frequently in college-level writing.   5
For example, on a psychology midterm, you may be asked to explain Carl Jung's theory of the collective unconscious and to show how it

differs from Sigmund Freud's theory of the personal unconscious. You may have read about this theory in your textbook or in a supplementary article, or your instructor may have outlined it in his or her lecture. You can best demonstrate your understanding of Jung's theory by summarizing it. Then you'll proceed to contrast it with Freud's theory—which, of course, you must also summarize.

WHERE DO WE FIND WRITTEN SUMMARIES?

Here are a few types of writing that involve summary:

Academic Writing

- **Critique papers.** Summarize material in order to critique it.
- **Synthesis papers.** Summarize to show relationships between sources.
- **Analysis papers.** Summarize theoretical perspectives before applying them.
- **Research papers.** Take notes and report on research through summary.
- **Literature reviews.** Analyze work through brief summaries.
- **Argument papers.** Summarize evidence and opposing arguments.
- **Essay exams.** Demonstrate understanding of course materials through summary.

Workplace Writing

- **Policy briefs.** Condense complex public policy.
- **Business plans.** Summarize costs, relevant environmental impacts, and other important matters.
- **Memos, letters, and reports.** Summarize procedures, meetings, product assessments, expenditures, and more.
- **Medical charts.** Record patient data in summarized form.
- **Legal briefs.** Summarize relevant facts of cases.

The Reading Process

It may seem to you that being able to tell (or retell) in summary form exactly what a passage says is a skill that ought to be taken for granted in anyone who can read at high school level. Unfortunately, this is not so: For all kinds of reasons, people don't always read carefully. In fact, it's probably safe to say that usually they don't. Either they read so inattentively that they skip over words, phrases, or even whole sentences, or, if they do see the words in front of them, they see them without registering their significance.

When a reader fails to pick up the meaning and implications of a sentence or two, usually there's no real harm done. (An exception: You could lose credit on an exam or paper because you failed to read or to realize the significance of a crucial direction by your instructor.) But over longer stretches—the paragraph, the section, the article, or the chapter—inattentive or haphazard reading interferes with your goals as a reader: to perceive the shape of the argument, to grasp the central idea, to determine the main points that compose it, to relate the parts of the whole, and to note key examples. This kind of reading takes a lot more energy and determination than casual reading. But, in the long run, it's an energy-saving method because it enables you to retain the content of the material and to use that content as a basis for your own responses. In other words, it allows you to develop an accurate and coherent written discussion that goes beyond summary.

CRITICAL READING FOR SUMMARY

- *Examine the context.* Note the credentials, occupation, and publications of the author. Identify the source in which the piece originally appeared. This information helps illuminate the author's perspective on the topic he or she is addressing.

- *Note the title and subtitle.* Some titles are straightforward, whereas the meanings of others become clearer as you read. In either case, titles typically identify the topic being addressed and often reveal the author's attitude toward that topic.

- *Identify the main point.* Whether a piece of writing contains a thesis statement in the first few paragraphs or

---

builds its main point without stating it up front, look at the entire piece to arrive at an understanding of the overall point being made.

- **Identify the subordinate points.** Notice the smaller subpoints that make up the main point, and make sure you understand how they relate to the main point. If a particular subpoint doesn't clearly relate to the main point you've identified, you may need to modify your understanding of the main point.

- **Break the reading into sections.** Notice which paragraph(s) make up the introduction, body, and conclusion of a piece. Break up the body paragraphs into sections that address the writer's various subpoints.

- **Distinguish between points, examples, and counterarguments.** Critical reading requires careful attention to what writers are *doing* as well as what they are *saying*. When a writer quotes someone else, or relays an example of something, ask yourself why this is being done. What point is the example supporting? Is another source being quoted as support for a point, or as a counterargument that the writer sets out to address?

- **Watch for transitions within and between paragraphs.** In order to follow the logic of a piece of writing, as well as to distinguish between points, examples, and counterarguments, pay attention to the transitional words and phrases writers use. Transitions function like road signs, preparing the reader for what's next.

- **Read actively and recursively.** Don't treat reading as a passive, linear progression through a text. Instead, read as though you are engaged in a dialogue with the writer: Ask questions of the text as you read, make notes in the margin, underline key ideas in pencil, put question or exclamation marks next to passages that confuse or excite you. Go back to earlier points once you finish a reading, stop during your reading to recap what's been presented so far, and move back and forth through a text.

How to Write Summaries

Every article you read will present a unique challenge as you work to summarize it. As you'll discover, saying in a few words what has taken someone else a great many can be difficult. But like any other skill, the ability to summarize improves with practice.

GUIDELINES FOR WRITING SUMMARIES

- **Read the passage carefully.** Determine its structure. Identify the author's purpose in writing. (Thins will help you distinguish between more important and less important information.) Make a note in the margin when you get confused or when you think something is important; highlight or underline points sparingly, if at all.

- **Reread the passage.** This time divide the passage into sections or stages of though. The author's use of paragraphing will often be a useful guide. On the passage itself, *label* each section or stage of thought. *Underline* key ideas and terms. Write notes in the margin.

- **Write one-sentence summaries**, on a separate sheet of paper, of each stage of thought.

- **Write a thesis—a one-or two-sentence summary of the entire passage.** The thesis should express the central idea of the passage, as you have determined it from the preceding steps. You may find it useful to follow the approach of most newspaper stories—naming the *what, who, why, where, when,* and *how* of the matter. For persuasive passages, summarize in a sentence the author's conclusion. For descriptive passages, indicate the subject of the description and its key feature(s). (Note: In some cases, *a suitable thesis may already be in the original passage.* If so, you may want to quote it directly in your summary.)

- **Write the first draft of your summary** by (1) combining the thesis with your list of one-sentence summaries or (2) combining the thesis with one-sentence summaries *plus* significant details from the passage. In either case,

---

eliminate repetition and less important information. Disregard minor details or generalize them (e.g., George H.W. Bush and Bill Clinton might be generalized as "recent presidents"). Use as few words as possible to convey the main ideas.

- ***Check your summary against the original passage*** and make whatever adjustments are necessary for accuracy and completeness.

- ***Revise your summary,*** inserting transitional words and phrases where necessary to ensure coherence. Check for style. *Avoid a series of short, choppy sentences.* Combine sentences for a smooth, logical flow of ideas. Check for grammatical correctness, punctuation, and spelling.

Analysis

What Is an Analysis?

1　An *analysis* is an argument in which you study the parts of something to understand how it works, what it means, or why it might be significant. The writer of an analysis uses an analytical tool: a *principle* or *definition* on the basis of which an object, an event, or behavior can be divided into parts and examined. Here are excerpts from two analyses of L. Frank Baum's *The Wizard of Oz*:

> At the dawn of adolescence, the very time she should start to distance herself from Aunt Em and Uncle Henry, the surrogate parents who raised her on their Kansas farm, Dorothy Gale experiences a hurtful reawakening of her fear that these loved ones will be rudely ripped from her, especially her Aunt (Em—M for Mother!).*

> [*The Wizard of Oz*] was originally written as a political allegory about grassroots protest. It may seem harder to believe than Emerald City, but the Tin Woodsman is the industrial worker, the Scarecrow [is] the struggling farmer, and the Wizard is the president, who is powerful only as long as he succeeds in deceiving the people.†

As these paragraphs suggest, what you discover through an analysis depends entirely on the principle or definition you use to make your insights. Is *The Wizard of Oz* the story of a girl's psychological development, or is it a story about politics? The answer is *both*. In the first example, psychiatrist Harvey Greenberg applies the principles of his profession and, not surprisingly, sees *The Wizard of Oz* in psychological terms. In the second example, a newspaper reporter applies the political

---

*Harvey Greenberg, *The Movies on Your Mind* (New York: Dutton, 1975) 16.
†Peter Dreier, "Oz Was Almost Reality," *Cleveland Plain Dealer* 3 Sept. 1989.

13

theories of Karl Marx and, again not surprisingly, discovers a story about politics.

Different as they are, these analyses share an important quality: Each is the result of a specific principle or definition used as a tool to divide an object into parts to see what it means and how it works. The writer's choice of analytical tool simultaneously creates and limits the possibilities for analysis. Thus, working with the principles of Freud, Harvey Greenberg sees *The Wizard of Oz* in psychological, not political, terms; working with the theories of Karl Marx, Peter Dreier understands the movie in terms of the economic relationships among characters. It's as if the writer of an analysis who adopts one analytical tool puts on a pair of glasses and sees an object in a specific way. Another writer, using a different tool (and a different pair of glasses), sees the object differently.

WHERE DO WE FIND WRITTEN ANALYSES?

Here are just a few types of writing that involve analysis:

Academic Writing

- **Experimental and lab reports.** Analyze the meaning or implications of the study results in your Discussion section.

- **Research papers.** Analyze information in sources; apply theories to material being reported.

- **Process analysis.** Break down the steps or stages involved in completing a process.

- **Literary analysis.** Analyze characterization, plot, imagery, or other elements in works of literature.

- **Essay exams.** Demonstrate understanding of course material by analyzing data using course concepts.

Workplace Writing

- **Grant proposals.** Analyze the issues you seek funding for in order to address them.

- **Reviews of the arts.** Employ dramatic or literary analysis to assess artistic works.

- **Business plans.** Break down and analyze capital outlays, expenditures, profits, materials, and the like.

- **Medical charts.** Review patient symptoms and explore treatment options.
- **Legal briefs.** Break down and analyze facts of cases and elements of legal precedents; apply legal rulings and precedents to new situations.
- **Case studies.** Describe and analyze the particulars of a specific medical, social service, advertising, or business case.

At this point, you may be a bit skeptical. Are there as many analyses of *The Wizard of Oz* as there are people to read it? Yes, or at least as many analyses as there are analytical tools. This does not mean that all analyses are equally valid or useful. The writer must convince the reader. In creating an essay of analysis, the writer must organize a series of related insights, using the analytical tool to examine first one part and then another of the object being studied. To read Harvey Greenberg's essay on *The Wizard of Oz* is to find paragraph after paragraph of related insights—first about Aunt Em, then the Wicked Witch, then Toto, and then the Wizard. All these insights point to Greenberg's single conclusion that "Dorothy's 'trip' is a marvelous metaphor for the psychological journey every adolescent must make."* Without Greenberg's analysis, we probably would not have thought about the movie as a psychological journey. This is precisely the power of an analysis: its ability to reveal objects or events in ways we would not otherwise have considered.

5   The writer's challenge is to convince readers that (1) the analytical tool being applied is legitimate and well matched to the object being studied; and (2) the analytical tool is being used systematically to divide the object into parts and to make a coherent, meaningful statement about these parts and the object as a whole.

Formulate the Argument

An analysis is an argument with two components. The first component states and establishes the writer's agreement with a certain principle or definition.

---

*Harvey Greenberg, *The Movies on Your Mind* (New York: Dutton, 1975) 16.

Part 1 of the Argument

This component of the argument essentially takes the following form:

Claim 1: Principle X (or definition X) is valuable.

Principle X can be a theory as encompassing and abstract as the statement that *myths are the enemy of truth.* Principle X can be as modest as the definition of a term—for instance, "addiction" or "comfort." As you move from one subject area to another, the principles and definitions you use for analysis will change, as these assignments illustrate:

Sociology: Write a paper in which you place yourself in American society by locating both your absolute position and relative rank on each single criterion of social stratification used by Lenski and Lenski. For each criterion, state whether you have attained your social position by yourself or if you have "inherited" that status from your parents.

Literature: Apply principles of Jungian psychology to Hawthorne's "Young Goodman Brown." In your reading of the story, apply Jung's principles of the *shadow, persona,* and *anima.*

Physics: Use Newton's second law $(F = ma)$ to analyze the acceleration of a fixed pulley, from which two weights hang: m_1 (.45 kg) and m_2 (.90 kg). Explain in a paragraph the principle of Newton's law and your method of applying it to solve the problem. Assume that your reader is not comfortable with mathematical explanations: do not use equations in your paragraph.

Finance: Using Guidford C. Babcock's "Concept of Sustainable Growth" [*Financial Analysis* 26 (May–June 1970): 108–14], analyze the stock price appreciation of the XYZ Corporation, figures for which are attached.

The analytical tools to be applied in these assignments change from discipline to discipline. Writing in response to the sociology assignment, you would use sociological principles developed by Lenski and Lenski. In your literature class, you would use principles of Jungian psychology; in physics, Newton's second law; and in finance, a particular writer's concept of "sustainable growth." But whatever discipline you are working in, the first part of your analysis will clearly state which (and whose) principles and definitions you are applying. For audiences unfamiliar with these principles, you will need to explain them; if you anticipate objections, you will need to argue that they are legitimate principles capable of helping you as you conduct an analysis.

Part 2 of the Argument

10 In the second component of your argument, you *apply* specific parts 10 of your principle or definition to the topic at hand. Regardless of how it is worded, this second argument in an analysis can be rephrased to take the following form:

> **Claim 2:** By applying Principle (or definition) X, we can understand *(topic)* as *(conclusion based on analysis).*

This is your thesis, the main idea of your analytical essay. Fill in the first blank with the specific object, event, or behavior you are examining. Fill in the second blank with your conclusion about the meaning or significance of this object, based on the insights made during your analysis.

GUIDELINES FOR WRITING ANALYSIS

Unless you are asked to follow a specialized format, especially in the sciences or the social sciences, you can present your analysis as a paper by following the guidelines below. As you move from one class to another, from discipline to discipline, the principles and definitions you use as the basis for your analyses will change, but the following basic steps will remain the same:

- *Create a context for your analysis.* Introduce and summarize for readers the object, event, or behavior to be analyzed. Present a strong case about why an analysis is needed: Give yourself a motivation to write, and give readers a motivation to read. Consider setting out a problem, puzzle, or question to be investigated.

- ***Introduce and summarize the key definition or principle that will form the basis of your analysis.*** Plan to devote the first part of your analysis to arguing for the validity of

---

this principle or definition *if* your audience is not likely to understand it or if they are likely to think that the principle or definition is *not* valuable.

- **Analyze your topic.** Systematically apply elements of this definition or principle to parts of the activity or object under study. You can do this by posing specific questions, based on your analytic principle or definition, about the object. Discuss what you find part by part (organized perhaps by question), in clearly defined sections of the essay.

- **Conclude by stating clearly what is significant about your analysis.** When considering your essay as a whole, what new or interesting insights have you made concerning the object under study? To what extent has your application of the definition or principle helped you to explain how the object works, what it might mean, or why it is significant?

CRITICAL READING FOR ANALYSIS

- **Read to get a sense of the whole in relation to its parts.** Whether you are clarifying for yourself a principle or definition to be used in an analysis, or reading a text that you will analyze, understand how parts function to create the whole. If a definition or principle consists of parts, use these to organize sections of your analysis. If your goal is to analyze a text, be aware of its structure: note the title and subtitle; identify the main point and subordinate points and where they are located; break the material into sections.

- **Read to discover relationships within the object being analyzed.** Watch for patterns. When you find them, be alert—for you create an occasion to analyze, to use a principle or definition as a guide in discussing what the pattern may mean:

In fiction, a pattern might involve responses of characters to events or to each other, recurrence of certain words or phrasings, images, themes, or turns of plot, to name a few.

> In poetry, a pattern might involve rhyme schemes, rhythm, imagery, figurative or literal language, and more.
>
> Your challenge as a reader is first to see a pattern (perhaps using a guiding principle or definition to do so) and then to locate other instances of that pattern. By reading carefully in this way, you prepare yourself to conduct an analysis.

Draft and Revise Your Analysis

You will usually need at least two drafts to produce a paper that presents your idea clearly. The biggest changes in your paper will typically come between your first and second drafts. No paper that you write, including an analysis, will be complete until you revise and refine your single compelling idea: your analytical conclusion about what the object, event, or behavior being examined means or how it is significant. You revise and refine by evaluating your first draft, bringing to it many of the same questions you pose when evaluating any piece of writing, including these:

- Are the facts accurate?
- Are my opinions supported by evidence?
- Are the opinions of others authoritative?
- Are my assumptions clearly stated?
- Are key terms clearly defined?
- Is the presentation logical?
- Are all parts of the presentation well developed?
- Are dissenting points of view presented?

Address these same questions on the first draft of your analysis, and you will have solid information to guide your revision.

Write an Analysis, Not a Summary

The most common error made in writing analyses—which is *fatal* to the form—is to present readers with a summary only. For analyses to succeed, you must *apply* a principle or definition and reach a conclusion about the object, event, or behavior you are examining. By definition, a summary includes none of your own conclusions. Summary is naturally a part of analysis; you will need to summarize the object or activity being examined and, depending on the audience's needs, summarize the principle or definition being applied. But in an analysis, you must take the next step and share insights that suggest the meaning or significance of some object, event, or behavior.

Make Your Analysis Systematic

15 Analyses should give the reader the sense of a systematic, purposeful examination.

Imagine an analysis in which a writer lays out four elements of a definition but then applies only two, without explaining the logic for omitting the others. Or imagine an analysis in which the writer offers a principle for analysis but directs it to only a half or a third of the object being discussed, without providing a rationale for doing so. In both cases, the writer would be failing to deliver on a promise basic to analyses: Once a principle or definition is presented, it should be thoroughly and systematically applied.

Answer the "So What?" Question

An analysis should make readers *want* to read. It should give readers a sense of getting to the heart of the matter, that what is important in the object or activity under analysis is being laid bare and discussed in revealing ways. If when rereading the first draft of your essay, you cannot imagine readers saying, "I never thought of _____ this way," then something may be seriously wrong. Reread closely to determine why the paper might leave readers flat and exhausted, as opposed to feeling that they have gained new and important insights. Closely reexamine your own motivations for writing. Have *you* learned anything significant through the analysis? If not, neither will readers, and they will turn away. If you have gained important insights through your analysis, communicate them clearly. At some point, pull together your related insights and say, in effect: "Here's how it all adds up."

Attribute Sources Appropriately

In an analysis the nature of the form dictates that you work with one or two sources and apply insights from those to some object or phenomenon you want to understand more thoroughly. The strength of an analysis derives mostly from *your* application of a principle or definition. You will have fewer sources to cite in an analysis than in a synthesis. Nevertheless, take special care to cite and quote, as necessary, the one or two sources you use throughout the analysis.

Synthesis

What Is a Synthesis?

1   A *synthesis* is a written discussion that draws on two or more sources. It follows that your ability to write syntheses depends on your ability to infer relationships among sources—essays, articles, and fiction as well as nonwritten sources such as lectures, interviews, and observations. This process is nothing new for you, since you infer relationships all the time—say, between something you've read in the newspaper and something you've seen for yourself, or between the teaching styles of your favorite and least favorite instructors. In fact, if you've written research papers, you've already written syntheses. In an *academic synthesis*, you make explicit the relationships that you have inferred among separate sources.

The skills you've already learned and practiced in the previous two chapters will be vital in writing syntheses. Clearly, before you're in a position to draw relationships between two or more sources, you must understand what those sources say; in other words, you must be able to *summarize* those sources. Readers will frequently benefit from at least partial summaries of sources in your synthesis essays. At the same time, you must go beyond summary to make judgments—judgments based, of course, on your *critical reading* of your sources: what conclusions you've drawn about the quality and validity of these sources, whether you agree or disagree with the points made in your sources, and why you agree or disagree.

Further, you must go beyond the critique of individual sources to determine the relationships among them. Is the information in source B, for example, an extended illustration of the generalizations in source A? Would it be useful to compare and contrast source C with source B? Having read and considered sources A, B, and C, can you infer something else—D (not a source, but your own idea)?

Because a synthesis is based on two or more sources, you will need to be selective when choosing information from each. It would

---

Reprinted from *Writing and Reading Across the Curriculum* (2007), by permission of Pearson Education.

be neither possible nor desirable, for instance, to discuss in a ten-page paper on the American Civil War every point that the authors of two books make about their subject. What you as a writer must do is select from each source the ideas and information that best allow you to achieve your purpose.

WHERE DO WE FIND WRITTEN SYNTHESES?

Here are just a few of the types of writing that involve synthesis:

Academic Writing

- **Analysis papers.** Synthesize and apply several related theoretical approaches.
- **Research papers.** Synthesize multiple sources.
- **Argument papers.** Synthesize different points into a coherent claim or position.
- **Essay exams.** Demonstrate understanding of course material through comparing and contrasting theories, viewpoints, or approaches in a particular field.

Workplace Writing

- **Newspaper and magazine articles.** Synthesize primary and secondary sources.
- **Position papers and policy briefs.** Compare and contrast solutions for solving problems.
- **Business plans.** Synthesize ideas and proposals into one coherent plan.
- **Memos and letters.** Synthesize multiple ideas, events, and proposals into concise form.
- **Web sites.** Synthesize information from various sources to present in Web pages and related links.

How to Write Syntheses

5   Although writing syntheses can't be reduced to a lockstep method, it   5
should help you to follow the guidelines listed in the box below.

GUIDELINES FOR WRITING SYNTHESES

- *Consider your purpose in writing.* What are you trying to accomplish in your essay? How will this purpose shape the way you approach your sources?

- *Select and carefully read your sources,* according to your purpose. Then reread the passages, mentally summarizing each. Identify those aspects or parts of your sources that will help you fulfill your purpose. When rereading, *label* or *underline* the sources for main ideas, key terms, and any details you want to use in the synthesis.

- *Take notes on your reading.* In addition to labeling or underlining key points in the readings, you might write brief one- or two-sentence summaries of each source. This will help you in formulating your thesis statement and in choosing an organizing your sources later.

- *Formulate a thesis.* Your thesis is the main idea that you want to present in your synthesis. It should be expressed as a complete sentence. You might do some predrafting about the ideas discussed in the readings in order to help you work out a thesis. If you've written one-sentence summaries of the readings, looking these over will help you to brainstorm connections between readings and to devise a thesis.

  When you write your essay drafts, you will need to consider where your thesis fits in your paper. Sometimes the thesis is the first sentence, but more often it is *the final sentence of the first paragraph.* If you are writing an *inductively arranged* synthesis the thesis sentence may not appear until the final paragraphs.

- *Decide how you will use your source material.* How will the information and the ideas in the passages help you fulfill your purpose?

- *Develop an organizational plan,* according to your thesis. How will you arrange your material? It is not necessary to prepare a formal outline. But you should have some plan that will indicate the order in which you will present your material and that will indicate the relationships among your sources.

24

- **Draft the topic sentences for the main sections.** This is an optional step, but you may find it a helpful transition from organizational plan to first draft.

- **Write the first draft of your synthesis,** following your organizational plan. Be flexible with your plan, however. Frequently, you will use an outline to get started. As you write, you may discover new ideas and make room for them by adjusting the outline. When this happens, reread your work frequently, making sure that your thesis still accounts for what follows and that what follows still logically supports your thesis.

- **Document your sources.** You must do this by crediting them within the body of the synthesis—citing the author's last name and page number from which the point was taken and by providing full citation information in a list of "Works Cited" at the end. Don't open yourself to charges of plagiarism!

- **Revise your synthesis,** inserting transitional words and phrases where necessary. Make sure that the synthesis reads smoothly, logically, and clearly from beginning to end. Check for grammatical correctness, punctuation, and spelling.

Note: The writing of syntheses is a recursive process, and you should accept a certain amount of backtracking and reformulating as inevitable. For instance, in developing an organizational plan (point 6 of the procedure), you may discover a gap in your presentation that will send you scrambling for another source— back to point 2. You may find that formulating a thesis and making inferences among sources occur simultaneously; indeed, inference are often made before a thesis is formulated. Our recommendations for writing syntheses will give you a structure; they will get you started. But be flexible in your approach; expect discontinuity and, if possible, be comforted that through backtracking and reformulating you will eventually produce a coherent, well-crafted essay.

Use Comparison and Contrast Synthesis

A particularly important type of synthesis is built on patterns of comparison and contrast. Techniques of comparison and contrast enable you to examine two subjects (or sources) in terms of one another. When you compare, you consider *similarities*. When you contrast, you consider *differences*. By comparing and contrasting, you perform a multifaceted analysis that often suggests subtleties that otherwise might not have come to your (or your reader's) attention.

To organize a comparison-and-contrast synthesis, you must carefully read sources in order to discover *significant criteria for analysis*. A *criterion* is a specific point to which both of your authors refer and about which they may agree or disagree. (For example, in a comparative report on compact cars, criteria for *comparison and contrast* might be road handling, fuel economy, and comfort of ride.) The best criteria are those that allow you not only to account for obvious similarities and differences—those concerning the main aspects of your sources or subjects—but also to plumb deeper, exploring subtle yet significant comparisons and contrasts among details or subcomponents, which you can then relate to your overall thesis.

Organizing Comparison-and-Contrast Syntheses

Two basic approaches to organizing a comparison-and-contrast argument synthesis are available: organization by *source or subject* and organization by *criteria*.

Organizing by Source or Subject

You can organize a comparative synthesis by first summarizing each of your sources or subjects and then discussing significant similarities and differences between them. Having read the summaries and become familiar with the distinguishing features of each source, your readers will most likely be able to appreciate the more obvious similarities and differences. In the discussion, your task is to focus on both the obvious and subtle comparisons and contrasts—that is, on those that most clearly support your thesis.

Organization by source or subject is best saved for passages that can be briefly summarized. If the summary of your source or subject becomes too long, your readers might forget the points you made in the first summary as they are reading the second. A comparison-and-contrast synthesis organized by source or subject might proceed like this:

I. Introduce the paper; lead to thesis.

II. Summarize source / subject A by discussing its significant features.

III. Summarize source / subject B by discussing its significant features.

IV. Write a paragraph (or two) in which you discuss the significant points of comparison and contrast between sources or subjects A and B. Alternatively, begin comparison-contrast in section III upon introducing source or subject B.

End with a conclusion in which you summarize your points and, perhaps, raise and respond to pertinent questions.

Organizing by Criteria

Instead of summarizing entire sources one at a time with the intention of comparing them later, you could discuss two sources simultaneously, examining the views of each author point by point (criterion by criterion), comparing and contrasting these views in the process. The criterion approach is best used when you have a number of points to discuss or when passages or subjects are long and/or complex. A comparison-and-contrast synthesis organized by criteria might look like this:

I. Introduce the paper; lead to thesis.

II. Criterion 1

a. Discuss what author A says about this point.

b. Discuss what author B says about this point, comparing and contrasting B's treatment of the point with A's.

III. Criterion 2

a. Discuss what author A says about this point.

b. Discuss what author B says about this point, comparing and contrasting B's treatment of the point with A's.

And so on. Proceed criterion by criterion until you have completed your discussion. Be sure to arrange criteria with a clear method; knowing how the discussion of one criterion leads to the next will ensure smooth transitions throughout your paper. End by summarizing your key points and, perhaps, raising and responding to pertinent questions.

However you organize your comparison-and-contrast synthesis, keep in mind that comparing and contrasting are not ends in themselves. Your discussion should point somewhere: to a conclusion, an answer to "So what—why bother to compare and contrast in the first place?" If your discussion is part of a larger synthesis, point to and support the larger claim. If you write a stand-alone comparison-and-contrast, though, you must by the final paragraph answer the "why bother?" question.

Avoiding Plagiarism

1 Plagiarism is generally defined as the attempt to pass off the work of 1 another as one's own. Whether born out of calculation or desperation, plagiarism is the least tolerated offense in the academic world. The fact that most plagiarism is unintentional—arising from ignorance of conventions rather than deceitfulness—makes no difference to many professors.

The ease of cutting and pasting whole blocks of text from Web sources into one's own paper makes it tempting for some to take the easy way out and avoid doing their own research and writing. But apart from the serious ethical issues involved, the same technology that makes such acts possible also makes it possible for instructors to detect them. Software marketed to instructors allows them to conduct Web searches, using suspicious phrases as keywords. The results often provide irrefutable evidence of plagiarism.

Of course, plagiarism is not confined to students. Recent years have seen a number of high-profile cases—some of them reaching the front pages of newspapers—of well-known scholars who were shown to have copied passages from sources into their own book manuscripts, without proper attribution. In some cases, the scholars maintained that these appropriations were simply a matter of carelessness, and that in the press and volume of work, they had lost track of which words were theirs and which were the words of their sources. But such excuses sounded hollow: These careless acts inevitably embarrassed the scholars professionally, disappointed their many admirers, and tarnished their otherwise fine work and reputations.

The following is an excerpt from an article by Richard Rovere on Senator Joseph P. McCarthy, along with several student versions of the ideas represented:

> McCarthy never seemed to belieeve in himself or in anything he had said. He knew that Communists were not in charge of American foreign policy. He knew that they weren't running the United States Army. He knew that he had spent five

Reprinted from *Writing and Reading Across the Curriculum* (2007), by permission of Pearson Education.

years looking for Communists in the government and that—although some must certainly have been there, since Communists had turned up in practically every other major government in the world—he hadn't come up with even one.*

5   One student wrote the following version of this passage: 5

> McCarthy never believed in himself or in anything he had said. He knew that Communists were not in charge of American foreign policy and weren't running the United States Army. He knew that he had spent five years looking for Communists in the government, and although there must certainly have been some there, since Communists were in practically every other major government in the world, he hadn't come up with even one.

Clearly, this is intentional plagiarism. The student has copied the original passage almost word for word.

Here is another version of the same passage:

> McCarthy knew that Communists were not running foreign policy or the Army. He also knew that although there must have been some Communists in the government, he hadn't found a single one, even though he had spent five years looking.

This student has attempted to put the ideas into her own words, but both the wording and the sentence structure still are so heavily dependent on the original passage that even if it *were* citied, most professors would consider it plagiarism.

In the following version, the student has sufficiently changed the wording and sentence structure, and she uses a signal phrase (a phrase used to introduce a quotation or paraphrase, signaling to the reader that the words to follow come from someone else) to properly credit the information to Rovere, so that there is no question of plagiarism:

> According to Richard Rovere, McCarthy was fully aware that Communists were running neither the government nor the Army. He also knew that he hadn't found a single Communist in government, even after a lengthy search (192).

---

*Richard Rovere, "The Most Gifted and Successful Demagogue This Country Has Ever Known," *New York Times Magazine* 30 Apr. 1967: 192+.

10   And although this is not a matter of plagiarism, as noted above, it's   10
essential to quote accurately. You are not permitted to change any part of
a quotation or to omit any part of it without using brackets or ellipses.

RULES FOR AVOIDING PLAGIARISM

- Cite *all* quoted material and *all* summarized and paraphrased material, unless the information is common knowledge (e.g., the Civil War was fought from 1861 to 1865).

- Make sure that both the *wording* and the *sentence structure* of your summaries and paraphrases are substantially your own.

How to Mark a Book

Mortimer Adler

Mortimer Adler (1902–2001) received his Ph.D. from Columbia University in 1928. A conservative thinker, Adler advocated education based on the "truths" found in the classical works of Western civilization. Many academic intellectuals have scorned his simple formulas for progress, but the larger culture has often embraced his ideas, as his post as chairman of the editorial board of the Encyclopedia Britannica *indicated. His Great Books project, for which he is widely known, resulted in the publication and wide circulation of handsome bound sets of important works of world literature. As you read his essay on how to mark a book, you will see a man who thought that the world is, or ought to be, clear and simple.*

1 You know you have to read "between the lines" to get the most out of anything. I want to persuade you to do something equally important in the course of your reading. I want to persuade you to "write between the lines." Unless you do, you are not likely to do the most efficient kind of reading.

I contend, quite bluntly, that marking up a book is not an act of mutilation but of love.

You shouldn't mark up a book which isn't yours. Librarians (or your friends) who lend you books expect you to keep them clean, and you should. If you decide that I am right about the usefulness of marking books, you will have to buy them. Most of the world's great books are available today, in reprint editions, at less than a dollar.

There are two ways in which you can own a book. The first is the property right you establish by paying for it, just as you pay for clothes and furniture. But this act of purchase is only the prelude to

From *Saturday Review,* 1940. Published by Omni Publications, Ltd. Copyright © 1940. Copyright renewed by General Media International.

possession. Full ownership comes only when you have made it a part of yourself, and the best way to make yourself a part of it is by writing in it. An illustration may make the point clear. You buy a beefsteak and transfer it from the butcher's ice-box to your own. But you do not own the beefsteak in the most important sense until you consume it and get it into your bloodstream. I am arguing that books, too, must be absorbed in your bloodstream to do you any good.

5   Confusion about what it means to *own* a book leads people to a   5 false reverence for paper, binding, and type—a respect for the physical thing—the craft of the printer rather than the genius of the author. They forget that it is possible for a man to acquire the idea, to possess the beauty, which a great book contains, without staking his claim by pasting his bookplate inside the cover. Having a fine library doesn't prove that its owner has a mind enriched by books; it proves nothing more than that he, his father, or his wife, was rich enough to buy them.

There are three kinds of book owners. The first has all the standard sets and best-sellers—unread, untouched. (This deluded individual owns woodpulp and ink, not books.) The second has a great many books—a few of them read through, most of them dipped into, but all of them as clean and shiny as the day they were bought. (This person would probably like to make books his own, but is restrained by a false respect for their physical appearance.) The third has a few books or many—everyone of them dog-eared and dilapidated, shaken and loosened by continual use, marked and scribbled in from front to back. (This man owns books.)

Is it false respect, you may ask, to preserve intact and unblemished a beautifully printed book, an elegantly bound edition? Of course not. I'd no more scribble all over a first edition of *Paradise Lost* than I'd give my baby a set of crayons and an original Rembrandt! I wouldn't mark up a painting or a statue. Its soul, so to speak, is inseparable from its body. And the beauty of a rare edition or of a richly manufactured volume is like that of a painting or a statue.

But the soul of a book *can* be separated from its body. A book is more like the score of a piece of music than it is like a painting. No great musician confuses a symphony with the printed sheets of music. Arturo Toscanini reveres Brahms, but Toscanini's score of the C-minor Symphony is so thoroughly marked up that no one but the maestro himself can read it. The reason why a great conductor makes notations on his musical scores—marks them up again and again each time he returns to study them—is the reason why you should mark your books.

If your respect for magnificent binding or typography gets in the way, buy yourself a cheap edition and pay your respects to the author.

Why is marking up a book indispensable to reading? First, it keeps you awake. (And I don't mean merely conscious; I mean wide awake.) In the second place, reading, if it is active, is thinking, and thinking tends to express itself in words, spoken or written. The marked book is usually the thought-through book. Finally, writing helps you remember the thoughts you had, or the thoughts the author expressed. Let me develop these three points.

10 If reading is to accomplish anything more than passing time, it 10 must be active. You can't let your eyes glide across the lines of a book and come up with an understanding of what you have read. Now an ordinary piece of light fiction, like say, *Gone With the Wind*, doesn't require the most active kind of reading. The books you read for pleasure can be read in a state of relaxation, and nothing is lost. But a great book, rich in ideas and beauty, a book that raises and tries to answer great fundamental questions, demands the most active reading of which you are capable. You don't absorb the ideas of John Dewey the way you absorb the crooning of Mr. Vallee. You have to reach for them. That you cannot do while you're asleep.

If, when you've finished reading a book, the pages are filled with your notes, you know that you read actively. The most famous *active* reader of great books I know is President Hutchins, of the University of Chicago. He also has the hardest schedule of business activities of any man I know. He invariably reads with a pencil, and sometimes, when he picks up a book and pencil in the evening, he finds himself, instead of making intelligent notes, drawing what he calls "caviar factories" on the margins. When that happens, he puts the book down. He knows he's too tired to read, and he's just wasting time.

But, you may ask, why is writing necessary? Well, the physical act of writing, with your own hand, brings words and sentences more sharply before your mind and preserves them better in your memory. To set down your reaction to important words and sentences you have read, and the questions they have raised in your mind, is to preserve those reactions and sharpen those questions.

Even if you wrote on a scratch pad, and threw the paper away when you had finished writing, your grasp of the book would be surer. But you don't have to throw the paper away. The margins (top and bottom, as well as side), the end-papers, the very space between the lines, are all available. They aren't sacred. And, best of all, your marks and notes become an integral part of the book and stay there forever. You can pick up the book the following week or year, and there are all your points of agreement, disagreement, doubt, and inquiry. It's like resuming an interrupted conversation with the advantage of being able to pick up where you left off.

And that is exactly what reading a book should be: a conversation between you and the author. Presumably he knows more about the subject than you do; naturally, you'll have the proper humility as you approach him. But don't let anybody tell you that a reader is supposed to be solely on the receiving end. Understanding is a two-way operation; learning doesn't consist in being an empty receptacle. The learner has to question himself and question the teacher. He even has to argue with the teacher, once he understands what the teacher is saying. And marking a book is literally an expression of your differences, or agreements of opinion, with the author.

15 There are all kinds of devices for marking a book intelligently and 15 fruitfully. Here's the way I do it:

1. *Underlining:* Of major points, of important or forceful statements.
2. *Vertical lines at the margin:* To emphasize a statement already underlined.
3. *Star, asterisk, or other doo-dad at the margin:* To be used sparingly, to emphasize the ten or twenty most important statements in the book. (You may want to fold the bottom corner of each page on which you use such marks. It won't hurt the sturdy paper on which most modern books are printed, and you will be able to take the book off the shelf at any time and, by opening it at the folded corner page, refresh your recollection of the book.)
4. *Numbers in the margin:* To indicate the sequence of points the author makes in developing a single argument.
20 5. *Numbers of other pages in the margin:* To indicate where else in the 20 book the author made points relevant to the point marked; to tie up the ideas in a book, which, though they may be separated by many pages, belong together.
6. *Circling of key words or phrases.*
7. *Writing in the margin, or at the top or bottom of the page, for the sake of:* Recording questions (and perhaps answers) which a passage raised in your mind; reducing a complicated discussion to a simple statement; recording the sequence of major points right through the books. I use the end-papers at the back of the book

to make a personal index of the author's points in the order of their appearance.

The front end-papers are, to me, the most important. Some people reserve them for a fancy bookplate. I reserve them for fancy thinking. After I have finished reading the book and making my personal index on the back end-papers, I turn to the front and try to outline the book, not page by page, or point by point (I've already done that at the back), but as an integrated structure, with a basic unity and an order of parts. This outline is, to me, the measure of my understanding of the work.

If you're a die-hard anti-book-marker, you may object that the margins, the space between the lines, and the end-papers don't give you room enough. All right. How about using a scratch pad slightly smaller than the page-size of the book—so that the edges of the sheets won't protrude? Make your index, outlines, and even your notes on the pad, and then insert these sheets permanently inside the front and back covers of the book.

25 Or, you may say that this business of marking books is going to 25 slow up your reading. It probably will. That's one of the reasons for doing it. Most of us have been taken in by the notion that speed of reading is a measure of our intelligence. There is no such thing as the right speed for intelligent reading. Some things should be read quickly and effortlessly, and some should be read slowly and even laboriously. The sign of intelligence in reading is the ability to read different things differently according to their worth. In the case of good books, the point is not to see how many of them you can get through, but rather how many can get through you—how many you can make your own. A few friends are better than a thousand acquaintances. If this be your aim, as it should be, you will not be impatient if it takes more time and effort to read a great book than it does a newspaper.

You may have one final objection to marking books. You can't lend them to your friends because nobody else can read them without being distracted by your notes. Furthermore, you won't want to lend them because a marked copy is a kind of intellectual diary, and lending it is almost like giving your mind away.

If your friend wishes to read your *Plutarch's Lives*, "Shakespeare," or *The Federalist Papers*, tell him gently but firmly to buy a copy. You will lend him your car or your coat—but your books are as much a part of you as your head or your heart.

Women's Right to Vote

Susan B. Anthony

Susan B. Anthony (1820–1906) was born in Adams, Massachusetts. Raised as a Quaker, Anthony attended Deborah Moulson's Seminary for Females in Philadelphia for a short period, and then began teaching. From 1845 to 1848 she served as headmistress as the Canajoharie (New York) Academy. In her late twenties, Anthony began to dedicate herself to reform issues—temperance, the abolition of slavery, and, for the most part, women's rights. In 1850, Anthony met Elizabeth Cady Stanton, a feminist who had helped conduct the 1848 Seneca Falls Convention (a watershed meeting of women's rights activists). In 1860, Anthony and Stanton succeeded in convincing New York state to pass the Married Women's Property Act. From 1868 to 1870, Anthony helped publish the Revolution, *a women's suffrage paper. In 1869, she and Stanton founded the National Woman Suffrage Association. In 1988, Anthony founded the International Council of Women. From 1892 to 1900, she was president of the National American Woman Suffrage Association. In 1904, Anthony organized the International Woman Suf-frage Alliance in Berlin, Germany. In her later years, she concentrated on the passage of a constitutional amendment that would allow women to vote. Her books include the four-volume* The History of Woman Suffrage *(1881–1902), a collaboration with Stanton. In this speech, presented after she was arrested for attempting to vote in 1872, Anthony describes the injustice of women's legal status and argues that women* do *have the right to vote.*

1   "**I** stand before you under indictment for the alleged crime of hav-   1
ing voted at the last presidential election, without having a lawful right to vote. It shall be my work this evening to prove to you
that in thus doing, I not only committed no crime, but instead simply exercised my citizen's rights, guaranteed to me and all United
States citizens by the National Constitution beyond the power of any
State to deny.

Our democratic-republican government is based on the idea of
the natural right of every individual member thereof to a voice and a
vote in making and executing the laws. We assert the province of government to be to secure the people in the enjoyment of their inalienable rights. We throw to the winds the old dogma that government
can give rights. No one denies that before governments were organized each individual possessed the right to protect his own life, liberty and property. When 100 to 1,000,000 people enter into a free
government they do not barter away their natural rights; they simply
pledge themselves to protect each other in the enjoyment of them
through prescribed judicial and legislative tribunals. They agree to
abandon the methods of brute force in the adjustment of their differences and adopt those of civilization. . . . The Declaration of Independence, the United States Constitution, the constitutions of the
several States and the organic laws of the Territories, all alike propose
to *protect* the people in the exercise of their God-given rights. Not one
of them pretends to bestow rights.

> All men are created equal, and endowed by their Creator
> with certain inalienable rights. Among these are life, liberty
> and the pursuit of happiness. To secure these, governments
> are instituted among men, deriving their just powers from
> the consent of the governed.

Here is no shadow of government authority over rights, or exclu-
sion of any class from their full and equal enjoyment. Here is pronounced the right of all men, and "consequently," as the Quaker
preacher said, "of all women," to a voice in the government. And
here, in this first paragraph of the Declaration, is the assertion of the
natural right of all to the ballot; for how can "the consent of the governed" be given, if the right to vote be denied. . . . The women, dis-
satisfied as they are with this form of government, that enforces
taxation without representation—that compels them to obey laws to
which they never have given their consent—that imprisons and hangs

them without a trial by a jury of their peers—that robs them, in marriage, of the custody of their own persons, wages, and children—are this half of the people who are left wholly at the mercy of the other half, in direct violation of the spirit and letter of the declarations of the framers of this government, every one of which was based on the immutable principle of equal rights to all. By these declarations, kings, popes, priests, aristocrats, all were alike dethroned and placed on a common level, politically, with the lowliest born subject or serf. By them, too, men, as such, were deprived of their divine right to rule and placed on a political level with women. By the practice of these declarations all class and caste distinctions would be abolished, and slave, serf, plebeian, wife, woman, all alike rise from their subject position to the broader platform of equality.

The preamble of the Federal Constitution says:

> We, the people of the United States, in order to form a more perfect union, establish justice, insure domestic tranquillity, provide for the common defence, promote the general welfare and secure the blessings of liberty to ourselves and our posterity, do ordain and establish this Constitution for the United States of America.

It was we, the people, not we, the white male citizens, nor we, the male citizens; but we, the whole people, who formed this Union. We formed it not to give the blessings of liberty but to secure them; not to the half of ourselves and the half of our posterity, but to the whole people—women as well as men. It is downright mockery to talk to women of their enjoyment of the blessings of liberty while they are denied the only means of securing them provided by this democratic-republican government—the ballot. . . .

When, in 1871, I asked [Senator Charles Sumner] to declare the power of the United States Constitution to protect women in their right to vote—as he had done for black men—he handed me a copy of all his speeches during that reconstruction period, and said:

> Put "sex" where I have "race" or "color," and you have here the best and strongest argument I can make for woman. There is not a doubt but women have the constitutional right to vote, and I will never vote for a Sixteenth Amendment to guarantee it to them. I voted for both the Fourteenth and Fifteenth under protest; would never have done it but for the pressing emergency of that hour; would have

insisted that the power of the original Constitution to protect all citizens in the equal enjoyment of their rights should
have been vindicated through the courts. But the newly-
made freedmen had neither the intelligence, wealth nor time
to await that slow process. Women do possess all these in an
eminent degree, and I insist that they shall appeal to the
courts and through them establish the powers of our American magna charta to protect every citizen of the republic.

But, friends, when in accordance with Senator Sumner's counsel I
went to the ballot-box, last November, and exercised my citizen's right
to vote, the courts did not wait for me to appeal to them—they
appealed to me, and indicted me on the charge of having voted
illegally. . . .

For any State to make sex a qualification, which must ever result
in the disfranchisement of one entire half of the people, is to pass a
bill of attainder, an ex post facto law, and is therefore a violation of
the supreme law of the land. By it the blessings of liberty are forever
withheld from women and their female posterity. For them, this government has no just powers derived from the consent of the governed.
For them this government is not a democracy; it is not a republic. It is
the most odious aristocracy ever established on the face of the globe.
An oligarchy of wealth, where the rich govern the poor; an oligarchy
of learning, where the educated govern the ignorant; or even an oligarchy of race, where the Saxon rules the African, might be endured;
but this oligarchy of sex which makes father, brothers, husband, sons,
the oligarchs over the mother and sisters, the wife and daughters of
every household; which ordains all men sovereigns, all women subjects—carries discord and rebellion into every home of the nation. . . .

It is urged that the use of the masculine pronouns *he, his* and *him*
in all the constitutions and laws, is proof that only men were meant
to be included in their provisions. If you insist on this version of the
letter of the law, we shall insist that you be consistent and accept the
other horn of the dilemma, which would compel you to exempt
women from taxation for the support of the government and from
penalties for the violation of laws. There is no *she* or *her* or *hers* in the
tax laws, and this is equally true of all the criminal laws.

Take for example, the civil rights law which I am charged with
having violated; not only are all the pronouns in it masculine, but
everybody knows that it was intended expressly to hinder the rebel

men from voting. It reads, "If any person shall knowingly vote with-out *his* having a lawful right." . . . I insist if government officials may thus manipulate the pronouns to tax, fine, imprison and hang women, it is their duty to thus change them in order to protect us in our right to vote. . . .

Though the words persons, people, inhabitants, electors, citizens, are all used indiscriminately in the national and State constitutions, there was always a conflict of opinion, prior to the war, as to whether they were synonymous terms, but whatever room there was for doubt, under the old regime, the adoption of the Fourteenth Amend-ment settled that question forever in its first sentence:

All persons born or naturalized in the United States, and subject to the jurisdiction thereof, are citizens of the United States, and of the State wherein they reside.

The second settles the equal status of all citizens:

No State shall make or enforce any law which shall abridge the privileges or immunities of citizens of the United States; nor shall any State deprive any person of life, liberty or property without due process of law, or deny to any person within its jurisdiction the equal protection of the laws.

The only question left to be settled now is: Are women persons? I scarcely believe any of our opponents will have the hardihood to say they are not. Being persons, then, women are citizens, and no State has a right to make any new law, or to enforce any old law, which shall abridge their privileges or immunities. Hence, every discrimina-tion against women in the constitutions and laws of the several States is today null and void, precisely as is every one against negroes.

Is the right to vote one of the privileges or immunities of citizens? I think the disfranchised ex-rebels and ex-State prisoners all will agree that it is not only one of them, but the one without which all the oth-ers are nothing. Seek first the kingdom of the ballot and all things else shall be added, is the political injunction. . . .

However much the doctors of the law may disagree as to whether people and citizens, in the original Constitution, were one and the same, or whether the privileges and immunities in the Fourteenth Amendment include the right of suffrage, the question of the citizen's right to vote is forever settled by the Fifteenth Amendment. "The right of citizens of the United States to vote shall not be denied or abridged by the United States, or by any State, on account of race, color or previous condition of servitude." How can the State deny or abridge the right of the citizen, if the citizen does not possess it? There is no escape from the conclusion that to vote is the citizen's right, and the specifications of race, color or previous condition of servitude can in no way impair the force of that emphatic assertion that the citizen's right to vote shall not be denied or abridged. . . .

If, however, you will insist that the Fifteenth Amendment's emphatic interdiction against robbing United States citizens of their suffrage "on account of race, color or previous condition of servitude," is a recognition of the right of either the United States or any State to deprive them of the ballot for any or all other reasons, I will prove to you that the class of citizens for whom I now plead are, by all the principles of our government and many of the laws of the States, included under the term "previous conditions of servitude."

Consider first married women and their legal status. What is servitude? "The condition of a slave." What is a slave? "A person who is robbed of the proceeds of his labor; a person who is subject to the will of another." By the laws of Georgia, South Carolina and all the States of the South, the negro had no right to the custody and control of his person. He belonged to his master. If he were disobedient, the master had the right to use correction. If the negro did not like the correction and ran away, the master had the right to use coercion to bring him back. By the laws of almost every State in this Union today, North as well as South, the married woman has no right to the custody and control of her person. The wife belongs to the husband; and if she refuse obedience he may use moderate correction, and if she do not like his moderate correction and leave his "bed and board," the husband may use moderate coercion to bring her back. The little word "moderate," you see, is the saving clause for the wife, and would doubtless be overstepped should her offended husband administer his correction with the "cat-o'-nine-tails," or accomplish his coercion with blood-hounds.

Again the slave had no right to the earnings of his hands, they belonged to his master; no right to the custody of his children, they belonged to his master; no right to sue or be sued, or to testify in the courts. If he committed a crime, it was the master who must sue or be sued. In many of the States there has been special legislation, giving married women the right to property inherited or received by bequest, or earned by the pursuit of any avocation outside the home;

also giving them the right to sue and be sued in matters pertaining to such separate property; but not a single State of this Union has ever secured the wife in the enjoyment of her right to equal ownership of the joint earnings of the marriage copartnership. And since, in the nature of things, the vast majority of married women never earn a dollar by work outside their families, or inherit a dollar from their fathers, it follows that from the day of their marriage to the day of the death of their husbands not one of them ever has a dollar, except it shall please her husband to let her have it. . . .

20   Is anything further needed to prove woman's condition of servi-   20
tude sufficient to entitle her to the guarantees of the Fifteenth Amendment? Is there a man who will not agree with me that to talk of freedom without the ballot is mockery to the women of this republic, precisely as New England's orator, Wendell Phillips, at the close of the late war declared it to be to the newly emancipated black man? I admit that, prior to the rebellion, by common consent, the right to enslave, as well as to disfranchise both native and foreign born persons, was conceded to the States. But the one grand principle settled by the war and the reconstruction legislation, is the supremacy of the national government to protect the citizens of the United States in their right to freedom and the elective franchise, against any and every interference on the part of the several States; and again and again have the American people asserted the triumph of this principle by their overwhelming majorities for Lincoln and Grant.

The one issue of the last two presidential elections was whether the Fourteenth and Fifteenth Amendments should be considered the irrevocable will of the people; and the decision was that they should be, and that it is not only the right, but the duty of the national government to protect all United States citizens in the full enjoyment and free exercise of their privileges and immunities against the attempt of any State to deny or abridge. . . .

It is upon this just interpretation of the United States Constitution that our National Woman Suffrage Association, which celebrates the twenty-fifth anniversary of the woman's rights movement next May in New York City, has based all its arguments and action since the passage of these amendments. We no longer petition legislature or Congress to give us the right to vote, but appeal to women everywhere to exercise their too long neglected "citizen's right." We appeal to the inspectors of election to receive the votes of all United States citizens, as it is their duty to do. We appeal to United States commissioners and marshals to arrest, as is their duty, the inspectors who reject the votes of United States citizens, and leave alone those who perform their duties and accept these votes. We ask the juries to return verdicts of "not guilty" in the cases of law-abiding United States citizens who cast their votes, and inspectors of election who receive and count them.

We ask the judges to render unprejudiced opinions of the law, and wherever there is room for doubt to give the benefit to the side of liberty and equal rights for women, remembering that, as Sumner says, "The true rule of intepretation under our National Constitution, especially since its amendments, is that anything *for* human rights is constitutional, everything *against* human rights unconstitutional." It is on this line that we propose to fight our battle for the ballot—peaceably but nevertheless persistently—until we achieve complete triumph and all United States citizens, men and women alike, are recognized as equals in the government.

The Discovery of What It Means to Be an American

James Baldwin

James Baldwin (1924–1987) was born in poverty in the Harlem district of New York City, where he lived until he was eighteen. From age fourteen to seventeen he was a revivalist minister, manifesting a religious intensity seen in much of his work. After high school he worked various jobs in Greenwich Village while studying and writing on his own. He then moved to Paris for eight years, and thereafter much of his life was spent back and forth between New York and Europe. In the early 1960s Baldwin worked in the civil rights movement. At the time the following essay was written, in 1961, Baldwin had already written and published several successful novels, and he continued writing until his death in France. His novels include Go Tell It on the Mountain *(1953),* Giovanni's Room *(1956), and* Another Country *(1967). His best-known collections of essays are* Notes of a Native Son *(1955),* Nobody Knows My Name *(1961), and* The Fire Next Time. *His play* Blues for Mister Charley *(1964) is equally powerful. In the following autobiographical sketch written midway through his career, Baldwin analyzes how he came to understand his American self only after having gone to Europe. Consider whether his comments are as true of other Americans.*

1   "It is a complex fate to be an American," Henry James observed, and the principal discovery an American writer makes in Europe is just how complex this fate is. America's history, her aspirations, her peculiar triumphs, her even more peculiar defeats,

and her position in the world—yesterday and today—are all so profoundly and stubbornly unique that the very word "America" remains
a new, almost completely undefined and extremely controversial
proper noun. No one in the world seems to know exactly what it describes, not even we motley millions who call ourselves Americans.

I left America because I doubted my ability to survive the fury of
the color problem here. (Sometimes I still do.) I wanted to prevent
myself from becoming *merely* a Negro; or, even, merely a Negro writer.
I wanted to find in what way the *specialness* of my experience could be
made to connect me with other people instead of dividing me from
them. (I was as isolated from Negroes as I was from whites, which is
what happens when a Negro begins, at bottom, to believe what white
people say about him.)

In my necessity to find the terms on which my experience could
be related to that of others, Negroes and whites, writers and non-writ-
ers, I proved, to my astonishment, to be as American as any Texas G.I.
And I found my experience was shared by every American writer I
knew in Paris. Like me, they had been divorced from their origins, and
it turned out to make very little difference that the origins of white
Americans were European and mine were African—they were no
more at home in Europe than I was.

The fact that I was the son of a slave and they were the sons of
free men meant less, by the time we confronted each other on European soil, than the fact that we were both searching for our separate
identities. When we had found these, we seemed to be saying, why,
then, we would no longer need to cling to the shame and bitterness
which had divided us so long.

5   It became terribly clear in Europe, as it never had been here, that   5
we knew more about each other than any European ever could. And
it also became clear that, no matter where our fathers had been born,
or what they had endured, the fact of Europe had formed us both, was
part of our identity and part of our inheritance.

I had been in Paris a couple of years before any of this became
clear to me. When it did, I, like many a writer before me upon the
discovery that his props have all been knocked out from under him,
suffered a species of breakdown and was carried off to the mountains
of Switzerland. There, in that absolutely alabaster landscape, armed
with two Bessie Smith records and a typewriter, I began to try to

re-create the life that I had first known as a child and from which I had spent so many years in flight.

It was Bessie Smith, through her tone and her cadence, who helped me to dig back to the way I myself must have spoken when I was a pickaninny, and to remember the things I had heard and seen and felt. I had buried them very deep. I had never listened to Bessie Smith in America (in the same way that, for years, I would not touch watermelon), but in Europe she helped to reconcile me to being a "nigger."

I do not think that I could have made this reconciliation here. Once I was able to accept my role—as distinguished, I must say, from my "place"—in the extraordinary drama which is America, I was re-leased from the illusion that I hated America.

The story of what can happen to an American Negro writer in Europe simply illustrates, in some relief, what can happen to any American writer there. It is not meant, of course, to imply that it happens to them all, for Europe can be very crippling, too; and, anyway, a writer, when he has made his first breakthrough, has simply won a crucial skirmish in a dangerous, unending and unpredictable battle. Still, the breakthrough is important, and the point is that an American writer, in order to achieve it, very often has to leave this country.

The American writer, in Europe, is released, first of all, from the necessity of apologizing for himself. It is not until he *is* released from the habit of flexing his muscles and proving that he is just a "regular guy" that he realizes how crippling this habit has been. It is not necessary for him, there, to pretend to be something he is not, for the artist does not encounter in Europe the same suspicion he encounters here. Whatever the Europeans may actually think of artists, they have killed enough of them off by now to know that they are as real—and as persistent—as rain, snow, taxes or businessmen.

Of course, the reason for Europe's comparative clarity concerning the different functions of men in society is that European society has always been divided into classes in a way that American society never has been. A European writer considers himself to be part of an old and honorable tradition—of intellectual activity, of letters—and his choice of a vocation does not cause him any uneasy wonder as to whether or not it will cost him all his friends. But this tradition does not exist in America.

On the contrary, we have a very deep-seated distrust of real intellectual effort (probably because we suspect that it will destroy, as I hope it does, that myth of America to which we cling so desperately). An American writer fights his way to one of the lowest rungs on the American social ladder by means of pure bull-headedness and an indescribable series of odd jobs. He probably *has* been a "regular fellow" for much of his adult life, and it is not easy for him to step out of that lukewarm bath.

We must, however, consider a rather serious paradox: though American society is more mobile than Europe's, it is easier to cut across social and occupational lines there than it is here. This has something to do, I think, with the problem of status in American life. Where everyone has status, it is also perfectly possible, after all, that no one has. It seems inevitable, in any case, that a man may become uneasy as to just what his status is.

But Europeans have lived with the idea of status for a long time. A man can be as proud of being a good waiter as of being a good actor, and, in neither case, feel threatened. And this means that the actor and the waiter can have a freer and more genuinely friendly relationship in Europe than they are likely to have here. The waiter does not feel, with obscure resentment, that the actor has "made it," and the actor is not tormented by the fear that he may find himself, tomorrow, once again a waiter.

15   This lack of what may roughly be called social paranoia causes the   15 American writer in Europe to feel—almost certainly for the first time in his life—that he can reach out to everyone, that he is accessible to everyone and open to everything. This is an extraordinary feeling. He feels, so to speak, his own weight, his own value.

It is as though he suddenly came out of a dark tunnel and found himself beneath the open sky. And, in fact, in Paris, I began to see the sky for what seemed to be the first time. It was borne in on me—and it did not make me feel melancholy—that this sky had been there before I was born and would be there when I was dead. And it was up to me, therefore, to make of my brief opportunity the most that could be made.

I was born in New York, but have lived only in pockets of it. In Paris, I lived in all parts of the city—on the Right Bank and the Left, among the bourgeoisie and among *les misérables,* and knew all kinds of people, from pimps and prostitutes in Pigalle to Egyptian bankers in Neuilly. This may sound extremely unprincipled or even obscurely immoral: I found it healthy. I love to talk to people, all kinds of people, and almost everyone, as I hope we still know, loves a man who loves to listen.

This perpetual dealing with people very different from myself caused a shattering in me of preconceptions I scarcely knew I held. The writer is meeting in Europe people who are not American, whose sense of reality is entirely different from his own. They may love or hate or admire or fear or envy this country—they see it, in any case, from another point of view, and this forces the writer to reconsider many things he had always taken for granted. This reassessment, which can be very painful, is also very valuable.

This freedom, like all freedom, has its dangers and its responsibilities. One day it begins to be borne in on the writer, and with great force, that he is living in Europe as an American. If he were living there as a European, he would be living on a different and far less attractive continent.

20   This crucial day may be the day on which an Algerian taxi-driver 20 tells him how it feels to be an Algerian in Paris. It may be the day on which he passes a café terrace and catches a glimpse of the tense, intelligent and troubled face of Albert Camus. Or it may be the day on which someone asks him to explain Little Rock and he begins to feel that it would be simpler—and, corny as the words may sound, more honorable—to *go* to Little Rock than sit in Europe, on an American passport, trying to explain it.

This is a personal day, a terrible day, the day to which his entire sojourn has been tending. It is the day he realizes that there are no untroubled countries in this fearfully troubled world; that if he has been preparing himself for anything in Europe, he has been preparing himself—for America. In short, the freedom that the American writer finds in Europe brings him, full circle, back to himself, with the responsibility for his development where it always was: in his own hands.

Even the most incorrigible maverick has to be born somewhere. He may leave the group that produced him—he may be forced to— but nothing will efface his origins, the marks of which he carries with him everywhere. I think it is important to know this and even find it a matter for rejoicing, as the strongest people do, regardless of their station. On this acceptance, literally, the life of a writer depends.

The charge has often been made against American writers that they do not describe society, and have no interest in it. Of course, what the American writer is describing is his own situation. But what is *Anna Karenina* describing if not the tragic fate of the isolated individual, at odds with her time and place?

The real difference is that Tolstoy was describing an old and dense society in which everything seemed—to the people in it, though not to Tolstoy—to be fixed forever. And the book is a masterpiece because Tolstoy was able to fathom, and make us see, the hidden laws which really governed this society and made Anna's doom inevitable.

American writers do not have a fixed society to describe. The only society they know is one in which nothing is fixed and in which the individual must fight for his identity. This is a rich confusion, indeed, and it creates for the American writer unprecedented opportunities.

That the tensions of American life, as well as the possibilities, are tremendous is certainly not even a question. But these are dealt with in contemporary literature mainly compulsively; that is, the book is more likely to be a symptom of our tension than an examination of it. The time has come, God knows, for us to examine ourselves, but we can only do this if we are willing to free ourselves of the myth of America and try to find out what is really happening here.

Every society is really governed by hidden laws, by unspoken but profound assumptions on the part of the people, and ours is no exception. It is up to the American writer to find out what these laws and assumptions are. In a society much given to smashing taboos without thereby managing to be liberated from them, it will be no easy matter.

It is no wonder, in the meantime, that the American writer keeps running off to Europe. He needs sustenance for his journey and the best models he can find. Europe has what we do not have yet, a sense of the mysterious and inexorable limits of life, a sense, in a word, of tragedy. And we have what they sorely need: a new sense of life's possibilities.

In this endeavor to wed the vision of the Old World with that of the New, it is the writer, not the statesman, who is our strongest arm. Though we do not wholly believe it yet, the interior life is a real life, and the intangible dreams of people have a tangible effect on the world.

Of Studies
Francis Bacon

*Francis Bacon (1561–1626) was born in London, stud-
ied at Trinity College, Cambridge, and trained for law at
Gray's Inn. He served the courts of Queen Elizabeth and
then King James I, was knighted in 1603, and was made
a baron in 1618 and then a viscount in 1621. He was
later accused of accepting bribes at court and was convicted
and briefly imprisoned before being pardoned. Bacon is
known both for his* Essays or Counsels, Civil and Moral
*and his discourses on the "new science" methods of induc-
tive observation and experimentation. Interestingly, perhaps because he was often adept at turning a phrase, some
have theorized (falsely, according to most critics) that
Bacon is the true author of some of Shakespeare's plays. As
perhaps the originator of the essay genre in English, Bacon
was influenced by the French essayist Montaigne. "Of
Studies" is typical of many of Bacon's essays as a brief ex-
ploration of an idea, described with a flourish of rhetoric
and extended figures of speech. Modern readers are sometimes impatient with Bacon's style, but if you read the essay
without haste you may find yourself appreciating the ebb
and flow of his phrases. An interesting effect can be
achieved by reading this essay aloud, with a slightly
pompous tone, as if to a court or congregation.*

Studies serve for delight, for ornament, and for ability. Their chief
use for delight is in privateness, and retiring; for ornament, is in
discourse; and for ability, is in the judgment and disposition of
business; for, expert men can execute, and perhaps judge of particulars, one by one; but the general counsels, and the plots and marshal-
ing of affairs, come best from those that are learned. To spend too
much time in studies, is sloth; to use them too much for ornament, is
affectation; to make judgment wholly by their rules, is the humour of

a scholar; they perfect nature, and are perfected by experience—for natural abilities are like natural plants, that need pruning by study; and studies themselves do give forth directions too much at large, except they be bounded in by experience. Crafty men condemn studies, simple men admire them, and wise men use them, for they teach not their own use; but that is a wisdom without them, and above them, won by observation. Read not to contradict and confute nor to believe and take for granted, nor to find talk and discourse, but to weigh and consider. Some books are to be tasted, others to be swallowed, and some few to be chewed and digested; that is, some books are to be read only in parts; others to be read, but not curiously; and some few to be read wholly, and with diligence and attention. Some books also may be read by deputy, and extracts made of them by others; but that would be only in the less important arguments, and the meaner sort of books; else distilled books are, like common distilled waters, flashy things. Reading maketh a full man, conference a ready man, and writing an exact man; and, therefore, if a man write little, he had need have a great memory; if he confer little, he had need have a present wit; and if he read little, he had need have much cunning, to seem to know that he doth not. Histories make men wise; poets witty; the mathematics subtle; natural philosophy deep; moral, grave; logic and rhetoric, able to contend: *abeunt studia in mores.*—Nay, there is no stond or impediment in the wit, but may be wrought out by fit studies, like as diseases of the body may have appropriate exercises—bowling is good for the stone and reins, shooting for the lungs and breast, gentle walking for the stomach, riding for the head, and the like; so, if a man's wit be wandering, let him study the mathematics, for in demonstrations, if his wit be called away never so little, he must begin again; if his wit be not apt to distinguish or find differences, let him study the schoolmen, for they are *cymini sectores,* if he be not apt to beat over matters, and to call upon one thing to prove and illustrate another, let him study the lawyers' cases—so every defect of the mind may have a special receipt.

The Holocaust

Bruno Bettelheim

Bruno Bettelheim (1903–1990), a noted psychotherapist, was born in Vienna, Austria. He graduated from the University of Vienna (1938), where he studied with Sigmund Freud. Bettelheim was imprisoned by the Nazis at Dachau and Buchenwald from 1938 to 1939. After his release from prison, Bettelheim emigrated to the United States, where he went to work at the University of Chicago. In 1944, he became director of the University's Sonia Shankman Orthogenic School, a treatment facility for severely disturbed children. Bettelheim gained international recognition for his work with autistic children, although not without some controversy over his methodologies. He published many books on psychotherapy, including Love Is Not Enough: The Treatment of Emotionally Disturbed Children *(1950),* The Children of the Dream *(1969),* The Uses of Enchantment: The Meaning and Importance of Fairy Tales *(1976),* Freud and Man's Soul *(1982), and* A Good Enough Parent *(1987). He also wrote articles on rearing normal children for lay audiences. In addition to a well-known article on his experiences in Nazi concentration camps (1943), Bettelheim published two books on the death camps,* The Informed Heart: Autonomy in a Mass Age *(1960) and* Surviving and Other Essays *(1979), reprinted as* Surviving the Holocaust *(1986). In this essay, Bettelheim argues against some of the common terminology used to describe the Nazi killing of Jews, such as "holocaust" and "martyrs."*

1 To begin with, it was not the hapless victims of the Nazis who   1
named their incomprehensible and totally unmasterable fate
the "holocaust." It was the Americans who applied this artificial and highly technical term to the Nazi extermination of the European Jews. But while the event when named as mass murder most foul
evokes the most immediate, most powerful revulsion, when it is des-
ignated by a rare technical term, we must first in our minds translate
it back into emotionally meaningful language. Using technical or spe-
cially created terms instead of words from our common vocabulary is
one of the best-known and most widely used distancing devices, separating the intellectual from the emotional experience. Talking about
"the holocaust" permits us to manage it intellectually where the raw
facts, when given their ordinary names, would overwhelm us emotionally—because it was catastrophe beyond comprehension, beyond
the limits of our imagination, unless we force ourselves against our desire to extend it to encompass these terrible events.

This linguistic circumlocution began while it all was only in the
planning stage. Even the Nazis—usually given to grossness in language and action—shied away from facing openly what they were up
to and called this vile mass murder "the final solution of the Jewish
problem." After all, solving a problem can be made to appear like an
honorable enterprise, as long as we are not forced to recognize that the
solution we are about to embark on consists of the completely un-
provoked, vicious murder of millions of helpless men, women, and
children. The Nuremberg judges of these Nazi criminals followed
their example of circumlocution by coining a neologism out of one
Greek and one Latin root: genocide. These artificially created technical terms fail to connect with our strongest feelings. The horror of
murder is part of our most common human heritage. From earliest infancy on, it arouses violent abhorrence in us. Therefore in whatever
form it appears we should give such an act its true designation and not
hide it behind polite, erudite terms created out of classical words.

To call this vile mass murder "the holocaust" is not to give it a special name emphasizing its uniqueness which would permit, over time,
the word becoming invested with feelings germane to the event it
refers to. The correct definition of *holocaust* is "burnt offering." As
such, it is part of the language of the psalmist, a meaningful word to
all who have some acquaintance with the Bible, full of the richest emotional connotations. By using the term "holocaust," entirely false associations are established through conscious and unconscious

connotations between the most vicious of mass murders and ancient rituals of a deeply religious nature.

Using a word with such strong unconscious religious connotations when speaking of the murder of millions of Jews robs the victims of this abominable mass murder of the only thing left to them: their uniqueness. Calling the most callous, most brutal, most horrid, most heinous mass murder a burnt offering is a sacrilege, a profanation of God and man.

5 Martyrdom is part of our religious heritage. A martyr, burned at 5 the stake, is a burnt offering to his god. And it is true that after the Jews were asphyxiated, the victims' corpses were burned. But I believe we fool ourselves if we think we are honoring the victims of systematic murder by using this term, which has the highest moral connotations. By doing so, we connect for our own psychological reasons what happened in the extermination camps with historical events we deeply regret, but also greatly admire. We do so because this makes it easier for us to cope; only in doing so we cope with our distorted image of what happened, not with the events the way they did happen.

By calling the victims of the Nazis "martyrs," we falsify their fate. The true meaning of *martyr* is: "One who voluntarily undergoes the penalty of death for refusing to renounce his faith" (*Oxford English Dictionary*). The Nazis made sure that nobody could mistakenly think that their victims were murdered for their religious beliefs. Renouncing their faith would have saved none of them. Those who had converted to Christianity were gassed, as were those who were atheists, and those who were deeply religious Jews. They did not die for any conviction, and certainly not out of choice.

Millions of Jews were systematically slaughtered, as were untold other "undesirables," not for any convictions of theirs, but only because they stood in the way of the realization of an illusion. They neither died for their convictions, nor were they slaughtered because of their convictions, but only in consequence of the Nazis' delusional belief about what was required to protect the purity of their assumed superior racial endowment, and what they thought necessary to guarantee them the living space they believed they needed and were entitled to. Thus while these millions were slaughtered for an idea, they did not die for one.

Millions—men, women, and children—were processed after they had been utterly brutalized, their humanity destroyed, their clothes torn from their bodies. Naked, they were sorted into those who were destined to be murdered immediately, and those others who had a short-term usefulness as slave labor. But after a brief interval they, too, were to be herded into the same gas chambers into which the others were immediately piled, there to be asphyxiated so that, in their last moments, they could not prevent themselves from fighting each other in vain for a last breath of air.

To call these most wretched victims of a murderous delusion, of destructive drives run rampant, martyrs or a burnt offering is a distortion invented for our comfort, small as it may be. It pretends that this most vicious of mass murders had some deeper meaning; that in some fashion the victims either offered themselves or at least became sacrifices to a higher cause. It robs them of the last recognition which could be theirs, denies them the last dignity we could accord them: to face and accept what their death was all about, not embellishing it for the small psychological relief this may give us.

10   We could feel so much better if the victims had acted out of   10 choice. For our emotional relief, therefore, we dwell on the tiny minority who did exercise some choice: the resistance fighters of the Warsaw ghetto, for example, and others like them. We are ready to overlook the fact that these people fought back only at a time when everything was lost, when the overwhelming majority of those who had been forced into the ghettos had already been exterminated without resisting. Certainly those few who finally fought for their survival and their convictions, risking and losing their lives in doing so, deserve our admiration; their deeds give us a moral lift. But the more we dwell on these few, the more unfair are we to the memory of the millions who were slaughtered—who gave in, did not fight back—because we deny them the only thing which up to the very end remained uniquely their own: their fate.

"I'm Not Racist But . . ."

Neil Bissoondath

Born in Trinidad, Neil Bissoondath (1955–) moved to Canada at age 18 to attend York University. Upon receiving a degree in French, Bissoondath taught both French and English before beginning his writing career. In choosing to be a full-time writer, he followed in the footsteps of his internationally known uncles, Shiva and V.S. Naipaul. Bissoondath's first book, the short story collection Digging Up the Mountains *(1985), received significant critical praise, and his nonfiction critique of multiculturalism,* Selling Illusions: The Cult of Multiculturalism in Canada *(1994), stirred a good deal of controversy. His book* The Innocence of Age *(1992) won the Canadian Authors Association Prize for fiction. Most of Bissoondath's work, both fiction and nonfiction, deals with the dislocation, alienation, and racial tension of non-white immigrants in Canadian society. In the following essay, the author questions the legitimacy of labeling all insensitive ethnic language as racism.*

1   Someone recently said that racism is as Canadian as maple syrup. I have no argument with that. History provides us with ample proof. But, for proper perspective, let us remember that it is also as American as apple pie, as French as croissants, as Jamaican as ackee, as Indian as aloo, as Chinese as chow mein, as. . . . Well, there's an entire menu to be written. This is not by way of excusing it. Murder and rape, too, are international, multicultural, as innate to the darker side of the human experience. But we must be careful that the inevitable rage evoked does not blind us to the larger context.

The word "racism" is a discomforting one: It is so vulnerable to manipulation. We can, if we so wish, apply it to any incident involving people of different colour. And therein lies the danger. During the heat of altercation, we seize, as terms of abuse, on whatever is most obvious about the person. It is, often, a question of unfortunate convenience. A woman, because of her sex, easily becomes a female dog or an intimate part of her anatomy. A large person might be dubbed "a stupid ox," a small person "a little" whatever. And so a black might become "a nigger," a white "a honky," an Asian "a paki," a Chinese "a chink," an Italian "a wop," a French-Canadian "a frog."

There is nothing pleasant about these terms; they assault every decent sensibility. Even so, I once met someone who, in a stunning surge of naiveté, used them as simple descriptives and not as terms of racial abuse. She was horrified to learn the truth. While this may have been an extreme case, the point is that the use of such patently abusive words may not always indicate racial or cultural distaste. They may indicate ignorance or stupidity or insensitivity, but pure racial hatred—such as the Nazis held for Jews, or the Ku Klux Klan for blacks—is a thankfully rare commodity.

Ignorance, not the willful kind but that which comes from lack of experience, is often indicated by that wonderful phrase, "I'm not racist but. . . ." I think of the mover, a friendly man, who said, "I'm not racist, but the Chinese are the worst drivers on the road." He was convinced this was so because the shape of their eyes, as far as he could surmise, denied them peripheral vision.

5 Or the oil company executive, an equally warm and friendly man, who, looking for an apartment in Toronto, rejected buildings with East Indian tenants not because of their race—he was telling me this, after all—but because he was given to understand that cockroaches were symbols of good luck in their culture and that, when they moved into a new home, friends came by with gift-wrapped cockroaches.

Neither of these men thought of himself as racist, and I believe they were not, deep down. (The oil company executive made it clear he would not hesitate to have me as a neighbour; my East Indian descent was of no consequence to him, my horror of cockroaches was.) Yet their comments, so innocently delivered, would open them to the accusation, justifiably so if this were all one knew about them. But it is a charge which would undoubtedly be wounding to them. It is difficult to recognize one's own misconceptions.

True racism is based, more often than not, on willful ignorance, and an acceptance of—and comfort with—stereotype. We like to think, in this country, that our multicultural mosaic will help nudge us into a greater openness. But multiculturalism as we know it indulges in stereotype, depends on it for a dash of colour and the flash of dance. It fails to address the most basic questions people have about each other. Do those men doing the Dragon Dance really all belong to secret criminal societies? Do those women dressed in saris really coddle cockroaches for luck? Do those people in dreadlocks all smoke marijuana and live on welfare? Such questions do not seem to be the concern of the government's multicultural programs, superficial and exhibitionistic as they have become.

So the struggle against stereotype, the basis of all racism, becomes a purely personal one. We must beware of the impressions we create. A friend of mine once commented that, from talking to West Indians, she has the impression that their one great cultural contribution to the world is in the oft-repeated boast that "We (unlike everyone else) know how to party."

There are dangers, too, in community response. We must be wary of the self-appointed activists who seem to pop up in the media at every given opportunity spouting the rhetoric of retribution, mining distress for personal, political and professional gain. We must be skeptical about those who depend on conflict for their sense of self, the non-whites who need to feel themselves victims of racism, the whites who need to feel themselves purveyors of it. And we must be sure that, in addressing the problem, we do not end up creating it. Does the *Miss Black Canada Beauty Contest* still exist? I hope not. Not only do I find beauty contests offensive, but a racially segregated one even more so. What would the public reaction be, I wonder, if every year CTV broadcast the *Miss White Canada Beauty Pageant?* We give community-service awards only to blacks: Would we be comfortable with such awards only for whites? In Quebec, there are The Association of Black Nurses, The Association of Black Artists, The Congress of Black Jurists. Play tit for tat: The Association of White Nurses, White Artists, White Jurists: visions of apartheid. Let us be frank, racism for one is racism for others.

10 Finally, and perhaps most important, let us beware of abusing the 10 word itself.

The Gender Blur

Deborah Blum

Deborah Blum (1954–   ) was born in Urbana, Illinois to an entomologist and a legal scholar. Educated in journalism at the University of Georgia (B.A.) and the University of Wisconsin (M.A.), she has worked as a reporter for several newspapers in Georgia and Florida, and as a science writer for the Sacramento, California Bee. *Currently, Blum is professor of journalism at the University of Wisconsin. Her first book,* The Monkey Wars, *explored the issue of medical and psychological experimentation on primates. Lauded for its balanced approach, the book grew out of a Pulitzer Prize-winning series she had written on the subject in 1992. Her work has also earned her other awards, among them a Westinghouse Award from the American Academy of Arts and Sciences and a Clarion Award for Investigative Reporting, both in 1992; and a National Award for Non-Deadline Reporting from the Society of Professional Journalists in 1996. In 1997 she co-edited* A Field Guide for Science Writers. *Her most recent book,* Sex on the Brain: The Biological Differences Between Men and Women *(1997), explores the roles of biology and environment in determining gender. In this selection, based on that book, Blum describes how imprecise biological determiners of sex can be. Using extensive examples of indeterminate sexual identity, Blum raises questions about the rigid classification of male and female in the human race.*

I was raised in one of those university-based, liberal elite families that politicians like to ridicule. In my childhood, every human being—regardless of gender—was exactly alike under the skin, and I mean exactly, barring his or her different opportunities. My parents wasted no opportunity to bring this point home. One Christmas, I received a Barbie doll and a softball glove. Another brought a green enamel stove, which baked tiny cakes by the heat of a lightbulb, and also a set of steel-tipped darts and competition-quality dartboard. Did I mention the year of the chemistry set and the ballerina doll?

It wasn't until I became a parent—I should say, a parent of two boys—that I realized I had been fed a line and swallowed it like a sucker (barring the part about opportunities, which I still believe). This dawned on me during my older son's dinosaur phase, which began when he was about 2 1/2. Oh, he loved dinosaurs, all right, but only the blood-swilling carnivores. Plant-eaters were wimps and losers, and he refused to wear a T-shirt marred by a picture of a stegosaur. I looked down at him one day, as he was snarling around my feet and doing his toddler best to gnaw off my right leg, and I thought: This goes a lot deeper than culture.

Raising children tends to bring on this kind of politically incorrect reaction. Another friend came to the same conclusion watching a son determinedly bite his breakfast toast into the shape of a pistol he hoped would blow away—or at least terrify—his younger brother. Once you get past the guilt part—Did I do this? Should I have bought him that plastic allosaur with the oversized teeth?—such revelations can lead you to consider the far more interesting field of gender biology, where the questions take a different shape: Does love of carnage begin in culture or genetics, and which drives which? Do the gender roles of our culture reflect an underlying biology, and, in turn, does the way we behave influence that biology?

The point I'm leading up to—through the example of my son's innocent love of predatory dinosaurs—is actually one of the most straightforward in this debate. One of the reasons we're so fascinated by childhood behaviors is that, as the old saying goes, the child becomes the man (or woman, of course.) Most girls don't spend their preschool years snarling around the house and pretending to chew off their companion's legs. And they—mostly—don't grow up to be as aggressive as men. Do the ways that we amplify those early differences in childhood shape the adults we become?

Absolutely. But it's worth exploring the starting place—the faint signal that somehow gets amplified.

"There's plenty of room in society to influence sex differences," says Marc Breedlove, a behavioral endocrinologist at the University of California at Berkeley and a pioneer in defining how hormones can help build sexually different nervous systems. "Yes, we're born with predispositions, but it's society that amplifies them, exaggerates them. I believe that—except for the sex differences in aggression. Those [differences] are too massive to be explained simply by society."

Aggression does allow a straightforward look at the issue. Consider the following statistics: Crime reports in both the United States and Europe record between 10 and 15 robberies committed by men for every one by a woman. At one point, people argued that this was explained by size difference. Women weren't big enough to intimidate, but that would change, they predicted, with the availability of compact weapons. But just as little girls don't routinely make weapons out of toast, women—even criminal ones—don't seem drawn to weaponry in the same way that men are. Almost twice as many male thieves and robbers use guns as their female counterparts do.

Or you can look at more personal crimes: domestic partner murders. Three-fourths of men use guns in those killings; 50 percent of women do. Here's more from the domestic front: In conflicts in which a woman killed a man, he tended to be the one who had started the fight—in 51.8 percent of the cases, to be exact. When the man was the killer, he again was the likely first aggressor, and by an even more dramatic margin. In fights in which women died, they had started the argument only 12.5 percent of the time.

Enough. You can parade endless similar statistics but the point is this: Males are more aggressive, not just among humans but among almost all species on earth. Male chimpanzees, for instance, declare war on neighboring troops, and one of their strategies is a warning strike: They kill females and infants to terrorize and intimidate. In terms of simple, reproductive genetics, it's an advantage of males to be aggressive: You can muscle you way into dominance, winning more sexual encounters, more offspring, more genetic future. For the female—especially in a species like ours, with time for just one successful pregnancy a year—what's the genetic advantage in brawling?

Thus the issue becomes not whether there is a biologically influenced sex difference in aggression—the answer being a solid, technical

"You betcha"—but rather how rigid that difference is. The best science, in my opinion, tends to align with basic common sense. We all know that there are extraordinarily gentle men and murderous women. Sex differences are always generalizations: They refer to a behavior, with some evolutionary rationale behind it. They never define, entirely, an individual. And that fact alone should tell us that there's always—even in the most biologically dominated traits—some flexibility, an instinctive ability to respond, for better and worse, to the world around us.

10 This is true even with physical characteristics that we've often 10 assumed are nailed down by genetics. Scientists now believe height, for instance, is only about 90 percent heritable. A person's genes might code for a six-foot-tall body, but malnutrition could literally cut that short. And there's also some evidence, in girls anyway, that children with stressful childhoods tend to become shorter adults. So while some factors are predetermined, there's evidence that the prototypical male/female body design can be readily altered.

It's a given that humans, like most other species—bananas, spiders, sharks, ducks, any rabbit you pull out of a hat—rely on two sexes for reproduction. So basic is that requirement that we have chromosomes whose primary purpose is to deliver the genes that order up a male or a female. All other chromosomes are numbered, but we label the sex chromosomes with the letters X and Y. We get one each from our mother and our father, and the basic combinations are these: XX makes female, XY makes male.

There are two important—and little known—points about these chromosomal matches. One is that even with this apparently precise system, there's nothing precise—or guaranteed—about the physical construction of male and female. The other point makes that possible. It appears that sex doesn't matter in the early stages of embryonic development. We are unisex at the point of conception.

If you examine an embryo at about six weeks, you see that it has the ability to develop in either direction. The fledgling embryo has two sets of ducts—Wolffian for male, Muellerian for female—an either/or structure, held in readiness for further development. If testosterone and other androgens are released by hormone-producing cells, then the Wolffian ducts develop into the channel that connects penis to testes, and the female ducts wither away.

Without testosterone, the embryo takes on a female form; the male ducts vanish and the Muellerian ducts expand into oviducts, uterus, and vagina. In other words, in humans, anyway (the opposite is true in birds), the female is the default sex. Back in the 1950s, the famed biologist Alfred Jost showed that if you castrate a male rabbit fetus, choking off testosterone, you produce a completely feminized rabbit.

15   We don't do these experiments in humans—for obvious reasons— 15 but there are naturally occurring instances that prove the same point. For instance: In the fetal testes are a group of cells called Leydig cells, that make testosterone. In rare cases, the fetus doesn't make enough of these cells (a defect known as Leydig cell hypoplasia). In this circumstance we see the limited power of the XY chromosome. These boys have the right chromosomes and the right genes to be boys; they just don't grow a penis. Obstetricians and parents often think they see a baby girl, and these children are routinely raised as daughters. Usually, the "mistake" is caught about the time of puberty, when menstruation doesn't start. A doctor's examination shows the child to be internally male; there are usually small testes, often tucked with the abdomen. As the researchers put it, if the condition had been known from the beginning, "the sisters would have been born as brothers."

Just to emphasize how tricky all this body-building can get, there's a peculiar genetic defect that seems to be clustered by heredity in a small group of villages in the Dominican Republic. The result of the defect is a failure to produce an enzyme that concentrates testosterone, specifically for building genitals. One obscure little enzyme only, but here's what happens without it: You get a boy with undescended testes and a penis so short and stubby that it resembles an oversized clitoris.

In the mountain villages of this Caribbean nation, people are used to it. The children are usually raised as "conditional" girls. At puberty, the secondary tide of androgens rises and is apparently enough to finish the construction project. The scrotum suddenly descends, the phallus grows, and the child develops a distinctly male body—narrow hips, muscular build, and even slight beard growth. At that point, the family shifts the child over from daughter to son. The dresses are thrown out. He begins to wear male clothes and starts dating girls. People in the Dominican Republic are so familiar with this condition that there's a colloquial name for it: *guevedoces*, meaning "eggs (or testes) at 12."

It's the comfort level with this slip-slide of sexual identity that's so remarkable and, I imagine, so comforting to the children involved. I'm positive that the sexual transition of these children is less traumatic than the abrupt awareness of the "sisters who would have been brothers." There's a message of tolerance there, well worth repeating, and there are some other key lessons too.

These defects are rare and don't alter the basic male-female division of our species. They do emphasize how fragile those divisions can be. Biology allows flexibility, room to change, to vary and grow. With that comes room for error as well. That it's possible to live with these genetic defects, that they don't merely kill us off, is a reminder that we, male and female alike, exist on a continuum of biological possibilities that can overlap and sustain either sex.

20 Marc Breedlove points out that the most difficult task may be 20 separating how the brain responds to hormones from how the brain responds to the *results* of hormones. Which brings us back, briefly, below the belt: In this context, the penis is just a result, the product of androgens at work before birth. "And after birth," says Breedlove, "virtually everyone who interacts with that individual will note that he has a penis, and will, in many instances, behave differently than if the individual was a female."

Do the ways that we amplify physical and behavioral differences in childhood shape who we become as adults? Absolutely. But to understand that, you have to understand the differences themselves—their beginning and the very real biochemistry that may lie behind them.

Here is a good place to focus on testosterone—a hormone that is both well-studied and generally underrated. First, however, I want to acknowledge that there are many other hormones and neurotransmitters that appear to influence behavior. Preliminary work shows that fetal boys are a little more active than fetal girls. It's pretty difficult to argue socialization at that point. There's a strong suspicion that testosterone may create the difference.

And there are a couple of relevant animal models to emphasize the point. Back in the 1960s, Robert Goy, a psychologist at the University of Wisconsin at Madison, first documented that young male monkeys play much more roughly than young females. Goy went on to show that if you manipulate testosterone level—raising it in females, damping it down in males—you can reverse those effects, creating sweet little male monkeys and rowdy young females.

Is testosterone the only factor at work here? I don't think so. But clearly we can argue a strong influence, and, interestingly, studies have found that girls with congenital adrenal hypoplasia—who run high in testosterone—tend to be far more fascinated by trucks and toy weaponry than most little girls are. They lean toward rough-and-tumble play, too. As it turns out, the strongest influence on this "abnormal" behavior is not parental disapproval, but the company of other little girls, who tone them down and direct them toward more routine girl games.

25   And that reinforces an early point: If there is indeed a biology to   25
sex differences, we amplify it. At some point—when it is still up for debate—we gain a sense of our gender, and with it a sense of "gender-appropriate" behavior.

Some scientists argue for some evidence of gender awareness in infancy, perhaps by the age of 12 months. The consensus seems to be that full-blown "I'm a girl" or "I'm a boy" instincts arrive between the ages of 2 and 3. Research shows that if a family operates in a very traditional, Beaver Cleaver kind of environment, filled with awareness of and association with "proper" gender behaviors, the "boys do trucks, girls do dolls" attitude seems to come very early. If a child grows up in a less traditional family, with an emphasis on partnership and sharing—"We all do the dishes, Joshua"—children maintain a more flexible sense of gender roles until about age 6.

In this period, too, relationships between boys and girls tend to fall into remarkably strict lines. Interviews with children find that 3-year-olds say that about half their friendships are with the opposite sex. By the age of 5, that drops to 20 percent. By 7, almost no boys or girls have, or will admit to having, best friends of the opposite sex. They still hang out on the same playground, play on the same soccer teams. They may be friendly, but the real friendships tend to be boy-to-boy or girl-to-girl.

There's some interesting science that suggests that the space between boys and girls is a normal part of development; there are periods during which children may thrive and learn from hanging out with peers of the same sex. Do we, as parents, as a culture at large, reinforce such separations? Is the pope Catholic? One of my favorite studies looked at little boys who asked for toys. If they asked for a heavily armed action figure, they got the soldier about 70 percent of the time. If they asked for a "girl" toy, like a baby doll or a Barbie, their parents purchased it maybe 40 percent of the time. Name a child who won't figure out to work *that* system.

How does all this fit together—toys and testosterone, biology and behavior, the development of the child into the adult, the way that men and women relate to one another?

Let me make a cautious statement about testosterone: It not only has some body-building functions, it influences some behaviors as well. Let's make that a little less cautious: These behaviors include rowdy play, sex drive, competitiveness, and an in-your-face attitude. Males tend to have a higher baseline of testosterone than females—in our species, about seven to ten times as much—and therefore you would predict (correctly, I think) that all of those behaviors would be more generally found in men than in women.

But testosterone is also one of my favorite examples of how responsive biology is, how attuned it is to the way we live our lives. Testosterone, it turns out, rises in response to competition and threat. In the days of our ancestors, this might have been hand-to-hand combat or high-risk hunting endeavors. Today, scientists have measured testosterone rise in athletes preparing for a game, in chess players awaiting a match, in spectators following a soccer competition.

If a person—or even just a person's favored team—wins, testosterone continues to rise. It falls with a loss. (This also makes sense in an evolutionary perspective. If one was being clobbered with a club, it would be extremely unhelpful to have a hormone urging one to battle on.) Testosterone also rises in the competitive world of dating, settles down with a stable and supportive relationship, climbs again if the relationship starts to falter.

It's been known for years that men in high-stress professions—say, police work or corporate law—have higher testosterone levels than men in the ministry. It turns out that women in the same kind of strong-attitude professions have higher testosterone than women who choose to stay home. What I like about this is the chicken-or-egg aspect. If you argue that testosterone influenced the behavior of those women, which came first? Did they have high testosterone and choose the law? Or did they choose the law, and the competitive environment ratcheted them up on the androgen scale? Or could both be at work?

And, returning to children for a moment, there's an ongoing study by Pennsylvania researchers, tracking that question in adolescent girls, who are being encouraged by their parents to engage in competitive activities that were once for boys only. As they do so, the researchers are monitoring, regularly, two hormones: testosterone and cortisol, a stress hormone. Will these hormones rise in response to this new, more traditionally male environment? What if more girls choose the competitive path; more boys choose the other? Will female testosterone levels rise, male levels fall? Will that wonderful, unpredictable, flexible biology that we've been given allow a shift, so that one day, we will literally be far more alike?

35   We may not have answers to all those questions, but we can ask them, and we can expect that the answers will come someday, because science clearly shows us that such possibilities exist. In this most important sense, sex differences offer us a paradox. It is only through exploring and understanding what makes us different that we can begin to understand what binds us together.   35

Lies for the Public Good

Sissela Bok

Sissela Bok (1934–) was born in Stockholm, Sweden. A naturalized American citizen (1959), Bok graduated from George Washington University (B. A., 1957, and M. A., 1958) and Harvard University (Ph.D. in philosophy, 1970). She has taught philosophy and ethics (her specialty) at Brandeis University and Harvard and has served on medical ethics advisory boards. Bok's articles have been published in Ethics, Scientific American, *and other periodicals. Her books include* Lying: Moral Choice in Public, Private Life (1978) and Secrets: On the Ethics of Concealment and Revelation *(1983),* A Strategy for Peace *(1989), and* Alva Myrdal: A Daughter's Memoir *(1991). This essay, taken from* Lying, *explores the acceptability of government lies told to protect the public from unpleasant or hurtful truths.*

1   But the most characteristic defense for these [noble] lies is a separate one, based on the benefits they may confer and the long-range harm they can avoid. The intention may be broadly paternalistic, as when citizens are deceived "for their own good," or only a few may be lied to for the benefit of the community at large. Error and self-deception mingle with these altruistic purposes and blur them; the filters through which we must try to peer at lying are thicker and more distorting than ever in these practices. But I shall try to single out, among these lies, the elements that are consciously and purposely intended to benefit society.

A long tradition in political philosophy endorses some lies for the sake of the public. Plato . . . first used the expression "noble lie" for the fanciful story that might be told to people in order to persuade them to accept class distinctions and thereby safeguard social harmony. According to this story, God Himself mingled gold, silver, iron, and brass in fashioning rulers, auxiliaries, farmers, and craftsmen, intending these groups for separate tasks in a harmonious hierarchy.

The Greek adjective which Plato used to characterize this falsehood expresses a most important fact about lies by those in power: this adjective is *"gennaion,"* which means "noble" in the sense of both "high-minded" and "well-bred." The same assumption of nobility, good breeding, and superiority to those deceived is also present in Disraeli's statement that a gentleman is one who knows when to tell the truth and when not to. In other words, lying is excusable when undertaken for "noble" ends by those trained to discern these purposes.

Rulers, both temporal and spiritual, have seen their deceits in the benign light of such social purposes. They have propagated and maintained myths played on the gullibility of the ignorant, and sought stability in shared beliefs. They have seen themselves as high-minded and well-bred—whether by birth or by training—and as superior to those they deceive. Some have gone so far as to claim that those who govern have a *right* to lie.[1] The powerful tell lies believing that they have greater than ordinary understanding of what is at stake; very often, they regard their dupes as having inadequate judgment, or as likely to respond in the wrong way to truthful information.

At times, those who govern also regard particular circumstances as too uncomfortable, too painful, for most people to be able to cope with rationally. They may believe, for instance, that their country must prepare for long-term challenges of great importance, such as a war, an epidemic, or a belt-tightening in the face of future shortages. Yet they may fear that citizens will be able to respond only to short-range dangers. Deception at such times may seem to the government leaders as the only means of attaining the necessary results.

The perspective of the liar is paramount in all such decisions to tell "noble" lies. If the liar considers the responses of the deceived at

---

[1]Arthur Sylvester, "The Government Has the Right to Lie," *Saturday Evening Post,* 18 November 1967, p. 10.

all, he assumes that they will, once the deceit comes to light and its benefits are understood, be uncomplaining if not positively grateful. The lies are often seen as necessary merely at one *stage* in the education of the public. . . .

Some experienced public officials are impatient with any effort to question the ethics of such deceptive practices (except actions obviously taken for private ends). They argue that vital objectives in the national interest require a measure of deception to succeed in the face of powerful obstacles. Negotiations must be carried on that are best left hidden from public view; bargains must be struck that simply cannot be comprehended by a politically unsophisticated electorate. A certain amount of illusion is needed in order for public servants to be effective. Every government, therefore, has to deceive people to some extent in order to lead them.

These officials view the public's concern for ethics as understandable but hardly realistic. Such "moralistic" concerns, put forth without any understanding of practical exigencies, may lead to the setting of impossible standards; these could seriously hamper work without actually changing the underlying practices. Government officials could then feel so beleaguered that some of them might quit their jobs; inefficiency and incompetence would then increasingly afflict the work of the rest.

If we assume the perspective of the deceived—those who experience the consequences of government deception—such arguments are not persuasive. We cannot take for granted either the altruism or the good judgment of those who lie to us, no matter how much they intend to benefit us. We have learned that much deceit for private gain masquerades as being in the public interest. We know how deception, even for the most unselfish motive, corrupts and spreads. And we have lived through the consequences of lies told for what were believed to be noble purposes.

10 Equally unpersuasive is the argument that there always has been 10 government deception, and always will be, and that efforts to draw lines and set standards are therefore useless annoyances. It is certainly true that deception can never be completely absent from most human practices. But there are great differences among societies in the kinds of deceit that exist and the extent to which they are practiced, differences also among individuals in the same government and among successive governments within the same society. This strongly suggests

that it is worthwhile trying to discover why such differences exist and to seek ways of raising the standards of truthfulness.

The argument that those who raise moral concerns are ignorant of political realities, finally, ought to lead, not to a dismissal of such inquiries, but to a more articulate description of what these realities are, so that a more careful and informed debate could begin. We have every reason to regard government as more profoundly injured by a dismissal of criticism and a failure to consider standards than by efforts to discuss them openly. If duplicity is to be allowed in exceptional cases, the criteria for these exceptions should themselves be openly debated and publicly chosen. Otherwise government leaders will have free rein to manipulate and distort the facts and thus escape accountability to the public.

The effort to question political deception cannot be ruled out so summarily. The disparagement of inquiries into such practices has to be seen as the defense of unwarranted power—power bypassing the consent of the governed. In the pages to come I shall take up just a few cases to illustrate both the clear breaches of trust that no group of citizens could desire, and circumstances where it is more difficult to render a judgment.

Examples of Political Deception

In September 1964, a State Department official, reflecting a growing administration consensus, wrote a memorandum advocating a momentous deceit of the American public.[2] He outlined possible courses of action to cope with the deteriorating military situation in South Vietnam. These included a stepping up of American participation in the "pacification" in South Vietnam and a "crescendo" of military action against North Vietnam, involving heavy bombing by the United States. But an election campaign was going on; the President's Republican opponent, Senator Goldwater, was suspected by the electorate of favoring escalation of the war in Vietnam and of brandishing nuclear threats to the communist world. In keeping with President Johnson's efforts to portray Senator Goldwater as an irresponsible war

---

[2]The Senator Gravel Edition, *The Pentagon Papers* (Boston: Beacon Press, 1971), 3:556–59.

hawk, the memorandum ended with a paragraph entitled "Special considerations during the next two months," holding that:

During the next two months, because of the lack of "rebuttal time" before election to justify particular actions which may be distorted to the U.S. public, we must act with special care—signaling to . . . [the South Vietnamese] that we are behaving energetically despite the restraints of our political season, and to the U.S. public that we are behaving with good purpose and restraint.

As the campaign wore on, President Johnson increasingly professed to be the candidate of peace. He gave no indication of the growing pressure for escalation from high administrative officials who would remain in office should he win; no hint of the hard choice he knew he would face if elected.[3] Rather he repeated over and over again that:

[[T]he first responsibility, the only real issue in this campaign, the only thing you ought to be concerned about at all, is: Who can best keep the peace?[4]

15   The stratagem succeeded; the election was won; the war escalat-   15
ed. Under the name of Operation Rolling Thunder, the United States launched massive bombing raids over North Vietnam early in 1965. In suppressing genuine debate about these plans during the election campaign and masquerading as the party of peace, government members privy to the maneuver believed that they knew what was best for the country and that history would vindicate them. They meant to benefit the nation and the world by keeping the danger of a communist victory at bay. If a sense of crisis was needed for added justification, the Domino Theory strained for it: one regime after another was seen as toppling should the first domino be pushed over.

But why the deceit, if the purposes were so altruistic? Why not espouse these purposes openly before the election? The reason must have been that the government could not count on popular support for the scheme. In the first place, the sense of crisis and threat from North

---

[3]As early as March 1964, Lyndon Johnson knew that such a hard choice might have to be made. See telephone transcript cited by Doris Kearns in *Lyndon Johnson and the American Dream* (New York: Harper & Row, 1976), p. 197.

[4]Theodore H, White, *The Making of the President 1964* (New York: Atheneum, 1965), p. 373.

Vietnam would have been far from universally shared. To be forthright about the likelihood of escalation might lose many votes; it certainly could not fit with the campaign to portray President Johnson as the candidate most likely to keep the peace. Second, the government feared that its explanations might be "distorted" in the election campaign, so that the voters would not have the correct information before them, Third, time was lacking for the government to make an effort at educating the people about all that was at issue. Finally, the plans were not definitive; changes were possible, and the Vietnamese situation itself very unstable. For all these reasons, it seemed best to campaign for negotiation and restraint and let the Republican opponent be the target for the fear of United States belligerence.

President Johnson thus denied the electorate any chance to give or to refuse consent to the escalation of the war in Vietnam. Believing they had voted for the candidate of peace, American citizens were, within months, deeply embroiled in one of the cruelest wars in their history. Deception of this kind strikes at the very essence of democratic government. It allows those in power to override or nullify the right vested in the people to cast an informed vote in critical elections. Deceiving the people for the sake of the people is a self-contradictory notion in a democracy, unless it can be shown that there has been genuine consent to deceit. The actions of President Johnson were therefore inconsistent with the most basic principle of our political system.

What if all government officials felt similarly free to deceive provided they believed the deception genuinely necessary to achieve some important public end? The trouble is that those who make such calculations are always susceptible to bias. They overestimate the likelihood that the benefit will occur and that the harm will be averted; they underestimate the chances that the deceit will be discovered and ignore the effects of such a discovery on trust; they underrate the comprehension of the deceived citizens, as well as their ability and their right to make a reasoned choice. And, most important, such a benevolent self-righteousness disguises the many motives for political lying which could not serve as moral excuses: the need to cover up past mistakes; the vindictiveness; the desire to stay in power. These self-serving ends provide the impetus for countless lies that are rationalized as "necessary" for the public good.

As political leaders become accustomed to making such excuses, they grow insensitive to fairness and to veracity. Some come to believe that any lie can be told so long as they can convince themselves that people will be better off in the long run. From there, it is a short step to the conclusion that, even if people will not be better off from a particular lie, they will benefit by all maneuvers to keep the right people in office. Once public servants lose their bearings in this way, all the shabby deceits of Watergate—the fake telegrams, the erased tapes, the elaborate cover-ups, the bribing of witnesses to make them lie, the televised pleas for trust—become possible.

While Watergate may be unusual in its scope, most observers would agree that deception is part and parcel of many everyday decisions in government. Statistics may be presented in such a way as to diminish the gravity of embarrassing problems. Civil servants may lie to members of Congress in order to protect programs they judge important, or to guard secrets they have been ordered not to divulge. If asked, members of Congress who make deals with one another to vote for measures they would otherwise oppose deny having made such deals. False rumors may be leaked by subordinates who believe that unwise executive action is about to be taken. Or the leak may be correct, but falsely attributed in order to protect the source. . . .

These common lies are now so widely suspected that voters are at a loss to know when they can and cannot believe what a candidate says in campaigning. The damage to trust has been immense. I have already referred to the poll which found 69 percent of Americans agreeing, both in 1975 and 1976, that the country's leaders had consistently lied to the American people over the past ten years. Over 40 percent of the respondents also agreed that:

> *Most politicians are so similar that it doesn't really make much difference who gets elected.*[5]

Many refuse to vote under such circumstances. Others look to appearance or to personality factors for clues as to which candidate might be more honest than the others. Voters and candidates alike are the losers when a political system has reached such a low level of trust. Once elected, officials find that their warnings and their calls to common sacrifice meet with disbelief and apathy, even when cooperation is most urgently needed. Law suits and investigations multiply. And the fact that candidates, should they win, are not expected

---

[5] *Cambridge Survey Research,* 1975, 1976.

to have meant what they said while campaigning, nor held account-able for discrepancies, only reinforces the incentives for them to bend the truth the next time, thus adding further to the distrust of the voters.

Political lies, so often assumed to be trivial by those who tell them, rarely are. They cannot be trivial when they affect so many people and when they are so peculiarly likely to be imitated, used to retaliate, and spread from a few to many. When political representatives or entire governments arrogate to themselves the right to lie, they take power from the public that would not have been given up voluntarily.

Deception and Consent

Can there be exceptions to the well-founded distrust of deception in public life? Are there times when the public itself might truly not care about possible lies, or might even prefer to be deceived: Are some white lies so trivial or so transparent that they can be ignored? And can we envisage public discussion of more seriously misleading government statements such that reasonable persons could consent to them in advance?

White lies, first of all, are as common to political and diplomatic affairs as they are to the private lives of most people. Feigning enjoy-ment of an embassy gathering or a political rally, toasting the longevity of a dubious regime or an unimpressive candidate for office—these are forms of politeness that mislead few. It is difficult to regard them as threats to either individuals or communities. As with all white lies, however, the problem is that they spread so easily, and that lines are very hard to draw. Is it still a white lie for a secretary of state to an-nounce that he is going to one country when in reality he travels to another? Or for a president to issue a "cover story" to the effect that a cold is forcing him to return to the White House, when in reality an international crisis made him cancel the rest of his campaign trip? Is it a white lie to issue a letter of praise for a public servant one has just fired? Given the vulnerability of public trust, it is never more impor-tant than in public life to keep the deceptive element of white lies to an absolute minimum, and to hold down the danger of their turning into more widespread deceitful practices.

Certain additional forms of deception may be debated and au-thorized in advance by elected representatives of the public. The use of unmarked police cars to discourage speeding by drivers is an example of such a practice. Various forms of unannounced, sometimes covert, auditing of business and government operations are others. Whenever these practices are publicly regulated, they can be limited so that abuses are avoided. But they must be openly debated and agreed to in advance, with every precaution against abuses of privacy and the rights of individuals, and against the spread of such covert activities. It is not enough that a public official assumes that consent would be given to such practices. . . .

Another form of deception takes place when the government regards the public as frightened, or hostile, and highly volatile. In order not to create a panic, information about early signs of an epidemic may be suppressed or distorted. And the lie to a mob seeking its victim is like lying to the murderer asking where the person he is pursuing has gone. It can be acknowledged and defended as soon as the threat is over. In such cases, one may at times be justified in withholding information; perhaps on rare occasions, even in lying. But such cases are so rare that they hardly exist for practical purposes.

The fact that rare circumstances exist where the justification for government lying seems powerful creates a difficulty—these same excuses will often be made to serve a great many more purposes. For some governments or public officials, the information they wish to conceal is almost never of the requisite certainty, the time never the right one, and the public never sufficiently dispassionate. For these reasons, it is hard to see how a practice of lying to the public about devaluation or changes in taxation or epidemics could be consented to in advance, and therefore justified.

Are there any exceptionally dangerous circumstances where the state of crisis is such as to justify lies to the public for its own protection? We have already discussed lying to enemies in an acute crisis. Sometimes the domestic public is then also deceived, at least temporarily, as in the case of the U-2 incident. Wherever there is a threat—from a future enemy, as before World War II, or from a shortage of energy—the temptation to draw upon the excuses for deceiving citizens is very strong. The government may sincerely doubt that the electorate is capable of making the immediate sacrifices needed to confront the growing danger. (Or one branch of the government may lack confidence in another, for similar reasons, as when the administration mistrusts Congress.) The public may seem too emotional, the time not yet ripe for disclosure. Are there crises so exceptional that deceptive strategies are justifiable? . . .

30   Do we want to live in a society where public officials can resort to deceit and manipulation whenever they decide that an exceptional crisis has arisen? Would we not, on balance, prefer to run the risk of failing to rise to a crisis honestly explained to us, from which the government might have saved us through manipulation? And what protection from abuse do we foresee should we surrender this choice?

In considering answers to these questions, we must take into account more than the short-run effects of government manipulation. President Roosevelt's manner of bringing the American people to accept first the possibility, then the likelihood, of war [World War II] was used as an example by those who wanted to justify President Johnson's acts of dissimulation. And these acts in turn were pointed to by those who resorted to so many forms of duplicity in the Nixon administration. Secrecy and deceit grew at least in part because of existing precedents.[6]

The consequences of spreading deception, alienation, and lack of trust could not have been documented for us more concretely than they have in the past decades. We have had a very vivid illustration of how lies undermine our political system. While deception under the circumstances confronting President Roosevelt may in hindsight be more excusable than much that followed, we could no more consent to it in advance than to all that come later.

Wherever lies to the public have become routine, then, very special safeguards should be required. The test of public justification of deceptive practices is more needed than ever. It will be a hard test to satisfy, the more so the more trust is invested in those who lie and the more power they wield. Those in government and other positions of trust should be held to the highest standards. Their lies are not ennobled by their positions; quite the contrary. Some lies—notably minor white lies and emergency lies rapidly acknowledged—may be more *excusable* than others, but only those deceptive practices which can be openly debated and consented to in advance are *justifiable* in a democracy.

---

[6]See Arthur M. Schlesinger, Jr., *The Imperial Presidency* (Boston: Houghton Mifflin, 1973, p. 356: "The power to withhold and the power to leak led on inexorably to the power to lie . . . uncontrolled secrecy made it easy for lying to become routine." See also David Wise, *The Politics of Lying* (New York: Random House, 1973).

Civic Engagement: The University as a Public Good

Nancy E. Cantor

Nancy Cantor (1952–) graduated from Sarah Lawrence College (1974) and Stanford University (Ph.D. 1978). She taught at Princeton where she chaired the Department of Psychology. She moved on to be dean of the graduate schools at the University of Michigan, where she led the university's defense of affirmative action in the cases Grutter v. Bollinger *and* Gratz v. Bollinger—*which were decided by the Supreme Court in 2003. She wrote several papers on the issues involved in those decisions. She then became chancellor at the University of Illinois-Urbana-Champaign (2001). She is now chancellor at Syracuse University. She is a fellow of the American Academy of Arts and Sciences and has served as chair of the board of directors of the American Association of Higher Education. Her awards include Distinguished Scientific Award for an Early Career Contribution to Psychology, awarded by the American Psychological Association (1985), and Woman of Achievement Award, given by the Anti-Defamation League (2001). She co-authored* Personality and Social Intelligence, *Century Psychology Series, (Prentice Hall, 1987) and* Personality Psychology: Recent Trends and Emerging Directions *(Springer, 1989); and she edited* Personality, Cognition, and Social Interaction *(1981).*

Civic engagement at a great public university requires many kinds of involvement, including work across colleges

and departments and work across student boundaries. In
this speech, Cantor explains her views of civic engagement
and academic diversity.

1   A s a public good, universities have a rare and critical role to   1
play. While we educate leaders for the future, we also address
important societal issues of the day. Our discoveries can and
do change the world. We lay the groundwork for the future as we
work to preserve the culture of the past. At the same time, we try out
new ways to build community.

The university's role is "rare" because it is positioned to the side
of everyday life, unconstrained by requirements for rigid adherence to
social norms or intellectual paradigms. The university can foster an
experimental attitude—playful, if you will—that can give rise to both
intellectual discovery and social innovation.

The university takes on a "critical" role when it opens its gates far
enough to listen to the different voices in the debate over the issues of
greatest concern to society and to learn about them firsthand. The
university must face outward toward work that changes the culture of
the day.

We are at our best when we build a community of scholars and
learners who feel empowered to be both playful in examining their
world and responsible for affecting societal progress. Just as we want
to open our gates and look outward, we also want to build model
communities on campus to invite the world in as partners.

Liberal learning and civic engagement

5   As AAC&U eloquently states in its Statement on Liberal Learning: 5
"Liberal learning is society's best investment in our shared future." Likewise I would argue that the best way for society to fulfill its dreams of a
shared, productive, and harmonious future is to maintain universities as
public goods. We can do this by intertwining the playfulness of liberal
learning as a mode of thought and action with the responsibility of civic
engagement with diverse stakeholders whose voices need to matter
more in our shared future. In so doing, we will be able to educate
socially responsible citizens who will not be complacent in the face of
entrenched societal norms, but will take the initiative in shaping our
diverse democracy and its global interconnections.[1]

This can happen because, at their best, liberal education and civic engagement have much in common. Each requires vibrant and sustained exchanges of both people and ideas. Universities can offer safe havens for people from different backgrounds, races, ethnic groups, and generations to talk, argue, and reflect as equals in exchanges that can and should bridge the boundaries between the university and the wider world.

Now, just one generation away from a time when white children will be the minority in our public schools, children of different races still grow up in different neighborhoods without attending each other's birthday parties, proms, weddings, and funerals. Because they and we do not know each other, the stereotypes that result have led to great inequality and injustice in such vital areas as employment, health care, and the criminal justice system.

Mirroring our divisions at home is ethnic, religious, and intergroup conflict in virtually every corner of the globe. The result is untold human and cultural carnage. To make matters worse, we have reacted to the very real pain and losses we have suffered on our own shores by turning inward, "battening the hatches" if you will, presenting real problems for the free and vital exchanges of people and ideas that are the foundation of our democracy.

The task of universities is urgent: to build on themes of diversity, not only in admissions and in recruiting, but also in creating living and learning communities that will produce a citizenry that is both engaged and informed. It is not enough to affirmatively provide access to educational opportunity. We must also create opportunities and settings in which to pursue true integration. Universities can take a leadership role in shaping a dialogue that goes beyond differences by supporting environments in which students learn from and about each other—environments in which differences are neither privileged nor ignored. (See Patricia Gurin's discussion of Benjamin Barber's distinction between ignoring and privileging differences in *Defending Diversity*, 2004.)

Building sustained exchanges: The arts as a prototype

10 Universities can fulfill this mission by offering contexts for the 10
exchanges of people and ideas that are sustained, rather than one-shot efforts over a day, a week, or even a semester. These exchanges must

appeal to people of different expertise and backgrounds. They should allow for open-mindedness, permit the suspension of everyday norms and judgments, and give standing to everyone, across generations.

In trying to envision how such exchanges might actually work, we might look to the arts—which I would define broadly as "expressive culture" in all forms—for a natural prototype. The arts stand to the side of daily life, and they allow the expression of self and of social tensions in a safe way. They can also forge sustained connections between peoples and ideas and cultures that otherwise either simply remain invisible, unexpressed, or worse yet, clash in destructive ways.

As an example, I invite you to consider the blues, a creation of African-Americans that made its way from rural slavery to our nation's cities, to people and places all over the world with different musical traditions, to young and old, and to other art forms. It is shown in a brilliant traveling exhibition entitled "Visualizing the Blues," photographs of the Mississippi Delta collected by the Dixon Gallery and Gardens in Memphis.

In the catalog for this exhibition, which was shown at the Krannert Art Museum at the University of Illinois, Deborah Willis Kennedy (2000) writes, "The blues is a life-and-death struggle. The blues permits the living to defend life/living." To visualize the blues, one must contend with prejudice and racism, blood and spit, malice and murder.

Ernest Withers took a photograph that illustrates this point. Its title is "Boarding House Bathroom From Which James Earl Ray Shot Dr. King, 422 South Main Street, Memphis, April 1968." The photograph shows a filthy toilet, an old tub, a pockmarked wall, the open window from which a killer silenced our nation's greatest voice for peace in the twentieth century. The room is repellent. Normally, we would turn away, but as soon as we realize where we are, we stay to stare. We are at the vantage point of the assassin. The image draws us into dialogue, across history and between groups.

The arts often serve this way, as the medium, not just the reflection, of intergroup dialogue. They offer an escape from the silencing that tends to come in "normal" society, making it possible to face highly charged and even taboo subjects. And everyone has some "standing" in the "conversation" that ensues. In the arts, for example, it is not only diplomats who can discuss and negotiate peace. Without money, limousines, or hotel reservations, children are taking it up, one-to-one, through a "Peace through Poetry" exchange on the Internet, sponsored by iEARN, an international educational and resource network. The sixteen schools participating in this project are located in Chicago, Lithuania, Japan, Bulgaria, Moscow, and in Urbana, a few blocks from our campus at Illinois.

"Before the war commences the end is clear," writes Rositsa Kuneva, a student from Bulgaria. "All taking part are losers, nobody wins/Never wins the one who fights against his fear/Sluicing down the earth with bloody rinse."[2]

Dialogues such as these strip away the armor that we think we need to protect our place in the world, and there is nothing quite like the voices of students when they are given standing through artistic expression. The arts demonstrate that the kinds of exchanges we need in the nation's colleges and universities are possible, but we must construct ways for these exchanges to occur.

Exchanges across the boundaries of race and ethnicity

In our increasingly multiracial democracy it is vital that universities create exchanges across the rigid boundaries of race and ethnicity, religion and culture. But the exchanges that come so naturally in the arts need something more in higher education: structures that let these exchanges happen.

Our students, faculty, and community partners need settings in which we can let down our guard, acknowledge each other's standing in the conversation, and feel able to express both discomfort and ignorance. We need to be able to do this formally and informally, on and off campus, and across the groups in which we have been socialized. Then and only then will our nation come close to realizing the educational benefits of diversity. Then and only then will we begin to more fully embrace the fifty-year-old promise of *Brown v. Board of Education*.

So, why are we in higher education still talking about race? Because our failure to discard the legacy of Jim Crow has left our nation so segregated that our students, for the most part, do not meet as equals until they arrive at our doors. I will never forget a Latina student who told me, "I've never lived with so many white people before." It is up to us to shift that perspective to: "They've never had

83

the chance to live with ME before," with all the opportunities and optimism that implies. We must create learning and living communities that will make true integration possible, and we must create ways to assess how well we're doing.

We must understand that the idea of "civic engagement" goes beyond service or volunteer work. We must immerse ourselves in environments of genuine exchange, and these can start at home, on our own campuses. Vibrant multiracial/multicultural exchanges that bring the issues of society to our doorstep are as much about civic engagement as are our programs in neighboring communities. We should also take the extra step of inviting our community neighbors onto our campuses as we build new models of community.

Experiments in exchange at Illinois

What would such communities look like? And how can we use what we know about the arts as a model? At Illinois, as on many campuses, we have been asking these questions for several years and I thought it might be useful to describe a few of our efforts, keeping in mind the analogies with the artistic exchanges I have already described.

Exchanges that eschew boundaries. One of the most powerful aspects of artistic exchanges is that they eschew the "normal" boundaries and distinctions of social life—anyone and everyone can be engaged in artistic expression, and frequently these exchanges draw diverse peoples and generations together. In a similar vein, when we created our new Center for Democracy in a Multiracial Society in 2002, we resolved that it would bring together scholars, students, and community activists to engage in conversation about the many racialized positions of different groups and individuals in our society.

The Center drew its advisory board from the leadership of all of our ethnic studies programs on campus. It invited community activists to come to campus for sabbaticals at the Center. It engaged students from different campus communities in intergroup conversations and analyses that go beyond "black and white." And it funded projects to examine the experience of democracy in daily life from these different positions.

25 Many of the Center's initiatives intentionally engage multiple 25 generations of both novices and experts. They circumvent the "silencing" that comes with power and status, and they give "standing" to

those who often are the most affected but the least heard. For example, the Center faculty have mobilized with Latino/a community activists in Illinois to address two issues of critical importance to their community—narrowing the K-12 achievement gap and lobbying for the rights of children of undocumented families. As they define what it means to "mobilize with the community," the goal is to position the families and the students to be heard.

It is the families themselves who are helping to design interventions in the schools. It is our students, many of whom have firsthand experience with being excluded by virtue of their parents' status, who are speaking to the legislators in Springfield, dialoguing at the Center with statewide leaders of the newest Freedom Rides, and learning in action as they take part in opening up educational opportunity to our fastest-growing student population in Illinois. Their voices have authenticity and power when they are finally given the stage. Listen to the words of Yesenia Sanchez, who came to our campus on a Freedom Ride:

> I am fighting for my dignity. I am an undocumented student and, just like many others, feel helpless because my dreams and goals are being snatched away. I wake up every morning and feel that my life is in limbo, nothing is certain . . . I am also here for my mother. When she was a young girl, she was only able to go up to the sixth grade because she was a woman and was supposed to be at home. She tells me how every night she dreamed about going to school. Her dreams are also mine, and I am determined to be someone.

Exchanges that take a lesson from history. We also take a lesson from the arts in trying to encourage cross-talk about race and opportunity, contrasting historical dreams and contemporary realities. At the moment, for example, we are in the middle of a year-long commemoration of the fiftieth anniversary of *Brown v. Board,* honoring those who put their lives on the line for the cause of justice, reexamining their struggle, and rededicating ourselves to their still unfulfilled dream.

At our entering student convocation last August, we began with a speech from the director of our women's studies program, Professor Kal Alston, about what *Brown v. Board* had meant to her African-American family and to her own education in predominantly white schools. We'll end the year with a commencement address by legal scholar and activist, Professor Lani Guinier. In between we have sponsored symposia, performances, book clubs, community research projects and partnerships, and dialogues. We are seeing both synergy and exchange.

As part of the commemoration, we invited back to campus alumni from Project 500, which in 1968 recruited African-American students from all over the nation to enroll at Illinois. As graduates, many continued the struggle for civil rights their entire lives and our current students took note of their lessons. Numbers of current students told us later they were so moved by hearing the stories of this older generation that afterwards they met as a group on their own to do some soul-searching about themselves.

In fact, that kind of storytelling and social introspection is a key component in creating new contexts for exchange on campus. The *Brown v. Board* commemoration itself, for example, is now the object of study by undergraduates participating in a new initiative we are calling The Ethnography of the University. This initiative is giving students the opportunity to examine deliberately their own and their peers' experiences of race at the university and then to report their work, their interviews, their data, and their conclusions on a Web archive for future use by other students as well as faculty, staff, and members of our larger community. As the Web archive develops, we too will be able to better assess the impact of our efforts to foster multiracial exchange.

So far, the students' research on the *Brown v. Board* commemoration indicates that a big event, such as the convocation that all first year students are expected to attend, can make a big difference. Their interviews showed that, while only some of our 38,000 students knew about *Brown,* and many did not, every single first-year student interviewed knew something about it and had something to say. A massive one-time effort can create interest that then carries over to the book clubs, symposia, performances, and other venues that offer smaller, ongoing contexts for exchange.

Understanding difference in the service of building common cause happens one person at a time, and it requires that we be able to reflect on our experience and see it in relation to the experiences of others. This, of course, is what happens frequently between artist and audience, as each critiques the other's expressions. It is also what is happening to the students who are doing the research in the Ethnography of the University initiative and we hope it is happening with other students as they gather together to reflect on *Brown*.

Living and learning together in safe havens. Of course, nothing can quite match the awakening that occurs when students come together informally as peers, and in those rare but critical moments, let down their guard, shed their protective armor, and enter into what can then become sustained dialogues about diversity.

35 In this light, I'd like to share a comment from a University of 35 Michigan undergraduate who answered an e-mail request to all students from the president of the Michigan Student Assembly, to describe the impact, positive or negative, of diversity on their lives. This is what she said, in her words, in 1997:

> My roommate and I roomed blind. I had no idea whom I would end up with. In mid-August I found out all about her. She was from Detroit and black. This didn't bother me one bit. So far we have gotten along great. . . . Here is one thing that I found funny. . . . My roommate has a flat iron that she uses to straighten AND curl her hair with. She had been bugging me for a while to let her try it on my hair. This one Friday night I decided to let her give it a try. . . . So she reached for my hair with her hand so that she could grab a chunk to brush. "EEEE," she shrieked. "What is that? . . . No, nothing is wrong. I just can't believe what your hair feels like! . . . I've never felt any white girl's hair before," she said. "I had no idea it was so different." We spent the next hour discussing how we take care of our hair, how much it costs to get it done, and we also argued about what a perm is. This isn't a great educational story, but now I feel a little more "worldly" and not as sheltered as I had before. It's the little things like this that make impacts on my life. Small, but nonetheless important. Diversity helps to make the world a little smaller.

In one brief moment, two students who were already friends and even shared the same room really *saw* each other in new ways, as women with hair that was different and bad hair days that were the same. One more blind spot disappeared in the slow way things happen when real integration finally occurs, when differences can be affirmed, talked about, and shared.

So how do we foster this sense of safety to express the self and social tensions in nonjudgmental and authentic ways in both living and learning environments—and preferably at the place that living and learning intersect? Again using the insight we can get from the arts, compare the difference in the courage of expression we typically see in campus theater to the muted "politeness" of many classroom discussions.

Classroom conversations can be just as courageous, but first we must structure the context to provide just enough safety for students to try to get to know each other and experience alternative perspectives on the world. At Illinois, we are building on the work of a model developed at Michigan in our Program in Intergroup Relations, which facilitates structured dialogues across small groups to create environments in which discomfort, ignorance, and even conflict are tolerated in the service of building trust and a sense of common fate.

40 Next fall, we will take another step by opening a new living and 40 learning residence for first and second year students. It will be dedicated to Intergroup Relations and Multiracial Integration, with cultural programming, structured dialogues, and classes taught by faculty fellows from our Center for Democracy. The idea here is a simple one: Since most students have had very little, if any, experience in crossing the boundaries of race and ethnicity in their daily lives, we need to structure safe environments for integration, for learning how to do the hard work of reaching out and living and learning in a multiracial community.

We know that most students, majority and minority, will say that there are substantial racial tensions on campus. At the same time, they will also say that at college they have made, often for the first time in their lives, some very good, close relationships with persons of other races and ethnicities. It is our responsibility to foster these kinds of intergroup experiences, preparing the ground of daily life in our campus community. We want to encourage the actual reaching out, on the ground, from one person to another. And we recognize that if we want students to become engaged citizens of the world, people who can question that world and prod it to be a better place—somewhere they want to live—we must invite them to change higher education, to share it, and to make it stretch to fit them. We want our students to change our university and to make it better.

Knowing the other, shaping the self

We have a hope in this nation that we can draw on the talent, skill, insight, and imagination of all of our citizens, and higher education must help to lead the way. With a nod to Walt Whitman, the poet Langston Hughes expressed this hope—this conviction—in an equally powerful way, in a poem entitled "I, Too."[3]

> *I, too, sing America.*
>
> *I am the darker brother.*
> *They send me to eat in the kitchen*
> *When company comes,*
> *But I laugh,*
> *And eat well,*
> *And grow strong.*
>
> *Tomorrow,*
> *I'll be at the table*
> *When company comes.*
> *Nobody'll dare*
> *Say to me,*
> *"Eat in the kitchen,"*
> *Then.*
>
> *Besides,*
> *They'll see how beautiful I am*
> *And be ashamed—*
>
> *I, too, am America.*

To lead the way toward fulfilling this hope, we in higher education must figure out how to sit together around our table and engage with difference. It is through this social introspection, done in the company of others and informed by the clash of perspectives, that liberal learning occurs, sustained by difference and strengthened by the solidarity that follows.

End Notes

1. See the Guiding Principles for the Center for Liberal Education and Civic Engagement, a cooperative effort of AAC&U and Campus Compact.

2. www.vceducation.org/peace/schools/ukraine208.html.
3. From *The Collected Poems of Langston Hughes,* by Langston Hughes, copyright © 1994 by The Estate of Langston Hughes. Used by permission of Alfred A. Knof, a division of Random House, Inc.

Works Cited

Grutter v. Bollinger, U.S. Supreme Court, No. 02–214, June 23, 2003.

Gurin, Patricia, ed., Earl Lewis, Eric Dey, Sylvia Hurtado, Jeffrey S. Lehman. 2004. *Defending diversity: Affirmative Action at the University of Michigan.* Ann Arbor: University of Michigan Press.

Kennedy, Deborah Willis. 2000. Coda: Imagine the blues. In Wendy McDoris, *Visualizing the blues: Images of the American South.* Memphis: The Dixon Gallery and Garden.

National Advisory Commission on Civil Disorders. 1968. *Report of the National Advisory Commission on Civil Disorders.* Washington, DC: Government Printing Office, March 1.

The Obligation to Endure

Rachel Carson

Rachel Carson (1907–1964), a pioneer of the environmental movement, was born in Pennsylvania. A naturalist by training, she specialized in marine biology and developed a particular affection for the rocky coast of Maine. Her seminal book Silent Spring *(1962), resulted from her work as an aquatic biologist for the U.S. Fish and Wildlife service, during which she became acutely aware of the ecological hazards of herbicides and insecticides. She also wrote* The Sea Around Us *(1951), for which she received the National Book Award,* Under the Sea Wind *(1952), and* The Edge of the Sea *(1955). Although Carson's writing was not without controversy, and for many years she was criticized as being an alarmist, she is now credited with being one of America's most important environmentalists. In this classic essay, Carson clearly implicates chemical pollutants—and people's careless use of them—in the degradation of the environment.*

1   The history of life on earth has been a history of interaction between living things and their surroundings. To a large extent, the physical form and the habits of the earth's vegetation and its animal life have been molded by the environment. Considering the whole span of earthly time, the opposite effect, in which life actually modifies its surroundings, has been relatively slight. Only within the moment of time represented by the present century has one species—man—acquired significant power to alter the nature of his world.

During the past quarter century this power has not only increased to one of disturbing magnitude but it has changed in character. The most alarming of all man's assaults upon the environment is the contamination of air, earth, rivers, and sea with dangerous and even lethal materials. This pollution is for the most part irrecoverable; the chain of evil it initiates not only in the world that must support life but in living tissues is for the most part irreversible. In this now universal contamination of the environment, chemicals are the sinister and little-recognized partners of radiation in changing the very nature of the world—the very nature of its life. Strontium 90, released through nuclear explosions into the air, comes to earth in rain or drifts down in fallout, lodges in soil, enters into the grass or corn or wheat grown there, and in time takes up its abode in the bones of a human being, there to remain until his death. Similarly, chemicals sprayed on croplands or forests or gardens lie long in soil, entering into living organisms, passing from one to another in a chain of poisoning and death. Or they pass mysteriously by underground streams until they emerge and, through the alchemy of air and sunlight, combine into new forms that kill vegetation, sicken cattle, and work unknown harm on those who drink from once pure wells. As Albert Schweitzer has said, "Man can hardly even recognize the devils of his own creation."

It took hundreds of millions of years to produce the life that now inhabits the earth—eons of time in which that developing and evolving and diversifying life reached a state of adjustment and balance with its surroundings. The environment, rigorously shaping and directing the life it supported, contained elements that were hostile as well as supporting. Certain rocks gave out dangerous radiation; even within the light of the sun, from which all life draws its energy, there were short-wave radiations with power to injure. Given time—time not in years but in millennia—life adjusts, and a balance has been reached. For time is the essential ingredient; but in the modern world there is no time.

The rapidity of change and the speed with which new situations are created follow the impetuous and heedless pace of man rather than the deliberate pace of nature. Radiation is no longer merely the background radiation of rocks, the bombardment of cosmic rays, the ultraviolet of the sun that have existed before there was any life on earth; radiation is now the unnatural creation of man's tampering with the atom. The chemicals to which life is asked to make its adjustment are no longer merely the calcium and silica and copper and all the rest of the minerals washed out of the rocks and carried in rivers to the sea; they are the synthetic creations of man's inventive mind, brewed in his laboratories, and having no counterparts in nature.

5   To adjust to these chemicals would require time on the scale that   5 is nature's; it would require not merely the years of a man's life but the life of generations. And even this, were it by some miracle possible, would be futile, for the new chemicals come from our laboratories in an endless stream; almost five hundred annually find their way into actual use in the United States alone. The figure is staggering and its implications are not easily grasped—500 new chemicals to which the bodies of men and animals are required somehow to adapt each year, chemically totally outside the limits of biologic experience.

    Among them are many that are used in man's war against nature. Since the mid-1940s over 200 basic chemicals have been created for use in killing insects, weeds, rodents, and other organisms described in the modern vernacular as "pests"; and they are sold under several thousand different brand names.

    These sprays, dusts, and aerosols are now applied almost universally to farms, gardens, forests, and homes—nonselective chemicals that have the power to kill every insect, the "good" and the "bad," to still the songs of birds and the leaping of fish in the streams, to coat the leaves with a deadly film, and to linger on in soil—all this though the intended target may be only a few weeds or insects. Can anyone believe it is possible to lay down such a barrage of poisons on the surface of the earth without making it unfit for all life? They should not be called "insecticides," but "biocides."

    The whole process of spraying seems caught up in an endless spiral. Since DDT was released for civilian use, a process of escalation has been going on in which ever more toxic materials must be found. This has happened because insects, in a triumphant vindication of Darwin's principle of the survival of the fittest, have evolved super races immune to the particular insecticide used, hence a deadlier one has always to be developed—and then a deadlier one than that. It has happened also because, for reasons to be described later, destructive insects often undergo a "flare-back" or resurgence, after spraying in numbers greater than before. Thus the chemical war is never won, and all life is caught in its violent crossfire.

10   Along with the possibility of the extinction of mankind by nu-   10 clear war, the central problem of our age has therefore become the

contamination of man's total environment with such substances of incredible potential for harm—substances that accumulate in the tissues of plants and animals and even penetrate the germ cells to shatter or alter the very material of heredity upon which the shape of the future depends. Some would-be architects of our future look toward a time when it will be possible to alter the human germ plasm by design. But we may easily be doing so now by inadvertence, for many chemicals, like radiation, bring about gene mutations. It is ironic to think that man might determine his own future by something so seemingly trivial as the choice of an insect spray.

All this has been risked—for what? Future historians may well be amazed by our distorted sense of proportion. How could intelligent beings seek to control a few unwanted species by a method that contaminated the entire environment and brought the threat of disease and death even to their own kind? Yet this is precisely what we have done. We have done it, moreover, for reasons that collapse the moment we examine them. We are told that the enormous and expanding use of pesticides is necessary to maintain farm production. Yet is our real problem not one of *overproduction?* Our farms, despite measures to remove acreages from production and to pay farmers *not* to produce, have yielded such a staggering excess of crops that the American taxpayer in 1962 paid out more than one billion dollars a year as the total carrying cost of the surplus-food storage program. And is the situation helped when one branch of the Agriculture Department tries to reduce production while another states, as it did in 1958, "It is believed generally that reduction of crop acreages under provisions of the Soil Bank will stimulate interest in use of chemicals to obtain maximum production on the land retained in crops."

All this is not to say there is no insect problem and no need of control. I am saying, rather, that control must be geared to realities, not to mythical situations, and that the methods employed must be such that they do not destroy us along with the insects.

The problem whose attempted solution has brought such a train of disaster in its wake is an accomplishment of our modern way of life. Long before the age of man, insects inhabited the earth—a group of extraordinarily varied and adaptable beings. Over the course of time since man's advent, a small percentage of the more than half a million species of insects have come into conflict with human welfare in two principal ways: as competitors for the food supply and as carriers of human disease.

Disease-carrying insects become important where human beings are crowded together, especially under conditions where sanitation is poor, as in time of natural disaster or war or in situations of extreme poverty and deprivation. Then control of some sort becomes necessary. It is a sobering fact, however, as we shall presently see, that the method of massive chemical control has had only limited success, and also threatens to worsen the very conditions it is intended to curb.

15   Under primitive agricultural conditions the farmer had few insect   15
problems. These arose with the intensification of agriculture—the devotion of immense acreages to a single crop. Such a system set the stage for explosive increases in specific insect populations. Single-crop farming does not take advantage of the principles by which nature works; it is agriculture as an engineer might conceive it to be. Nature has introduced great variety into the landscape, but man has displayed a passion for simplifying it. Thus he undoes the built-in checks and balances by which nature holds the species within bounds. One important natural check is a limit on the amount of suitable habitat for each species. Obviously then, an insect that lives on wheat can build up its population to much higher levels on a farm devoted to wheat than on one in which wheat is intermingled with other crops to which the insect is not adapted.

The same thing happens in other situations. A generation or more ago, the towns of large areas of the United States lined their streets with the noble elm tree. Now the beauty they hopefully created is threatened with complete destruction as disease sweeps through the elms, carried by a beetle that would have only limited chance to build up large populations and to spread from tree to tree if the elms were only occasional trees in a richly diversified planting.

Another factor in the modern insect problem is one that must be viewed against a background of geologic and human history: the spreading of thousands of different kinds of organisms from their native homes to invade new territories. This worldwide migration has been studied and graphically described by the British ecologist Charles Elton in his recent book *The Ecology of Invasions*. During the Cretaceous Period, some hundred million years ago, flooding seas cut many land bridges between continents and living things found themselves confined in what Elton calls "colossal separate nature reserves." There, isolated from others of their kind, they developed many new species. When some of the land masses were joined again, about 15 million years ago, these species began to move out into new territories—a movement that is not only still in progress but is now receiving considerable assistance from man.

The importation of plants is the primary agent in the modern spread of species, for animals have almost invariably gone along with the plants, quarantine being a comparatively recent and not completely effective innovation. The United States Office of Plant Introduction alone has introduced almost 200,000 species and varieties of plants from all over the world. Nearly half of the 180 or so major insect enemies of plants in the United States are accidental imports from abroad, and most of them have come as hitchhikers on plants.

In new territory, out of reach of the restraining hand of the natural enemies that kept down its numbers in its native land, an invading plant or animal is able to become enormously abundant. Thus it is no accident that our most troublesome insects are introduced species.

These invasions, both the naturally occurring and those dependent on human assistance, are likely to continue indefinitely. Quarantine and massive chemical campaigns are only extremely expensive ways of buying time. We are faced, according to Dr. Elton, "with a life-and-death need not just to find new technological means of suppressing this plant or that animal"; instead we need the basic knowledge of animal populations and their relations to their surroundings that will "promote an even balance and damp down the explosive power of outbreaks and new invasions."

Much of the necessary knowledge is now available but we do not use it. We train ecologists in our universities and even employ them in our governmental agencies but we seldom take their advice. We allow the chemical death rain to fall as though there were no alternative, whereas in fact there are many, and our ingenuity could soon discover many more if given opportunity.

Have we fallen into a mesmerized state that makes us accept as inevitable that which is inferior or detrimental, as though having lost the will or the vision to demand that which is good? Such thinking, in the words of the ecologist Paul Shepard, "idealizes life with only its head out of water, inches above the limits of toleration of the corruption of its own environment . . . Why should we tolerate a diet of weak poisons, a home in insipid surroundings, a circle of acquaintances who are not quite our enemies, the noise of motors with just enough relief to prevent insanity? Who would want to live in a world which is just not quite fatal?"

Yet such a world is pressed upon us. The crusade to create a chemically sterile, insect-free world seems to have engendered a fanatic zeal on the part of many specialists and most of the so-called control agencies. On every hand there is evidence that those engaged in spraying operations exercise a ruthless power. "The regulatory entomologists . . . function as prosecutor, judge and jury, tax assessor and collector and sheriff to enforce their own orders," said Connecticut entomologist Neely Turner. The most flagrant abuses go unchecked in both state and federal agencies.

It is not my contention that chemical insecticides must never be used. I do contend that we have put poisonous and biologically potent chemicals indiscriminately into the hands of persons largely or wholly ignorant of their potentials for harm. We have subjected enormous numbers of people to contact with these poisons, without their consent and often without their knowledge. If the Bill of Rights contains no guarantee that a citizen shall be secure against lethal poisons distributed either by private individuals or by public officials, it is surely only because our forefathers, despite their considerable wisdom and foresight, could conceive of no such problem.

25   I contend, furthermore, that we have allowed these chemicals to   25 be used with little or no advance investigation of their effect on soil, water, wildlife, and man himself. Future generations are unlikely to condone our lack of prudent concern for the integrity of the natural world that supports all life.

There is still very limited awareness of the nature of the threat. This is an era of specialists, each of whom sees his own problem and is unaware of or intolerant of the larger frame into which it fits. It is also an era dominated by industry, in which the right to make a dollar at whatever cost is seldom challenged. When the public protests, confronted with some obvious evidence of damaging results of pesticide applications, it is fed little tranquilizing pills of half truth. We urgently need an end to these false assurances, to the sugar coating of unpalatable facts. It is the public that is being asked to assume the risks that the insect controllers calculate. The public must decide whether it wishes to continue on the present road, and it can do so only when in full possession of the facts. In the words of Jean Rostand, "The obligation to endure gives us the right to know."

Grant and Lee: A Study in Contrasts

Bruce Catton

*Bruce Catton (1899–1978) is best known for his popular
histories of the American Civil War. He wrote a dozen
books and many articles about the War, including* A Still-
ness at Appomattox, *which won the Pulitzer Prize and
the National Book Award in 1954. Having first worked as
a newspaper journalist, Catton was interested in writing
for the popular press rather than scholarly historians, and
his writing always sought to make history real and living.
"Grant and Lee: A Study in Contrasts" was published in
1956 in a book of essays by various historians called* The
American Story. *As you read it, notice how Catton takes
us far beyond just the story of these two Civil War generals
meeting at the end of the War—he is indeed writing a
chapter in an American story. As you read this focused ex-
ploration of the character of these two men and the times
they embody, you will also be learning something about the
Civil War itself and the nature of great men.*

1   When Ulysses S. Grant and Robert E. Lee met in the parlor
of a modest house at Appomattox Court House, Virginia,
on April 9, 1865, to work out the terms for the surrender
of Lee's Army of Northern Virginia, a great chapter in American life
came to a close, and a great new chapter began.

These men were bringing the Civil War to its virtual finish. To be
sure, other armies had yet to surrender, and for a few days the fugitive
Confederate government would struggle desperately and vainly, trying
to find some way to go on living now that its chief support was gone.

From *The American Story,* edited by Earl Schenck Miers. Published by the U.S. Capi-
tol Historical Society.

But in effect it was all over when Grant and Lee signed the papers. And the little room where they wrote out the terms was the scene of one of the poignant, dramatic contrasts in American history.

They were two strong men, these oddly different generals, and they represented the strengths of two conflicting currents that, through them, had come into final collision.

Back of Robert E. Lee was the notion that the old aristocratic concept might somehow survive and be dominant in American life.

5   Lee was tidewater Virginia, and in his background were family,   5
culture, and tradition . . . the age of chivalry transplanted to a New World which was making its own legends and its own myths. He embodied a way of life that had come down through the age of knighthood and the English country squire. America was a land that was beginning all over again, dedicated to nothing much more complicated than the rather hazy belief that all men had equal rights and should have an equal chance in the world. In such a land Lee stood for the feeling that it was somehow of advantage to human society to have a pronounced inequality in the social structure. There should be a leisure class, backed by ownership of land; in turn, society itself should be keyed to the land as the chief source of wealth and influence. It would bring forth (according to this ideal) a class of men with a strong sense of obligation to the community; men who lived not to gain advantage for themselves, but to meet the solemn obligations which had been laid on them by the very fact that they were privileged. From them the country would get its leadership; to them it could look for the higher values—of thought, of conduct, of personal deportment—to give it strength and virtue.

Lee embodied the noblest elements of this aristocratic ideal. Through him, the landed nobility justified itself. For four years, the Southern states had fought a desperate war to uphold the ideals for which Lee stood. In the end, it almost seemed as if the Confederacy fought for Lee; as if he himself was the Confederacy . . . the best thing that the way of life for which the Confederacy stood could ever have to offer. He had passed into legend before Appomattox. Thousands of tired, underfed, poorly clothed Confederate soldiers, long since past the simple enthusiasm of the early days of the struggle, somehow considered Lee the symbol of everything for which they had been willing to die. But they could not quite put this feeling into words. If the Lost Cause, sanctified by so much heroism and so many deaths, had a living justification, its justification was General Lee.

Grant, the son of a tanner on the Western frontier, was everything Lee was not. He had come up the hard way and embodied nothing in particular except the eternal toughness and sinewy fiber of the men who grew up beyond the mountains. He was one of a body of men who owed reverence and obeisance to no one, who were self-reliant to a fault, who cared hardly anything for the past but who had a sharp eye for the future.

These frontier men were the precise opposites of the tidewater aristocrats. Back of them, in the great surge that had taken people over the Alleghenies and into the opening Western country, there was a deep, implicit dissatisfaction with a past that had settled into grooves. They stood for democracy, not from any reasoned conclusion about the proper ordering of human society, but simply because they had grown up in the middle of democracy and knew how it worked. Their society might have privileges, but they would be privileges each man had won for himself. Forms and patterns meant nothing. No man was born to anything, except perhaps to a chance to show how far he could rise. Life was competition.

Yet along with this feeling had come a deep sense of belonging to a national community. The Westerner who developed a farm, opened a shop, or set up in business as a trader, could hope to prosper only as his own community prospered—and his community ran from the Atlantic to the Pacific and from Canada down to Mexico. If the land was settled, with towns and highways and accessible markets, he could better himself. He saw his fate in terms of the nation's own destiny. As its horizons expanded, so did his. He had, in other words, an acute dollars-and-cents stake in the continued growth and development of his country.

10   And that, perhaps, is where the contrast between Grant and Lee   10 becomes most striking. The Virginia aristocrat, inevitably, saw himself in relation to his own region. He lived in a static society which could endure almost anything except change. Instinctively, his first loyalty would go to the locality in which that society existed. He would fight to the limit of endurance to defend it, because in defending it he was defending everything that gave his own life its deepest meaning.

The Westerner, on the other hand, would fight with an equal tenacity for the broader concept of society. He fought so because everything he lived by was tied to growth, expansion, and a constantly widening horizon. What he lived by would survive or fall with the nation itself. He could not possibly stand by unmoved in the face of an attempt to destroy the Union. He would combat it with everything he had, because he could only see it as an effort to cut the ground out from under his feet.

So Grant and Lee were in complete contrast, representing two diametrically opposed elements in American life. Grant was the modern man emerging; beyond him, ready to come on the stage, was the great age of steel and machinery, of crowded cities and a restless burgeoning vitality. Lee might have ridden down from the old age of chivalry, lance in hand, silken banner fluttering over his head. Each man was the perfect champion of his cause, drawing both his strengths and his weaknesses from the people he led.

Yet it was not all contrast, after all. Different as they were—in background, in personality, in underlying aspiration—these two great soldiers had much in common. Under everything else, they were marvelous fighters. Furthermore, their fighting qualities were really very much alike.

Each man had, to begin with, the great virtue of utter tenacity and fidelity. Grant fought his way down the Mississippi Valley in spite of acute personal discouragement and profound military handicaps. Lee hung on in the trenches at Petersburg after hope itself had died. In each man there was an indomitable quality . . . the born fighter's refusal to give up as long as he can still remain on his feet and lift his two fists.

15 Daring and resourcefulness they had, too; the ability to think 15 faster and move faster than the enemy. These were the qualities which gave Lee the dazzling campaigns of Second Manassas and Chancellorsville and won Vicksburg for Grant.

Lastly, and perhaps greatest of all, there was the ability, at the end, to turn quickly from war to peace once the fighting was over. Out of the way these two men behaved at Appomattox came the possibility of a peace of reconciliation. It was a possibility not wholly realized, in the years to come, but which did, in the end, help the two sections to become one nation again . . . after a war whose bitterness might have seemed to make such a reunion wholly impossible. No part of either man's life became him more than the part he played in this brief meeting in the McLean house at Appomattox. Their behavior there put all succeeding generations of Americans in their debt. Two great Americans, Grant and Lee—very different, yet under everything very much alike. Their encounter at Appomattox was one of the great moments of American history.

Children of Affluence

Robert Coles

*Robert Coles (1929–), born in Boston, has been affiliated
with the Harvard Medical School since the 1970s. A noted
child psychiatrist, Coles has studied the problems of children in many countries and socioeconomc situations. His
emphases include social reform and civil rights as well as
child psychology. His most important work is the Pulitzer
Prize–winning five-volume* Children of Crisis *(1967–
1978), from which the following selection is excerpted. As
you read this essay, note Coles's personal response to what he
observes, even how he admits how he might occasionally be
misinterpreting or misjudging what he observes. Coles
demonstrates that the social scientist too can have feelings
for his subject, here the problems and issues children face.
Note also that even though Coles is clearly an authority on
his subject, he refrains from authoritarian pronouncements
about what these children are like, favoring a more quiet,
compassionate tone.*

1   It won't do to talk of *the* affluent in America. It won't do to say that   1
in our upper-middle-class suburbs, or among our wealthy, one ob-
serves clear-cut, consistent psychological or cultural characteristics. Even in relatively homogeneous places there are substantial
differences in homelife, in values taught, hobbies encouraged, beliefs
advocated or sometimes virtually instilled. But it is the obligation of
a psychological observer like me, who wants to know how children
make sense of a certain kind of life, to document as faithfully as possible the way a common heritage of money and power affects the assumptions of particular boys and girls.

Adapted from "The Children of Affluence" from *Privileged Ones,* Volume V of *Children of Crisis* by Robert Coles. Published by Little, Brown and Company. Copyright
© 1977 by Robert Coles.

I started my work with affluent children by seeing troubled boys and girls; they were the ones I saw as a child psychiatrist *before* I began my years of "field work" in the South, then Appalachia, then the North, then the West. There are only a few hundred child psychiatrists in the United States, and often their time is claimed by those who have money. After a while, if one is not careful, the well-off and the rich come to be seen exclusively through a clinician's eye: homes full of bitterness, deceit, snobbishness, neuroses, psychoses; homes with young children in mental pain, and with older children, adolescents and young adults, who use drugs, drink, run away, rebel constantly and disruptively, become truants, delinquents, addicts, alcoholics, become compulsively promiscuous, go crazy, go wild, go to ruin.

We blame the alcoholism, insanity, meanness, apathy, drug usage, despondency, and, not least, cruelty to children we see or are told exists in the ghetto or among the rural poor upon various "socioeconomic factors." All of those signs of psychological deterioration can be found among quite privileged families, too—and so we remind ourselves, perhaps, that wealth corrupts.

No—it is not that simple. Wealth does not corrupt nor does it ennoble. But wealth does govern the minds of privileged children, gives them a peculiar kind of identity which they never lose, whether they grow up to be stockbrokers or communards, and whether they lead healthy or unstable lives. There is, I think, a message that virtually all quite well-off American families transmit to their children—an emotional expression of those familiar, classbound prerogatives, money and power. I use the word "entitlement" to describe that message.

The word was given to me by the rather rich parents of a child I began to talk with almost two decades ago, in 1959. I have watched those parents become grandparents, and have seen what they described as "the responsibilities of entitlement" handed down to a new generation. When the father, a lawyer and stockbroker from a prominent and quietly influential family, referred to the "entitlement" his children were growing up to know, he had in mind a social rather than a psychological phenomenon: the various juries or committees that select the Mardi Gras participants in New Orlean's annual parade and celebration. He knew that his daughter was "entitled" to be invited.

He wanted, however, to go beyond that social fact. He talked about what he had received from his parents and what he would give to his children, "automatically, without any thought," and what they too would pass on. The father was careful to distinguish between the social entitlement and "something else," a "something else" he couldn't quite define but knew he had to try to evoke if he was to be psychologically candid: "I mean they should be responsible, and try to live up to their ideals, and not just sit around wondering which island in the Caribbean to visit this year, and where to go next summer to get away from the heat and humidity here in New Orleans."

He was worried about what a lot of money can do to a personality. When his young daughter, during a Mardi Gras season, kept *assuming* she would one day become a Mardi Gras queen, he realized that his notion of "entitlement" was not quite hers. Noblesse oblige requires a gesture toward others.

He was not the only parent to express such a concern to me in the course of my work. In homes where mothers and fathers profess no explicit reformist persuasions, they nevertheless worry about what happens to children who grow up surrounded by just about everything they want, virtually on demand. "When they're like that, they've gone from spoiled to spoiled rotten—and beyond, to some state I don't know how to describe."

Obviously, it is possible for parents to have a lot of money yet avoid bringing up their children in such a way that they feel like members of a royal family. But even parents determined not to spoil their children often recognize what might be called the existential (as opposed to strictly psychological) aspects of their situation. A father may begin rather early on lecturing his children about the meaning of money; a mother may do her share by saying no, even when yes is so easy to say. And a child, by the age of five or six, has very definite notions of what is possible, even if it is not always permitted. That child, in conversation, and without embarrassment or the kind of reticence and secretiveness that come later, may reveal a substantial knowledge of economic affairs. A six-year-old girl I spoke to knew that she would, at twenty-one, inherit half a million dollars. She also knew that her father "only" gave her twenty-five cents a week, whereas some friends of hers received as much as a dollar. She was vexed; she asked her parents why they were so "strict." One friend had even used the word "stingy" for the parents. The father, in a matter-of-fact way, pointed out to the daughter that she did, after all, get "anything she really wants." Why, then, the need for an extravagant allowance? The girl was won over.

But admonitions don't always modify the quite realistic appraisal children make of what they are heir to; and they don't diminish their sense of entitlement—a state of mind that pervades their view of the world. In an Appalachian home, for instance, a boy of seven made the following comment in 1963, after a mine his father owned had suffered an explosion, killing two men and injuring seriously nine others: "I heard my mother saying she felt sorry for the families of the miners. I feel sorry for them, too. I hope the men who got hurt get better. I'm sure they will. My father has called in doctors from Lexington. He wants the best doctors in all Kentucky for those miners. Daddy says it was the miners' fault; they get careless, and the next thing you know, there's an explosion. It's too bad. I guess there are a lot of kids who are praying hard for their fathers. I wish God was nice to everyone. He's been very good to us. My daddy says it's been hard work, running the mine, and another one he has. It's just as hard to run a mine as it is to go down and dig the coal! I'm glad my father is the owner, though. I wouldn't want him to get killed or hurt bad down there, way underground. Daddy has given us a good life. We have a lot of fun coming up, he says, in the next few years. We're going on some trips. Daddy deserves his vacations. He says he's happy because he can keep us happy, and he does."

Abundance is this boy's destiny, he has every reason to believe, abundance and limitless possibility. He may even land on the stars. Certainly he has traveled widely in this country. He associates the seasons with travel. In winter, there is a trip south, to one or another Caribbean island. He worries, on these trips, about his two dogs, and the other animals—the guinea pigs, hamsters, rabbits, chickens. There is always someone in the house, a maid, a handyman. Still it is sad to say goodbye. Now if the family owned a plane, the animals could come along on those trips!

The boy doesn't really believe that his father will ever own a Lear jet; yet he can construct a fantasy: "I had this dream. In it I was walking through the woods with Daddy, and all of a sudden there was an open field, and I looked, and I saw a hawk, and it was circling and circling. I like going hunting with Daddy, and I thought we were hunting. But when I looked at him, he didn't have his gun. Then he pointed at the hawk, and it was coming down. It landed ahead of us, and it was real strange—because the hawk turned into an airplane! I couldn't believe it. We went toward the plane, and Daddy said we could get a ride anytime we wanted, because it was ours; he'd just bought it. That's when I woke up, I think."

Four years after the boy dreamed that his father owned a plane, the father got one. The boom of the 1970s in the coal fields made his father even richer. The boy was, of course, eager to go on flying trips; eager, also, to learn to fly. At thirteen, he dreamed (by day) of becoming an astronaut, or of going to the Air Force Academy and afterwards becoming a "supersonic pilot."

He would never become a commercial pilot, however; and his reasons were interesting. "I've gone on a lot of commercial flights, and there are a lot of people on board, and the pilot has to be nice to everyone, and he makes all these announcements about the seat belts, and stuff like that. My dad's pilot was in the Air Force, and then he flew commercial. He was glad to get out, though. He says you have to be like a waiter; you have to answer complaints from the customers, and apologize to them, just because the ride gets bumpy. It's best to work for yourself, or work for another person, if you trust him and like him. If you go commercial, like our pilot says, you're a servant."

15   Many of the children I have worked with are similarly disposed; they do not like large groups of people in public places—in fact, have been taught the value not only of privacy but of the quiet that goes with being relatively alone. Some of the children are afraid of those crowds, can't imagine how it would be possible to survive them. Of course, what is strange, unknown, or portrayed as unattractive, uncomfortable, or just to be avoided as a nuisance can for a given child become a source of curiosity, like an event to be experienced at all costs. An eight-year-old girl who lived on a farm well outside Boston wanted desperately to go to the city and see Santa Claus—not because she believed in him, but because she wanted to see "those crowds" she had seen on television. She got her wish, was excited at first, then became quite disappointed, and ultimately uncomfortable. She didn't like being jostled, shoved, and ignored when she protested.

A week after the girl had gone through her Boston "adventure" (as she had called the trip *before* she embarked upon it), each student in her third-grade class was asked to draw a picture in some way connected to the Christmas season, and the girl obliged eagerly. She drew Santa Claus standing beside a pile of packages, presents for the many children who stood near him. They blended into one another—a mob scene. Watching them but removed from them was one child, bigger and on a higher level—suspended in space, it seemed, and partially surrounded by a thin but visible line. The girl wrote on the bottom of the drawing, "I saw Santa Claus." She made it quite clear what she had intended to portray. "He was standing there, handing out these gifts. They were all the same, I think, and they were plastic squirt guns for the boys and little dolls for the girls. I felt sorry for the kids. I asked my mother why kids wanted to push each other, just to get that junk. My mother said a lot of people just don't know any better. I was going to force my way up to Santa Claus and tell him to stop being so dumb! My mother said he was probably a drunk, trying to make a few dollars so he could spend it in a bar that evening! I don't want to be in a store like that again. We went up to a balcony and watched and then we got out of the place and came home. I told my mother that I didn't care if I ever went to Boston again. I have two friends, and they've never been to Boston, and they don't want to go there, except to ride through on the way to the airport."

She sounded at that moment more aloof, condescending, and snobbish than she ordinarily is. She spends her time with two or three girls who live on nearby estates. Those girls don't see each other regularly, and each of them is quite able to be alone—in fact, rather anxious for those times of solitude. Sometimes a day or two goes by with no formal arrangement to play. They meet in school, and that seems to be enough. Each girl has obligations—a horse to groom, a stall to work on. They are quite "self-sufficient," a word they have heard used repeatedly by their parents. Even with one's own social circle there is no point surrendering to excessive gregariousness!

Once up on her own horse, she is (by her own description) in her "own world." She has heard her mother use that expression. The mother is not boasting, or dismissing others who live in other worlds. The mother is describing, as does the child, a state of progressive withdrawal from people, and the familiar routines or objects of the environment, in favor of a mixture of reverie and disciplined activity.

Nothing seems impossible, burdensome, difficult. There are no distractions, petty or boring details to attend to. And one is closer to one's "self." The mother talks about the "self," and the child does, too. "It is strange," the girl comments, "because you forget yourself riding or skiing, but you also remember yourself the way you don't when you're just sitting around watching television or reading or playing in your room."

None of the other American children I have worked with have placed such a continuous and strong emphasis on the "self"—its display, its possibilities, its cultivation and development, even the repeated use of the word *self.* A ten-year-old boy who lived in Westchester County made this very clear. I met him originally because his parents were lawyers, and active in the civil rights movement. His father, a patrician Yankee, very much endorsed the students who went south in the early 1960s, and worked on behalf of integrated schools up north. The boy, however, attended private schools—a source of anguish to both father and son, who do not lend themselves to a description that suggests hypocrisy.

The boy knew that he, also, *would* be (as opposed to *wanted* to be) a lawyer. He was quick to perceive and acknowledge his situation, and as he did so, he brought his "self" right into the discussion: "I don't want to tell other kids what to do. I told my father I should be going to the public schools myself. Then I could say anything. Then I could ask why we don't have black kids with us in school. But you have to try to do what's best for your own life, even if you can't speak up for the black people. When I'm grown up I'll be like my father; I'll help the black people all I can. It's this way: first you build *yourself* up. You learn all you can. Later, you can *give of yourself.* That's what Dad says: you can't help others until you've learned to help yourself. It's not that you're being selfish, if you're going to a private school and your parents have a lot of money. We had a maid here, and she wasn't right in the head. She lost her temper and told Daddy that he's a phony, and he's out for himself and no one else, and the same goes for my sister and me. Then she quit. Daddy tried to get her to talk with us, but she wouldn't. She said that's all we ever do—talk, talk. I told Daddy she was contradicting herself, because she told me a few weeks ago that I'm always doing something, and I should sit down and talk with her. But I don't know what to say to her! I think she got angry with me, because I was putting on my skis, for cross-country skiing, and she said I had too much, that was my problem. I asked her where the regular skis were, and she said she wouldn't tell me, even if she knew! It's too bad, what happened to her.

"I feel sorry for her, though. It's not fun to be a maid. The poor woman doesn't look very good. She weighs too much. She's only forty, my mother thinks, but she looks as if she's sixty, and is sick. She should take better care of herself. Now she's thrown away this job, and she told my mother last year that it was the best one she'd ever had, so she's her own worst enemy. I wonder what she'll think when she looks at herself in the mirror."

This boy was no budding egotist. If anything, he was less self-centered at ten than many other children of his community and others like it. He was willing to think about those less fortunate than himself—the maid, and black people in general. True, he would often repeat uncritically his father's words, or a version of them. But he was trying to respond to his father's wishes and beliefs as well as his words. It was impossible for him, no matter how compassionate his nature, to conceive of life as others live it—the maid and, yes, millions of children his age, who don't look in the mirror very often, and may not even own one; who don't worry about how one looks, and what is said, and how one sounds, and how one smells.

It is important that a child's sense of entitlement be distinguished not only from the psychiatric dangers of narcissism but from the less pathological and not all that uncommon phenomenon known as being "spoiled." It is a matter of degree; "spoiled" children are self-centered all right, petulant and demanding—but not as grandiose or, alas, saddled with illusions (or delusions) as the children clinicians have in mind when using the phrase "narcissistic entitlement." The rich or quite well-to-do are all too commonly charged with producing spoiled children. Yet one sees spoiled children everywhere, among the very poor as well as the inordinately rich.

25   In one of the first wealthy families I came to know there was a girl   25 who was described by both parents as "spoiled." At the time, I fear, I was ready to pronounce every child in New Orleans's Garden District spoiled. Were they not all living comfortable, indeed luxurious, lives, as compared to the lives of the black or working-class white children I was getting to know in other sections of that city?

Nevertheless, I soon began to realize that it wouldn't do to characterize without qualification one set of children as spoiled, by virtue of their social and economic background, as against another set of children who were obviously less fortunate in many respects. One meets, among the rich, restrained, disciplined, and by no means indulged children; sometimes, even, boys and girls who have learned to be remarkably self-critical, even ascetic—anything but "spoiled" in the conventional sense of the word. True, one can find a touch and more of arrogance, or at least sustained self-assurance, in those apparently spartan boys and girls who seem quite anxious to deny themselves all sorts of presumably accessible privileges if not luxuries. But one also finds in these children a consistent willingness to place serious and not always pleasant burdens on themselves—to the point where they often struck me, when I came to their homes fresh from visits with much poorer age-mates, as remarkably *less* spoiled: not so much whining or crying; fewer demands for candy or other sweets; even, sometimes, a relative indifference to toys, however near at hand and expensive they may have been; a disregard of television—so often demanded by the children that I was seeing.

A New Orleans black woman said to me in 1961: "I don't know how to figure out these rich white kids. They're something! I used to think, before I took a job with this family, that the only difference between a rich kid and a poor kid is that the rich kid knows he has a lot of money and he grows up and becomes spoiled rotten. That's what my mother told me; she took care of a white girl, and the girl was an only child, and her father owned a department store in McComb, Mississippi, and that girl thought she was God's special creature. My mother used to come home and tell us about the 'little princess;' but she turned out to be no good. She was so pampered, she couldn't do a thing for herself. All she knew how to do was order people around.

"It's different with these two children. I've never seen such a boy and such a girl. They think they're the best ones who ever lived—like that girl in McComb—but they don't behave like her. They're never asking me to do much of anything. They even ask if they can help me! They tell me that they want to know how to do everything. The girl says she wants to learn how to run the washing machine and the dishwasher. She says she wants to learn all my secret recipes. She says she'd like to give the best parties in the Garden District when she grows up, and she'd like to be able to give them without anyone's help. She says I could serve the food, but she would like to make it. The boy says he's going to be a lawyer and a banker, so he wants to know how much everything costs. He doesn't want to waste anything. He'll see me throw something away, and he wants to know why. I only wish that my own kids were like him!

"But these children here are special, and don't they know it! That's what being rich is: you know you're different from most people. These two kids act as if they're going to be tops in everything, and they're pleased as can be with themselves, because there is nothing they can't do, and there's nothing they can't get, and there's nothing they can't win, and they're always showing off what they can do, and then before you can tell them how good they are, they're telling the same thing to themselves. It's confusing! They're not spoiled one bit, but oh, they have a high opinion of themselves!"

30   Actually, children like the ones she speaks of don't allow themselves   30
quite the unqualified confidence she describes, though she certainly has correctly conveyed the appearance they give. Boys and girls may seem without anxiety or self-doubt; they have been brought up, as the maid suggests, to feel important, superior, destined for a satisfying, rewarding life—and at, say, eight or nine they already appear to know all that. Yet there are moments of hesitation, if not apprehension. An eleven-year-old boy from a prominent and quite brilliant Massachusetts family told his teachers, in an autobiographical composition about the vicissitudes of "entitlement": "I don't always do everything right. I'd like to be able to say I don't make any mistakes, but I do, and when I do, I feel bad. My father and mother say that if you train yourself, you can be right *almost* 100 percent of the time. Even they make mistakes, though. I like to be first in sports. I like to beat my brothers at skiing. But I don't always go down the slopes as fast as I could and I sometimes fall down. Last year I broke my leg. When I get a bad cold, I feel disappointed in myself. I don't think it's right to be easy on yourself. If you are, then you slip back, and you don't get a lot of the rewards in life. If you really work for the rewards, you'll get them."

A platitude—the kind of assurance his teachers, as a matter of fact, have rather often given him. In the fourth grade, for instance, the teacher had this written on the blackboard (and kept it there for weeks): "Those who want something badly enough get it, provided they are willing to wait and work." The boy considers that assertion neither banal nor unrealistic. He has been brought up to believe that such is and will be (for him) the case. He knows that others are not so lucky, but he hasn't really met those "others," and they don't cross his mind at all. What does occur to him sometimes is the need for constant exertion, lest he fail to "measure up." One "measures up" when one tries hard and succeeds. If one slackens or stumbles, one ought to be firm with oneself—but not in any self-pitying or self-excusing or self-paralyzing way. The emphasis is on a quick and efficient moment of scrutiny followed by "a fast pick-up."

Such counsel is not as callous as it may sound—or, ironically, as it may well have been intended to sound. The child who hears it gets, briefly, upset; but unless he or she stops heeding what has been said, quite often "a fast pick-up" does indeed take place—an effort to redeem what has been missed or lost, or only somewhat accomplished. Again, it is a matter of feeling entitled. A child who has been told repeatedly that all he or she needs to do is try hard does not feel inclined to allow himself or herself long stretches of time for skeptical self-examination. The point is to feel *entitled*—then act upon that feeling. The boy whose composition was just quoted from used the word "entitled" in another essay he wrote, this one meant to be a description of his younger (age five) brother. The writing was not, however, without an autobiographical strain to it: "I was watching my brother from my bedroom window. He was climbing up the fence we built for our corral. He got to the top, and then he just stood there and waved and shouted. No one was there. He was talking to himself. He was very happy. Then he would fall. He would be upset for a few seconds, but he would climb right back up again. Then he would be even happier! He was entitled to be happy. It is his fence, and he has learned to climb it, and stay up, and balance himself."

Sins Leave Scars

J. California Cooper

Born in Berkeley, Calif., J. California Cooper (1966–) has also written under the names of Joan California Cooper, Joan Cooper, and Juan Andres Correa Guzman. Cooper began as a playwright and was named Black Play- wright of the Year in 1978 for Strangers. *With the encouragement of Alice Walker, Cooper wrote her first col- lection of short stories,* A Piece of Mine, *in 1984. A num- ber of short story collections and novels followed, including* Some Soul to Keep *(stories, 1988),* Family: A Novel *(1991), the novel* The Wake of the Wind *(1999), and* The Matter Is Life *(stories, 1992). She has received numerous awards, including the American Library Asso- ciation's James Baldwin Award, the American Book Award, and the Best Female Writer in Texas Award. This selection from her first collection features Cooper's trade- mark narrator, who recounts with sympathy and humor the tale of a young girl's futile struggle to escape her world of poverty, promiscuity, and brutality.*

1   W hen Lida Mae was born the ninth of nine children, she   1
had a 90% possibility to do and be anything she would
choose. She had a good brain and disposition, good
health and body, excellent looks and big legs to come in the future!
She was going to be neat, petite and all reet! As they say!

During the first 12 years as she was realizing her world of food,
animals, insects, trees and flowers, school and other people, people,
mostly men, were realizing her. Even brothers and uncles like to put
their hands and anything else they could where they shouldn't have

Reprinted from *A Piece of Mine,* by permission of Doubleday, a division of Random House, Inc. Copyright © 1984 by J. California Cooper.

been. She always had some change to spend and she was generous and kind to everyone and shared always. She like to laugh. I mean, what did she know to cry about? So she was fun to be with.

Her mother, Sissy, was tired and worn out early from having fun because is seemed every time she had some fun, she had another baby! They were beautiful children though and each one a memory of some good time! The first one was her husband's and maybe one or two of the others. She didn't know and it didn't matter no-way! She had some money from the state and her own little odd jobs (not too many tho, she had been tired a long time now) so that in case, as usual, her husband didn't bring nothing home, she could feed them and him, too. Sissy was like that, treated everybody alike.

So Lida Mae hurried to school and to play, even to household chores with a smile on her pretty face. She lived by rote that way til she was 14 years old and was coming home from school and got a ride from one of her mother's friends, Smokey, who had a run-down raggedy car but acted like it was a new Oldsmobile or something. During the ride he drove real slow, the long way, cause he couldn't get enough of feasting his eyes on Lida Mae and all her innocent peachy splendor. She shone like a brilliant star in that dirty beat-up old pile of junk. She had accepted the ride cheerfully enough so he asked her to accept $1.00 first then changed it to $2.00 to let him touch her in her very own private spot. She seemed disappointed for a moment, but Lida Mae kept looking at the $2.00 on the seat til she said "I ain't gonna pull my panties down!" He said he could manage that and she opened her young legs and he managed it as she picked up her $2.00 and rolled it deep into her fist. She got out at home, at last, and he whispered "Don't tell your mama!" She answered "Are you a fool? I ain't gonna give her my $2.00!" and slammed the door and bounced on in her house!

Now, people don't have to be there to "know," you know? Somehow some people just looked at Lida Mae and knew something from their own experiences. Lida Mae had a few boyfriends her own age she laughed and talked and kissed with and sometimes at a show or playing hide and seek, they did just that: played hide and seek. She was not really a loose young girl or a prudish one, just caught up in the middle of life and didn't know a damn thing about it so she just "felt" her way through. Then, when she was 15 years old she was still a virgin because she also liked her school work, books and the teachers. She knew all about love leading to marriage and all that but she wanted something out of life because her teachers told her there was something to get out of life. She wasn't always thinking about boys.

But the unexpected is so unexpected it's expected! One day going home from school (she was really a doll at 15 going on 16) the man who owned the filling-station called to her and said, "Hey, little-bit! come over here and have a Coke with me! It's on the house!" Lida Mae, because of her fight for survival at the dinner table at home, seldom refused something to eat or drink for free. She smiled as she turned her feet toward the station, "O.K. Mr. Hammon!" He grinned down at her. "Let's sit inside, it's too hot out here!" "O.K." She smiled as she followed him. He opened the Cokes asking her if she wanted some whiskey in it and when she said "No thank you" gave her plain Coke. He sat down in the only chair pulling her by her dresstail down on his lap. "Sit down here girl, ain't got no other chair for you to sit on." Now, Lida had known him all her life it seemed so she wasn't nervous, she sat! He rubbed her leg through her dress while he talked to her, "Who your boyfriend girl?" he grinned. (He wasn't a bad looking man.)

"I don't know," she said smiling.

"You don't know who you love?" He looked shocked.

"I don't love none of em, I just like em!" She took a drink.

10 "I know they like you." He lowered his voice. 10

"How come?" She grinned.

"Girl, you know you pretty, pretty as a picture!" He rubbed her leg. "Even I could like you!" He was serious now.

"Oh, Mr. Hammon, you wouldn't! I'm too young for you and Mrs. Hammon wouldn't like that!" She took another drink.

"Mrs. Hammon don't know everything!" He smiled then noticed she was almost through with the Coke. "Wanna nother Coke?"

15 "No, I got to go now! I'll take one with me if you want to!" She 15 set the empty bottle down and prepared to get off his lap.

Mr. Hammon moved his knees and Lida Mae almost fell backwards and Mr. Hammon grabbed her around the waist and under her dress as she struggled to get up. He said, "Oh! Oh! Lookit here what I got my hand on! I didn't mean to do it, but I couldn't let you fall!" He grinned.

"Well help me up!" She cried.

"I can't!" He grinned. "I can't move my hand!" But he was moving his hand and when he let Lida Mae up, she was mad! She left there with six Cokes tho and her virginity intact.

Lida Mae didn't play so hard with the boys for the next week or so. Something told her it wasn't so innocent and she felt a little grown up in a way they weren't.

20   Somehow on the next hot day after school when Lida Mae had   20
no money, her long braids freely flying behind her, she turned into Mr. Hammon's filling-station. He was just a man after all and she felt grown so she went and got her own Coke and sat down in the chair herself! Mr. Hammon watched awhile as he worked on his customer, one of the few in this little small town, then she was leaving with six more Cokes, waving good-by. In a few days she stopped again and reached for a Coke but the Coke freezer was locked. Mr. Hammon walked over to her smiling as he unlocked it and held it open for her and told her to take two out. This day when she sat on his lap, she opened her legs and he smiled with the devil looking out of his eyes and she looked at him with eyes wide open to receive the devil.

It wasn't long before Lida Mae was not a virgin anymore and really liked Mr. Hammon. She had all the Coke she wanted to drink and kept a nice little piece of change in her pockets. She had new sweaters, blouses, skirts and shoes to wear. Things she had never had too much of except at Christmas, maybe. She didn't play with the boys her age anymore cause "she had a MAN," a grown man with money! She felt above her friends, girls and boys, until sometimes she forgot and played as hard as they did at games the way a young girl her age should have!

Mr. Hammon didn't care nothing bout no school; sometimes he told his wife he was going fishing instead of working and closed the garage and Lida Mae skipped school. He and Lida Mae stayed in back of the garage on the little cot Mr. Hammon had kept for such purposes for the last 20 years anyway. They drank Coke, only now they had whiskey in it and Lida Mae would get home drunk but nobody paid it no mind, there was so much else to pay attention to in a house full of nine grown and half grown kids: some of the older ones coming in drunk too. There were still some there that were 25 years old or bout! Just lazy, do-nothings most of them. Some bringing a wife or husband home or go live off with one and be back and forth so you sometimes didn't know who was living at home and who was not!

116

Sissy didn't get drunk so much anymore after the doctor warned her. Just laid around and never smiled, eating and sleeping and getting fat, but when she did get drunk they gave her plenty space cause she would tell them to get their grown asses out of her house! Then, she would grab her coat and stagger out the door to they didn't know where and they didn't care where! Just don't mess with their lives! I'm sure the devil used to look in on the situation and be amused!

Lida Mae liked herself because she had more sense than to settle for boys who could only make babies. Mr. Hammon wouldn't do that to her! He gave her money too! Now, how you like that!? She smiled to herself. SHE had a future! She was gonna stop cutting school too! The teachers had spoken to her and she was getting ready to graduate, but she had missed a few tests and things that she had to make up! So! This was the last day she was going to let him talk her into cutting class in the afternoon, she thought to herself as she turned into the filling-station.

She was telling him that as he was undressing her, he was already undressed when he let her in the back door. She was also taking a drink of her Coke and whiskey as he laid her down and was kissing her beautiful body all over, loving its smoothness and softness. He excited her body and she put the drink down tho she wished he wouldn't hurry so! They were moving up an old road for him and a new and unfamiliar one for her.

25   BAM! The window next to the door was broken in and Mrs. Hammon looked through the opening! "Andy! Open this got-damn door!" She screamed, looking like a crazy woman in a frame. Mr. Hammon was speechless and could only stare at the broken window and shift his gaze to the door as she kicked it! He wished he could stop moving on top of Lida Mae, who was trying to push him off, but he couldn't. Lida was scared and wanted to run but he wouldn't stop and she began to have a climax just as Mrs. Hammon came through the window and lifted her knife and started trying to cut Lida Mae's face (which Lida hid with her arms) but cut her arms instead; then her husband was reaching for her, trying to stop her and hollering to Lida Mae to run! Get her things and run! Which Lida Mae, wide-eyed and frightened nearly to death and bleeding from numerous cuts, tried to do! She had to grab clothes, dodge the knife, open the door all at the same time. She was crying too and couldn't always see. Finally she got the door open and there were all those people who had heard

the noise and come to see what was happening. Lida was naked and bleeding . . . what a sight! She had just begun to run when the knife flicked across her buttocks and she screamed as she ran into the arms of Smokey who "just happened" to be standing there with what looked like hate in his face. He grabbed her and helped fight Mrs. Hammon off because Mr. Hammon couldn't stay outside long with no clothes on, til he hit her on the chin, knocking her out, and put Lida Mae in his car to take her to the hospital.

They were almost there when he stopped the car near a wooded area. He slapped her already bloody face saying "Whatcha wanna go with that sucker for? I'm glad I told on you cause that'll keep your ass away from there!!!" She was in shock, so she couldn't say nothin as he wiped the blood away from her face and kissed her as he removed the clothes from her, laying her back. She started to struggle and he said "I just saved your life, bitch!" He slapped her again so hard her earring flew off through the window. He made sex with her, dirty as she was, and bloody, then drove her to the hospital and helped her go in. Needless to say she carried those scars the rest of her life, the ones outside . . . and the ones inside.

Lida Mae didn't get to her graduation. She did not want anyone to see her again, ever. The doctor had sewn her up; 72 stitches on her arms and buttocks. They had also decided to fix her insides (since she had already started trouble so young) so she would not be bothering the state with bills for children. She didn't know it, no one but the doctor and the nurse did.

When she went home, she was so unhappy there, her mother sent her to live with a sister of hers about 15 miles away in another little town. Lida Mae was glad to go. She packed her new long-sleeved blouses and the rest of her things and left without looking back.

She was very quiet the first month or two she lived in the new town. Going to church with her aunt who was very religious. School was out, so she helped around the house and with the few animals they had. Everything was fine and Aunty was pleased cause Lida was no trouble at all and she must be a good person cause the preacher started stopping by two or three times a week to visit and he never had before. He was watching his flock . . . he said.

Lida Mae knew why he was coming by cause he was always touching her when it was accompanied by words of the Lord. But, she wasn't having any of that! She thought about the graduation she had missed and her future that had stopped. She didn't want to be a domestic or a waitress so she had to think of going back to school or something! Well, "something" came up first, in the person of a friend of her uncle's. A nice older man about 55 years old, James Winston. His wife had passed on and he had a house, car, some land and some money and even tho he had another girl friend, Josie B., he was falling in love with Lida Mae. He wanted to marry her.

Lida Mae took about a week to think about it. She kept picturing the house and the car. She could have her OWN! Her aunt kept urging her by saying, "HOUSE, HOUSE, HOUSE." Her uncle kept saying, "Money, money, money." So Lida Mae took her young, inexperienced, naive self and married him and went home to her house!

Now, in the country, if you don't work or have something to do, the time stretches out long, long, long. You fill the days with eating, gossip or making love. Lida Mae's largest outlet was gossip! She didn't really know she was gossiping, she thought she was just telling a friend the truth about what she thought. But people can take your truth and stretch it, twist it, tear it apart, turn it inside out and when you get it back, you are making enemies and when you try to straighten it out, you talk a whole lot more and give the people new ammunition to shoot back at you and then you have made more enemies! So the days come to be filled with stinky shit and then you don't feel so good (unless it's natural to you) and you don't always know why. Then, you go to church and sing and shout and get a little off your chest and then feel better all day Sunday . . . for awhile.

It wasn't long before Lida Mae was going with the preacher. She just seemed to move naturally into situations without much forethought, but she really hadn't ever known anyone who gave her any idea of how or why this was done; only a few teachers in school regarding the future through education, and there was so much in her life that diluted those urgings to wise decisions.

Lida Mae was kind tho, she was good to her husband. The house was clean, his meals were cooked, his clothes were clean, but he drank quite a bit now and was usually sleeping it off nights. She was drinking more now and with some kind of confrontation at least three times a week on account of her mouth, she naturally turned to the preacher. It made her feel the affair was O.K. with God. It wasn't O.K. with God and it wasn't O.K. with Mrs. Preacher either cause one night she came over to see Lida Mae and when Lida Mae came to the door,

Mrs. Preacher threw a pot full of lye water in Lida's face. It was a good thing her aunt was there; she cared for Lida's face and got her taken to the doctor. Lida's skin was young and healed well but her eyes were affected and they were cloudy and dim when she came from the hospital. I went by to see her and she said to me "Well, here I am, still young, done been cut up and now almost had my eyes burnt up! I can see, but not much. Not the things I want to see. Not the pretty world outside and not my pretty clothes. I don't want to go anywhere again. But, this is my house! I have given up a lot for it and done a lot to it and I don't want to leave it again ever, tho I do want to leave this town. I don't want no more of Mr. Preacher either! Oh he calls, and comes around! But I wouldn't open the door and if my husband let him in I went in my bedroom and shut the door til he was gone!"

35   But time passed and soon everything was back to "normal?" Lida   35 Mae thought of school only briefly, just couldn't get the grit up to go. Thought of eye operations, but since she had to go out to some big city and she didn't want to do that either and her husband didn't want to spend all his money (course they wasn't his eyes) she didn't go. She seem to be seeing a little better every day anyway.

Time went by and this Josie B., who used to be Lida's husband's girl-friend, came to be friends with Lida Mae. I could have told Lida she didn't mean her no good cause Josie B. was still mad bout losing that house and money and a man. But Lida Mae seem to listen to you, then when she talked back to you seem like she ain't heard nothing you said! Anyway they became friends and they started going out together to these juke joints that they have round here. Between that gossip and liquor and backbiting, Josie somehow got things fixed so one day when Lida Mae was high and sitting on a stool in one of those joints, Leella and Bertha jumped on her and beat Lida up! Even busting a bottle cross her mouth so that she lost four or five teeth right there in front. Well Lida Mae went right back in the house again and stayed there and in church for three or four months. She was about 20 years old now, but drinking so heavy (used to send her husband to the liquor store every day!) she looked like she was 50! Skin still smooth and all but them eyes and that mouth and them scars! Lord have mercy!

Then, one day, her husband stepped on a nail and only soaked his foot and in two weeks he was dead! Josie B. and Bertha came and sat outside the cemetery and laughed, drinking in their car with hatred in Josie B.'s eyes. I went to see Lida after the funeral, she was sitting on the screened in front porch still in her black dress with a record playing real loud saying "The sun gonna shine in my backdoor some day!" I talked to her awhile and she said one thing; she say "You know, I got this house, I got some money and a car . . . but I keep trying to see, in my mind, would I rather have my eyes, and my teeth . . . and my looks back and all these scars off . . . I believe I rather have nothing if I could just have myself back. OR SOME REAL LOVE! Ain't nothin left for me but love. I'm all gone."

She was young, but she was old! And through! But somewhere inside of me I didn't think she had to be.

Something good happens to everybody and about a year or so later a man came back to this town who had grown up here. He came to see his mama and saw Lida Mae at church (that's the only day she sobered up) and gave her his heart and stayed longer than he had planned. She took him in, used him, abused him . . . just tried to use that poor man up! She seemed to be mean, mean, mean! He was a neat, clean person with a little money, I guess, cause he was always running to the liquor store for Lida or bringing her candy, flowers and sweaters and things. Got her car fixed and all the work in her house that needed a man's touch. But she put him out every day when she through needing him for that day, cussing him. Now, she was playing that record bout the sunshine was coming in her back door some day and here the sunshine was coming in her front door and she didn't see it! Well, she was making him eat shit and nothing but a fool want to eat the same thing every day so he finally kissed his mama good-by and left, looking back, but leaving anyway! Lida Mae say "He'll be back! I put some of this good stuff on him! He be back!"

But he never came back.

The years have passed and we have really sure nuff got old. Lida Mae looks like she is 150 years old and she is only 45 or so. I stop over to see her on my way to my son's house to get my grandchild sometime and she still be setting on the porch, drinking and she say things I don't know if I believe them. She say, "Life ain't shit, you know that? It ain't never done a fuckin thing for me!!"

When I leave, thoughts be zooming round in my head and I think of those words I got on a 15¢ postcard go like this:

Some people watch things happen.
Some people make things happen.
Some people don't even know nothing happened.

Then I go on over to pick up my grandbaby and thank God, ugly as I may be, I am who I am.

The Ethic of Compassion
The Dalai Lama

His Holiness the Dalai Lama (1935–) was born a peasant in Taktser, Tibet under the birth name of Lhamo Dhondrub. He is the fourteenth Dalai Lama (spiritual leader of Tibet, reincarnation of the thirteenth Dalai Lama, and an incarnation of the Buddha of Compassion). He lives in Dharamsala, India. He was recognized at age two as the Dalai Lama and was enthroned on February 22, 1940. He completed the Geshe Lharampa Degree (equivalent to a Doctorate of Buddhist Philosophy) in 1959 and became head of Tibet—but was driven out by a Chinese invasion. He has worked on behalf of Tibet from India, asking the United Nations for help and working to bring Buddhist beliefs back to the country. He received the Albert Schweitzer Humanitarian Award (1987); Raoul Wallenberg Congressional Human Rights Award (1989); the Nobel Peace Prize (1989); Franklin D. Roosevelt Freedom Medal (1994); and the Hessian Peace Prize (2005). His books include Kindness, Clarity and Insight *(Snow Lion, 1984);* Compassion and the Individual *(Wisdom Publications, 1991); and* The Power of Compassion *(Harper Collins, 1995).*

Compassion is good when first considered, for it is easy to feel compassion for one who suffers. Compassion is harder to muster for wealthy and powerful people and even harder to feel when true compassion leads to a career change or an even greater life upheaval.

We noted earlier that all the world's major religions stress the importance of cultivating love and compassion. In the Buddhist philosophical tradition, different levels of attainment

Reprinted from *Ethics for the New Millennium,* by permission of Riverhead Books, an imprint of Penguin Group (USA) Inc. and The Wylie Agency. Copyright © 1999, 2001 by Kyabje Tenzin Gyatso, 14th Dalai Lama of Tibet.

are described. At a basic level, compassion (*nying je*) is understood mainly in terms of empathy—our ability to enter into and, to some extent, share others' suffering. But Buddhist—and perhaps others—believe that this can be developed to such a degree that not only does our compassion arise without any effort, but it is unconditional, undifferentiated, and universal in scope. A feeling of intimacy toward all other sentient beings, including of course those who would harm us, is generated, which is likened in the literature to the love a mother has for her only child.

But this sense of equanimity toward all others is not seen as an end in itself. Rather, it is seen as the springboard to a love still greater. Because our capacity for empathy is innate, and because the ability to reason is also an innate faculty, compassion shares the characteristics of consciousness itself. The potential we have to develop it is therefore stable and continuous. It is not a resource which can be used up—as water is used up when we boil it. And though it can be described in terms of activity, it is not like a physical activity which we train for, like jumping, where once we reach a certain height we can go no further. On the contrary, when we enhance our sensitivity toward others' suffering through deliberately opening ourselves up to it, it is believed that we can gradually extend out compassion to the point where the individual feels so moved by even the subtlest suffering of others that they come to have an over-whelming sense of responsibility toward those others. This causes the one who is compassionate to dedicate themselves entirely to helping others overcome both their suffering and the causes of their suffering. In Tibetan, this ultimate level of attainment is called *nying je chenmo,* literally "great compassion."

Now I am not suggesting that each individual must attain these advanced states of spiritual development in order to lead an ethically wholesome life. I have described *nying je chenmo* not because it is a precondition of ethical conduct but rather because I believe that pushing the logic of compassion to the highest level can act as a powerful inspiration. If we can just keep the aspiration to develop *nying je chenmo,* or great compassion, as an ideal, it will naturally have a significant impact on our outlook. Based on the simple recognition that, just as I do, so do all others desire to be happy and not to suffer, it will serve as a constant reminder against selfishness and partiality. It will remind us that there is little to be gained from being kind and generous because we hope to win something in return. It will remind us that actions motivated by the desire to create a good name for ourselves are still selfish, however much they may appear to be acts of kindness. It will also remind us that there is nothing exceptional about acts of charity toward those we already feel close to. And it will help us to recognize that the bias we naturally feel toward our families and friends is actually a highly unreliable thing on which to base ethical conduct. If we reserve ethical conduct for those whom we feel close to, the danger is that we will neglect our responsibilities toward those outside this circle.

Why is this? So long as the individuals in question continue to meet our expectations, all is well. But should they fail to do so, someone we consider a dear friend one day can become our sworn enemy the next. As we saw earlier, we have a tendency to react badly to all who threaten fulfillment of our cherished desires, though they may be our closest relations. For this reason, compassion and mutual respect offer a much more solid basis for our relations with others. This is also true of partnerships. If our love for someone is based largely on attraction, whether it be their looks or some other superficial characteristic, our feelings for that person are liable, over time, to evaporate. When they lose the quality we found alluring, or when we find ourselves no longer satisfied by it, the situation can change completely, this despite their being the same person. This is why relationships based purely on attraction are almost always unstable. On the other hand, when we begin to perfect our compassion, neither the other's appearance nor their behavior affects our underlying attitude.

Consider, too, that habitually our feelings toward others depend very much on their circumstances. Most people, when they see someone who is handicapped, feel sympathetic toward that person. But then when they see others who are wealthier, or better educated, or better placed socially, they immediately feel envious and competitive toward them. Our negative feelings prevent us from seeing the sameness of ourselves and all others. We forget that just like us, whether fortunate or unfortunate, distant or near, they desire to be happy and not to suffer.

The struggle is thus to overcome these feelings of partiality. Certainly, developing genuine compassion for our loved ones is the obvious and appropriate place to start. The impact our actions have on our close ones will generally be much greater than on others, and therefore our responsibilities toward them are greater. Yet we need to recognize that, ultimately, there are no grounds for discriminating in their favor. In this sense, we are all in the same position as a doctor confronted by ten patients suffering the same serious illness. They are each equally deserving of treatment. The reader should not suppose that what is being advocated here is a state of detached indifference, however. The further essential challenge, as we begin to extend our compassion toward all others, is to maintain the same level of intimacy as we feel toward those closest to us. In other words, what is being suggested is that we need to strive for even-handedness in our approach toward all others, a level ground into which we can plant the seed of *nying je chenmo,* of great love and compassion.

If we can begin to relate to others on the basis of such equanimity, our compassion will not depend on the fact that so and so is my husband, my wife, my relative, my friend. Rather, a feeling of closeness toward all others can be developed based on the simple recognition that, just like myself, all wish to be happy and to avoid suffering. In other words, we will start to relate to others on the basis of their sentient nature. Again, we can think of this in terms of an ideal, one which it is immensely difficult to attain. But, for myself, I find it one which is profoundly inspiring and helpful.

Let us now consider the role of compassionate love and kindheartedness in our daily lives. Does the ideal of developing it to the point where it is unconditional mean that we must abandon our own interests entirely? Not at all. In fact, it is the best way of serving them—indeed, it could even be said to constitute the wisest course for fulfilling self-interest. For if it is correct that those qualities such as love, patience, tolerance, and forgiveness are what happiness consists in, and if it is also correct that *nying je,* or compassion, as I have defined it, is both the source and the fruit of these qualities, then the more we are compassionate, the more we provide for our own happiness. Thus, any idea that concern for others, though a noble quality, is a matter for our private lives only, is simply short-sighted. Compassion belongs to every sphere of activity, including, of course, the workplace.

Here, though, I must acknowledge the existence of a perception—shared by many, it seems—that compassion is, if not actually an impediment, at least irrelevant to professional life. Personally, I would argue that not only is it relevant, but that when compassion is lacking, our activities are in danger of becoming destructive. This is because when we ignore the question of the impact our actions have on others' well-being, inevitably we end up hurting them. The ethic of compassion helps provide the necessary foundation and motivation for both restraint and the cultivation of virtue. When we begin to develop a genuine appreciation of the value of compassion, our outlook on others begins automatically to change. This alone can serve as a powerful influence on the conduct of our lives. When, for example, the temptation to deceive others arises, our compassion for them will prevent us from entertaining the idea. And when we realize that our work itself is in danger of being exploited to the detriment of others, compassion will cause us to disengage from it. So to take an imaginary case of a scientist whose research seems likely to be a source of suffering, they will recognize this and act accordingly, even if this means abandoning the project.

10   I do not deny that genuine problems can arise when we dedicate   10
ourselves to the ideal of compassion. In the case of a scientist who felt unable to continue in the direction their work was taking them, this could have profound consequences both for themselves and for their families. Likewise, those engaged in the caring professions—in medicine, counseling, social work, and so on—or even those looking after someone at home may sometimes become so exhausted by their duties that they feel overwhelmed. Constant exposure to suffering, coupled occasionally with a feeling of being taken for granted, can induce feelings of helplessness and even despair. Or it can happen that individuals may find themselves performing outwardly generous actions merely for the sake of it—simply going through the motions, as it were. Of course this is better than nothing. But when left unchecked, this can lead to insensitivity toward others' suffering. If this starts to happen, it is best to disengage for a short while and make a deliberate effort to reawaken that sensitivity. In this it can be helpful to remember that despair is never a solution. It is, rather, the ultimate failure. Therefore, as the Tibetan expression has it, even if the rope breaks nine times, we must splice it back together a tenth time. In this way, even if ultimately we do fail, at least there will be no feelings of regret. And when we combine this insight with a clear appreciation of our potential to benefit others, we find that we can begin to restore our hope and confidence.

Some people may object to this ideal on the grounds that by entering into others' suffering, we bring suffering on ourselves. To an extent, this is true. But I suggest that there is an important qualitative distinction to be made between experiencing one's own suffering and experiencing suffering in the course of sharing in others'. In the case of one's own suffering, given that it is involuntary, there is a sense of oppression: it seems to come from outside us. By contrast, sharing in someone else's suffering must at some level involve a degree of voluntariness, which itself is indicative of a certain inner strength. For this reason, the disturbance it may cause is considerably less likely to paralyze us than our own suffering.

Of course, even as an ideal, the notion of developing unconditional compassion is daunting. Most people, including myself, must struggle even to reach the point where putting others' interests on a par with our own becomes easy. We should not allow this to put us off, however. And while undoubtedly there will be obstacles on the way to developing a genuinely warm heart, there is the deep consolation of knowing that in doing so we are creating the conditions for our own happiness. As I mentioned earlier, the more we truly desire to benefit others, the greater the strength and confidence we develop and the greater the peace and happiness we experience. If this still seems unlikely, it is worth asking ourselves how else we are to do so. With violence and aggression? Of course not. With money? Perhaps up to a point, but no further. But with love, by sharing in others' suffering, by recognizing ourselves clearly in all others—especially those who are disadvantaged and those whose rights are not respected—by helping them to, be happy: yes. Through love, through kindness, through compassion we establish understanding between ourselves and others. This is how we forge unity and harmony.

Compassion and love are not mere luxuries. As the source both of inner and external peace, they are fundamental to the continued survival of our species. On the one hand, they constitute non-violence in action. On the other, they are the source of all spiritual qualities: of forgiveness, tolerance, and all the virtues. Moreover, they are the very thing that gives meaning to our activities and makes them constructive. There is nothing amazing about being highly educated; there is nothing amazing about being rich. Only when the individual has a warm heart do these attributes become worthwhile.

So to those who say that the Dalai Lama is being unrealistic in advocating this ideal of unconditional love, I urge them to experiment with it nonetheless. They will discover that when we reach beyond the confines of narrow self-interest, our hearts become filled with strength. Peace and joy become our constant companion. It breaks down barriers of every kind and in the end destroys the notion of my interest as independent from others' interest. But most important, so far as ethics is concerned, where love of one's neighbor, affection, kindness, and compassion live, we find that ethical conduct is automatic. Ethically wholesome actions arise naturally in the context of compassion.

Understanding Natural Selection
Charles Darwin

Charles Darwin (1809–1892), the famed scientist credited with discovering natural selection, was born in Shrewsbury, England. The grandson of a noted physician/scientist, Darwin studied medicine at Edinburgh, then biology at Cambridge. In 1835, at age 26, he embarked on a 5-year scientific survey of South American waters. In 1839, he married a cousin, Emma Wedgewood; shortly after, Darwin began a period of intensive research and writing. By the mid-1840s, he had published several works on his geological and zoological discoveries and had become recognized as one of the leading scientists of the day. Darwin's best-known work, On the Origin of Species by Means of Natural Selection *(1859), received mixed reaction initially, but over time it has become known as a central document of scientific writing. This essay, which comes from that work, presents some of the basic theories of the scientist whose concept of evolution has become a household world—Darwinism. As you read the essay, be alert to the various rhetorical strategies Darwin uses to transform hard science into good reading.*

1   It may be said that natural selection is daily and hourly scrutiniz-   1
ing, throughout the world, every variation, even the slightest; rejecting that which is bad, preserving and adding up all that is
good; silently and insensibly working, whenever and wherever opportunity offers, at the improvement of each organic being in relation to
its organic and inorganic conditions of life. We see nothing of these
slow changes in progress, until the hand of time has marked the long
lapses of ages, and then so imperfect is our view into long past

geological ages, that we only see that the forms of life are now different from what they formerly were.

Although natural selection can act only through and for the good of each being, yet characters and structures, which we are apt to consider as of very trifling importance, may thus be acted on. When we see leaf-eating insects green, and bark-feeders mottled-grey; the alpine ptarmigan white in winter, the red-grouse the color of heather, and the black-grouse that of peaty earth, we must believe that these tints are of service to these birds and insects in preserving them from danger. Grouse, if not destroyed at some period of their lives, would increase in countless numbers; they are known to suffer largely from birds of prey; and hawks are guided by eyesight to their prey—so much so, that on parts of the Continent persons are warned not to keep white pigeons, as being the most liable to destruction. Hence I can see no reason to doubt that natural selection might be most effective in giving the proper color to each kind of grouse, and in keeping that color, when once acquired, true and constant. Nor ought we to think that the occasional destruction of an animal of any particular color would produce little effect: we should remember how essential it is in a flock of white sheep to destroy every lamb with the faintest trace of black. In plants the down on the fruit and the color of the flesh are considered by botanists as characters of the most trifling importance: yet we hear from an excellent horticulturist, Downing, that in the United States smooth-skinned fruits suffer far more from a beetle, a curculio, than those with down; that purple plums suffer far more from a certain disease than yellow plums; whereas another disease attacks yellow-fleshed peaches far more than those with other colored flesh. If, with all the aids of art, these slight differences make a great difference in cultivating the several varieties, assuredly, in a state of nature, where the trees would have to struggle with other trees and with a host of enemies, such differences would effectually settle which variety, whether a smooth or downy, a yellow or purple fleshed fruit, should succeed.

In looking at many small points of difference between species, which, as far as our ignorance permits us to judge, seem to be quite unimportant, we must not forget that climate, food, and so on probably produce some slight and direct effect. It is, however, far more necessary to bear in mind that there are many unknown laws of correlation to growth, which, when one part of the organization is modified through variation, and the modifications are accumulated by natural selection for the good of the being, will cause other modifications, often of the most unexpected nature.

As we see that those variations which under domestication appear at any particular period of life, tend to reappear in the offspring of the same period; for instance, in the seeds of the many varieties of our culinary and agricultural plants; in the caterpillar and cocoon stages of the varieties of the silkworm; in the eggs of poultry, and in the color of the down of their chickens; in the horns of our sheep and cattle when nearly adult; so in a state of nature, natural selection will be enabled to act on and modify organic beings at any age, by the accumulation of profitable variations at that age, and by their inheritance at a corresponding age. If it profit a plant to have its seeds more and more widely disseminated by the wind, I can see no greater difficulty in this being effected through natural selection, than in the cotton-planter increasing and improving by selection the down in the pods on his cotton-trees. Natural selection may modify and adapt the larva of an insect to a score of contingencies, wholly different from those which concern the mature insect. These modifications will no doubt affect, through the laws of correlation, the structure of the adult; and probably in the case of those insects which live only for a few hours, and which never feed, a large part of their structure is merely the correlated result of successive changes in the structure of their larvae. So, conversely, modifications in the adult will probably often affect the structure of the larva; but in all cases natural selection will ensure that modifications consequent on other modifications at a different period of life, shall not be in the least degree injurious: for if they became so, they would cause the extinction of the species.

Natural selection will modify the structure of the young in relation to the parent, and of the parent in relation to the young. In social animals it will adapt the structure of each individual for the benefit of the community; if each in consequence profits by the selected change. What natural selection cannot do, is to modify the structure of one species, without giving it any advantage, for the good of another species; and though statements to this effect may be found in works of natural history, I cannot find one case which will bear investigation. A structure used only once in an animal's whole life, if of high importance to it, might be modified to any extent by natural selection; for instance, the great jaws possessed by certain insects, and

132

used exclusively for opening the cocoon; or the hard tip to the beak of nestling birds, used for breaking the egg. It has been asserted, that of the best short-beaked tumbler-pigeons more perish in the egg than are able to get out of it; so that fanciers assist in the act of hatching. Now, if nature had to make the beak of a full-grown pigeon very short for the bird's own advantage, the process of modification would be very slow, and there would be simultaneously the most rigorous selection of the young birds within the egg, which had the most powerful and hardest beaks, for all with weak beaks would inevitably perish: or, more delicate and more easily broken shells might be selected, the thickness of the shell being known to vary like every other structure.

Sexual Selection

Inasmuch as peculiarities often appear under domestication in one sex and become hereditarily attached to that sex, the same fact probably occurs under nature, and if so, natural selection will be able to modify one sex in its functional relations to the other sex, or in relation to wholly different habits of life in the two sexes, as is sometimes the case with insects. And this leads me to say a few words on what I call sexual selection. This depends, not on a struggle for existence, but on a struggle between the males for possession of the females; the result is not death to the unsuccessful competitor, but few or no offspring. Sexual selection is, therefore, less rigorous than natural selection. Generally, the most vigorous males, those which are best fitted for their places in nature, will leave most progeny. But in many cases, victory will depend not on general vigor, but on having special weapons, confined to the male sex. A hornless stag or spurless cock would have a poor chance of leaving offspring. Sexual selection by always allowing the victor to breed might surely give indomitable courage, length to the spur, and strength to the wing to strike in the spurred leg, as well as the brutal cock-fighter, who knows well that he can improve his breed by careful selection of the best cocks. How low in the scale of nature this law of battle descends, I know not; male alligators have been described as fighting, bellowing, and whirling round, like Indians in a war dance, for the possession of the females; male salmons have been seen fighting all day long; male stag-beetles often bear wounds from the huge mandibles of other males. The war is, perhaps, severest between the males of polygamous animals, and these seem oftenest provided with special weapons. The males of carnivorous animals are already well armed; though to them and to others, special means of defence may be given through means of sexual selection, as the mane to the lion, the shoulder-pad to the boar, and the hooked jaw to the male salmon; for the shield may be as important for victory, as the sword or spear.

Amongst birds, the contest is often of a more peaceful character. All those who have attended to the subject, believe that there is the severest rivalry between the males of many species to attract by singing the females. The rock-thrush of Guiana, birds of Paradise, and some others, congregate; and successive males display their gorgeous plumage and perform strange antics before the females, which standing by as spectators, at last choose the most attractive partner. Those who have closely attended to birds in confinement well know that they often take individual preferences and dislikes: thus Sir R. Heron has described how one pied peacock was eminently attractive to all his hen birds. It may appear childish to attribute any effect to such apparently weak means: I cannot here enter on the details necessary to support this view; but if man can in a short time give elegant carriage and beauty to his bantams, according to his standard of beauty, I can see no good reason to doubt that female birds, by selecting, during thousands of generations, the most melodious or beautiful males, according to their standard of beauty, might produce a marked effect. I strongly suspect that some well-known laws with respect to the plumage of male and female birds, in comparison with the plumage of the young, can be explained on the view of plumage having been chiefly modified by sexual selection, acting when the birds have come to the breeding age or during the breeding season; the modifications thus produced being inherited at corresponding ages or seasons, either by the males alone, or by the males and females; but I have not space here to enter on this subject.

Thus it is, as I believe, that when the males and females of any animal have the same general habits of life, but differ in structure, color, or ornament, such differences have been mainly caused by sexual selection; that is, individual males have had, in successive generations, some slight advantage over other males, in their weapons, means of defence, or charms; and have transmitted these advantages to their male offspring. Yet, I would not wish to attribute all such sexual differences to this agency: for we see peculiarities arising and becoming attached to the male sex in our domestic animals (as the wattle in male carriers, horn-like protuberances in the cocks of certain fowls, and so on), which we cannot believe to be either useful to the males in battle, or attractive to the females. We see analogous cases under nature, for instance, the tuft of hair on the breast of the turkey-cock, which can hardly be either useful or ornamental to this bird; indeed, had the tuft appeared under domestication, it would have been called a monstrosity.

Illustration of the Action of Natural Selection

. . . Let us take the case of a wolf, which preys on various animals, securing some by craft, some by strength, and some by fleetness; and let us suppose that the fleetest prey, a deer for instance, had from any change in the country increased in numbers, or that other prey had decreased in numbers, during that season of the year when the wolf is hardest pressed for food. I can under such circumstances see no reason to doubt that the swiftest and slimmest wolves would have the best chance of surviving, and so be preserved or selected—provided always that they retained strength to master their prey at this or at some other period of the year, when they might be compelled to prey on other animals. I can see no more reason to doubt this, than that man can improve the fleetness of his greyhounds by careful and methodical selection, or by that unconscious selection which results from each man trying to keep the best dogs without any thought of modifying the breed.

10   Even without any change in the proportional numbers of the an- 10
imals on which our wolf preyed, a cub might be born with an innate tendency to pursue certain kinds of prey. Nor can this be thought very improbable; for we often observe great differences in the natural tendencies of our domestic animals; one cat, for instance, taking to catch rats, another mice; one cat . . . bringing home winged game, another hares or rabbits, and another hunting on marshy ground and almost nightly catching woodcocks or snipes. The tendency to catch rats rather than mice is known to be inherited. Now, if any slight innate change of habit or of structure benefited an individual wolf, it would have the best chance of surviving and of leaving offspring. Some of its young would probably inherit the same habits or structure, and by the repetition of this process, a new variety might be formed which would

either supplant or coexist with the parent-form of wolf. Or, again, the wolves inhabiting a mountainous district, and those frequenting the lowlands, would naturally be forced to hunt different prey; and from the continued preservation of the individuals best fitted for the two sites, two varieties might slowly be formed. These varieties would cross and blend where they met; but to this subject of intercrossing we shall soon have to return. I may add, that . . . there are two varieties of the wolf inhabiting the Catskill Mountains in the United States, one with a light greyhound-like form, which pursues deer, and the other more bulky, with shorter legs, which more frequently attacks the shepherd's flocks.

Learning to Read and Write

Frederick Douglass

Frederick Douglass (1817–1895)—abolitionist, author, and the first black American to become a prominent public figure—was born into slavery near Tuckahoe, Maryland. As a youth, Douglass worked as a household servant, a field hand, and a shipyard apprentice. In 1838, after several failed attempts to escape (for which he received beatings), he successfully reached New York. He took the surname "Douglass" and eventually settled in New Bedford, Massachusetts. In 1841, the Massachusetts Anti-Slavery League, impressed by his great oratory skills, hired Douglass to help promote the abolition of slavery. Douglass bought his freedom in 1847, using money contributed both by Americans and by sympathizers in England, where he had fled to preserve his freedom. For the next 13 years, Douglass edited the abolitionist periodical North Star *(changed to* Frederick Douglass's Paper *in 1851). During the Civil War, Douglass urged President Lincoln to emancipate the slaves and helped recruit black troops. After the war, he held a series of government posts, including Assistant Secretary to the Santo Domingo Commission, Marshall of the District of Columbia, District Recorder of Deeds, and Ambassador to Haiti. This essay, which comes from Douglass's autobiography,* Narrative of the Life of Frederick Douglass, an American Slave *(1845), reveals the guile and determination that Douglass employed to teach himself to read. As you read the words of a former slave, written more than a century ago, think of how closed the world was to Douglass, yet how he recognized that literacy could help open the door.*

1

I lived in Master Hugh's family about seven years. During this time, I succeeded in learning to read and write. In accomplishing this, I was compelled to resort to various stratagems. I had no regular teacher. My mistress, who had kindly commenced to instruct me, had, in compliance with the advice and direction of her husband, not only ceased to instruct, but had set her face against my being instructed by any one else. It is due, however, to my mistress to say of her, that she did not adopt this course of treatment immediately. She at first lacked the depravity indispensable to shutting me up in mental darkness. It was at least necessary for her to have some training in the exercise of irresponsible power, to make her equal to the task of treating me as though I were a brute.

My mistress was, as I have said, a kind and tender-hearted woman; and in the simplicity of her soul she commenced, when I first went to live with her, to treat me as she supposed one human being ought to treat another. In entering upon the duties of a slaveholder, she did not seem to perceive that I sustained to her the relation of a mere chattel, and that for her to treat me as a human being was not only wrong, but dangerously so. Slavery proved as injurious to her as it did to me. When I went there, she was a pious, warm, and tender-hearted woman. There was no sorrow or suffering for which she had not a tear. She had bread for the hungry, clothes for the naked, and comfort for every mourner that came within her reach. Slavery soon proved its ability to divest her of these heavenly qualities. Under its influence, the tender heart became stone, and the lamb-like disposition gave way to one of tiger-like fierceness. The first step in her downward course was in her ceasing to instruct me. She now commenced to practise her husband's precepts. She finally became even more violent in her opposition than her husband himself. She was not satisfied with simply doing as well as he had commanded; she seemed anxious to do better. Nothing seemed to make her more angry than to see me with a newspaper. She seemed to think that here lay the danger. I have had her rush at me with a face made all up of fury, and snatch from me a newspaper, in a manner that fully revealed her apprehension. She was an apt woman; and a little experience soon demonstrated, to her satisfaction, that education and slavery were incompatible with each other.

From this time I was most narrowly watched. If I was in a separate room any considerable length of time, I was sure to be suspected

1

of having a book, and was at once called to give an account of myself. All this, however, was too late. The first step had been taken. Mistress, in teaching me the alphabet, had given me the *inch,* and no precaution could prevent me from taking the *ell.*

The plan which I adopted, and the one by which I was most successful, was that of making friends of all the little white boys whom I met in the street. As many of these as I could, I converted into teachers. With their kindly aid, obtained at different times and in different places, I finally succeeded in learning to read. When I was sent on errands, I always took my book with me, and by going one part of my errand quickly, I found time to get a lesson before my return. I used also to carry bread with me, enough of which was always in the house, and to which I was always welcome; for I was much better off in this regard than many of the poor white children in our neighborhood. This bread I used to bestow upon the hungry little urchins, who, in return, would give me that more valuable bread of knowledge. I am strongly tempted to give the names of two or three of those little boys, as a testimonial of the gratitude and affection I bear them; but prudence forbids;—not that it would injure me, but it might embarrass them; for it is almost an unpardonable offense to teach slaves to read in this Christian country. It is enough to say of the dear little fellows, that they lived on Philpot Street, very near Durgin and Bailey's shipyard. I used to talk this matter of slavery over with them. I would sometimes say to them, I wished I could be as free as they would be when they got to be men. "You will be free as soon as you are twenty-one, *but I am a slave for life!* Have not I as good a right to be free as you have?" These words used to trouble them; they would express for me the liveliest sympathy, and console me with the hope that something would occur by which I might be free.

I was now about twelve years old, and the thought of being *a slave for life* began to bear heavily upon my heart. Just about this time, I got hold of a book entitled "The Columbian Orator." Every opportunity I got, I used to read this book. Among much of other interesting matter, I found in it a dialogue between a master and his slave. The slave was represented as having run away from his master three times. The dialogue represented the conversation which took place between them, when the slave was retaken the third time. In this dialogue, the whole argument in behalf of slavery was brought forward by the master, all of which was disposed of by the slave. The slave was made to say some very smart as well as impressive things in reply to his master—things which had the desired though unexpected effect; for the conversation resulted in the voluntary emancipation of the slave on the part of the master.

In the same book, I met with one of Sheridan's mighty speeches on and in behalf of Catholic emancipation. These were choice documents to me. I read them over and over again with unabated interest. They gave tongue to interesting thoughts of my own soul, which had frequently flashed through my mind, and died away for want of utterance. The moral which I gained from the dialogue was the power of truth over the conscience of even a slaveholder. What I got from Sheridan was a bold denunciation of slavery, and a powerful vindication of human rights. The reading of these documents enabled me to utter my thoughts, and to meet the arguments brought forward to sustain slavery; but while they relieved me of one difficulty, they brought on another even more painful than the one of which I was relieved. The more I read, the more I was led to abhor and detest my enslavers. I could regard them in no other light than a band of successful robbers, who had left their homes, and gone to Africa, and stolen us from our homes, and in a strange land reduced us to slavery. I loathed them as being the meanest as well as the most wicked of men. As I read and contemplated the subject, behold! that very discontentment which Master Hugh had predicted would follow my learning to read had already come, to torment and sting my soul to unutterable anguish. As I writhed under it, I would at times feel that learning to read had been a curse rather than a blessing. It had given me a view of my wretched condition, without the remedy. It opened my eyes to the horrible pit, but to no ladder upon which to get out. In moments of agony, I envied my fellow-slaves for their stupidity. I have often wished myself a beast. I preferred the condition of the meanest reptile to my own. Any thing, no matter what, to get rid of thinking! It was this everlasting thinking of my condition that tormented me. There was no getting rid of it. It was pressed upon me by every object within sight or hearing, animate or inanimate. The silver trump of freedom had roused my soul to eternal wakefulness. Freedom now appeared, to disappear no more forever. It was heard in every sound, and seen in every thing. It was ever present to torment me with a sense of my wretched condition. I saw nothing without seeing it, I heard nothing without hearing it, and felt nothing without feeling it. It looked from every star, it smiled in every calm, breathed in every wind, and moved in every storm.

I often found myself regretting my own existence, and wishing myself dead; and but for the hope of being free, I have no doubt but that I should have killed myself, or done something for which I should have been killed. While in this state of mind, I was eager to hear any one speak of slavery. I was a ready listener. Every little while, I could hear something about the abolitionists. It was some time before I found what the word meant. It was always used in such connections as to make it an interesting word to me. If a slave ran away and succeeded in getting clear, or if a slave killed his master, set fire to a barn, or did any thing very wrong in the mind of a slaveholder, it was spoken of as the fruit of *abolition*. Hearing the word in this connection very often, I set about learning what it meant. The dictionary afforded me little or no help. I found it was "the act of abolishing," but then I did not know what was to be abolished. Here I was perplexed. I did not dare to ask any one about its meaning, for I was satisfied that it was something they wanted me to know very little about. After a patient waiting, I got one of our city papers, containing an account of the number of petitions from the north, praying for the abolition of slavery in the District of Columbia, and of the slave trade between the States. From this time I understood the words *abolition* and *abolitionist,* and always drew near when that word was spoken, expecting to hear something of importance to myself and fellow-slaves. The light broke in upon me by degrees. I went one day down on the wharf of Mr. Waters; and seeing two Irishmen unloading a scow of stone, I went, unasked, and helped them. When we had finished, one of them came to me and asked me if I were a slave. I told him I was. He asked, "Are ye a slave for life?" I told him that I was. The good Irishman seemed to be deeply affected by the statement. He said to the other that it was a pity so fine a little fellow as myself should be a slave for life. He said it was a shame to hold me. They both advised me to run away to the north; that I should find friends there, and that I should be free. I pretended not to be interested in what they said, and treated them as if I did not understand them; for I feared they might be treacherous. White men have been known to encourage slaves to escape, and then, to get the reward, catch them and return them to their masters. I was afraid that these seemingly good men might use me so; but I nevertheless remembered their advice, and from that time I resolved to run away. I looked forward to a time at which it would be safe for me to escape. I was too young to think of doing so immediately; besides, I wished to learn how to write, as I might have occasion to write my own pass. I consoled myself with the hope that I should one day find a good chance. Meanwhile, I would learn to write.

The idea as to how I might learn to write was suggested to me by being in Durgin and Bailey's ship-yard, and frequently seeing the ship carpenters, after hewing, and getting a piece of timber ready for use, write on the timber the name of that part of the ship for which it was intended. When a piece of timber was intended for the larboard side, it would be marked thus—"L." When a piece was for the starboard side, it would be marked thus—"S." A piece for the larboard side forward, would be marked thus—"L. F." When a piece was for starboard side forward, it would be marked thus—"S. F." For larboard aft, it would be marked thus—"L. A." For starboard aft, it would be marked thus—"S. A." I soon learned the names of these letters, and for what they were intended when placed upon a piece of timber in the shipyard. I immediately commenced copying them, and in a short time was able to make the four letters named. After that, when I met with any boy who I knew could write, I would tell him I could write as well as he. The next word would be, "I don't believe you. Let me see you try it." I would then make the letters which I had been so fortunate as to learn, and ask him to beat that. In this way I got a good many lessons in writing, which it is quite possible I should never have gotten in any other way. During this time, my copy-book was the board fence, brick wall, and pavement; my pen and ink was a lump of chalk. With these, I learned mainly how to write. I then commenced and continued copying the Italics in Webster's Spelling Book, until I could make them all without looking on the book. By this time, my little Master Thomas had gone to school, and learned how to write, and had written over a number of copy-books. These had been brought home, and shown to some of our near neighbors, and then laid aside. My mistress used to go to class meeting at the Wilk Street meetinghouse every Monday afternoon, and leave me to take care of the house. When left thus, I used to spend the time in writing in the spaces left in Master Thomas's copy-book, copying what he had written. I continued to do this until I could write a hand very similar to that of Master Thomas. Thus, after a long, tedious effort for years, I finally succeeded in learning how to write.

The Myth of Man as Hunter

Barbara Ehrenreich

Barbara Ehrenreich (1941–) was born in Montana and earned her Ph.D. from Rockefeller University. She is known as—and speaks of herself as—an independent and outspoken feminist, liberal, and democratic socialist. Most of her non-fiction writing could be classified as social criticism, including a number of books: The Hearts of Men *(1983),* Fear of Falling *(1989),* The Worst Years of Our Lives *(1990), and* Bait and Switch: The (Futile) Pursuit of the American Dream *(2005). Her* New York Times *best seller* Nickel and Dimed: On (Not) Getting By in America *(2001) exposed the reality of the working poor. Her novel,* Kipper's Game *was published in 1993. She is a regular essayist for* Time *magazine, where the essay "The Myth of Man as Hunter" was first published. A hallmark of Ehrenreich's writing is her tendency to challenge accepted beliefs and attempt to shock the reader out of intellectual complacency. She is viewed by many as a controversial thinker.*

1   It must seem odd to the duck and deer populations that Americans have paid more than $255 million this summer for the experience of being prey. In *Jurassic Park* we had the supreme thrill of being hunted for food by creatures far larger, faster, and—counting teeth and claws—better armed than we are. With the raptors closing in, we saw how vulnerable the human body is—no claws, no exoskeleton, no blinding poison sprays. Take away our guns and high-voltage fences and we are, from a typical predator perspective, tasty mounds of unwrapped meat.

     If the experience resonates to the most ancient layers of our brains, it's probably because we spent our first million years or so not just hunting and gathering, but being hunted and gathered. *T. Rex* had been gone for 60 million years when our progenitors came along, but there were saber-toothed tigers, lions, cougars, leopards, bears, wolves and wild boars waiting at the edge of every human settlement and campground.

The myth of "man the hunter" has flatteringly obscured our true prehistory as prey. According to the myth, "man" climbed down from the trees one day, strode out into the savanna with a sharpened stick in his hand and started slaughtering the local ungulates. After that, supposedly, the only violence prehumans had to worry about was from other stick-wielding bipeds like themselves. Thus some punctured australopithecine skulls found in Africa were at first chalked up to "intentional armed assault"—until someone pointed out that the punctures precisely fit the tooth gap of the leopard.

Humans didn't even invent effective action-at-a-distance weapons until a mere 40,000 or so years ago. Only with these new tools, like the bow and arrow and the spear thrower, could our ancestors begin to mimic the speed and sharpness of a big cat's claws. Even so, predator animals remained a major threat. As late as the 7th century B.C., a stela erected by the Assyrian King Assurbanipal recounts the ferocity of the lions and tigers after torrential rains had flushed them out of their lairs; the great King, of course, stamped out the beasts.

Our collective memory of the war against the predator beasts is preserved in myth and fairy tale. Typically, a mythical hero starts out by taking on the carnivorous monster that is ravaging the land: Perseus saves Andromeda from becoming a sea monster's snack. Theseus conquers the Minotaur who likes to munch on Athenian youth. Beowulf destroys the loathsome night-feeding Grendel. Heracles takes on a whole zoo of horrors: lions, hydras, boars. In European fairy tales it's the wolves you have to watch out for—if the cannibal witches don't get you first.

No doubt the greatest single leap in human prehistory was the one we made from being helpless prey to becoming formidable predators of other living creatures, including, eventually, the ones with claws and fangs. This is the theme that is acted out over and over, obsessively, in the initiation rites of tribal cultures. In the drama of initiation, the young (usually men) are first humiliated and sometimes tortured, only to be "reborn" as hunters and warriors. Very often the initial torment includes the threat of being eaten by costumed humans or actual beasts. Orokaiva children in Papua New Guinea are told they will be devoured like pigs; among Indians of the Pacific Northwest, the initiates were kidnapped or menaced by wolves; young Norwegian men, at least in the sagas, had to tackle bears single-handedly.

As a species, we've been fabulously successful at predation. We enslaved the wild ungulates, turning them into our cattle and sheep, pushing them into ever narrower habitats. We tamed some of the wolves and big cats, trivializing them as household pets. We can dine on shark or alligator fillets if we want, and the only bears we're likely to know are the ones whose name is teddy. In fact, horror movies wouldn't be much fun if real monsters lurked outside our theaters. We can enjoy screaming at the alien or the raptor or the blob because we know, historically speaking, it was our side that won.

But the defeat of the animal predators was not a clear-cut victory for us. With the big land carnivores out of the way, humans decided that the only worthwhile enemy was others like themselves—"enemy" individuals or tribes or nations or ethnic groups. The criminal stalking his victim, the soldiers roaring into battle, are enacting an archaic drama in which the other player was originally nonhuman, either something to eat or be eaten by. For millenniums now, the earth's scariest predator has been ourselves.

In our arrogance, we have tended to forget that our own most formidable enemies may still be of the nonhuman kind. Instead of hungry tigers or fresh-cloned dinosaurs, we face equally deadly microscopic life forms. It will take a whole new set of skills and attitudes to defeat HIV or the TB bacterium—not the raging charge on the field of battle, but the cunning ambush of the lab.

10 And then there are all the nonliving enemies—Pinatubo, Andrew, 10 the murderously bloated Mississippi—to remind us that the earth has not passively accepted our dominion over it. We will go down, locked in incestuous combat with our own kind, while the earth quakes, the meteors hit and the viruses mindlessly duplicate in our living organs. Or we will take another great leap like the one our protohuman ancestors took so long ago when the threat was still from predator beasts: We will marshal all our skills and resources, our tools and talents, and face the enemy without.

What Is the Theory of Relativity?

Albert Einstein

Albert Einstein (1879–1955) was born in Germany. After receiving a Ph.D. in 1905, he was unable to secure an academic position, so he took a job in a patent office in Bern, Switzerland. It was during this time that he produced his groundbreaking work, Special Theory of Relativity *(1905). In* General Theory of Relativity *(1916), Einstein concluded that mass caused space to curve, and objects traveling in that curved space have their paths deflected. This theory significantly revised scientific assumption about gravitation, space, and time, and in 1921 Einstein was awarded the Nobel Prize for Physics. In 1933 he accepted a post at Princeton University's Institute for Advanced Study, where he remained until his death in 1955. The following essay originally appeared in the* London Times *in 1919.*

1   I gladly accede to the request of your colleague to write something   1
for *The Times* on relativity. After the lamentable breakdown of the
old active intercourse between men of learning, I welcome this
opportunity of expressing my feelings of joy and gratitude toward the
astronomers and physicists of England. It is thoroughly in keeping
with the great and proud traditions of scientific work in your country
that eminent scientists should have spent much time and trouble, and
your scientific institutions have spared no expense, to test the implications of a theory which was perfected and published during the war
in the land of your enemies. Even though the investigation of the

From the *London Times*, 1919.

influence of the gravitational field of the sun on light rays is a purely objective matter, I cannot forbear to express my personal thanks to my English colleagues for their work; for without it I could hardly have lived to see the most important implication of my theory tested.

We can distinguish various kinds of theories in physics. Most of them are constructive. They attempt to build up a picture of the more complex phenomena out of the materials of a relatively simply formal scheme from which they start out. Thus the kinetic theory of gases seeks to reduce mechanical, thermal, and diffusional processes to movements of molecules—i.e., to build them up out of the hypothesis of molecular motion. When we say that we have succeeded in understanding a group of natural processes, we invariably mean that a constructive theory has been found which covers the processes in question.

Along with this most important class of theories there exists a second, which I will call "principle-theories." These employ the analytic, not the synthetic, method. The elements which form their basis and starting-point are not hypothetically constructed but empirically discovered ones, general characteristics of natural processes, principles that give rise to mathematically formulated criteria which the separate processes or the theoretical representations of them have to satisfy. Thus the science of thermodynamics seeks by analytical means to deduce necessary conditions, which separate events have to satisfy, from the universally experienced fact that perpetual motion is impossible.

The advantages of the constructive theory are completeness, adaptability, and clearness, those of the principle theory are logical perfection and security of the foundations.

The theory of relativity belongs to the latter class. In order to grasp its nature, one needs first of all to become acquainted with the principles on which it is based. Before I go into these, however, I must observe that the theory of relativity resembles a building consisting of two separate stories, the special theory and the general theory. The special theory, on which the general theory rests, applies to all physical phenomena with the exception of gravitation; the general theory provides the law of gravitation and its relations to the other forces of nature.

It has, of course, been known since the days of the ancient Greeks that in order to describe the movement of a body, a second body is needed to which the movement of the first is referred. The movement of a vehicle is considered in reference to the earth's surface, that of a planet to the totality of the visible fixed stars. In physics the body to which events are spatially referred is called the coordinate system. The laws of the mechanics of Galileo and Newton, for instance, can only be formulated with the aid of a coordinate system.

The state of motion of the coordinate system may not, however, be arbitrarily chosen, if the laws of mechanics are to be valid (it must be free from rotation and acceleration). A coordinate system which is admitted in mechanics is called an "inertial system." The state of motion of an inertial system is according to mechanics not one that is determined uniquely by nature. On the contrary, the following definition holds good: a coordinate system that is moved uniformly and in a straight line relative to an inertial system is likewise an inertial system. By the "special principle of relativity" is meant the generalization of this definition to include any natural event whatever: thus, every universal law of nature which is valid in relation to a coordinate system C, must also be valid, as it stands, in relation to a coordinate system C', which is in uniform translatory motion relatively to C.

The second principle, on which the special theory of relativity rests, is the "principle of the constant velocity of light in vacuo." This principle asserts that light in vacuo always has a definite velocity of propagation (independent of the state of motion of the observer or of the source of the light). The confidence which physicists place in this principle springs from the successes achieved by the electrodynamics of Maxwell and Lorentz.

Both the above-mentioned principles are powerfully supported by experience, but appear not to be logically reconcilable. The special theory of relativity finally succeeded in reconciling them logically by a modification of kinematics—i.e., of the doctrine of the laws relating to space and time (from the point of view of physics). It became clear that to speak of the simultaneity of two events had no meaning except in relation to a given coordinate system, and that the shape of measuring devices and the speed at which clocks move depend on their state of motion with respect to the coordinate system.

10 But the old physics, including the laws of motion of Galileo and 10 Newton, did not fit in with the suggested relativist kinematics. From the latter, general mathematical conditions issued, to which natural laws had to conform, if the above-mentioned two principles were really to apply. To these, physics had to be adapted. In particular, sci-

entists arrived at a new law of motion for (rapidly moving) mass points, which was admirably confirmed in the case of electrically charged particles. The most important upshot of the special theory of relativity concerned the inert masses of corporeal systems. It turned out that the inertia of a system necessarily depends on its energy-content, and this led straight to the notion that inert mass is simply latent energy. The principle of the conservation of mass lost its independence and became fused with that of the conservation of energy.

The special theory of relativity, which was simply a systematic development of the electrodynamics of Maxwell and Lorentz, pointed beyond itself, however. Should the independence of physical laws of the state of motion of the coordinate system be restricted to the uniform translatory motion of coordinate systems in respect to each other? What has nature to do with our coordinate systems and their state of motion? If it is necessary for the purpose of describing nature, to make use of a coordinate system arbitrarily introduced by us, then the choice of its state of motion ought to be subject to no restriction; the laws ought to be entirely independent of this choice (general principle of relativity).

The establishment of this general principle of relativity is made easier by a fact of experience that has long been known, namely, that the weight and the inertia of a body are controlled by the same constant (equality of inertial and gravitational mass). Imagine a coordinate system which is rotating uniformly with respect to an inertial system in the Newtonian manner. The centrifugal forces which manifest themselves in relation to this system must, according to Newton's teaching, be regarded as effects of inertia. But these centrifugal forces are, exactly like the forces of gravity, proportional to the masses of the bodies. Ought it not to be possible in this case to regard the coordinate system as stationary and the centrifugal forces as gravitational forces? This seems the obvious view, but classical mechanics forbid it.

This hasty consideration suggests that a general theory of relativity must supply the laws of gravitation, and the consistent following up of the idea has justified our hopes.

But the path was thornier than one might suppose, because it demanded the abandonment of Euclidean geometry. This is to say, the laws according to which solid bodies may be arranged in space do not completely accord with the spatial laws attributed to bodies by Euclidean geometry. This is what we mean when we talk of the "curvature of space." The fundamental concepts of the "straight line," the "plane," etc., thereby lose their precise significance in physics.

In the general theory of relativity the doctrine of space and time, or kinematics, no longer figures as a fundamental independent of the rest of physics. The geometrical behavior of bodies and the motion of clocks rather depend on gravitational fields, which in their turn are produced by matter.

The new theory of gravitation diverges considerably, as regards principles, from Newton's theory. But its practical results agree so nearly with those of Newton's theory that it is difficult to find criteria for distinguishing them which are accessible to experience. Such have been discovered so far:

1. In the revolution of the ellipses of the planetary orbits around the sun (confirmed in the case of Mercury).
2. In the curving of light rays by the action of gravitational fields (confirmed by the English photographs of eclipses).
3. In a displacement of the spectral lines toward the red end of the spectrum in the case of light transmitted to us from stars of considerable magnitude (unconfirmed so far).

The chief attraction of the theory lies in its logical completeness. If a single one of the conclusions drawn from it proves wrong, it must be given up; to modify it without destroying the whole structure seems to be impossible.

Let no one suppose, however, that the mighty work of Newton can really be superseded by this or any other theory. His great and lucid ideas will retain their unique significance for all time as the foundation of our whole modern conceptual structure in the sphere of natural philosophy.

Note: Some of the statements in your paper concerning my life and person owe their origin to the lively imagination of the writer. Here is yet another application of the principle of relativity for the delectation of the reader: today I am described in Germany as a "German savant," and in England as a "Swiss Jew." Should it ever be my fate to be represented as a *bête noire,* I should, on the contrary, become a "Swiss Jew" for the Germans and a "German savant" for the English.

The Brown Wasps

Loren Eiseley

Loren Eiseley (1907–1977) was born in Lincoln, Nebraska. A noted anthropologist, educator, poet, and author, Eiseley was lauded for his beautiful prose and his ability to make science interesting and entertaining to lay readers. Eiseley taught at the University of Kansas at Lawrence, Oberlin College, and the University of Pennsylvania. His books include The Immense Journey *(1957),* Darwin's Century *(1958),* The Firmament of Time *(rev. ed. 1960), and* Night Country *(1971). In this essay, Eiseley notes the ability of humans as well as other animals to hold an image in the mind—the homing instinct—despite the proof of reality.*

1　There is a corner in the waiting room of one of the great Eastern stations where women never sit. It is always in the shadow and overhung by rows of lockers. It is, however, always frequented—not so much by genuine travelers as by the dying. It is here that a certain element of the abandoned poor seeks a refuge out of the weather, clinging for a few hours longer to the city that has fathered them. In a precisely similar manner I have seen, on a sunny day in midwinter, a few old brown wasps creep slowly over an abandoned wasp nest in a thicket. Numbed and forgetful and frost-blackened, the hum of the spring hive still resounded faintly in their sodden tissues. Then the temperature would fall and they would drop away into the white oblivion of the snow. Here in the station it is in no way different save that the city is busy in its snows. But the old ones cling to their seats as though these were symbolic and could not be given up. Now and then they sleep, their gray old heads resting with painful awkwardness on the backs of the benches.

Also they are not at rest. For an hour they may sleep in the gasping exhaustion of the ill-nourished and aged who have to walk in the night. Then a policeman comes by on his round and nudges them upright.

"You can't sleep here," he growls.

A strange ritual then begins. An old man is difficult to waken. After a muttered conversation the policeman presses a coin into his hand and passes fiercely along the benches prodding and gesturing toward the door. In his wake, like birds rising and settling behind the passage of a farmer through a cornfield, the men totter up, move a few paces and subside once more upon the benches.

One man, after a slight, apologetic lurch, does not move at all. Tubercularly thin, he sleeps on steadily. The policeman does not look back. To him, too, this has become a ritual. He will not have to notice it again officially for another hour.

Once in a while one of the sleepers will not awake. Like the brown wasps, he will have had his wish to die in the great droning center of the hive rather than in some lonely room. It is not so bad here with the shuffle of footsteps and the knowledge that there are others who share the bad luck of the world. There are also the whistles and the sounds of everyone, everyone in the world, starting on journeys. Amidst so many journeys somebody is bound to come out all right. Somebody.

Maybe it was on a like thought that the brown wasps fell away from the old paper nest in the thicket. You hold till the last, even if it is only to a public seat in a railroad station. You want your place in the hive more than you want a room or a place where the aged can be eased gently out of the way. It is the place that matters, the place at the heart of things. It is life that you want, that bruises your gray old head with the hard chairs; a man has a right to his place.

But sometimes the place is lost in the years behind us. Or sometimes it is a thing of air, a kind of vaporous distortion above a heap of rubble. We cling to a time and place because without them man is lost, not only man but life. This is why the voices, real or unreal, which speak from the floating trumpets at spiritualist seances are so unnerving. They are voices out of nowhere whose only reality lies in their ability to stir the memory of a living person with some fragment of the past. Before the medium's cabinet both the dead and the living revolve endlessly about an episode, a place, an event that has already been engulfed by time.

153

This feeling runs deep in life; it brings stray cats running over endless miles, and birds homing from the ends of the earth. It is as though all living creatures, and particularly the more intelligent, can survive only by fixing or transforming a bit of time into space or by securing a bit of space with its objects immortalized and made permanent in time. For example, I once saw, on a flower pot in my own living room, the efforts of a field mouse to build a remembered field. I have lived to see this episode repeated in a thousand guises, and since I have spent a large portion of my life in the shade of a nonexistent tree, I think I am entitled to speak for the field mouse.

One day as I cut across the field which at the time extended on one side of our suburban shopping center, I found a giant slug feeding from a runnel of pink ice cream in an abandoned Dixie cup. I could see his eyes telescope and protrude in a kind of dim, uncertain ecstasy as his dark body bunched and elongated in the curve of the cup. Then, as I stood there at the edge of the concrete, contemplating the slug, I began to realize it was like standing on a shore where a different type of life creeps up and fumbles tentatively among the rocks and sea wrack. It knows its place and will only creep so far until something changes. Little by little as I stood there I began to see more of this shore that surrounds the place of man. I looked with sudden care and attention at things I had been running over thoughtlessly for years. I even waded out a short way into the grass and the wild-rose thickets to see more. A huge black-belted bee went droning by and there were some indistinct scurrying in the underbrush.

Then I came to a sign which informed me that this field was to be the site of a new Wanamaker suburban store. Thousands of obscure lives were about to perish, the spores of puffballs would go smoking off to new fields, and the bodies of little white-footed mice would be crunched under the inexorable wheels of the bulldozers. Life disappears or modifies its appearances so fast that everything takes on an aspect of illusion—a momentary fizzing and boiling with smoke rings, like pouring dissident chemicals into a retort. Here man was advancing, but in a few years his plaster and bricks would be disappearing once more into the insatiable maw of the clover. Being of an archaeological cast of mind, I thought of this fact with an obscure sense of satisfaction and waded back through the rose thickets to the concrete parking lot. As I did so, a mouse scurried ahead of me, frightened of my steps if not of that ominous Wanamaker sign. I saw him vanish in the general direction of my apartment house, his little body quivering with fear in the great open sun on the blazing concrete. Blinded and confused, he was running straight away from his field. In another week scores would follow him.

I forgot the episode then and went home to the quiet of my living room. It was not until a week later, letting myself into the apartment, that I realized I had a visitor. I am fond of plants and had several ferns standing on the floor in pots to avoid the noon glare by the south window.

As I snapped on the light and glanced carelessly around the room, I saw a little heap of earth on the carpet and a scrabble of pebbles that had been kicked merrily over the edge of one of the flower pots. To my astonishment I discovered a full-fledged burrow delving downward among the fern roots. I waited silently. The creature who had made the burrow did not appear. I remembered the wild field then, and the flight of the mice. No house mouse, no *Mus domesticus,* had kicked up this little heap of earth or sought refuge under a fern root in a flower pot. I thought of the desperate little creature I had seen fleeing from the wild-rose thicket. Through intricacies of pipes and attics, he, or one of his fellows, had climbed to this high green solitary room. I could visualize what had occurred. He had an image in his head, a world of seed pods and quiet, of green sheltering leaves in the dim light among the weed stems. It was the only world he knew and it was gone.

Somehow in his flight he had found his way to this room with drawn shades where no one would come till nightfall. And here he had smelled garden leaves and run quickly up the flower pot to dabble his paws in common earth. He had even struggled half the afternoon to carry his burrow deeper and had failed. I examined the hole, but no whiskered twitching face appeared. He was gone. I gathered up the earth and refilled the burrow. I did not expect to find traces of him again.

15   Yet for three nights thereafter I came home to the darkened room   15
and my ferns to find the dirt kicked gaily about the rug and the burrow reopened, though I was never able to catch the field mouse within it. I dropped a little food about the mouth of the burrow, but it was never touched. I looked under beds or sat reading with one ear cocked for rustlings in the ferns. It was all in vain; I never saw him. Probably he ended in a trap in some other tenant's room.

But before he disappeared I had come to look hopefully for his evening burrow. About my ferns there had begun to linger the insubstantial vapor of an autumn field, the distilled essence, as it were, of a mouse brain in exile from its home. It was a small dream, like our dreams, carried a long and weary journey along pipes and through spider webs, past holes over which loomed the shadows of waiting cats, and finally, desperately, into this room where he had played in the shuttered daylight for an hour among the green ferns on the floor. Every day these invisible dreams pass us on the street, or rise from beneath our feet, or look out upon us from beneath a bush.

Some years ago the old elevated railway in Philadelphia was torn down and replaced by a subway system. This ancient El with its barnlike stations containing nut-vending machines and scattered food scraps had, for generations, been the favorite feeding ground of flocks of pigeons, generally one flock to a station along the route of the El. Hundreds of pigeons were dependent upon the system. They flapped in and out of its stanchions and steel work or gathered in watchful little audiences about the feet of anyone who rattled the peanut-vending machines. They even watched people who jingled change in their hands, and prospected for food under the feet of the crowds who gathered between trains. Probably very few among the waiting people who tossed a crumb to an eager pigeon realized that this El was like a food-bearing river, and that the life which haunted its banks was dependent upon the running of the trains with their human freight.

I saw the river stop.

The time came when the underground tubes were ready; the traffic was transferred to a realm unreachable by pigeons. It was like a great river subsiding suddenly into desert sands. For a day, for two days, pigeons continued to circle over the El or stand close to the red vending machines. They were patient birds, and surely this great river which had flowed through the lives of unnumbered generations were merely suffering from some momentary drought.

They listened for the familiar vibrations that had always heralded an approaching train; they flapped hopefully about the head of an occasional workman walking along the steel runways. They passed from one empty station to another, all the while growing hungrier. Finally they flew away.

I thought I had seen the last of them about the El, but there was a revival and it provided a curious instance of the memory of living things for a way of life or a locality that has long been cherished. Some weeks after the El was abandoned workmen began to tear it down. I went to work every morning by one particular station, and the time came when the demolition crews reached this spot. Acetylene torches showered passersby with sparks, pneumatic drills hammered at the base of the structure, and a blind man who, like the pigeons, had clung with his cup to a stairway leading to the change booth, was forced to give up his place.

It was then, strangely, momentarily, one morning that I witnessed the return of a little band of the familiar pigeons. I even recognized one or two members of the flock that had lived around this particular station before they were dispersed into the streets. They flew bravely in and out among the sparks and the hammers and the shouting workmen. They had returned—and they had returned because the hubbub of the wreckers had convinced them that the river was about to flow once more. For several hours they flapped in and out through the empty windows, nodding their heads and watching the fall of girders with attentive little eyes. By the following morning the station was reduced to some burned-off stanchions in the street. My bird friends had gone. It was plain, however, that they retained a memory for an insubstantial structure now compounded of air and time. Even the blind man clung to it. Someone had provided him with a chair, and he sat at the same corner staring sightlessly at an invisible stairway where, so far as he was concerned, the crowds were still ascending to the trains.

I have said my life has been passed in the shade of a nonexistent tree, so that such sights do not offend me. Prematurely I am one of the brown wasps and I often sit with them in the great droning hive of the station, dreaming sometimes of a certain tree. It was planted sixty years ago by a boy with a bucket and a toy spade in a little Nebraska town. That boy was myself. It was a cottonwood sapling and the boy remembered it because of some words spoken by his father and because everyone died or moved away who was supposed to wait and grow old under its shade. The boy was passed from hand to hand, but the tree for some intangible reason had taken root in his mind. It was under its branches that he sheltered; it was from this tree that his memories, which are my memories, led away into the world.

After sixty years the mood of the brown wasps grows heavier upon one. During a long inward struggle I thought it would do me good to go and look upon that actual tree. I found a rational excuse in which to clothe this madness. I purchased a ticket and at the end of two thousand miles I walked another mile to an address that was still the same. The house had not been altered.

25 I came close to the white picket fence and reluctantly, with great 25 effort, looked down the long vista of the yard. There was nothing there to see. For sixty years that cottonwood had been growing in my mind. Season by season its seeds had been floating farther on the hot prairie winds. We had planted it lovingly there, my father and I, because he had a great hunger for soil and live things growing, and because none of these things had long been ours to protect. We had planted the little sapling and watered it faithfully, and I remembered that I had run out with my small bucket to drench its roots the day we moved away. And all the years since it had been growing in my mind, a huge tree that somehow stood for my father and the love I bore him. I took a grasp on the picket fence and forced myself to look again.

A boy with the hard bird eye of youth pedaled a tricycle slowly up beside me.

"What'cha lookin' at?" he asked curiously.

"A tree," I said.

"What for?" he said.

30 "It isn't there," I said, to myself mostly, and began to walk away 30 at a pace just slow enough not to seem to be running.

"What isn't there?" the boy asked. I didn't answer. It was obvious I was attached by a thread to a thing that had never been there, or certainly not for long. Something that had to be held in the air, or sustained in the mind, because it was part of my orientation in the universe and I could not survive without it. There was more than an animal's attachment to a place. There was something else, the attachment of the spirit to a grouping of events in time; it was part of our morality.

So I had come home at last, driven by a memory in the brain as surely as the field mouse who had delved long ago into my flower pot or the pigeons flying forever amidst the rattle of nut-vending machines. These, the burrow under the greenery in my living room and the red-bellied bowls of peanuts now hovering in midair in the minds of pigeons, were all part of an elusive world that existed nowhere and yet everywhere. I looked once at the real world about me while the persistent boy pedaled at my heels.

It was without meaning, though my feet took a remembered path. In sixty years the house and street had rotted out of my mind. But the tree, the tree that no longer was, that had perished in its first season, bloomed on in my individual mind, unblemished as my father's words. "We'll plant a tree here, son, and we're not going to move any more. And when you're an old, old man you can sit under it and think how we planted it here, you and me, together."

I began to outpace the boy on the tricycle.

35 "Do you live here, Mister?" he shouted after me suspiciously I 35 took a firm grasp on airy nothing—to be precise, on the bole of a great tree. "I do," I said. I spoke for myself, one field mouse, and several pigeons. We were all out of touch but somehow permanent. It was the world that had changed.

Don't You Think It's Time to Start Thinking?

Northrop Frye

*Northrop Frye (1912–1991), one of Canada's most dis-
tinguished scholars, was reared in New Brunswick, and
after attending school in Canada, received his MA from
Oxford University, in England (1940). In 1939 Frye
became a professor at the University of Toronto, where he
wrote and taught until his death. His interests were literary criticism and school curriculum; his books include* On
Education *and* Myth and Metaphor. *The following essay
insists that thinking happens only when a person writes
down ideas "in the right words."*

1   A student often leaves high school today without any sense of   1
language as a structure.
     He may also have the idea that reading and writing are ele-
mentary skills that he mastered in childhood, never having grasped the
fact that there are differences in levels of reading and writing as there
are in mathematics between short division and integral calculus.
     Yet, in spite of his limited verbal skills, he firmly believes that he
can think, that he has ideas, and that if he is just given the opportunity to express them he will be all right. Of course, when you look at
what he's written you find it doesn't make any sense. When you tell
him this he is devastated.
     Part of his confusion here stems from the fact that we use the word
"think" in so many bad, punning ways. Remember James Thurber's
Walter Mitty who was always dreaming great dreams of glory. When
his wife asked him what he was doing he would say, "Has it ever
occurred to you that I might be thinking?"

5   But, of course, he wasn't thinking at all. Because we use it for every-   5
thing our minds do, worrying, remembering, daydreaming, we imagine that thinking is something that can be achieved without any training.
But again it's a matter of practice. How well we can think depends on
how much of it we have already done. Most students need to be taught,
very carefully and patiently, that there is no such thing as an inarticu-
late idea waiting to have the right words wrapped around it.

They have to learn that ideas do not exist until they have been
incorporated into words. Until that point you don't know whether you
are pregnant or just have gas on the stomach.

The operation of thinking is the practice of articulating ideas
until they are in the right words. And we can't think at random either.
We can only add one more idea to the body of something we have
already thought about. Most of us spend very little time doing this,
and that is why there are so few people whom we regard as having
any power to articulate at all. When such a person appears in public life, like Mr. Trudeau, we tend to regard him as possessing a gigantic intellect.

A society like ours doesn't have very much interest in literacy.
It is compulsory to read and write because society must have docile
and obedient citizens. We are taught to read so that we can obey
the traffic signs and to cipher so that we can make out our income
tax, but development of verbal competency is very much left to the
individual.

And when we look at our day-to-day existence we can see that there
are strong currents at work against the development of powers of articulateness. Young adolescents today often betray a curious sense of shame
about speaking articulately, of framing a sentence with a period at the
end of it.

10   Part of the reason for this is the powerful anti-intellectual drive   10
which is constantly present in our society. Articulate speech marks you
out as an individual, and in some settings this can be rather dangerous because people are often suspicious and frightened of articulateness. So if you say as little as possible and use only stereotyped,
ready-made phrases you can hide yourself in the mass.

Then there are various epidemics sweeping over society which
use unintelligibility as a weapon to preserve the present power structure. By making things as unintelligible as possible, to as many people as possible, you can hold the present power structure together.

Understanding and articulateness lead to its destruction. This is the kind of thing that George Orwell was talking about, not just in *Nineteen Eighty-Four,* but in all his work on language. The kernel of everything reactionary and tyrannical in society is the impoverishment of the means of verbal communication.

The vast majority of things that we hear today are prejudices and clichés, simply verbal formulas that have no thought behind them but are put up as pretence of thinking. It is not until we realize these things conceal meaning, rather than reveal it, that we can begin to develop our own powers of articulateness.

The teaching of humanities is, therefore, a militant job. Teachers are faced not simply with a mass of misconceptions and unexamined assumptions. They must engage in a fight to help the student confront and reject the verbal formulas and stock responses, to convert passive acceptance into active, constructive power. It is a fight against illiteracy and for the maturation of the mental process, for the development of skills which once acquired will never become obsolete.

What Is Style?

Mavis Gallant

Mavis Gallant (1922–), born Mavis Young, began her career as a journalist in Montreal but moved to Paris in 1950 and became a fiction writer. Gallant is best known for her short fiction, which has appeared in numerous publications, including the New Yorker *magazine, and in several volumes, including* Home Truths: Selected Canadian Stories *(1981). She has also published two novels, a play, and a collection of essays,* Paris Journals: Selected Essays and Reviews *(1986). The following essay addresses one of the most interesting and yet vexing questions about writing: How does a writer or a critic define style, and how do we identify a particular style?*

1   I do not reread my own work unless I have to; I fancy no writer does.   1
The reason why, probably, is that during the making of the story every line has been read and rewritten and read again to the point of glut. I am unable to "see" the style of "Baum, Gabriel, 1935–( )" and "His Mother," and would not recognize its characteristics if they were pointed out to me. Once too close, the stories are already too distant. If I read a passage aloud, I am conscious of a prose rhythm easy for me to follow, that must be near to the way I think and speak. It seems to be my only link with a finished work.

The manner of writing, the thread spun out of the story itself, may with time have grown instinctive. I know that the thread must hold from beginning to end, and that I would like to be invisible. Rereading "Baum, Gabriel" and "His Mother," all I can relate is that they are about loss and bewilderment, that I cannot imagine the people described living with any degree of willingness anywhere but in a city—in spite of Gabriel's imaginings about country life—and that a café as a home more congenial than home appears in both. The atmosphere, particularized, is of a fading world, though such a thing was far from my mind when the stories were written. It may be that the Europe of the nineteen-seventies already secreted the first dangerous sign of nostalgia, like a pervasive mist: I cannot say. And it is not what I have been asked to discuss.

Leaving aside the one analysis closed to me, of my own writing, let me say what style is *not:* it is not a last-minute addition to prose, a charming and universal slipcover, a coat of paint used to mask the failings of a structure. Style is inseparable from structure, part of the conformation of whatever the author has to say. What he says—this is what fiction is about—is that something is taking place and that nothing lasts. Against the sustained tick of a watch, fiction takes the measure of a life, a season, a look exchanged, the turning point, desire as brief as a dream, the grief and terror that after childhood we cease to express. The lie, the look, the grief are without permanence. The watch continues to tick where the story stops.

A loose, a wavering, a slipshod, an affected, a false way of transmitting even a fragment of this leaves the reader suspicious: What is this too elaborate or too simple language hiding? What is the author trying to disguise? Probably he doesn't know. He has shown the works of the watch instead of its message. He may be untalented, just as he may be a gifted author who for some deeply private reason (doubt, panic, the pressures of a life unsuited to writing) has taken to rearranging the works in increasingly meaningless patterns. All this is to say that content, meaning, intention and form must make up a whole, and must above all have a reason to be.

5   There are rules of style. By applying them doggedly any literate,   5
ambitious and determined person should be able to write like Somerset Maugham. Maugham was conscious of his limitations and deserves appreciation on that account: "I knew that I had no lyrical quality, had a small vocabulary . . . I had little gift for metaphors; the original or striking simile seldom occurred to me. Poetic flights and the great imaginative sweep were beyond my powers." He decided, sensibly, to write "as well as my natural defects allowed" and to aim at "lucidity, simplicity and euphony." The chance that some other indispensable quality had been overlooked must have been blanketed by a lifetime of celebrity. Now, of course, first principles are there to be heeded or, at the least, considered with care; but no guided tour of literature, no

commitment to the right formula or to good taste (which is change-able anyway), can provide, let alone supplant, the inborn vitality and tension of living prose.

Like every other form of art, literature is no more and nothing less than a matter of life and death. The only question worth asking about a story—or a poem, or a piece of sculpture, or a new concert hall—is, "Is it dead or alive?" If a work of the imagination needs to be coaxed into life, it is better scrapped and forgotten. Working to rule, trying to make a barely breathing work of fiction simpler and more lucid and more euphonious merely injects into the desperate author's voice a tone of suppressed hysteria, the result of what E.M. Forster called "confus-ing order with orders." And then, how reliable are the rules? Listen to Pablo Picasso's rejection of a fellow-artist: "He looks up at the sky and says, 'Ah, the sky is blue,' and he paints a blue sky. Then he takes another look and says, 'The sky is mauve, too,' and he adds some mauve. The next time he looks he notices a trace of pink, and he adds a little pink." It sounds a proper mess, but Picasso was talking about Pierre Bonnard. As soon as we learn the names, the blues, mauves and pinks acquire a meaning, a reason to be. Picasso was right, but only in theory. In the end, everything depends on the artist himself.

Style in writing, as in painting, is the author's thumbprint, his mark. I do not mean that it establishes him as finer or greater than other writers, though that can happen too. I am thinking now of prose style as a writer's armorial bearings, his name and address. In a privately printed and libellous pamphlet, Colette's first husband, Willy, who had fraudulently signed her early novels, tried to prove she had gone on to plagiarize and plunder different things he had written. As evidence he offered random sentences from work he was supposed to have influ-enced or inspired. Colette's manner, robust and personal, seems to leap from the page. Willy believed he had taught Colette "everything," and it may have been true—"everything," that is, except her instinct for language, her talent for perceiving the movement of life and fac-ulty for describing it. He was bound to have influenced her writing; it couldn't be helped. But by the time he chose to print a broadside on the subject, his influence had been absorbed, transmuted and—most humbling for the teacher—had left no visible trace.

There is no such a thing as a writer who has escaped being influ-enced. I have never heard a professional writer of any quality or stand-ing talk about "pure" style, or say he would not read this or that for fear of corrupting or affecting his own; but I have heard it from would-be writers and amateurs. Corruption—if that is the word—sets in from the moment a child learns to speak and to hear language used and mis-used. A young person who does not read, and read widely, will never write anything—at least, nothing of interest. From time to time, in France, a novel is published purporting to come from a shepherd whose only influence has been the baaing of lambs on some God-forsaken slope of the Pyrenees. His artless and untampered-with mode of expres-sion arouses the hope that there will be many more like him, but as a rule he is never heard from again. For "influences" I would be inclined to substitute "acquisitions." What they consist of, and amount to, are affected by taste and environment, preferences and upbringing (even, and sometimes particularly, where the latter has been rejected), instinc-tive selection. The beginning writer has to choose, tear to pieces, spit out, chew up and assimilate as naturally as a young animal—as natu-rally and as ruthlessly. Style cannot be copied, except by the untalented. It is, finally, the distillation of a lifetime of reading and listening, of selection and rejection. But if it is not a true voice, it is nothing.

The Tipping Point

Malcolm Gladwell

Malcolm Gladwell (1963–   ) was born in England but grew up in Canada. He majored in history at the University of Toronto, graduating in 1984. In 1987 he began as a reporter for the Washington Post *where he worked first as a science writer and then as New York bureau chief. In 1996 he moved to the* New Yorker *where he works as a staff writer.* The Tipping Point *(2001), his best-selling book, is the source of this essay. The book theorizes the impact of building trends on events and ideas, showing that change takes place in sudden events rather than by gradual shifting.*

1   For Hush Puppies—the classic American brushed-suede shoes with the lightweight crepe sole—the Tipping Point came somewhere between late 1994 and early 1995. The brand had been all but dead until that point. Sales were down to 30,000 pairs a year, mostly to backwoods outlets and small-town family stores. Wolverine, the company that makes Hush Puppies, was thinking of phasing out the shoes that made them famous. But then something strange happened. At a fashion shoot, two Hush Puppies executives—Owen Baxter and Geoffrey Lewis—ran into a stylist from New York who told them that the classic Hush Puppies had suddenly become hip in the clubs and bars of downtown Manhattan. "We were being told," Baxter recalls, "that there were resale shops in the Village, in Soho, where the shoes were being sold. People were going to the Ma and Pa stores, the little stores that still carried them, and buying them up." Baxter and Lewis were baffled at first. It made no sense to them that shoes that were so obviously out of fashion could make a comeback. "We were told that Isaac Mizrahi was wearing the shoes himself,"

Lewis says. "I think it's fair to say that at the time we had no idea who Isaac Mizrahi was."

By the fall of 1995, things began to happen in a rush. First the designer John Bartlett called. He wanted to use Hush Puppies in his spring collection. Then another Manhattan designer, Anna Sui, called, wanting shoes for her show as well. In Los Angeles, the designer Joe Fitzgerald put a twenty-five-foot inflatable basset hound—the symbol of the Hush Puppies brand—on the roof of his Hollywood store and gutted an adjoining art gallery to turn it into a Hush Puppies boutique. While he was still painting and putting up shelves, the actor Pee-wee Herman walked in and asked for a couple of pairs. "It was total word of mouth," Fitzgerald remembers.

In 1995, the company sold 430,000 pairs of the classic Hush Puppies, and the next year it sold four times that, and the year after that still more, until Hush Puppies were once again a staple of the wardrobe of the young American male. In 1996, Hush Puppies won the prize for best accessory at the Council of Fashion Designers awards dinner at Lincoln Center, and the president of the firm stood up on the stage with Calvin Klein and Donna Karan and accepted an award for an achievement that—as he would be the first to admit—his company had almost nothing to do with. Hush Puppies had suddenly exploded, and it all started with a handful of kids in the East Village and Soho.

How did that happen? Those first few kids, whoever they were, weren't deliberately trying to promote Hush Puppies. They were wearing them precisely because no one else would wear them. Then the fad spread to two fashion designers who used the shoes to peddle something else—haute couture. The shoes were an incidental touch. No one was trying to make Hush Puppies a trend. Yet, somehow, that's exactly what happened. The shoes passed a certain point in popularity and they tipped. How does a thirty-dollar pair of shoes go from a handful of downtown Manhattan hipsters and designers to every mall in America in the space of two years?

I

5   There was a time, not very long ago, in the desperately poor New   5
York City neighborhoods of Brownsville and East New York, when the streets would turn into ghost towns at dusk. Ordinary working

people wouldn't walk on the sidewalks. Children wouldn't ride their bicycles on the streets. Old folks wouldn't sit on stoops and park benches. The drug trade ran so rampant and gang warfare was so ubiquitous in that part of Brooklyn that most people would take to the safety of their apartment at nightfall. Police officers who served in Brownsville in the 1980s and early 1990s say that, in those years, as soon as the sun went down their radios exploded with chatter between beat officers and their dispatchers over every conceivable kind of violent and dangerous crime. In 1992, there were 2,154 murders in New York City and 626,182 serious crimes, with the weight of those crimes falling hardest in places like Brownsville and East New York. But then something strange happened. At some mysterious and critical point, the crime rate began to turn. It tipped. Within five years, murders had dropped 64.3 percent to 770 and total crimes had fallen by almost half to 355,893. In Brownsville and East New York, the sidewalks filled up again, the bicycles came back, and old folks reappeared on the stoops. "There was a time when it wasn't uncommon to hear rapid fire, like you would hear somewhere in the jungle in Vietnam," says Inspector Edward Messadri, who commands the police precinct in Brownsville. "I don't hear the gunfire anymore."[1]

The New York City police will tell you that what happened in New York was that the city's policing strategies dramatically improved. Criminologists point to the decline of the crack trade and the aging of the population. Economists, meanwhile, say that the gradual improvement in the city's economy over the course of the 1990s had the effect of employing those who might otherwise have become criminals. These are the conventional explanations for the rise and fall of social problems, but in the end none is any more satisfying than the statement that kids in the East Village caused the Hush Puppies revival. The changes in the drug trade, the population, and the economy are all long-term trends, happening all over the country. They don't explain why crime plunged in New York City so much more than in other cities around the country, and they don't explain why it all happened in such an extraordinarily short time. As for the improvements made by the police, they are important too. But there is a puzzling gap between the scale of the changes in policing and the size of the effect on places like Brownsville and East New York. After all, crime didn't just slowly ebb in New York as conditions gradually improved.

It plummeted. How can a change in a handful of economic and social indices cause murder rates to fall by two-thirds in five years?

II

The idea of the Tipping Point is very simple. It is that the best way to understand the emergence of fashion trends, the ebb and flow of crime waves, or, for that matter, the transformation of unknown books into bestsellers, or the rise of teenage smoking, or the phenomena of word of mouth, or any number of other mysterious changes that mark everyday life is to think of them as epidemics. Ideas and products and messages and behaviors spread just like viruses do.

The rise of Hush Puppies and the fall of New York's crime rate are textbook examples of epidemics in action. Although they may sound as if they don't have very much in common, they share a basic, underlying pattern. First of all, they are clear examples of contagious behavior. No one took out an advertisement and told people that the traditional Hush Puppies were cool and they should start wearing them. Those kids simply wore the shoes when they went to clubs or cafes or walked the streets of downtown New York, and in so doing exposed other people to their fashion sense. They infected them with the Hush Puppies "virus."

The crime decline in New York surely happened the same way. It wasn't that some huge percentage of would-be murderers suddenly sat up in 1993 and decided not to commit any more crimes. Nor was it that the police managed magically to intervene in a huge percentage of situations that would otherwise have turned deadly. What happened is that the small number of people in the small number of situations in which the police or the new social forces had some impact started behaving very differently, and that behavior somehow spread to other would-be criminals in similar situations. Somehow a large number of people in New York got "infected" with an anti-crime virus in a short time.

The second distinguishing characteristic of these two examples is that in both cases little changes had big effects. All of the possible reasons for why New York's crime rate dropped are changes that happened at the margin; they were incremental changes. The crack trade leveled off. The population got a little older. The police force got a little better. Yet the effect was dramatic. So too with Hush Puppies.

How many kids are we talking about who began wearing the shoes in downtown Manhattan? Twenty? Fifty? One hundred—at the most? Yet their actions seem to have single-handedly started an international fashion trend.

Finally, both changes happened in a hurry. They didn't build steadily and slowly. It is instructive to look at a chart of the crime rate in New York City from, say, the mid-1960s to the late 1990s. It looks like a giant arch. In 1965, there were 200,000 crimes in the city and from that point on the number begins a sharp rise, doubling in two years and continuing almost unbroken until it hits 650,000 crimes a year in the mid-1970s. It stays steady at that level for the next two decades, before plunging downward in 1992 as sharply as it rose thirty years earlier. Crime did not taper off. It didn't gently decelerate. It hit a certain point and jammed on the brakes.

These three characteristics—one, contagiousness; two, the fact that little causes can have big effects; and three, that change happens not gradually but at one dramatic moment—are the same three principles that define how measles moves through a grade-school classroom or the flu attacks every winter. Of the three, the third trait—the idea that epidemics can rise or fall in one dramatic moment—is the most important, because it is the principle that makes sense of the first two and that permits the greatest insight into why modern change happens the way it does. The name given to that one dramatic moment in an epidemic when everything can change all at once is the Tipping Point.

III

A world that follows the rules of epidemics is a very different place from the world we think we live in now. Think, for a moment, about the concept of contagiousness. If I say that word to you, you think of colds and the flu or perhaps something very dangerous like HIV or Ebola. We have, in our minds, a very specific, biological notion of what contagiousness means. But if there can be epidemics of crime or epidemics of fashion, there must be all kinds of things just as contagious as viruses. Have you ever thought about yawning, for instance? Yawning is a surprisingly powerful act. Just because you read the word "yawning" in the previous two sentences—and the two additional "yawns" in this sentence—a good number of you will probably yawn within the next few minutes. Even as I'm writing this, I've yawned twice. If you're reading this in a public place, and you've just yawned, chances are that a good proportion of everyone who saw you yawn is now yawning too, and a good proportion of the people watching the people who watched you yawn are now yawning as well, and on and on, in an ever-widening, yawning circle.[2]

Yawning is incredibly contagious. I made some of you reading this yawn simply by writing the word "yawn." The people who yawned when they saw you yawn, meanwhile, were infected by the sight of you yawning—which is a second kind of contagion. They might even have yawned if they only heard you yawn, because yawning is also aurally contagious: if you play an audiotape of a yawn to blind people, they'll yawn too. And finally, if you yawned as you read this, did the thought cross your mind—however unconsciously and fleetingly—that you might be tired? I suspect that for some of you it did, which means that yawns can also be emotionally contagious. Simply by writing the word, I can plant a feeling in your mind. Can the flu virus do that? Contagiousness, in other words, is an unexpected property of all kinds of things, and we have to remember that, if we are to recognize and diagnose epidemic change.

The second of the principles of epidemics—that little changes can somehow have big effects—is also a fairly radical notion. We are, as humans, heavily socialized to make a kind of rough approximation between cause and effect. If we want to communicate a strong emotion, if we want to convince someone that, say, we love them, we realize that we need to speak passionately and forthrightly. If we want to break bad news to someone, we lower our voices and choose our words carefully. We are trained to think that what goes into any transaction or relationship or system must be directly related, in intensity and dimension, to what comes out. Consider, for example, the following puzzle. I give you a large piece of paper, and I ask you to fold it over once, and then take that folded paper and fold it over again, and then again, and again, until you have refolded the original paper 50 times. How tall do you think the final stack is going to be? In answer to that question, most people will fold the sheet in their mind's eye, and guess that the pile would be as thick as a phone book, or, if they're really courageous, they'll say that it would be as tall as a refrigerator. But the real answer is that the height of the stack would approximate the distance to the sun. And if you folded it over one more time, the stack would be as high as the distance to the sun and back. This is an example of what in mathematics is called a geometric progression. Epidemics are another example of geometric progression: when a virus spreads through a population, it doubles and doubles again, until it has (figuratively) grown from a single sheet of paper all the way to the sun in fifty steps. As human beings we have a hard time with this kind of progression, because the end result—the effect—seems far out of proportion to the cause. To appreciate the power of epidemics, we have to abandon this expectation about pro-portionality. We need to prepare ourselves for the possibility that sometimes big changes follow from small events, and that sometimes these changes can happen very quickly.

This possibility of sudden change is at the center of the idea of the Tipping Point and might well be the hardest of all to accept. The expression first came into popular use in the 1970s to describe the flight to the suburbs of white living in the older cities of the American Northeast. When the number of incoming African Americans in a particular neighborhood reached a certain point—20 percent, say—sociologists observed that the community would "tip": most of the remaining whites would leave almost immediately. The Tipping Point is the moment of critical mass, the threshold, the boiling point. There was a Tipping Point for violent crime in New York in the early 1990s, and a Tipping Point for the reemergence of Hush Puppies, just as there is a Tipping Point for the introduction of any new technology. Sharp introduced the first low-priced fax machine in 1984, and sold about 80,000 of those machines in the United States in that first year. For the next three years, businesses slowly and steadily bought more and more faxes, until, in 1987, enough people had faxes that it made sense for everyone to get a fax. Nineteen eighty-seven was the fax machine Tipping Point. A million machines were sold that year, and by 1989 two million new machines had gone into operation. Cellular phones have followed the same trajectory. Through the 1990s, they got smaller and cheaper, and service got better until 1998, when the technology hit a Tipping Point and suddenly everyone had a cell phone[3]. . . .

All epidemics have Tipping Points. Jonathan Crane, a sociologist at the University of Illinois, has looked at the effect the number of role models in a community—the professionals, managers, teachers whom the Census Bureau has defined as "high status"—has on the lives of teenagers in the same neighborhood. He found little difference in pregnancy rates or school drop-out rates in neighborhoods of between 40 and 5 percent of high-status workers. But when the number of professionals dropped below 5 percent, the problems exploded. For black schoolchildren, for example, as the percentage of high-status workers falls just 2.2 percentage points—from 5.6 percent to 3.4 percent—drop-out rates more than double. At the same Tipping Point, the rates of childbearing for teenaged girls—which barely move at all up to that point—nearly double. We assume, intuitively, that neighborhoods and social problems decline in some kind of steady progression. But sometimes they may not decline steadily at all; at the Tipping Point, schools can lose control of their students, and family life can disintegrate all at once.

I remember once as a child seeing our family's puppy encounter snow for the first time. He was shocked and delighted and overwhelmed, wagging his tail nervously, sniffing about in this strange, fluffy substance, whimpering with the mystery of it all. It wasn't much colder on the morning of his first snowfall than it had been the evening before. It might have been 34 degrees the previous evening, and now it was 31 degrees. Almost nothing had changed, in other words, yet—and this was the amazing thing—everything had changed. Rain had become something entirely different. Snow! We are all, at heart, gradualists, our expectations set by the steady passage of time. But the world of the Tipping Point is a place where the unexpected becomes expected, where radical change is more than possibility. It is—contrary to all our expectations—a certainty. . . .

Notes

1. For a good summary of New York City crime statistics, see: Michael Massing, "The Blue Revolution," in the *New York Review of Books,* November 19, 1998, pp. 32–34. There is another good discussion of the anomalous nature of the New York crime drop in William Bratton and William Andrews, "What We've Learned About Policing," in *City Journal,* Spring 1999, p. 25.
2. The leader in research on yawning is Robert Provine, a psychologist at the University of Maryland. Among his papers on the subject are: Robert Provine, "Yawning as a Stereotyped Action Pattern and Releasing Stimulus," *Ethology* (1983), vol. 72, pp. 109–122.

Robert Provine, "Contagious Yawning and Infant Imitation," *Bulletin of the Psychonomic Society* (1989), vol. 27, no. 2, pp. 125–126.

3. The best way to understand the Tipping Point is to imagine a hypothetical outbreak of the flu. Suppose, for example, that one summer 1,000 tourists come to Manhattan from Canada carrying an untreatable strain of twenty-four-hour virus. This strain of flu has a 2 percent infection rate, which is to say that one out of every 50 people who come into close contact with someone carrying it catches the bug himself. Let's say that 50 is also exactly the number of people the average Manhattanite—in the course of riding the subways and mingling with colleagues at work—comes in contact with every day. What we have, then, is a disease in equilibrium. Those 1,000 Canadian tourists pass on the virus to 1,000 new people on the day they arrive. And the next day those 1,000 newly infected people pass on the virus to another 1,000 people, just as the original 1,000 tourists who started the epidemic are returning to health. With those getting sick and those getting well so perfectly in balance, the flu chugs along at a steady but unspectacular clip through the rest of the summer and the fall.

But then comes the Christmas season. The subways and buses get more crowded with tourists and shoppers, and instead of running into an even 50 people a day, the average Manhattanite now has close contact with, say, 55 people a day. All of a sudden, the equilibrium is disrupted. The 1,000 flu carriers now run into 55,000 people a day, and at a 2 percent infection rate, that translates into 1,100 cases the following day. Those 1,100, in turn, are now passing on their virus to 55,000 people as well, so that by day three there are 1,210 Manhattanites with the flu and by day four 1,331 and by the end of the week there are nearly 2,000, and so on up, in an exponential spiral, until Manhattan has a full-blown flu epidemic on its hands by Christmas Day. That moment when the average flu carrier went from running into 50 people a day to running into 55 people was the Tipping Point. It was the point at which an ordinary and stable phenomenon—a low-level flu outbreak—turned into a public health crisis. If you were to draw a graph of the progress of the Canadian flu epidemic, the Tipping Point would be the point on the graph where the line suddenly turned upward.

Tipping Points are moments of great sensitivity. Changes made right at the Tipping Point can have enormous consequences. Our Canadian flu became an epidemic when the number of New Yorkers running into a flu carrier jumped from 50 to 55 a day. But had that same small change happened in the opposite direction, if the number had dropped from 50 to 45, that change would have pushed the number of flu victims down to 478 within a week, and with a few weeks more at that rate, the Canadian flu would have vanished from Manhattan entirely. Cutting the number exposed from 70 to 65, or 65 to 60 or 60 to 55 would not have been sufficient to end the epidemic. But a change right at the Tipping Point, from 50 to 45, would.

The Tipping Point model has been described in several classic works of sociology. I suggest:

Mark Granovetter, "Threshold Models of Collective Behavior," *American Journal of Sociology* (1978), vol. 83, pp. 1420–1443.

Mark Granovetter and R. Soong, "Threshold Models of Diffusion and Collective Behavior," *Journal of Mathematical Sociology* (1983), vol. 9, pp. 165–179.

Thomas Schelling, "Dynamic Models of Segregation," *Journal of Mathematical Sociology* (1971), vol. I, pp. 143–186.

Thomas Schelling, *Micromotives and Macrobehavior* (New York: W. W. Norton, 1978).

Jonathan Crane, "The Epidemic Theory of Ghettos and Neighborhood Effects on Dropping Out and Teenage Childbearing," *American Journal of Sociology* (1989), vol. 95, no. 5, pp. 1226–1259.

The Median Isn't the Message

Stephen Jay Gould

Stephen Jay Gould (1941–2002) was born in New York City. A graduate of Antioch College (1963) and Columbia University (Ph.D., 1967) Gould joined the faculty of Harvard University in 1973, where he taught geology, biology, and the history of science. An evolutionist who enjoyed explaining complex scientific theories to lay audiences, Gould wrote extensively (often on the theory of evolution), including a monthly column for Natural History, *"This View of Life." Gould's books include* Ontogeny and Phylogeny *(1977),* The Mismeasure of Man *(1981),* Time's Arrow, Time's Cycle *(1987), and* Wonderful Life *(1989). His essay collections include* Ever Since Darwin *(1977),* The Panda's Thumb *(1980),* Hen's Teeth and Horse's Toes *(1983),* The Flamingo's Smile *(1985),* Urchin in the Storm: Essays About Books and Ideas *(1987),* Bully for Brontosaurus *(1991), and* Eight Little Piggies *(1993). Gould received a National Book Award and was named a MacArthur Prize Fellow. In this typically enlightening essay from* Bully for Brontosaurus, *Gould uses his 1982 diagnosis of cancer to expose common misinterpretations of statistics.*

1   My life has recently intersected, in a most personal way, two of Mark Twain's famous quips. One I shall defer to the end of this essay. The other (sometimes attributed to Disraeli

From *Bully for Brontosaurus: Reflections in Natural History* by Stephen Jay Gould. Published by W. W. Norton & Company, Inc. Copyright © 1991 by Stephen Jay Gould.

177

identified three species of mendacity, each worse than the one before—lies, damned lies, and statistics.

Consider the standard example of stretching truth with numbers—a case quite relevant to my story. Statistics recognizes different measures of an "average," or central tendency. The *mean* represents our usual concept of an overall average—add up the items and divide them by the number of sharers (100 candy bars collected for five kids next Halloween will yield 20 for each in a fair world). The *median,* a different measure of central tendency, is the halfway point. If I line up five kids by height, the median child is shorter than two and taller than the other two (who might have trouble getting their mean share of the candy). A politician in power might say with pride, "The mean income of our citizens is $15,000 per year." The leader of the opposition might retort, "But half our citizens make less than $10,000 per year." Both are right, but neither cites a statistic with impassive objectivity. The first invokes a mean, the second a median. (Means are higher than medians in such cases because one millionaire may outweigh hundreds of poor people in setting a mean, but can balance only one mendicant in calculating a median.)

The larger issue that creates a common distrust or contempt for statistics is more troubling. Many people make an unfortunate and invalid separation between heart and mind, or feeling and intellect. In some contemporary traditions, abetted by attitudes stereotypically centered upon Southern California, feelings are exalted as more "real" and the only proper basis for action, while intellect gets short shrift as a hang-up of outmoded elitism. Statistics, in this absurd dichotomy, often becomes the symbol of the enemy. As Hilaire Belloc wrote, "Statistics are the triumph of the quantitative method, and the quantitative method is the victory of sterility and death."

This is a personal story of statistics, properly interpreted, as profoundly nurturant and life-giving. It declares holy war on the downgrading of intellect by telling a small story to illustrate the utility of dry, academic knowledge about science. Heart and head are focal points of one body, one personality.

In July 1982, I learned that I was suffering from abdominal mesothelioma, a rare and serious cancer usually associated with exposure to asbestos. When I revived after surgery, I asked my first question of my doctor and chemotherapist: "What is the best technical literature about mesothelioma?" She replied, with a touch of diplomacy (the only departure she has ever made from direct frankness), that the medical literature contained nothing really worth reading.

Of course, trying to keep an intellectual away from literature works about as well as recommending chastity to *Homo sapiens,* the sexiest primate of all. As soon as I could walk, I made a beeline for Harvard's Countway medical library and punched mesothelioma into the computer's bibliographic search program. An hour later, surrounded by the latest literature on abdominal mesothelioma, I realized with a gulp why my doctor had offered that humane advice. The literature couldn't have been more brutally clear: Mesothelioma is incurable, with a median mortality of only eight months after discovery. I sat stunned for about fifteen minutes, then smiled and said to myself: So that's why they didn't give me anything to read. Then my mind started to work again, thank goodness.

If a little learning could ever be a dangerous thing, I had encountered a classic example. Attitude clearly matters in fighting cancer. We don't know why (from my old-style materialistic perspective, I suspect that mental states feed back upon the immune system). But match people with the same cancer for age, class, health, and socioeconomic status, and, in general, those with positive attitudes, with a strong will and purpose for living, with commitment to struggle, and with an active response to aiding their own treatment and not just a passive acceptance of anything doctors say, tend to live longer. A few months later I asked Sir Peter Medawar, my personal scientific guru and a Nobelist in immunology, what the best prescription for success against cancer might be. "A sanguine personality," he replied. Fortunately (since one can't reconstruct oneself at short notice and for a definite purpose), I am, if anything, even-tempered and confident in just this manner.

Hence the dilemma for humane doctors: Since attitude matters so critically, should such a somber conclusion be advertised, especially since few people have sufficient understanding of statistics to evaluate what the statements really mean? From years of experience with the small-scale evolution of Bahamian land snails treated quantitatively, I have developed this technical knowledge—and I am convinced that it played a major role in saving my life. Knowledge is indeed power, as Francis Bacon proclaimed.

The problem may be briefly stated: What does "median mortality of eight months" signify in our vernacular? I suspect that most people, without training in statistics, would read such a statement as "I will probably be dead in eight months"—the very conclusion that must be avoided, both because this formulation is false, and because attitude matters so much.

10   I was not, of course, overjoyed, but I didn't read the statement in   10 this vernacular way either. My technical training enjoined a different perspective on "eight months median mortality." The point may seem subtle, but the consequences can be profound. Moreover, this perspective embodies the distinctive way of thinking in my own field of evolutionary biology and natural history.

We still carry the historical baggage of a Platonic heritage that seeks sharp essences and definite boundaries. (Thus we hope to find an unambiguous "beginning of life" or "definition of death," although nature often comes to us as irreducible continua.) This Platonic heritage, with its emphasis on clear distinctions and separated immutable entities, leads us to view statistical measures of central tendency wrongly, indeed opposite to the appropriate interpretation in our actual world of variation, shadings, and continua. In short, we view means and medians as hard "realities," and the variation that permits their calculation as a set of transient and imperfect measurements of this hidden essence. If the median is the reality and variation around the median just a device for calculation, then "I will probably be dead in eight months" may pass as a reasonable interpretation.

But all evolutionary biologists know that variation itself is nature's only irreducible essence. Variation is the hard reality, not a set of imperfect measures for a central tendency. Means and medians are the abstractions. Therefore, I looked at the mesothelioma statistics quite differently—and not only because I am an optimist who tends to see the doughnut instead of the hole, but primarily because I know that variation itself is the reality. I had to place myself amidst the variation.

When I learned about the eight-month median, my first intellectual reaction was: Fine, half the people will live longer; now what are my chances of being in that half. I read for a furious and nervous hour and concluded, with relief: damned good. I possessed every one of the characteristics conferring a probability of longer life: I was young; my disease had been recognized in a relatively early state; I would receive the nation's best medical treatment; I had the world to live for; I knew how to read the data properly and not despair.

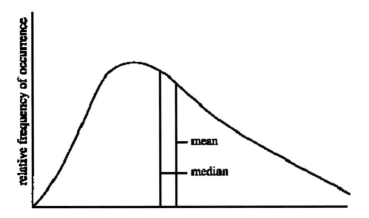

A right-skewed distribution showing that means must be higher than medians, and that the right side of the distribution extends out into a long tail.

Another technical point then added ever more solace. I immediately recognized that the distribution of variation about the eight-month median would almost surely be what statisticians call "right skewed." (In a symmetrical distribution, the profile of variation to the left of the central tendency is a mirror image of variation to the right. Skewed distributions are asymmetrical, with variation stretching out more in one direction than the other—left skewed if extended to the left, right skewed if stretched out to the right.) The distribution of variation had to be right skewed, I reasoned. After all, the left of the distribution contains an irrevocable lower boundary of zero (since mesothelioma can only be identified at death or before). Thus, little space exists for the distribution's lower (or left) half—it must be scrunched up between zero and eight months. But the upper (or right) half can extend out for years and years, even if nobody ultimately survives. The distribution must be right skewed, and I needed to know how long the extended tail ran—for I had already concluded that my favorable profile made me a good candidate for the right half of the curve.

The distribution was, indeed, strongly right skewed, with a long tail (however small) that extended for several years above the eight-month median. I saw no reason why I shouldn't be in that small tail, and I breathed a very long sigh of relief. My technical knowledge had helped. I had read the graph correctly. I had asked the right question and found the answers. I had obtained, in all probability, that most precious of all possible gifts in the circumstances—substantial time. I didn't have to stop and immediately follow Isaiah's injunction to Hezekiah—set thine house in order: for thou shalt die, and not live. I would have time to think, to plan, and to fight.

One final point about statistical distributions. They apply only to a prescribed set of circumstances—in this case to survival with mesothelioma under conventional modes of treatment. If circumstances change, the distribution may alter. I was placed on an experimental protocol of treatment and, if fortune holds, will be in the first cohort of a new distribution with a high median and a right tail extending to death by natural causes at advanced old age.*

It has become, in my view, a bit too trendy to regard the acceptance of death as something tantamount to intrinsic dignity. Of course I agree with the preacher of Ecclesiastes that there is a time to love and a time to die—and when my skein runs out I hope to face the end calmly and in my own way. For most situations, however, I prefer the more martial view that death is the ultimate enemy—and I find nothing reproachable in those who rage mightily against the dying of the light.

The swords of battle are numerous, and none more effective than humor. My death was announced at a meeting of my colleagues in Scotland, and I almost experienced the delicious pleasure of reading my obituary penned by one of my best friends (the so-and-so got suspicious and checked; he too is a statistician, and didn't expect to find me so far out on the left tail). Still, the incident provided my first good laugh after the diagnosis. Just think, I almost got to repeat Mark Twain's most famous line of all: The reports of my death are greatly exaggerated.**

---

*So far so good.

**Since writing this, my death has actually been reported in two European magazines, five years apart. *Fama volat* (and lasts a long time). I squawked very loudly both times and demanded a retraction; guess I just don't have Mr. Clemens's *savoir faire*.

Sex, Drugs, Disasters, and the Extinction of Dinosaurs

Stephen Jay Gould

Stephen Jay Gould (1941–2002) was born in New York City. A graduate of Antioch College (1963) and Columbia University (Ph.D., 1967) Gould joined the faculty of Harvard University in 1973, where he taught geology, biology, and the history of science. An evolutionist who enjoyed explaining complex scientific theories to lay audiences, Gould wrote extensively (often on the theory of evolution), including a monthly column for Natural History, *"This View of Life." Gould's books include* Ontogeny and Phylogeny *(1977),* The Mismeasure of Man *(1981),* Time's Arrow, Time's Cycle *(1987), and* Wonderful Life *(1989). His essay collections include* Ever Since Darwin *(1977),* The Panda's Thumb *(1980),* Hen's Teeth and Horse's Toes *(1983),* The Flamingo's Smile *(1985),* Urchin in the Storm: Essays About Books and Ideas *(1987),* Bully for Brontosaurus *(1991), and* Eight Little Piggies *(1993). Gould received a National Book Award and was named a MacArthur Prize Fellow. In this essay, Gould uses the dominant theories about how dinosaurs became extinct to teach the characteristics of good and bad scientific theories in this essay.*

1　Science, in its most fundamental definition, is a fruitful mode of inquiry, not a list of enticing conclusions. The conclusions are the consequence, not the essence.

My greatest unhappiness with most popular presentations of science concerns their failure to separate fascinating claims from the

Originally published in *Discover,* March 1984. Reprinted from *The Flamingo's Smile: Reflections in Natural History* by Stephen Jay Gould. Published by W. W. Norton & Co., Inc. Copyright © 1984, 1985 by Stephen Jay Gould.

methods that scientists use to establish the facts of nature. Journalists, and the public, thrive on controversial and stunning statements. But science is, basically, a way of knowing—in P. B. Medawar's apt words, "the art of the soluble." If the growing corps of popular science writers would focus on how scientists develop and defend those fascinating claims, they would make their greatest possible contribution to public understanding.

Consider three ideas, proposed in perfect seriousness to explain that greatest of all titillating puzzles—the extinction of dinosaurs. Since these three notions invoke the primally fascinating themes of our culture—sex, drugs, and violence—they surely reside in the category of fascinating claims. I want to show why two of them rank as silly speculation, while the other represents science at its grandest and most useful.

Science works with testable proposals. If, after much compilation and scrutiny of data, new information continues to affirm a hypothesis, we may accept it provisionally and gain confidence as further evidence mounts. We can never be completely sure that a hypothesis is right, though we may be able to show with confidence that it is wrong. The best scientific hypotheses are also generous and expansive: They suggest extensions and implications that enlighten related, and even far distant, subjects. Simply consider how the idea of evolution has influenced virtually every intellectual field.

5   Useless speculation, on the other hand, is restrictive. It generates   5
no testable hypothesis, and offers no way to obtain potentially refuting evidence. Please note that I am not speaking of truth or falsity. The speculation may well be true; still, if it provides, in principle, no material for affirmation or rejection, we can make nothing of it. It must simply stand forever as an intriguing idea. Useless speculation turns in on itself and leads nowhere; good science, containing both seeds for its potential refutation and implications for more and different testable knowledge, reaches out. But, enough preaching. Let's move on to dinosaurs, and the three proposals for their extinction.

1. *Sex.* Testes function only in a narrow range of temperature (those of mammals hang externally in a scrotal sac because internal body temperatures are too high for their proper function). A worldwide rise in temperature at the close of the Cretaceous period caused the testes of dinosaurs to stop functioning and led to their extinction by sterilization of males.

2. *Drugs.* Angiosperms (flowering plants) first evolved toward the end of the dinosaurs' reign. Many of these plants contain psychoactive agents, avoided by mammals today as a result of their bitter taste. Dinosaurs had neither means to taste the bitterness nor livers effective enough to detoxify the substances. They died of massive overdoses.

3. *Disasters.* A large comet or asteroid struck the earth some 65 million years ago, lofting a cloud of dust into the sky and blocking sunlight, thereby suppressing photosynthesis and so drastically lowering world temperatures that dinosaurs and hosts of other creatures became extinct.

Before analyzing these three tantalizing statements, we must establish a basic ground rule often violated in proposals for the dinosaurs' demise. *There is no separate problem of the extinction of dinosaurs.* Too often we divorce specific events from their wider contexts and systems of cause and effect. The fundamental fact of dinosaur extinction is its synchrony with the demise of so many other groups across a wide range of habitats, from terrestrial to marine.

The history of life has been punctuated by brief episodes of mass extinction. A recent analysis by University of Chicago paleontologists Jack Sepkoski and Dave Raup, based on the best and most exhaustive tabulation of data ever assembled, shows clearly that five episodes of mass dying stand well above the "background" extinctions of normal times (when we consider all mass extinctions, large and small, they seem to fall in a regular 26-million-year cycle). The Cretaceous debacle, occurring 65 million years ago and separating the Mesozoic and Cenozoic eras of our geological time scale, ranks prominently among the five. Nearly all the marine plankton (single-celled floating creatures) died with geological suddenness; among marine invertebrates, nearly 15 percent of all families perished, including many previously dominant groups, especially the ammonites (relatives of squids in coiled shells). On land, the dinosaurs disappeared after more than 100 million years of unchallenged domination.

In this context, speculations limited to dinosaurs alone ignore the larger phenomenon. We need a coordinated explanation for a system of events that includes the extinction of dinosaurs as one component. Thus it makes little sense, though it may fuel our desire to view mammals as inevitable inheritors of the earth, to guess that dinosaurs died because small mammals ate their eggs (a perennial favorite among untestable speculations). It seems most unlikely that some disaster peculiar to dinosaurs befell these massive beasts—and that the debacle happened to strike just when one of history's five great dyings had enveloped the earth for completely different reasons.

The testicular theory, an old favorite from the 1940s, had its root in an interesting and thoroughly respectable study of temperature tolerances in the American alligator, published in the staid *Bulletin of the American Museum of Natural History* in 1946 by three experts on living and fossil reptiles—E. H. Colbert, my own first teacher in paleontology; R. B. Cowles; and C. M. Bogert.

The first sentence of their summary reveals a purpose beyond alligators: "This report describes an attempt to infer the reactions of extinct reptiles, especially the dinosaurs, to high temperatures as based upon reactions observed in the modern alligator." They studied, by rectal thermometry, the body temperatures of alligators under changing conditions of heating and cooling. (Well, let's face it, you wouldn't want to try sticking a thermometer under a 'gator's tongue.) The predictions under test go way back to an old theory first stated by Galileo in the 1630s—the unequal scaling of surfaces and volumes. As an animal, or any object, grows (provided its shape doesn't change), surface areas must increase more slowly than volumes—since surfaces get larger as length squared, while volumes increase much more rapidly, as length cubed. Therefore, small animals have high ratios of surface to volume, while large animals cover themselves with relatively little surface.

Among cold-blooded animals lacking any physiological mechanism for keeping their temperatures constant, small creatures have a hell of a time keeping warm—because they lose so much heat through their relatively large surfaces. On the other hand, large animals, with their relatively small surfaces, may lose heat so slowly that, once warm, they may maintain effectively constant temperatures against ordinary fluctuations of climate. (In fact, the resolution of the "hot-blooded dinosaur" controversy that burned so brightly a few years back may simply be that, while large dinosaurs possessed no physiological mechanism for constant temperature, and were not therefore warm-blooded in the technical sense, their large size and relatively small surface area kept them warm.)

Colbert, Cowles, and Bogert compared the warming rates of small and large alligators. As predicted, the small fellows heated up (and cooled down) more quickly. When exposed to a warm sun, a tiny 50-gram (1.76-ounce) alligator heated up one degree Celsius every minute and a half, while a large alligator, 260 times bigger at 13,000 grams (28.7 pounds), took seven and a half minutes to gain a degree. Extrapolating up to an adult 10-ton dinosaur, they concluded that a one-degree rise in body temperature would take eighty-six hours. If large animals absorb heat so slowly (through their relatively small surfaces), they will also be unable to shed any excess heat gained when temperatures rise above a favorable level.

The authors then guessed that large dinosaurs lived at or near their optimum temperatures; Cowles suggested that a rise in global temperatures just before the Cretaceous extinction caused the dinosaurs to heat up beyond their optimal tolerance—and, being so large, they couldn't shed the unwanted heat. (In a most unusual statement within a scientific paper, Colbert and Bogert then explicitly disavowed this speculative extension of their empirical work on alligators.) Cowles conceded that this excess heat probably wasn't enough to kill or even to enervate the great beasts, but since testes often function only within a narrow range of temperature, he proposed that this global rise might have sterilized all the males, causing extinction by natural contraception.

The overdose theory has recently been supported by UCLA psychiatrist Ronald K. Siegel. Siegel has gathered, he claims, more than 2,000 records of animals who, when given access, administer various drugs to themselves—from a mere swig of alcohol to massive doses of the big H. Elephants will swill the equivalent of twenty beers at a time, but do not like alcohol in concentrations greater than 7 percent. In a silly bit of anthropocentric speculation, Siegel states that "elephants drink, perhaps, to forget . . . the anxiety produced by shrinking rangeland and the competition for food."

Since fertile imaginations can apply almost any hot idea to the extinction of dinosaurs, Siegel found a way. Flowering plants did not evolve until late in the dinosaurs' reign. These plants also produced an array of aromatic, amino-acid-based alkaloids—the major group of psychoactive agents. Most mammals are "smart" enough to avoid these potential poisons. The alkaloids simply don't taste good (they are bitter); in any case, we mammals have livers happily supplied with the capacity to detoxify them. But, Siegel speculates, perhaps dinosaurs could neither taste the bitterness nor detoxify the substances once ingested. He recently told members of the American Psychological Association: "I'm not suggesting that all dinosaurs OD'd on plant drugs, but it certainly was a factor." He also argued that death by overdose may help explain why so many dinosaur fossils are found in contorted positions. (Do not go gently into that good night.)

15 Extraterrestrial catastrophes have long pedigrees in the popular literature of extinction, but the subject exploded again in 1979, after a long lull, when the father-son, physicist-geologist team of Luis and Walter Alvarez proposed that an asteroid, some 10 km in diameter, struck the earth 65 million years ago (comets, rather than asteroids, have since gained favor. Good science is self-corrective).

The force of such a collision would be immense, greater by far than the megatonnage of all the world's nuclear weapons. In trying to reconstruct a scenario that would explain the simultaneous dying of dinosaurs on land and so many creatures in the sea, the Alvarezes proposed that a gigantic dust cloud, generated by particles blown aloft in the impact, would so darken the earth that photosynthesis would cease and temperatures drop precipitously. (Rage, rage against the dying of the light.) The single celled photosynthetic oceanic plankton, with life cycles measured in weeks, would perish outright, but land plants might survive through the dormancy of their seeds (land plants were not much affected by the Cretaceous extinction, and any adequate theory must account for the curious pattern of differential survival). Dinosaurs would die by starvation and freezing; small, warm-blooded mammals, with more modest requirements for food and better regulation of body temperature, would squeak through. "Let the bastards freeze in the dark," as bumper stickers of our chauvinistic neighbors in sunbelt states proclaimed several years ago during the Northeast's winter oil crisis.

All three theories, testicular malfunction, psychoactive overdosing, and asteroidal zapping, grab our attention mightily. As pure phenomenology, they rank about equally high on any hit parade of primal fascination. Yet one represents expansive science, the others restrictive and untestable speculation. The proper criterion lies in evidence and methodology; we must probe behind the superficial fascination of particular claims.

How could we possibly decide whether the hypothesis of testicular frying is right or wrong? We would have to know things that the fossil record cannot provide. What temperatures were optimal for dinosaurs? Could they avoid the absorption of excess heat by staying in the shade, or in caves? At what temperatures did their testicles cease to function? Were late Cretaceous climates ever warm enough to drive the internal temperatures of dinosaurs close to this ceiling? Testicles simply don't fossilize, and how could we infer their temperature tolerances even if they did? In short, Cowles's hypothesis is only an intriguing speculation leading nowhere. The most damning statement against it appeared right in the conclusion of Colbert, Cowles, and Bogert's paper, when they admitted: "It is difficult to advance any definite arguments against this hypothesis." My statement may seem paradoxical—isn't a hypothesis really good if you can't devise any arguments against it? Quite the contrary. It is simply untestable and unusable.

Siegel's overdosing has even less going for it. At least Cowles extrapolated his conclusion from some good data on alligators. And he didn't completely violate the primary guideline of siting dinosaur extinction in the context of a general mass dying—for rise in temperature could be the root cause of a general catastrophe, zapping dinosaurs by testicular malfunction and different groups for other reasons. But Siegel's speculation cannot touch the extinction of ammonites or oceanic plankton (diatoms make their own food with good sweet sunlight; they don't OD on the chemicals of terrestrial plants). It is simply a gratuitous, attention grabbing guess. It cannot be tested, for how can we know what dinosaurs tasted and what their livers could do? Livers don't fossilize any better than testicles.

20 The hypothesis doesn't even make any sense in its own context. 20 Angiosperms were in full flower ten million years before dinosaurs went the way of all flesh. Why did it take so long? As for the pains of a chemical death recorded in contortions of fossils, I regret to say (or rather I'm pleased to note for the dinosaurs' sake) that Siegel's knowledge of geology must be a bit deficient: Muscles contract after death and geological strata rise and fall with motions of the earth's crust after burial—more than enough reason to distort a fossil's pristine appearance.

The impact story, on the other hand, has a sound basis in evidence. It can be tested, extended, refined, and, if wrong, disproved. The Alvarezes did not just construct an arresting guess for public consumption. They proposed their hypothesis after laborious geochemical studies with Frank Asaro and Helen Michael had revealed a massive increase of iridium in rocks deposited right at the time of extinction. Iridium, a rare metal of the platinum group, is virtually absent from indigenous rocks of the earth's crust; most of our iridium arrives on extraterrestrial objects that strike the earth.

The Alvarez hypothesis bore immediate fruit. Based originally on evidence from two European localities, it led geochemists throughout the world to examine other sediments of the same age. They found abnormally high amounts of iridium everywhere—from continental rocks of the western United States to deep sea cores from the South Atlantic.

Cowles proposed his testicular hypothesis in the mid-1940s. Where has it gone since then? Absolutely nowhere, because scientists can do nothing with it. The hypothesis must stand as a curious appendage to a solid study of alligators. Siegel's overdose scenario will also win a few press notices and fade into oblivion. The Alvarezes' asteroid falls into a different category altogether, and much of the popular commentary has missed this essential distinction by focusing on the impact and its attendant results, and forgetting what really matters to a scientist—the iridium. If you talk just about asteroids, dust, and darkness, you tell stories no better and no more entertaining than fried testicles or terminal trips. It is the iridium—the source of testable evidence—that counts and forges the crucial distinction between speculation and science.

The proof, to twist a phrase, lies in the doing. Cowles's hypothesis has generated nothing in thirty-five years. Since its proposal in 1979, the Alvarez hypothesis has spawned hundreds of studies, a major conference, and attendant publications. Geologists are fired up. They are looking for iridium at all other extinction boundaries. Every week exposes a new wrinkle in the scientific press. Further evidence that the Cretaceous iridium represents extraterrestrial impact and not indigenous volcanism continues to accumulate. As I revise this essay in November 1984 (this paragraph will be out of date when [it] is published), new data include chemical "signatures" of other isotopes indicating unearthly provenance, glass spherules of a size and sort produced by impact and not by volcanic eruptions, and high-pressure varieties of silica formed (so far as we know) only under the tremendous shock of impact.

My point is simply this: Whatever the eventual outcome (I suspect it will be positive), the Alvarez hypothesis is exciting, fruitful science because it generates tests, provides us with things to do, and expands outward. We are having fun, battling back and forth, moving toward a resolution, and extending the hypothesis beyond its original scope.

As just one example of the unexpected, distant cross-fertilization that good science engenders, the Alvarez hypothesis made a major contribution to a theme that has riveted public attention in the past few months—so-called nuclear winter. In a speech delivered in April 1982, Luis Alvarez calculated the energy that a ten-kilometer asteroid would release on impact. He compared such an explosion with a full nuclear exchange and implied that all-out atomic war might unleash similar consequences.

This theme of impact leading to massive dust clouds and falling temperatures formed an important input to the decision of Carl Sagan and a group of colleagues to model the climatic consequences of nuclear holocaust. Full nuclear exchange would probably generate the same kind of dust cloud and darkening that may have wiped out the dinosaurs. Temperatures would drop precipitously and agriculture might become impossible. Avoidance of nuclear war is fundamentally an ethical and political imperative, but we must know the factual consequences to make firm judgments. I am heartened by a final link across disciplines and deep concerns—another criterion, by the way, of science at its best: A recognition of the very phenomenon that made our evolution possible by exterminating the previously dominant dinosaurs and clearing a way for the evolution of large mammals, including us, might actually help to save us from joining those magnificent beasts in contorted poses among the strata of the earth.

Women's Brains
Stephen Jay Gould

Stephen Jay Gould (1941–2002) was born in New York City. A graduate of Antioch College (1963) and Columbia University (Ph.D., 1967) Gould joined the faculty of Harvard University in 1973, where he taught geology, biology, and the history of science. An evolutionist who enjoyed explaining complex scientific theories to lay audiences, Gould wrote extensively (often on the theory of evolution), including a monthly column for Natural History, "This View of Life." *Gould's books include* Ontogeny and Phylogeny *(1977),* The Mismeasure of Man *(1981),* Time's Arrow, Time's Cycle *(1987), and* Wonderful Life *(1989). His essay collections include* Ever Since Darwin *(1977),* The Panda's Thumb *(1980),* Hen's Teeth and Horse's Toes *(1983),* The Flamingo's Smile *(1985),* Urchin in the Storm: Essays About Books and Ideas *(1987),* Bully for Brontosaurus *(1991), and* Eight Little Piggies *(1993). Gould received a National Book Award and was named a MacArthur Prize Fellow. Gould reveals in this essay how scientists have used theories about brain size to argue the "inferiority" of women.*

1   In the prelude to *Middlemarch*, George Eliot lamented the unfulfilled   1
lives of talented women:

> *Some have felt that these blundering lives are due to the inconvenient indefiniteness with which the Supreme Power has fashioned the natures of women: if there were one level of feminine incompetence as strict as the ability to count three and no more, the social lot of women might be treated with scientific certitude.*

From *The Panda's Thumb, More Reflections on Natural History,* by Stephen Jay Gould. Published by W. W. Norton & Company, Inc. Copyright © 1980 by Stephen Jay Gould.

Eliot goes on to discount the idea of innate limitation, but while she wrote in 1872, the leaders of European anthropometry were trying to measure "with scientific certitude" the inferiority of women. Anthropometry, or measurement of the human body, is not so fashionable a field these days, but it dominated the human sciences for much of the nineteenth century and remained popular until intelligence testing replaced skull measurement as a favored device for making invidious comparisons among races, classes, and sexes. Craniometry, or measurement of the skull, commanded the most attention and respect. Its unquestioned leader, Paul Broca (1824–80), professor of clinical surgery at the Faculty of Medicine in Paris, gathered a school of disciples and imitators around himself. Their work, so meticulous and apparently irrefutable, exerted great influence and won high esteem as a jewel of nineteenth-century science.

Broca's work seemed particularly invulnerable to refutation. Had he not measured with the most scrupulous care and accuracy? (Indeed, he had. I have the greatest respect for Broca's meticulous procedure. His numbers are sound. But science is an inferential exercise, not a catalog of facts. Numbers, by themselves, specify nothing. All depends upon what you do with them.) Broca depicted himself as an apostle of objectivity, a man who bowed before facts and cast aside superstition and sentimentality. He declared that "there is no faith, however respectable, no interest, however legitimate, which must not accommodate itself to the progress of human knowledge and bend before truth." Women, like it or not, had smaller brains than men and, therefore, could not equal them in intelligence. This fact, Broca argued, may reinforce a common prejudice in male society, but it is also a scientific truth. L. Manouvrier, a black sheep in Broca's fold, rejected the inferiority of women and wrote with feeling about the burden imposed upon them by Broca's numbers:

> *Women displayed their talents and their diplomas. They also invoked philosophical authorities. But they were opposed by numbers unknown to Condorcet or to John Stuart Mill. These numbers fell upon poor women like a sledge hammer, and they were accompanied by commentaries and sarcasms more ferocious than the most misogynist imprecations of certain church fathers. The theologians had asked if women had a soul. Several centuries later, some scientists were ready to refuse them a human intelligence.*

Broca's argument rested upon two sets of data: the larger brains of men in modern societies, and a supposed increase in male superiority through time. His most extensive data came from autopsies performed personally in four Parisian hospitals. For 292 male brains, he calculated an average weight of 1,325 grams; 140 female brains averaged 1,144 grams for a difference of 181 grams, or 14 percent of the male weight. Broca understood, of course, that part of this difference could be attributed to the greater height of males. Yet he made no attempt to measure the effect of size alone and actually stated that it cannot account for the entire difference because we know, a priori, that women are not as intelligent as men (a premise that the data were supposed to test, not rest upon):

> We might ask if the small size of the female brain depends exclusively upon the small size of her body. Tiedemann has proposed this explanation. But we must not forget that women are, on the average, a little less intelligent than men, a difference which we should not exaggerate but which is, nonetheless, real. We are therefore permitted to suppose that the relatively small size of the female brain depends in part upon her physical inferiority and in part upon her intellectual inferiority.

5   In 1873, the year after Eliot published *Middlemarch*, Broca measured the cranial capacities of prehistoric skulls from L'Homme Mort cave. Here he found a difference of only 99.5 cubic centimeters between males and females, while modern populations range from 129.5 to 220.7. Topinard, Broca's chief disciple, explained the increasing discrepancy through time as a result of differing evolutionary pressures upon dominant men and passive women:

> The man who fights for two or more in the struggle for existence, who has all the responsibility and the cares of tomorrow, who is constantly active in combating the environment and human rivals, needs more brain than the woman whom he must protect and nourish, the sedentary woman, lacking any interior occupations, whose role is to raise children, love, and be passive.

In 1879, Gustave Le Bon, chief misogynist of Broca's school, used these data to publish what must be the most vicious attack upon women in modern scientific literature (no one can top Aristotle). I do not claim his views were representative of Broca's school, but they were published in France's most respected anthropological journal. Le Bon concluded:

> *In the most intelligent races, as among the Parisians, there are a large number of women whose brains are closer in size to those of gorillas than to the most developed male brains. This inferiority is so obvious that no one can contest it for a moment; only its degree is worth discussion. All psychologists who have studied the intelligence of women, as well as poets and novelists, recognize today that they represent the most inferior forms of human evolution and that they are closer to children and savages than to an adult, civilized man. They excel in fickleness, inconstancy, absence of thought and logic, and incapacity to reason. Without doubt there exist some distinguished women, very superior to the average man, but they are as exceptional as the birth of any monstrosity, as, for example, of a gorilla with two heads; consequently, we may neglect them entirely.*

Nor did Le Bon shrink from the social implications of his views. He was horrified by the proposal of some American reformers to grant women higher education on the same basis as men:

> *A desire to give them the same education, and, as a consequence, to propose the same goals for them, is a dangerous chimera. . . . The day when, misunderstanding the inferior occupations which nature has given her, women leave the home and take part in our battles; on this day a social revolution will begin, and everything that maintains the sacred ties of the family will disappear.*

Sound familiar?[1]

I have reexamined Broca's data, the basis for all this derivative pronouncement, and I find his numbers sound but his interpretation ill-founded, to say the least. The data supporting his claim for increased difference through time can be easily dismissed. Broca based his contention on the samples from L'Homme Mort alone—only seven male and six female skulls in all. Never have so little data yielded such far ranging conclusions.

---

[1] When I wrote this essay, I assumed that Le Bon was a marginal, if colorful, figure. I have since learned that he was a leading scientist, one of the founders of social psychology, and best known for a seminal study on crowd behavior, still cited today (*La psychologie des foules*, 1895), and for his work on unconscious motivation.

10   In 1888, Topinard published Broca's more extensive data on the   10
Parisian hospitals. Since Broca recorded height and age as well as brain
size, we may use modern statistics to remove their effect. Brain weight
decreases with age, and Broca's women were, on average, considerably
older than his men. Brain weight increases with height, and his average man was almost half a foot taller than his average woman. I used
multiple regression, a technique that allowed me to assess simultaneously the influence of height and age upon brain size. In an analysis
of the data for women, I found that, at average male height and age,
a woman's brain would weigh 1,212 grams. Correction for height and
age reduces Broca's measured difference of 181 grams by more than a
third, to 113 grams.

I don't know what to make of this remaining difference because I
cannot assess other factors known to influence brain size in a major
way. Cause of death has an important effect: degenerative disease often
entails a substantial diminution of brain size. (This effect is separate
from the decrease attributed to age alone.) Eugene Schreider, also
working with Broca's data, found that men killed in accidents had
brains weighing, on average, 60 grams more than men dying of in-
fectious diseases. The best modern data I can find (from American
hospitals) records a full 100-gram difference between death by degenerative arteriosclerosis and by violence or accident. Since so many of
Broca's subjects were very elderly women, we may assume that lengthy
degenerative disease was more common among them than among the
men.

More importantly, modern students of brain size still have not
agreed on a proper measure for eliminating the powerful effect of body
size. Height is partly adequate, but men and women of the same
height do not share the same body build. Weight is even worse than
height, because most of its variation reflects nutrition rather than intrinsic size—fat versus skinny exerts little influence upon the brain.
Manouvrier took up this subject in the 1880s and argued that muscular mass and force should be used. He tried to measure this elusive
property in various ways and found a marked difference in favor of
men, even in men and women of the same height. When he corrected
for what he called "sexual mass," women actually came out slightly
ahead in brain size.

Thus, the corrected 113-gram difference is surely too large; the
true figure is probably close to zero and may as well favor women as

men. And 113 grams, by the way, is exactly the average difference between a 5 foot 4 inch and a 6 foot 4 inch male in Broca's data. We would not (especially us short folks) want to ascribe greater intelligence to tall men. In short, who knows what to do with Broca's data? They certainly don't permit any confident claim that men have bigger brains than women.

To appreciate the social role of Broca and his school, we must recognize that his statements about the brains of women do not reflect an isolated prejudice toward a single disadvantaged group. They must be weighed in the context of a general theory that supported contemporary social distinctions as biologically ordained. Women, blacks, and poor people suffered the same disparagement, but women bore the brunt of Broca's argument because he had easier access to data on women's brains. Women were singularly denigrated but they also stood as surrogates for other disenfranchised groups. As one of Broca's disciples wrote in 1881: "Men of the black races have a brain scarcely heavier than that of white women." This juxtaposition extended into many other realms of anthropological argument, particularly to claims that, anatomically and emotionally, both women and blacks were like white children—and that white children, by the theory of recapitulation, represented an ancestral (primitive) adult stage of human evolution. I do not regard as empty rhetoric the claim that women's battles are for all of us.

15 Maria Montessori did not confine her activities to educational reform for young children. She lectured on anthropology for several years at the University of Rome, and wrote an influential book entitled *Pedagogical Anthropology* (English edition, 1913). Montessori was no egalitarian. She supported most of Broca's work and the theory of innate criminality proposed by her compatriot Cesare Lombroso. She measured the circumference of children's heads in her schools and inferred that the best prospects had bigger brains. But she had no use for Broca's conclusions about women. She discussed Manouvrier's work at length and made much of his tentative claim that women, after proper correction of the data, had slightly larger brains than men. Women, she concluded, were intellectually superior, but men had prevailed heretofore by dint of physical force. Since technology has abolished force as an instrument of power, the era of women may soon be upon us: "In such an epoch there will really be superior human beings, there will really be men strong in morality and in sentiment.

Perhaps in this way the reign of women is approaching, when the enigma of her anthropological superiority will be deciphered. Woman was always the custodian of human sentiment, morality and honor."

This represents one possible antidote to "scientific" claims for the constitutional inferiority of certain groups. One may affirm the validity of biological distinctions but argue that the data have been misinterpreted by prejudiced men with a stake in the outcome, and that disadvantaged groups are truly superior. In recent years, Elaine Morgan has followed this strategy in her *Descent of Woman,* a speculative reconstruction of human prehistory from the woman's point of view—and as farcical as more famous tall tales by and for men.

I prefer another strategy. Montessori and Morgan followed Broca's philosophy to reach a more congenial conclusion. I would rather label the whole enterprise of setting a biological value upon groups for what it is: irrelevant and highly injurious. George Eliot well appreciated the special tragedy that biological labeling imposed upon members of disadvantaged groups. She expressed it for people like herself—women of extraordinary talent. I would apply it more widely—not only to those whose dreams are flouted but also to those who never realize that they may dream—but I cannot match her prose. In conclusion, then, the rest of Eliot's prelude to *Middlemarch:*

> *The limits of variation are really much wider than anyone would imagine from the sameness of women's coiffure and the favorite love stories in prose and verse. Here and there a cygnet is reared uneasily among the ducklings in the brown pond, and never finds the living stream in fellowship with its own oary-footed kind. Here and there is born a Saint Theresa, foundress of nothing, whose loving heart-beats and sobs after an unattained goodness tremble off and are dispersed among hindrances instead of centering in some long-recognizable deed.*

Steerage

Oscar Handlin

Background

1   Oscar Handlin, born in 1915 in New York City as the son of Jewish immigrants, received his Ph. D. from Harvard in 1935. A distinguished social historian, Handlin is the author of many definitive works, including *The Uprooted* (1951), which received the Pulitzer Prize; *Immigration as a Factor in American History* (1959); *Truth in History* (1979); and *The Distortion of America* (1981). He has also served as the editor of important works that interpret the immigrant experience in America, which include *Children of the Uprooted* (1966) and the *Harvard Encyclopedia of American Ethnic Groups* (1980). His most recent works include *The Road to Gettysburg* (1986) and a multivolume series (with Lillian Handlin), *Liberty in America, 1600 to the Present*, of which the latest is *Liberty and Equality, 1920–1994* (1994). "Steerage," drawn from the second chapter of *The Uprooted*, conveys Handlin's mastery in compressing a wealth of detail on the immigrant experience into a few telling pages.

Steerage

The difficulty of residence in the ports complicated the problems of security passage. The overpowering desire to get away as soon as possible took precedence over every other consideration. The temptation was to regard the ship quickest found, the best. Haste often led to unexpected and tragic consequences.

    Until after the middle of the nineteenth century, the emigrants were carried in sailing vessels, few in number, irregular in the routes

Reprinted from *Uprooted: The Epic Story of the Great Migrations That Made the American People* (1973), by permission of Little, Brown and Co.

they followed, and uncertain as to their destination. Often the masters of these craft did not know for which port they would head until the sails were set; generally the cargo dictated the course. But there was no assurance, even after the ship was under way, that wind or weather would not induce a change. Only rarely could the passengers protest or, as on the Mary Ann in 1817, actually revolt. The generality did not expect to be able to choose a precise place of landing in the New World; if they reached shore somewhere in America that was enough.

Nor could they be overly fastidious about the character of their conveyance. Reckoning up the sum of guarded coins, the emigrants knew how little power they had to command favorable terms. The fare could, of course, be haggled over; there were no established rates and those who shared the same steerage would later discover that the charge varied from two to five pounds, depending upon the bargaining power of the various parties. But in the long run the shipmasters held the more favorable situation and could push the rate nearer the higher than the lower limit.

5   Indeed, as the volume of traffic mounted, the captains no longer   5
had to trouble with these negotiations themselves. The business fell into the hands of middlemen. Enterprising brokers contracted for the steerage space of whole ships and then resold accommodations to prospective travelers. As might be expected, avarice magnified the fancied capacity of the vessels to an unbearable degree, in fact, to a degree that provoked government intervention. But even when the American and British governments began to regulate the number of passengers and, after 1850, even began to enforce those regulations, the emigrant was but poorly protected. The brokers continued to sell as many tickets as they could; and the purchasers above the legal limit, denied permission to board, could only hope to hunt up the swindler who had misled them and seek the return of their funds.

In time, at last, the day approached. On the morning the fortunate ones whose turn it was worriedly gathered their possessions, hastened from lodginghouse to ship's side. The children dragged along the trusses of straw on which they would sleep while the men wrestled onward with the cumbrous barrels that would hold their water, with the battered chests crammed with belongings. Not into the ship yet, but into a thronging expectant crowd they pushed their way, shoving to keep sight of each other, deafened by their own impatient noises and by the cries of peddlers who thrust at them now nuts and taffy for the moment, now pots and provisions for the way.

Some, having waited so long, would wait no more and tried to clamber up the dangling ropes. The most stayed anxiously still and when the moment came jostled along until they stood then upon the ship. And when they stood then upon the ship, when the Old Land was no longer beneath them, they sensed the sea in uneasy motion and knew they were committed to a new destiny. As they lined up for the roll call, their curious gaze sought out the features of this their unfamiliar home—the rising masts the great folds of sail, the web of rigging, and the bold, pointing bowsprit. Silenced and as if immobilized by the decisiveness of the moment, they remained for a while on deck; and some, raising their eyes from examination of the ship itself, noticed the shores of the Mersey or Weser move slowly by. There was time, before they passed through the estuary to the empty ocean, to reflect on the long way they had come, to mingle with the hope and gratitude of escape the sadness and resentment of flight.

In the early days there was leisure enough for reflection on these matters. The journey was long, the average from Liverpool to New York about forty days. Favorable weather might lower the figure to a month, unfavorable raise it to two or three. The span was uncertain, for the ship was at the mercy of the winds and tides, of the primitive navigation of its masters and of the ignorance of its barely skilled sailors.

These unsubstantial craft sailed always at the edge of danger from the elements. Wrecks were disastrous and frequent. A single year in the 1830's saw seventeen vessels founder on the run from Liverpool to Quebec alone. Occasional mutinies put the fate of all in dubious hands. Fire, caused by the carelessness of passengers or crew, added another hazard to the trials of the journey. At a blow, such catastrophes swept away scores of lives, ended without further ado many minor histories in the peopling of the new continent.

10 Other perils too, less dramatic but more pervasive, insidiously 10 made shipwreck of hopes. In the slow-elapsing crossing, the boat became a circumscribed universe of its own, with its own harsh little way of life determined by the absence of space. Down to midcentury the vessels were pitifully small; three hundred tons was a good size. Yet into these tiny craft were crammed anywhere from four hundred to a thousand passengers.

These numbers set the terms of shipboard life. If they talked of it later, the emigrants almost forgot that there had also been cabins for the other sort of men who could pay out twenty to forty pounds for passage. Their own world was the steerage.

Below decks is the place, its usual dimensions seventy-five feet long twenty-five wide, five and a half high. Descend. In the fitful light your eye will discover a middle aisle five feet wide. It will be a while before you can make out the separate shapes within it, the water closets at either end (for the women; the men must go above deck), one or several cooking stoves, the tables. The aisle itself, you will see, is formed by two rows of bunks that run to the side of the ship.

Examine a bunk. One wooden partition reaches from floor to ceiling to divide it from the aisle, another stretches horizontally from wall to aisle to create two decks. Within the partitions are the boxlike spaces, ten feet wide, five long, less than three high. For the months of the voyage, each is home for six to ten beings.

This was the steerage setting. Here the emigrants lived their lives, day and night. The more generous masters gave them access to a portion of the deck at certain hours. But bad weather often deprived the passengers of that privilege, kept them below for days on end.

Life was hard here. Each family received its daily ration of water, adding to it larger and larger doses of vinegar to conceal the odor. From the limited hoard of provisions brought along, the mother struggled to eke out food for the whole journey. She knew that if the potatoes ran out there would be only the captain to turn to, who could be counted on mercilessly to extort every last possession in return; some masters, in fact, deliberately deceived the emigrants as to the length of the journey, to be able to profit from the sale of food and grog. Later, at midcentury, the government would specify the supplies that had to be taken for each passenger. But there remained ways of avoiding such regulations; tenders followed the ships out of the harbor and carried back the casks checked on for the inspector.

It was no surprise that disease should be a familiar visitor. The only ventilation was through the hatches battened down in rough weather. When the close air was not stifling hot, it was bitter cold in the absence of fire. Rats were at home in the dirt and disorder. The result: cholera, dysentery, yellow fever, smallpox, measles, and the generic "ship fever" that might be anything. It was not always as bad as on the *April,* on which five hundred of eleven hundred Germans perished in the crossing; the normal mortality was about 10 per cent, although in the great year, 1847, it was closer to 20.

It was perhaps no consolation to these emigrants, but they were not the worst off. Among the Irish before 1850 there were some who had not the paltry price of a steerage passage, yet for whom there was no return from Liverpool. They had to find the means of a still cheaper crossing.

From Canada came awkward ships built expressly to bring eastward the tall timbers of American forests, lumbering vessels with great open holds not suited for the carriage of any west-bound cargo. From Nova Scotia and Newfoundland came fishing boats laden with the catch of the Grand Bank; these craft also could be entrusted with no cargo of value on their return. Formerly both types went back in ballast. Now they would bring the New World to Irishmen. The pittance these poor creatures could pay—ten to twenty shillings—was pure gain. As for the passengers, they would camp out in the empty stinking space below decks, spend an uneasy purgatory preparatory to the redemption by America.

Don't Let Stereotypes Warp Your Judgments

Robert Heilbroner

Robert Heilbroner (1919–2005) attended Harvard University and the New School for Social Research, where he taught economics for over thirty years. His books include the Future as History *(1960),* A Primer of Government Spending: Between Capitalism and Socialism *(1970), and* An Inquiry into the Human Prospect *(1974). This essay, published in* Reader's Digest, *highlights dangers of stereotyping—both to others as well as to ourselves—and suggests how we can correct this tendency.*

1   Is a girl called Gloria apt to be better-looking than one called Bertha? Are criminals more likely to be dark than blond? Can you tell a good deal about someone's personality from hearing his voice briefly over the phone? Can a person's nationality be pretty accurately guessed from his photograph? Does the fact that someone wears glasses imply that he is intelligent?

The answer to all these questions is obviously, "No."

Yet, from all the evidence at hand, most of us believe these things. Ask any college boy if he'd rather take his chances with a Gloria or a Bertha, or ask a college girl if she'd rather blind-date a Richard or a Cuthbert. In fact, you don't have to ask: college students in questionnaires have revealed that names conjure up the same images in their minds as they do in yours—and for as little reason.

Look into the favorite suspects of persons who report "suspicious characters" and you will find a large percentage of them to be "swarthy" or "dark and foreign-looking"—despite the testimony of criminologists that criminals do not tend to be dark, foreign or "wild-eyed." Delve into the main asset of a telephone stock swindler and you will find it to be a marvelously confidence-inspiring telephone

From *Reader's Digest.*

"personality." And whereas we all think we know what an Italian or a Swede looks like, it is the sad fact that when a group of Nebraska students sought to match faces and nationalities of 15 European countries, they were scored wrong in 93 percent of their identifications. Finally, for all the fact that horn-rimmed glasses have now become the standard television sign of an "intellectual," optometrists know that the main thing that distinguishes people with glasses is just bad eyes.

5   Stereotypes are a kind of gossip about the world, a gossip that makes   5 us pre-judge people before we ever lay eyes on them. Hence it is not surprising that stereotypes have something to do with the dark world of prejudice. Explore most prejudices (note that the word means prejudgment) and you will find a cruel stereotype at the core of each one.

For it is the extraordinary fact that once we have typecast the world, we tend to see people in terms of our standardized pictures. In another demonstration of the power of stereotypes to affect our vision, a number of Columbia and Barnard students were shown 30 photographs of pretty but unidentified girls, and asked to rate each in terms of "general liking," "intelligence," "beauty" and so on. Two months later, the same group were shown the same photographs, this time with fictitious Irish, Italian, Jewish and "American" names attached to the pictures. Right away the ratings changed. Faces which were now seen as representing a national group went down in looks and still farther down in likability, while the "American" girls suddenly looked decidedly prettier and nicer.

Why is it that we stereotype the world in such irrational and harmful fashion? In part, we begin to typecast people in our childhood years. Early in life, as every parent whose child has watched a TV Western knows, we learn to spot the Good Guys from the Bad Guys. Some years ago, a social psychologist showed very clearly how powerful these stereotypes of childhood vision are. He secretly asked the most popular youngsters in an elementary school to make errors in their morning gym exercises. Afterwards, he asked the class if anyone had noticed any mistakes during gym period. Oh, yes, said the children. But it was the *unpopular* members of the class—the "bad guys"—they remembered as being out of step.

We not only grow up with standardized pictures forming inside of us, but as grown-ups we are constantly having them thrust upon us. Some of them, like the half-joking, half-serious stereotypes of mothers-in-law, or country yokels, or psychiatrists, are dinned into us by the stock jokes we hear and repeat. In fact, without such stereotypes, there would be a lot fewer jokes. Still other stereotypes are perpetuated by the advertisements we read, the movies we see, the books we read.

And finally, we tend to stereotype because it helps us make sense out of a highly confusing world, a world which William James once described as "one great, blooming, buzzing confusion." It is a curious fact that if we don't *know* what we're looking at, we are often quite literally unable to *see* what we're looking at. People who recover their sight after a lifetime of blindness actually cannot at first tell a triangle from a square. A visitor to a factory sees only noisy chaos where the superintendent sees a perfectly synchronized flow of work. As Walter Lippmann has said, "For the most part we do not first see, and then define; we define first, and then we see."

10   Stereotypes are one way in which we "define" the world in order 10 to see it. They classify the infinite variety of human beings into a convenient handful of "types" towards whom we learn to act in stereotyped fashion. Life would be a wearing process if we had to start from scratch with each and every human contact. Stereotypes economize on our mental effort by covering up the blooming, buzzing confusion with big recognizable cut-outs. They save us the "trouble" of finding out what the world is like—they give it its accustomed look.

Thus the trouble is that stereotypes make us mentally lazy. As S. I. Hayakawa, the authority on semantics, has written: "The danger of stereotypes lies not in their existence, but in the fact that they become for all people some of the time, and for some people all the time, *substitutes for observation.*" Worse yet, stereotypes get in the way of our judgment, even when we do observe the world. Someone who has formed rigid preconceptions of all Latins as "excitable," or all teenagers as "wild," doesn't alter his point of view when he meets a calm and deliberate Genoese, or a serious-minded high school student. He brushes them aside as "exceptions that prove the rule." And, of course, if he meets someone true to type, he stands triumphantly vindicated. "They're all like that," he proclaims, having encountered an excited Latin, an ill-behaved adolescent.

Hence, quite aside from the injustice which stereotypes do to others, they impoverish ourselves. A person who lumps the world into simple categories, who type-casts all labor leaders as "racketeers," all businessmen as "reactionaries," all Harvard men as "snobs," and all Frenchmen as "sexy," is in danger of becoming a stereotype himself. He loses his capacity to be himself—which is to say, to see the world in his own absolutely unique, inimitable and independent fashion.

Instead, he votes for the man who fits his standardized picture of what a candidate "should" look like or sound like, buys the goods that someone in his "situation" in life "should" own, lives the life that others define for him. The mark of the stereotype person is that he never surprises us, that we do indeed have him "typed." And no one fits this straitjacket so perfectly as someone whose opinions about *other people* are fixed and inflexible.

Impoverishing as they are, stereotypes are not easy to get rid of. The world we type-cast may be no better than a Grade B movie, but at least we know what to expect of our stock characters. When we let them act for themselves in the strangely unpredictable way that people do act, who knows but that many of our fondest convictions will be proved wrong?

15   Nor do we suddenly drop our standardized pictures for a blinding vision of the Truth. Sharp swings of ideas about people often just substitute one stereotype for another. The true process of change is a slow one that adds bits and pieces of reality to the pictures in our heads, until gradually they take on some of the blurriness of life itself. Little by little, we learn not that Jews and Negroes and Catholics and Puerto Ricans are "just like everybody else"—for that, too, is a stereotype—but that each and every one of them is unique, special, different and individual. Often we do not even know that we have let a stereotype lapse until we hear someone saying, "all so-and-so's are like such-and-such, and we hear ourselves saying, "Well-maybe."

Can we speed the process along? Of course we can.

First, we can become *aware* of the standardized pictures in our heads, in other peoples' heads, in the world around us.

Second, we can become suspicious of all judgments that we allow exceptions to "prove." There is no more chastening thought than that in the vast intellectual adventure of science, it takes but one tiny exception to topple a whole edifice of ideas.

Third, we can learn to be chary of generalizations about people. As F. Scott Fitzgerald once wrote: "Begin with an individual, and before you know it you have created a type; begin with a type, and you find you have created—nothing."

20   Most of the time, when we type-cast the world, we are not in fact generalizing about people at all. We are only revealing the embarrassing facts about the pictures that hang in the gallery of stereotypes in our own heads.

The Declaration of Independence

Thomas Jefferson

Thomas Jefferson (1743–1826) was born in Virginia in a well-to-do land-owning family. He graduated from the College of William and Mary and then studied law. When he was elected at age 26 to the Virginia legislature, he had already begun forming his revolutionary views. As a delegate to the Second Continental Congress in 1775, he was the principal writer of the Declaration of Independence, which was adopted on July 4, 1776. After the Revolution he was Governor of Virginia from 1775 to 1777. From then until 1801, when he was elected the third President of the United States, Jefferson served in various federal positions, including secretary of state and ambassador to France. Jefferson was influential as an advocate of democracy in the early years of the United States, although his ideas were more typical of the eighteenth century "enlightened man" than original. The Declaration of Independence shows his ideas and style as well as those of the times and remains not merely an important historical document but also an eloquent statement of the founding principles of this country.

1 When in the course of human events, it becomes necessary for one people to dissolve the political bands which have connected them with another, and to assume among the powers of the earth, the separate and equal station to which the Laws of Nature and of Nature's God entitle them, a decent respect to the opinions of mankind requires that they should declare the causes which impel them to the separation.

We hold these truths to be self-evident, that all men are created equal, that they are endowed by their Creator with certain inalienable rights, that among these are life, liberty, and the pursuit of happiness. That to secure these rights, governments are instituted among men, deriving their just powers from the consent of the governed. That whenever any form of government becomes destructive of these ends, it is the right of the people to alter or to abolish it, and to institute new government, laying its foundation on such principles and organizing its powers in such form, as to them shall seem most likely to effect their safety and happiness. Prudence, indeed, will dictate that governments long established should not be changed for light and transient causes; and accordingly all experience hath shown, that mankind are more disposed to suffer, while evils are sufferable, than to right themselves by abolishing the forms to which they are accustomed. But when a long train of abuses and usurpations, pursuing invariably the same object, evinces a design to reduce them under absolute despotism, it is their right, it is their duty, to throw off such government, and to provide new guards for their future security. Such has been the patient sufferance of these Colonies; and such is now the necessity which constrains them to alter their former systems of government. The history of the present King of Great Britain is a history of repeated injuries and usurpations, all having in direct object the establishment of an absolute tyranny over these States. To prove this, let facts be submitted to a candid world.

He has refused his assent to laws, the most wholesome and necessary for the public good.

He has forbidden his Governors to pass laws of immediate and pressing importance, unless suspended in their operation till his assent should be obtained; and when so suspended, he has utterly neglected to attend to them.

He has refused to pass other laws for the accommodation of large districts of people, unless those people would relinquish the right of representation in the legislature, a right inestimable to them and formidable to tyrants only.

He has called together legislative bodies at places unusual, uncomfortable, and distant from the depository of their public records, for the sole purpose of fatiguing them into compliance with his measures.

He has dissolved representative houses repeatedly, for opposing with manly firmness his invasions on the rights of the people.

He has refused for a long time, after such dissolutions, to cause others to be elected; whereby the legislative powers, incapable of annihilation, have returned to the people at large for their exercise; the State remaining in the meantime exposed to all the dangers of invasion from without and convulsions within.

He has endeavoured to prevent the population of these states; for that purpose obstructing the laws for naturalization of foreigners; refusing to pass others to encourage their migration hither, and raising the conditions of new appropriations of lands.

10 He has obstructed the administration of justice, by refusing his assent to laws for establishing judiciary powers.

He has made judges dependent on his will alone, for the tenure of their offices, and the amount and payment of their salaries.

He has erected a multitude of new offices, and sent hither swarms of officers to harass our people, and eat out their substance.

He has kept among us, in times of peace, standing armies without the consent of our legislatures.

He has affected to render the military independent of and superior to the civil power.

15 He has combined with others to subject us to a jurisdiction foreign of our constitution, and unacknowledged by our laws; giving his assent to their acts of pretended legislation:

For quartering large bodies of armed troops among us:

For protecting them, by a mock trial, from punishment for any murders which they should commit on the inhabitants of these States:

For cutting off our trade with all parts of the world:

For imposing taxes on us without our consent:

20 For depriving us in many cases of the benefits of trial by jury:

For transporting us beyond seas to be tried for pretended offences:

For abolishing the free system of English laws in a neighbouring Province, establishing therein an arbitrary government, and enlarging its boundaries so as to render it at once an example and fit instrument for introducing the same absolute rule into these Colonies:

For taking away our Charters, abolishing our most valuable laws, and altering fundamentally the forms of our governments:

For suspending our own legislatures, and declaring themselves invested with power to legislate for us in all cases whatsoever.

25 He has abdicated government here, by declaring us out of his protection and waging war against us.

He has plundered our seas, ravaged our coasts, burnt our towns, and destroyed the lives of our people.

He is at this time transporting large armies of foreign mercenaries to complete the works of death, desolation, and tyranny, already begun with circumstances of cruelty and perfidy scarcely paralleled in the most barbarous ages, and totally unworthy the head of a civilized nation.

He has constrained our fellow citizens taken captive on the high seas to bear arms against their country, to become the executioners of their friends and brethren, or to fall themselves by their hands.

He has excited domestic insurrections amongst us, and has endeavoured to bring on the inhabitants of our frontiers, the merciless Indian savages, whose known rule of warfare, is an undistinguished destruction of all ages, sexes, and conditions.

30 In every stage of these oppressions we have petitioned for redress 30 in the most humble terms: our repeated petitions have been answered only by repeated injury. A prince whose character is thus marked by every act which may define a tyrant is unfit to be the ruler of a free people.

Nor have we been wanting in attention to our British brethren. We have warned them from time to time of attempts by their legislature to extend an unwarrantable jurisdiction over us. We have reminded them of the circumstances of our emigration and settlement here. We have appealed to their native justice and magnanimity, and we have conjured them by the ties of our common kindred to disavow these usurpations, which would inevitably interrupt our connections and correspondence. They too have been deaf to the voice of justice and of consanguinity. We must, therefore, acquiesce in the necessity, which denounces our separation, and hold them, as we hold the rest of mankind, enemies in war, in peace friends.

We, therefore, the Representatives of the United States of America, in General Congress assembled, appealing to the Supreme Judge of the world for the rectitude of our intentions, do, in the name, and by authority of the good people of these Colonies, solemnly publish and declare, That these United Colonies are, and of right ought to be, Free and Independent States; that they are absolved from all allegiance to the British Crown, and that all political connection between them and the state of Great Britain, is and ought to be totally dissolved; and that as Free and Independent States, they have full power to levy war, conclude peace, contract alliances, establish commerce, and to do all other acts and things which Independent States may of right do. And for the support of this declaration, with a firm reliance on the protection of Divine Providence, we mutually pledge to each other our lives, our fortunes, and our sacred honor.

The World in 2005: Hidden in Plain Sight

Robert D. Kaplan

Robert D. Kaplan is a correspondent for The Atlantic
Monthly *and has been on assignments in some of the
world's most dangerous places. His books include* Eastward
to Tartary: Travels in the Balkans, the Middle East, and
the Caucasus *(2000), and* The Coming Anarchy: Shattering the Dreams of the Post Cold War *(2000). As one
reviewer said of his work, "Kaplan explodes many of the
conventions and grammar by which foreign policy, conflict, and security threats have been thought and written
about. . . . [H]is ability to influence the way one looks at
the world is hard to resist."*

1   As Americans, we have a natural tendency to believe that world   1
events over the next few years will unfold from Septem-
ber 11. But in truth much of the world will evolve without
regard to September 11. Civil wars will continue, diseases will break
out, and local economic crises will run their course. The challenge is
to anticipate how these other processes will intersect with the war on
terrorism.

We saw an example of such intersection after the start of the air
campaign in Afghanistan, when anti-Americanism among Muslims in
northern Nigeria sparked a pogrom that left hundreds of local Christians dead or wounded. Intercommunal riots have been on the
increase in Nigeria for years—the result, in part, of rising numbers of
young males and the destabilizing effects of democratization, which
have strengthened the forces of religious mobilization. The collision

of these factors with America's anti-terror campaign ignited the recent violence.

What other existing trends are likely to collide with the war on terrorism—and how?

In the Middle East the war on terrorism could have the unintended consequence of disturbing regional politics to a degree unknown since the collapse of the Ottoman Empire after World War I. Remember that the war has been launched at a time when secular-nationalist regimes in Egypt, Syria, and Iraq are so vulnerable that only the sons of dictators are trusted to succeed the dictators. Morocco, Egypt, Syria, Jordan, and Saudi Arabia are all facing, at best, Mexican-style political and economic disorder, without Mexico's advantage of a long border with a First World country to which it can export millions of jobless workers and from which it can import billions of investment dollars. Because of economic and cultural transformation tied to urbanization, the next generation of Arab autocrats will, like their Mexican counterparts today, not be permitted to rule as autocratically as their predecessors. Yet none of these countries is capable of sustainable parliamentary democracy, not even to the limited degree that Mexico has achieved.

5   Aggravating the kind of political and economic turbulence that   5
has been a feature of Mexican society for more than a decade will be bulges in the number of youths across the Middle East, the most severe occurring in Yemen, Saudi Arabia, Oman, Gaza, and the West Bank. In Egypt, too, the percentage of males between the ages of fifteen and twenty-nine—the age group that traditionally stirs up unrest—will be dangerously high through 2020. Meanwhile, the amount of available water per capita will diminish by nearly half in many parts of the Middle East over the next twenty years. These inescapable realities will only become more troublesome if there is any sort of global economic downturn.

In Cairo, President Hosni Mubarak's banal authoritarianism represents the Egyptian equivalent of the Soviet Union's Brezhnev-Chernenko era. There is no Mikhail Gorbachev on the horizon. Saudi Arabia, despite its oil wealth, will prove even less governable than Egypt. It lacks the organizing geography of a great river valley, where most of the population lives within easy reach of central control. In stretches of Saudi Arabia, such a Nejd, the regime has already essentially lost its legitimacy. The experience of neighboring Yemen, with its brazen highwaymen and rampant kidnappings, may be what Saudi Arabia can look forward to—and that's the optimistic view.

Nominally pro-American regimes in the Arab heartland are not the only ones in a state of calcification. So is the anti-American regime in Iran. There the population of 66 million is refreshingly pro-American, owing to real-life experience with an Islamic revolution that has bankrupted the middle class and destroyed both the aura and the legitimacy of the clergy. In Iraq the level of repression is comparable to that in the Soviet Union under Stalin and in Romania under Nicolae Ceausescu. Once Saddam Hussein's regime is brought down, the reaction among the populace may be no less enthusiastic than it was in Afghanistan when the United States dismantled the Taliban regime.

The Middle East, then, may be poised for a flip-flop, with the United States having embassies a few years hence in Tehran and Baghdad but not in Cairo, and with U.S. forces withdrawing from bases in an increasingly volatile Saudi Arabia.

Although the American-led anti-terror campaign may stoke the flames of fundamentalism in some places, including Egypt, the new century will ultimately see the implosion of political Islam. Because there is "no Islamic way to fix a car," as the saying goes, Islamic regimes offer only the sterile repression of the Taliban or the incompetent economic management of the ayatollahs. The rise of militant Islam in Pakistan, if it continues, will not create a new anti-American force so much as it will further weaken the state itself. Pakistani Islamists, divided by ethnicity and subdivided by clan, lack a unifying, Khomeini-like figure.

10   Indeed, the most dangerous underlying trend in the Subcontinent is the weakening of central authority. This, in turn, intensifies bellicosity between Pakistan and India, because foreign policy represents the last arena in which the state can exert its traditional primacy. The fate of the war on terrorism will hinge to no small degree on the ability of the Bush Administration to manage the India-Pakistan rivalry. Pakistani intervention in the affairs of Afghanistan lay behind the radicalization of Afghanistan's politics in the first place. That intervention was driven by the need to create a rear wall of militant Islamic states to stand against predominantly Hindu India.

This brings us to Central Asia, which straddles the former Soviet Union and China. In the 1990s, even as the world witnessed ethnic warfare in the Caucasus and political chaos in Russia itself, the former

Soviet republics of Central Asia were quiet, their populations kept under tight control by ex-communist bosses such as Islam Karimov, in Uzbekistan, and Saparmurad Niyazov, in Turkmenistan. Because Central Asia experienced little of Gorbachev's glasnost or perestroika, it had too few reformed communists to provide the basis of a secular opposition. Therefore the only serious opposition to the region's stultifying autocracies has been Islamic. As that Islamic opposition grows in Central Asia, so will Russia's paranoia—and so will its incentive to cooperate with the United States against terrorism.

The same holds true for China, where further modernization, before leading to stable democracy, will heighten ethnic conflict between the Han Chinese and the Muslim Turkic Uighurs in the western part of the country (historically known as East Turkistan). Among the reasons the Chinese cooperated with our effort to topple the Taliban was that Uighur radicals were to be found in al Qaeda training camps.

The rising threat of militant Islam in the Asian steppes could usher in a new "concert of powers" that, while not ending competition among the United States, Russia, and China, will provide a framework for cooperation. Stability in Afghanistan can be achieved only by commanders and warlords, each fearful of the other, cutting deals that serve one another's self-interest; a modicum of order in a disorderly world can be had only on the basis of a similarly wary cooperation.

In Africa the rising tide of young males will be even more extreme than in the Middle East. The top ten "youth-bulge" countries are all in sub-Saharan Africa. Whereas the 1990s saw the implosion of small states (Somalia, Rwanda, and Sierra Leone), the next decade, judging by recent political violence that has devolved into gang warlordism in a number of African cities, could see the implosion of larger entities such as Côte d'Ivoire and Kenya. Nigeria is already crumbling, although too slowly to generate headlines. The loss of central authority may be part of a long-term transition that will ultimately yield positive results. But in the short term it will provide new opportunities and havens for global terrorist groups, which thrive in weakly governed realms.

As al Qaeda's 1998 bombing of the American missions in Kenya and Tanzania demonstrated, the safety of U.S. embassies in Africa has become increasingly difficult to guarantee. The years ahead could witness more embassy downsizings in Africa, together with commando raids on terrorist hideouts. Humanitarian crises in Africa will worsen in the near future, even as the United States pays less attention to the continent, because of other foreign-policy concerns and because America's diminished affluence will temper national idealism. If NATO does not begin to work through the United Nations to organize a global constabulary force for select humanitarian interventions, the application of American power against terrorists will run the risk of seeming narrowly self-serving—undermining America's reputation and thus its ability to be a benevolent global power.

Finally, in Latin America, as in so many other places, the teeming urban underclasses remain poor and politically disenfranchised. They are supporters-in-waiting for populist authoritarianism, as witnessed in Venezuela, under General Hugo Chavez. The United States is riding a tiger there: Venezuela is the third largest supplier of oil to the United States. Given global interconnection and the fragility of so many regimes, the possibilities for unintended consequences to foreign action are legion. The near future may see catastrophic chain reactions: a terrorist attack in one place may prompt a military attack someplace else, which sets off riots in yet another place, leading to a coup in a pivotal country elsewhere.

From the 1950s through the 1980s the existence of the Cold War justified media coverage of far-off countries in little-known parts of the world. The war on terror will do the same. It will provide a template for foreign news. But in the shadows will lurk a philosophical tension: A world that is closer and more dangerous than ever necessitates a heightened pragmatism in U.S. foreign policy. At the same time, global elites in this interconnected world will demand a heightened idealism from President Bush if he is to have legitimacy in their eyes. Presidential rhetoric may get nobler even as American policies become more ruthless. Closing the distance between the two—through a global constabulary force and similar measures—will constitute the principal challenge for American foreign policy.

Learning the Language

Perri Klass

Perri Klass (1958–) was born to American parents in Trinidad and earned her M. D. from Harvard in 1986, going on to become a pediatrician. She has been writing and publishing widely while pursuing her medical career. Her fiction includes two novels, Recombinations *(1985) and* Other Women's Children *(1990), and a collection of short stories,* I Am Having an Adventure *(1986). She published a collection of autobiographical essays,* A Not Entirely Benign Procedure *(1987) about her experience in medical school. The following selection, "Learning the Language," is excerpted from that book. Klass is sensitive to uses of language and understands how language affects thinking. As you read this essay, think about other special groups who also use language in unique ways.*

1 "**M**rs. Tolstoy is your basic LOL in NAD, admitted for a soft rule-out MI," the intern announces. I scribble that on my patient list. In other words, Mrs. Tolstoy is a Little Old Lady in No Apparent Distress who is in the hospital to make sure she hasn't had a heart attack (rule out a Myocardial Infarction). And we think it's unlikely that she has had a heart attack (a *soft* rule-out).

If I learned nothing else during my first three months of working in the hospital as a medical student, I learned endless jargon and abbreviations. I started out in a state of primeval innocence, in which I didn't even know that "s̄ CP, SOB, N/V" meant "without chest pain, shortness of breath, or nausea and vomiting." By the end I took the abbreviations so much for granted that I would complain to my mother the English professor, "And can you believe I had to put down three NG tubes last night?"

"You'll have to tell me what an NG tube is if you want me to sympathize properly," my mother said. NG, nasogastric—isn't it obvious?

I picked up not only the specific expressions but also the patterns of speech and the grammatical conventions; for example, you never say that a patient's blood pressure fell or that his cardiac enzymes rose. Instead, the patient is always the subject of the verb: "He dropped his pressure." "He bumped his enzymes." This sort of construction probably reflects the profound irritation of the intern when the nurses come in the middle of the night to say that Mr. Dickinson has disturbingly low blood pressure. "Oh, he's gonna hurt me bad tonight," the intern might say, inevitably angry at Mr. Dickinson for dropping his pressure and creating a problem.

5   When chemotherapy fails to cure Mrs. Bacon's cancer, what we   5 say is, "Mrs. Bacon failed chemotherapy."

"Well, we've already had one hit today, and we're up next, but at least we've got mostly stable players on our team." This means that our team (group of doctors and medical students) has already gotten one new admission today, and it is our turn again, so we'll get whoever is admitted next in emergency, but at least most of the patients we already have are fairly stable, that is, unlikely to drop their pressures or in any other way get suddenly sicker and hurt us bad. Baseball metaphor is pervasive. A no-hitter is a night without any new admissions. A player is always a patient—a nitrate player is a patient on nitrates, a unit player is a patient in the intensive care unit, and so on, until you reach the terminal player.

It is interesting to consider what it means to be winning, or doing well, in this perennial baseball game. When the intern hangs up the phone and announces, "I got a hit," that is not cause for congratulations. The team is not scoring points; rather, it is getting hit, being bombarded with new patients. The object of the game from the point of view of the doctors, considering the players for whom they are already responsible, is to get as few new hits as possible.

This special language contributes to a sense of closeness and professional spirit among people who are under a great deal of stress. As a medical student, I found it exciting to discover that I'd finally cracked the code, that I could understand what doctors said and wrote, and could use the same formulations myself. Some people seem to become enamored of the jargon for its own sake, perhaps because they are so deeply thrilled with the idea of medicine, with the idea of themselves as doctors.

I knew a medical student who was referred to by the interns on the team as Mr. Eponym because he was so infatuated with eponymous terminology, the more obscure the better. He never said "capillary pulsations" if he could say "Quincke's pulses." He would lovingly tell over the multinamed syndromes—Wolff-Parkinson-White, Lown-Ganong-Levine, Schönlein-Henoch—until the temptation to suggest Schleswig-Holstein or Stevenson-Kefauver or Baskin-Robbins became irresistible to his less reverent colleagues.

10 And there is the jargon that you don't ever want to hear yourself using. You know that your training is changing you, but there are certain changes you think would be going a little too far.

The resident was describing a man with devastating terminal pancreatic cancer. "Basically he's CTD," the resident concluded. I reminded myself that I had resolved not to be shy about asking when I didn't understand things. "CTD?" I asked timidly.

The resident smirked at me. "Circling The Drain."

The images are vivid and terrible. "What happened to Mrs. Melville?"

"Oh, she boxed last night." To box is to die, of course.

15 Then there are the more pompous locutions that can make the beginning medical student nervous about the effects of medical training. A friend of mine was told by his resident, "A pregnant woman with sickle-cell represents a failure of genetic counseling."

Mr. Eponym, who tried hard to talk like the doctors, once explained to me, "An infant is basically a brainstem preparation." The term "brainstem preparation," as used in neurological research, refers to an animal whose higher brain functions have been destroyed so that only the most primitive reflexes remain, like the sucking reflex, the startle reflex, and the rooting reflex.

And yet at other times the harshness dissipates into a strangely elusive euphemism. "As you know, this is a not entirely benign procedure," some doctor will say, and that will be understood to imply agony, risk of complications, and maybe even a significant mortality rate.

The more extreme forms aside, one most important function of medical jargon is to help doctors maintain some distance from their patients. By reformulating a patient's pain and problems into a language that the patient doesn't even speak, I suppose we are in some sense taking those pains and problems under our jurisdiction and also reducing their emotional impact. This linguistic separation between doctors and patients allows conversations to go on at the bedside that are unintelligible to the patient. "Naturally, we're worried about adeno-CA," the intern can say to the medical student, and lung cancer need never be mentioned.

I learned a new language this past summer. At times it thrills me to hear myself using it. It enables me to understand my colleagues, to communicate effectively in the hospital. Yet I am uncomfortably aware that I will never again notice the peculiarities and even atrocities of medical language as keenly as I did this summer. There may be specific expressions I manage to avoid, but even as I remark them, promising myself I will never use them, I find that this language is becoming my professional speech. It no longer sounds strange in my ears—or coming from my mouth. And I am afraid that as with any new language, to use it properly you must absorb not only the vocabulary but also the structure, the logic, the attitudes. At first you may notice these new and alien assumptions every time you put together a sentence, but with time and increased fluency you stop being aware of them at all. And as you lose that awareness, for better or for worse, you move closer and closer to being a doctor instead of just talking like one.

From Silence to Words: Writing as Struggle

Min-zhan Lu

Min-zhan Lu (1946–) was born in China. Lu, who grew up speaking English as well as a number of Chinese dialects, has taught composition and literary criticism at Drake University. She has published both academic articles related to composition issues and articles about her life in China. This article, published in College English *in 1987, relates Lu's challenges acquiring literacy in both China and the United States and how those challenges have affected her writing and teaching.*

Imagine that you enter a parlor. You come late. When you arrive, others have long preceded you, and they are engaged in a heated discussion. . . .You listen for a while, until you decide that you have caught the tenor of the argument; then you put in your oar. Someone answers; you answer him; another comes to your defense; another aligns himself against you, to either the embarrassment or gratification of your opponent, depending upon the quality of your ally's assistance. However, the discussion is interminable. The hour grows late, you must depart. And you do depart, with the discussion still vigorously in progress.

—Kenneth Burke, The Philosophy of Literary Form

Men are not built in silence, but in word, in work, in action-reflection.

—Paulo Freire, Pedagogy of the Oppressed

From *College English,* April, 1987. Copyright © 1987 by the National Council of Teachers of English.

1

y mother withdrew into silence two months before she
died. A few nights before she fell silent, she told me she re-
gretted the way she had raised me and my sisters. I knew
she was referring to the way we had been brought up in the midst of
two conflicting worlds—the world of home, dominated by the ideol-
ogy of the Western humanistic tradition, and the world of a society
dominated by Mao Tse-tung's Marxism. My mother had devoted her
life to our education, an education she knew had made us suffer political persecution during the Cultural Revolution. I wanted to find a
way to convince her that, in spite of the persecution, I had benefited
from the education she had worked so hard to give me. But I was
silent. My understanding of my education was so dominated by memories of confusion and frustration that I was unable to reflect on what
I could have gained from it.

This paper is my attempt to fill up that silence with words, words
I didn't have then, words that I have since come to by reflecting on
my earlier experience as a student in China and on my recent experience as a composition teacher in the United States. For in spite of the
frustration and confusion I experienced growing up caught between
two conflicting worlds, the conflict ultimately helped me to grow as a
reader and writer. Constantly having to switch back and forth between
the discourse of home and that of school made me sensitive and self-
conscious about the struggle I experienced every time I tried to read,
write, or think in either discourse. Eventually, it led me to search for
constructive uses for such struggle.

From early childhood, I had identified the differences between
home and the outside world by the different languages I used in each.
My parents had wanted my sisters and me to get the best education
they could conceive of—Cambridge. They had hired a live-in tutor, a
Scot, to make us bilingual. I learned to speak English with my parents, my tutor, and my sisters. I was allowed to speak Shanghai dialect
only with the servants. When I was four (the year after the Communist Revolution of 1949), my parents sent me to a local private school
where I learned to speak, read, and write in a new language—Standard
Chinese, the official written language of New China.

In those days I moved from home to school, from English to Standard Chinese to Shanghai dialect, with no apparent friction. I spoke
each language with those who spoke the language. All seemed quite
"natural"—servants spoke only Shanghai dialect because they were

servants; teachers spoke Standard Chinese because they were teachers; languages had different words because they were different languages. I thought of English as my family language, comparable to the many strange dialects I didn't speak but had often heard some of my classmates speak with their families. While I was happy to have a special family language, until second grade I didn't feel that my family language was any different than some of my classmates' family dialects.

5   My second grade homeroom teacher was a young graduate from a missionary school. When she found out I spoke English, she began to practice her English on me. One day she used English when asking me to run an errand for her. As I turned to close the door behind me, I noticed the puzzled faces of my classmates. I had the same sensation I had often experienced when some stranger in a crowd would turn on hearing me speak English. I was more intensely pleased on this occasion, however, because suddenly I felt that my family language had been singled out from the family languages of my classmates. Since we were not allowed to speak any dialect other than Standard Chinese in the classroom, having my teacher speak English to me in class made English an official language of the classroom. I began to take pride in my ability to speak it.

This incident confirmed in my mind what my parents had always told me about the importance of English to one's life. Time and again they had told me of how my paternal grandfather, who was well versed in classic Chinese, kept losing good-paying jobs because he couldn't speak English. My grandmother reminisced constantly about how she had slaved and saved to send my father to a first-rate missionary school. And we were made to understand that it was my father's fluent English that had opened the door to his success. Even though my family had always stressed the importance of English for my future, I used to complain bitterly about the extra English lessons we had to take after school. It was only after my homeroom teacher had "sanctified" English that I began to connect English with my education. I became a much more eager student in my tutorials.

What I learned from my tutorials seemed to enhance and reinforce what I was learning in my classroom. In those days each word had one meaning. One day I would be making a sentence at school: "The national flag of China is red." The next day I would recite at home, "My love is like a red, red rose." There seemed to be an agreement between the Chinese "red" and the English "red," and both corresponded to the patch of color printed next to the word. "Love" was my love for my mother at home and my love for my "motherland" at school; both "loves" meant how I felt about my mother. Having two loads of homework forced me to develop a quick memory for words and a sensitivity to form and style. What I learned in one language carried over to the other. I made sentences such as, "I saw a red, red rose among the green leaves," with both the English lyric and the classic Chinese lyric—red flower among green leaves—running through my mind, and I was praised by both teacher and tutor for being a good student.

Although my elementary schooling took place during the fifties, I was almost oblivious to the great political and social changes happening around me. Years later, I read in my history and political philosophy textbooks that the fifties were a time when "China was making a transition from a semi-feudal, semi-capitalist, and semi-colonial country into a socialist country," a period in which "the Proletarians were breaking into the educational territory dominated by Bourgeois Intellectuals." While people all over the country were being officially classified into Proletarians, Petty-bourgeois, National-bourgeois, Poor-peasants, and Intellectuals, and were trying to adjust to their new social identities, my parents were allowed to continue the upper middle-class life they had established before the 1949 Revolution because of my father's affiliation with British firms. I had always felt that my family was different from the families of my classmates, but I didn't perceive society's view of my family until the summer vacation before I entered high school.

First, my aunt was caught by her colleagues talking to her husband over the phone in English. Because of it, she was criticized and almost labeled a Rightist. (This was the year of the Anti-Rightist movement, a movement in which the Intellectuals became the target of the "socialist class-struggle.") I had heard others telling my mother that she was foolish to teach us English when Russian had replaced English as the "official" foreign language. I had also learned at school that the American and British Imperialists were the arch-enemies of New China. Yet I had made no connection between the arch-enemies and the English our family spoke. What happened to my aunt forced the connection on me. I began to see my parents' choice of a family language as an anti-Revolutionary act and was alarmed that I had participated in such an act. From then on, I took care not to use English outside home and to conceal my knowledge of English from my new classmates.

10   Certain words began to play important roles in my new life at the junior high. On the first day of school, we were handed forms to fill out with our parents' class, job, and income. Being one of the few people not employed by the government, my father had never been officially classified. Since he was a medical doctor, he told me to put him down as an Intellectual. My homeroom teacher called me into the office a couple of days afterwards and told me that my father couldn't be an Intellectual if his income far exceeded that of a Capitalist. He also told me that since my father worked for Foreign Imperialists, my father should be classified as an Imperialist Lackey. The teacher looked nonplussed when I told him that my father couldn't be an Imperialist Lackey because he was a medical doctor. But I could tell from the way he took notes on my form that my father's job had put me in an unfavorable position in his eyes.

The Standard Chinese term "class" was not a new word for me. Since first grade, I had been taught sentences such as, "The Working class are the masters of New China." I had always known that it was good to be a worker, but until then, I had never felt threatened for not being one. That fall, "class" began to take on a new meaning for me. I noticed a group of Working-class students and teachers at school. I was made to understand that because of my class background, I was excluded from that group.

Another word that became important was "consciousness." One of the slogans posted in the school building read, "Turn our students into future Proletarians with socialist consciousness and education!" For several weeks we studied this slogan in our political philosophy course, a subject I had never had in elementary school. I still remember the definition of "socialist consciousness" that we were repeatedly tested on through the years: "Socialist consciousness is a person's political soul. It is the consciousness of the Proletarians represented by Marxist Mao Tse-tung thought. It takes expression in one's action, language, and lifestyle. It is the task of every Chinese student to grow up into a Proletarian with a socialist consciousness so that he can serve the people and the motherland." To make the abstract concept accessible to us, our teacher pointed out that the immediate task for students from Working-class families was to strengthen their socialist consciousnesses. For those of us who were from other class

backgrounds, the task was to turn ourselves into Workers with socialist consciousnesses. The teacher never explained exactly how we were
supposed to "turn" into Workers. Instead, we were given samples of
the ritualistic annual plans we had to write at the beginning of each
term. In these plans, we performed "self-criticism" on our consciousnesses and made vows to turn ourselves into Workers with socialist
consciousnesses. The teacher's division between those who did and
those who didn't have a socialist consciousness led me to reify the notion of "consciousness" into a thing one possesses. I equated this intangible "thing" with a concrete way of dressing, speaking, and
writing. For instance, I never doubted that my political philosophy
teacher had a socialist consciousness because she was from a steel-
worker's family (she announced this the first day of class) and was a
party member who wore grey cadre suits and talked like a philosophy
textbook. I noticed other things about her. She had beautiful eyes and
spoke Standard Chinese with such a pure accent that I thought she
should be a film star. But I was embarrassed that I had noticed things
that ought not to have been associated with her. I blamed my observation on my Bourgeois consciousness.

At the same time, the way reading and writing were taught
through memorization and imitation also encouraged me to reduce
concepts and ideas to simple definitions. In literature and political
philosophy classes, we were taught a large number of quotations from
Marx, Lenin, and Mao Tse-tung. Each concept that appeared in these
quotations came with a definition. We were required to memorize the
definitions of the words along with the quotations. Every time I memorized a definition, I felt I had learned a word: "The national red flag
symbolizes the blood shed by Revolutionary ancestors for our socialist cause"; "New China rises like a red sun over the eastern horizon."
As I memorized these sentences, I reduced their metaphors to dictionary meanings: "red" meant "Revolution" and "red sun" meant "New
China" in the "language" of the Working class. I learned mechanically
but eagerly. I soon became quite fluent in this new language.

As school began to define me as a political subject, my parents
tried to build up my resistance to the "communist poisoning" by ex-
posing me to the "great books"—novels by Charles Dickens,
Nathaniel Hawthorne, Emily Brontë, Jane Austen, and writers from
around the turn of the century. My parents implied that these writers
represented how I, their child, should read and write. My parents

replaced the word "Bourgeois" with the word "cultured." They reminded me that I was in school only to learn math and science. I needed to pass the other courses to stay in school, but I was not to let the "Red doctrines" corrupt my mind. Gone were the days when I could innocently write, "I saw the red, red rose among the green leaves," collapsing, as I did, English and Chinese cultural traditions. "Red" came to mean Revolution at school, "the Commies" at home, and adultery in *The Scarlet Letter.* Since I took these symbols and metaphors as meanings natural to people of the same class, I abandoned my earlier definitions of English and Standard Chinese as the language of home and the language of school. I now defined English as the language of the Bourgeois and Standard Chinese as the language of the Working class. I thought of the language of the Working class as someone else's language and the language of the Bourgeois as my language. But I also believed that, although the language of the Bourgeois was my real language, I could and would adopt the language of the Working class when I was at school. I began to put on and take off my Working class language in the same way I put on and took off my school clothes to avoid being criticized for wearing Bourgeois clothes.

15   In my literature classes, I learned the Working-class formula for reading. Each work in the textbook had a short "Author's Biography": "X X X, born in 19—in the province of X X X, is from a Worker's family. He joined the Revolution in 19—. He is a Revolutionary realist with a passionate love for the Party and Chinese Revolution. His work expresses the thoughts and emotions of the masses and sings praise to the prosperous socialist construction on all fronts of China." The teacher used the "Author's Biography" as a yardstick to measure the texts. We were taught to locate details in the texts that illustrated these summaries, such as words that expressed Workers' thoughts and emotions or events that illustrated the Workers' lives.

I learned a formula for Working-class writing in the composition classes. We were given sample essays and told to imitate them. The theme was always about how the collective taught the individual a lesson. I would write papers about labor-learning experiences or school-cleaning days, depending on the occasion of the collective activity closest to the assignment. To make each paper look different, I dressed it up with details about the date, the weather, the environment, or the appearance of the Master-worker who had taught me "the lesson." But as I became more and more fluent in the generic voice of the Working-class Student, I also became more and more self-conscious about the language we used at home.

For instance, in senior high we began to have English classes ("to study English for the Revolution," as the slogan on the cover of the textbook said), and I was given my first Chinese-English dictionary. There I discovered the English version of the term "class-struggle." (The Chinese characters for a school "class" and for a social "class" are different.) I had often used the English word "class" at home in sentences such as, "So and so has class," but I had not connected this sense of "class" with "class-struggle." Once the connection was made, I heard a second layer of meaning every time someone at home said a person had "class." The expression began to mean the person had the style and sophistication characteristic of the bourgeoisie. The word lost its innocence. I was uneasy about hearing that second layer of meaning because I was sure my parents did not hear the word that way. I felt that therefore I should not be hearing it that way either. Hearing the second layer of meaning made me wonder if I was losing my English.

My suspicion deepened when I noticed myself unconsciously merging and switching between the "reading" of home and the "reading" of school. Once I had to write a report on *The Revolutionary Family*, a book about an illiterate woman's awakening and growth as a Revolutionary through the deaths of her husband and all her children for the cause of the Revolution. In one scene the woman deliberated over whether or not she should encourage her youngest son to join the Revolution. Her memory of her husband's death made her afraid to encourage her son. Yet she also remembered her earlier married life and the first time her husband tried to explain the meaning of the Revolution to her. These memories made her feel she should encourage her son to continue the cause his father had begun.

I was moved by this scene. "Moved" was a word my mother and sisters used a lot when we discussed books. Our favorite moments in novels were moments of what I would now call internal conflict, moments which we said "moved" us. I remember that we were "moved" by Jane Eyre when she was torn between her sense of ethics, which compelled her to leave the man she loved, and her impulse to stay with the only man who had ever loved her. We were also moved by Agnes in *David Copperfield* because of the way she restrained her love for

David so that he could live happily with the woman he loved. My standard method of doing a book report was to model it on the review by the Publishing Bureau and to dress it up with detailed quotations from the book. The review of *The Revolutionary Family* emphasized the woman's Revolutionary spirit. I decided to use the scene that had moved me to illustrate this point. I wrote the report the night before it was due. When I had finished, I realized I couldn't possibly hand it in. Instead of illustrating her Revolutionary spirit, I had dwelled on her internal conflict, which could be seen as a moment of weak sentimentality that I should never have emphasized in a Revolutionary heroine. I wrote another report, taking care to illustrate the grandeur of her Revolutionary spirit by expanding on a quotation in which she decided that if the life of her son could change the lives of millions of sons, she should not begrudge his life for the cause of Revolution. I handed in my second version but kept the first in my desk.

20   I never showed it to anyone. I could never show it to people out-   20
side my family, because it had deviated so much from the reading enacted by the jacket review. Neither could I show it to my mother or sisters, because I was ashamed to have been so moved by such a "Revolutionary" book. My parents would have been shocked to learn that I could like such a book in the same way they liked Dickens. Writing this book report increased my fear that I was losing the command over both the "language of home" and the "language of school" that I had worked so hard to gain. I tried to remind myself that, if I could still tell when my reading or writing sounded incorrect, then I had retained my command over both languages. Yet I could no longer be confident of my command over either language because I had discovered that when I was not careful—or even when I was—my reading and writing often surprised me with its impurity. To prevent such impurity, I became very suspicious of my thoughts when I read or wrote. I was always asking myself why I was using this word, how I was using it, always afraid that I wasn't reading or writing correctly. What confused and frustrated me most was that I could not figure out why I was no longer able to read or write correctly without such painful deliberation.

I continued to read only because reading allowed me to keep my thoughts and confusion private. I hoped that somehow, if I watched myself carefully, I would figure out from the way I read whether I had really mastered the "languages." But writing became a dreadful chore. When I tried to keep a diary, I was so afraid that the voice of school might slip in that I could only list my daily activities. When I wrote for school, I worried that my Bourgeois sensibilities would betray me.

The more suspicious I became about the way I read and wrote, the more guilty I felt for losing the spontaneity with which I had learned to "use" these "languages." Writing the book report made me feel that my reading and writing in the "language" of either home or school could not be free of the interference of the other. But I was unable to acknowledge, grasp, or grapple with what I was experiencing, for both my parents and my teachers had suggested that, if I were a good student, such interference would and should not take place. I assumed that once I had "acquired" a discourse, I could simply switch it on and off every time I read and wrote as I would some electronic tool. Furthermore, I expected my readings and writings to come out in their correct forms whenever I switched the proper discourse on. I still regarded the discourse of home as natural and the discourse of school alien, but I never had doubted before that I could acquire both and switch them on and off according to the occasion.

When my experience in writing conflicted with what I thought should happen when I used each discourse, I rejected my experience because it contradicted what my parents and teachers had taught me. I shied away from writing to avoid what I assumed I should not experience. But trying to avoid what should not happen did not keep it from recurring whenever I had to write. Eventually my confusion and frustration over these recurring experiences compelled me to search for an explanation: how and why had I failed to learn what my parents and teachers had worked so hard to teach me?

I now think of the internal scene for my reading and writing about *The Revolutionary Family* as a heated discussion between myself, the voices of home, and those of school. The review on the back of the book, the sample student papers I came across in my composition classes, my philosophy teacher—these I heard as voices of one group. My parents and my home readings were the voices of an opposing group. But the conversation between these opposing voices in the internal scene of my writing was not as polite and respectful as the parlor scene Kenneth Burke has portrayed (see epigraph). Rather, these voices struggled to dominate the discussion, constantly incorporating, dismissing, or suppressing the arguments of each other, like the battles between the hegemonic and counter-hegemonic forces described in Raymond Williams' *Marxism and Literature* (108–14).

25   When I read *The Revolutionary Family* and wrote the first version 25
of my report, I began with a quotation from the review. The voices of
both home and school answered, clamoring to be heard. I tried to listen to one group and turn a deaf ear to the other. Both persisted. I negotiated my way through these conflicting voices, now agreeing with
one, now agreeing with the other. I formed a reading out of my interaction with both. Yet I was afraid to have done so because both
home and school had implied that I should speak in unison with only
one of these groups and stand away from the discussion rather than
participate in it.

My teachers and parents had persistently called my attention to
the intensity of the discussion taking place on the external social scene.
The story of my grandfather's failure and my father's success had from
my early childhood made me aware of the conflict between Western
and traditional Chinese cultures. My political education at school
added another dimension to the conflict; the war of Marxist-Maoism
against them both. Yet when my parents and teachers called my attention to the conflict, they stressed the anxiety of having to live
through China's transformation from a semi-feudal, semi-capitalist,
and semi-colonial society to a socialist one. Acquiring the discourse of
the dominant group was, to them, a means of seeking alliance with
that group and thus of surviving the whirlpool of cultural currents
around them. As a result, they modeled their pedagogical practices on
this utilitarian view of language. Being the eager student, I adopted
this view of language as a tool for survival. It came to dominate my
understanding of the discussion on the social and historical scene and
to restrict my ability to participate in that discussion.

To begin with, the metaphor of language as a tool for survival led
me to be passive in my use of discourse, to be a bystander in the discussion. In Burke's "parlor," everyone is involved in the discussion. As
it goes on through history, what we call "communal discourses"—arguments specific to particular political, social, economic, ethnic, sexual, and family groups—form, re-form and transform. To use a
discourse in such a scene is to participate in the argument and to contribute to the formation of the discourse. But when I was growing up,
I could not take on the burden of such an active role in the discussion. For both home and school presented the existent conventions of
the discourse each taught me as absolute laws for my action. They
turned verbal action into a tool, a set of conventions produced and

shaped prior to and outside of my own verbal acts. Because I saw language as a tool, I separated the process of producing the tool from the process of using it. The tool was made by someone else and was then acquired and used by me. How the others made it before I acquired it determined and guaranteed what it produced when I used it. I imagined that the more experienced and powerful members of the community were the ones responsible for making the tool. They were the ones who participated in the discussion and fought with opponents. When I used what they made, their labor and accomplishments would ensure the quality of my reading and writing. By using it, I could survive the heated discussion. When my immediate experience in writing the book report suggested that knowing the conventions of school did not guarantee the form and content of my report, when it suggested that I had to write the report with the work and responsibility I had assigned to those who wrote book reviews in the Publishing bureau, I thought I had lost the tool I had earlier acquired.

Another reason I could not take up an active role in the argument was that my parents and teachers contrived to provide a scene free of conflict for practicing my various languages. It was as if their experience had made them aware of the conflict between their discourse and other discourses and of the struggle involved in reproducing the conventions of any discourse on a scene where more than one discourse exists. They seemed convinced that such conflict and struggle would overwhelm someone still learning the discourse. Home and school each contrived a purified space where only one discourse was spoken and heard. In their choice of textbooks, in the way they spoke, and in the way they required me to speak, each jealously silenced any voice that threatened to break the unison of the scene. The homogeneity of home and of school implied that only one discourse could and should be relevant in each place. It led me to believe I should leave behind, turn a deaf ear to, or forget the discourse of the other when I crossed the boundary dividing them. I expected myself to set down one discourse whenever I took up another just as I would take off or put on a particular set of clothes for school or home.

Despite my parents' and teachers' attempts to keep home and school discrete, the internal conflict between the two discourses continued whenever I read or wrote. Although I tried to suppress the voice of one discourse in the name of the other, having to speak aloud in the voice I had just silenced each time I crossed the boundary kept both voices active in my mind. Every "I think . . . " from the voice of home or school brought forth a "However . . . " or a "But. . ." from the voice of the opponents. To identify with the voice of home or school, I had to negotiate through the conflicting voices of both by restating, taking back, qualifying my thoughts. I was unconsciously doing so when I did my book report. But I could not use the interaction comfortably and constructively. Both my parents and my teachers had implied that my job was to prevent that interaction from happening. My sense of having failed to accomplish what they had taught silenced me.

30   To use the interaction between the discourses of home and school   30 constructively, I would have to have seen reading or writing as a process in which I worked my way towards a stance through a dialectical process of identification and division. To identify with an ally, I would have to have grasped the distance between where he or she stood and where I was positioning myself. In taking a stance against an opponent, I would have to have grasped where my stance identified with the stance of my allies. Teetering along the "wavering line of pressure and counter-pressure" from both allies and opponents, I might have worked my way towards a stance of my own (Burke, *A Rhetoric of Motives,* 23). Moreover, I would have to have understood that the voices in my mind, like the participants in the parlor scene, were in constant flux. As I came into contact with new and different groups of people or read different books, voices entered and left. Each time I read or wrote, the stance I negotiated out of these voices would always be at some distance from the stances I worked out in my previous and my later readings or writings.

I could not conceive such a form of action for myself because I saw reading and writing as an expression of an established stance. In delineating the conventions of a discourse, my parents and teachers had synthesized the stance they saw as typical for a representative member of the community. Burke calls this the stance of a "god" or the "prototype"; Williams calls it the "official" or "possible" stance of the community. Through the metaphor of the survival tool, my parents and teachers had led me to assume I could automatically reproduce the official stance of the discourse I used. Therefore, when I did my book report on *The Revolutionary Family,* I expected my knowledge of the official stance set by the book review to ensure the actual stance of my report. As it happened, I began by trying to take the official stance of the review. Other voices interrupted. I answered back. In the process, I worked out a stance approximate but not identical to the official stance I began with. Yet the experience of having to labor to realize my knowledge of the official stance or to prevent myself from wandering away from it frustrated and confused me. For even though I had been actually reading and writing in a Burkean scene, I was afraid to participate actively in the discussion. I assumed it was my role to survive by staying out of it.

Not long ago, my daughter told me that it bothered her to hear her friend "talk wrong." Having come to the United States from China with little English, my daughter has become sensitive to the way English, as spoken by her teachers, operates. As a result, she has amazed her teachers with her success in picking up the language and in adapting to life at school. Her concern to speak the English taught in the classroom "correctly" makes her uncomfortable when she hears people using "ain't" or double negatives, which her teacher considers "improper." I see in her the me that had eagerly learned and used the discourse of the Working class at school. Yet while I was torn between the two conflicting worlds of school and home, she moves with seeming ease from the conversations she hears over the dinner table to her teacher's words in the classroom. My husband and I are proud of the good work she does at school. We are glad she is spared the kinds of conflict between home and school I experienced at her age. Yet as we watch her becoming more and more fluent in the language of the classroom, we wonder if, by enabling her to "survive" school, her very fluency will silence her when the scene of her reading and writing expands beyond that of the composition classroom.

For when I listen to my daughter, to students, and to some composition teachers talking about the teaching and learning of writing, I am often alarmed by the degree to which the metaphor of a survival tool dominates their understanding of language as it once dominated my own. I am especially concerned with the way some composition classes focus on turning the classroom into a monological scene for the students' reading and writing. Most of our students live in a world similar to my daughter's, somewhere between the purified world of the classroom and the complex world of my adolescence. When composition classes encourage these students to ignore those voices that seem irrelevant to the purified world of the classroom, most students are often able to do so without much struggle. Some of them are so adept at doing it that the whole process has for them become automatic.

However, beyond the classroom and beyond the limited range of these students' immediate lives lies a much more complex and dynamic social and historical scene. To help these students become actors in such a scene, perhaps we need to call their attention to voices that may seem irrelevant to the discourse we teach rather than encourage them to shut them out. For example, we might intentionally complicate the classroom scene by bringing into it discourses that stand at varying distances from the one we teach. We might encourage students to explore ways of practicing the conventions of the discourse they are learning by negotiating through these conflicting voices. We could also encourage them to see themselves as responsible for forming or transforming as well as preserving the discourse they are learning.

35   As I think about what we might do to complicate the external and   35 internal scenes of our students' writing, I hear my parents and teachers saying: "Not now. Keep them from the wrangle of the marketplace until they have acquired the discourse and are skilled at using it." And I answer: "Don't teach them to 'survive' the whirlpool of crosscurrents by avoiding it. Use the classroom to moderate the currents. Moderate the currents, but teach them from the beginning to struggle." When I think of the ways in which the teaching of reading and writing as classroom activities can frustrate the development of students, I am almost grateful for the overwhelming complexity of the circumstances in which I grew up. For it was this complexity that kept me from losing sight of the effort and choice involved in reading or writing with and through a discourse.

References

Burke, Kenneth. *The Philosophy of Literary Form: Studies in Symbolic Action.* 2nd ed. Baton Rouge: Louisiana State UP, 1967.
———. *A Rhetoric of Motives.* Berkeley: U of California P, 1969.
Freire, Paulo. *Pedagogy of the Oppressed.* Trans. M. B. Ramos. New York: Continuum, 1970.
Williams, Raymond. *Marxism and Literature.* New York: Oxford UP, 1977.

On Friendship
Margaret Mead and Rhoda Metraux

Margaret Mead (1901–1978), an anthropologist with the American Museum of Natural History in New York City, conducted many field studies in Pacific areas, including Bali, New Guinea, and Samoa. Mead wrote both acade-mic and popular books, including Coming of Age in Samoa *(1928),* Growing Up in New Guinea *(1930), and* Sex and Temperament in Three Primitive Societies *(1935). Anthropologist Rhoda Metraux (1914–), who also worked at the American Museum of Natural History in New York City, performed field work in several Caribbean and South American countries. Mead and Me-traux coauthored* Themes in French Culture *and collab-orated on a series of articles written for* Redbook, *which were collected and published as* A Way of Seeing. *In this essay, an excerpt from* A Way of Seeing, *Mead and Me-traux discuss how the concept of friendship varies from country to country.*

1   ew Americans stay put for a lifetime. We move from town to   1
F city to suburb, from high school to college in a different state, from a job in one region to a better job elsewhere, from the home where we raise our children to the home where we plan to live in retirement. With each move we are forever making new friends, who become part of our new life at that time.

For many of us the summer is a special time for forming new friendships. Today millions of Americans vacation abroad, and they go not only to see new sights but also—in those places where they do not feel too strange—with the hope of meeting new people. No one really expects a vacation trip to produce a close friend. But surely the beginning of a friendship is possible? Surely in every country people value friendship?

They do. The difficulty when strangers from two countries meet is not a lack of appreciation of friendship, but different expectations about what constitutes friendship and how it comes into being. In those European countries that Americans are most likely to visit, friendship is quite sharply distinguished from other, more casual relations, and is differently related to family life. For a Frenchman, a German or an Englishman friendship is usually more particularized and carries a heavier burden of commitment.

But as we use the word, "friend" can be applied to a wide range of relationships—to someone one has known for a few weeks in a new place, to a close business associate, to a childhood playmate, to a man or woman, to a trusted confidant. There are real differences among these relations for Americans—a friendship may be superficial, casual, situational or deep and enduring. But to a European, who sees only our surface behavior, the differences are not clear.

5   As they see it, people known and accepted temporarily, casually,   5
flow in and out of Americans' homes with little ceremony and often with little personal commitment. They may be parents of the children's friends, house guests of neighbors, members of a committee, business associates from another town or even another country. Coming as a guest into an American home, the European visitor finds no visible landmarks. The atmosphere is relaxed. Most people, old and young, are called by first names.

Who, then, is a friend?

Even simple translation from one language to another is difficult. "You see," a Frenchman explains, "if I were to say to you in France, 'This is my good friend,' that person would not be as close to me as someone about whom I said only, 'This is my friend.' Anyone about whom I have to say *more* is really less."

In France, as in many European countries, friends generally are of the same sex, and friendship is seen as basically a relationship between men. Frenchwomen laugh at the idea that "women can't be friends," but they also admit sometimes that for women "it's a different thing." And many French people doubt the possibility of a friendship between a man and a woman. There is also the kind of relationship within a group—men and women who have worked together for a long time, who may be very close, sharing great loyalty and warmth of feeling. They may call one another *copains*—a word that in English becomes "friends" but has more the feeling of "pals" or "buddies." In French eyes this is not friendship, although two members of such a group may well be friends.

For the French, friendship is a one-to-one relationship that demands a keen awareness of the other person's intellect, temperament and particular interests. A friend is someone who draws out your own best qualities, with whom you sparkle and become more of whatever the friendship draws upon. Your political philosophy assumes more depth, appreciation of a play becomes sharper, taste in food or wine is accentuated, enjoyment of a sport is intensified.

10 And French friendships are compartmentalized. A man may play 10 chess with a friend for thirty years without knowing his political opinion, or he may talk politics with him for as long a time without knowing about his personal life. Different friends fill different niches in each person's life. These friendships are not made part of family life. A friend is not expected to spend evenings being nice to children or courteous to a deaf grandmother. These duties, also serious and enjoined, are primarily for relatives. Men who are friends may meet in a café. Intellectual friends may meet in larger groups for evenings of conversation. Working people may meet in the little *bistro* where they drink and talk, far from the family. Marriage does not affect such friendships; wives do not have to be taken into account.

In the past in France, friendships of this kind seldom were open to any but intellectual women. Since most women's lives centered on their homes, their warmest relations with other women often went back to their girlhood. The special relationship of friendship is based on what the French value most—on the mind, on compatibility of outlook, on vivid awareness of some chosen area of life.

Friendship heightens the sense of each person's individuality. Other relationships commanding as great loyalty and devotion have a different meaning. In World War II the first resistance groups formed in Paris were built on the foundation of *les copains*. But significantly, as time went on these little groups, whose lives rested in one another's hands, called themselves "families." Where each had a total responsibility for all, it was kinship ties that provided the model. And even today such ties, crossing every line of class and personal interest, remain binding on the survivors of these small, secret bands.

In Germany, in contrast with France, friendship is much more articulately a matter of feeling. Adolescents, boys and girls, form deeply sentimental attachments, walk and talk together—not so much to polish their wits as to share their hopes and fears and dreams, to form a common front against the world of schools and family and to join in a kind of mutual discovery of each other's and their own inner life. Within the family, the closest relationship over a lifetime is between brothers and sisters. Outside the family, men and women find in their closest friends of the same sex the devotion of a sister, the loyalty of a brother. Appropriately, in Germany friends usually are brought into the family. Children call their father's and their mother's friends "uncle" and "aunt." Between French friends, who have chosen each other for the congeniality of their point of view, lively disagreement and sharpness of argument are the breath of life. But for Germans, whose friendships are based on mutuality of feeling, deep disagreement on any subject that matters to both is regarded as a tragedy. Like ties of kinship, ties of friendship are meant to be irrevocably binding. Young Germans who come to the United States have a great difficulty in establishing such friendships with Americans. We view friendship more tentatively, subject to changes in intensity as people move, change their jobs, marry, or discover new interests.

English friendships follow still a different pattern. Their basis is shared activity. Activities at different stages of life may be of very different kinds—discovering a common interest in school, serving together in the armed forces, taking part in a foreign mission, staying in the same country house during a crisis. In the midst of the activity, whatever it may be, people fall into step—sometimes two men or two women, sometimes two couples, sometimes three people—and find that they walk or play a game or tell stories or serve on a tiresome and exacting committee with the same easy anticipation of what each will do day by day or in some critical situation. Americans who have made English friends comment that, even years later, "you can take up just where you left off." Meeting after a long interval, friends are like a couple who begin to dance again when the orchestra strikes up after a pause. English friendships are formed outside the family circle, but they are not, as in Germany, contrapuntal to the family nor are they, as in France, separated from the family. And a break in an English friendship comes not necessarily as a result of some irreconcilable difference of viewpoint or feeling but instead as a result of misjudgment, where one friend seriously misjudges how the other will think or feel or act, so that suddenly they are out of step.

15   What, then, is friendship? Looking at these different styles, in- 15 cluding our own, each of which is related to a whole way of life, are there common elements? There is the recognition that friendship, in contrast with kinship, invokes freedom of choice. A friend is someone who chooses and is chosen. Related to this is the sense each friend gives the other of being a special individual, on whatever grounds this recognition is based. And between friends there is inevitably a kind of equality of give and take. These similarities make the bridge between societies possible, and the American's characteristic openness to different styles of relationships makes it possible for him to find new friends abroad with whom he feels at home.

Territorial Behavior
Desmond Morris

Desmond Morris (1928-), an Englishman, studied at Birmingham University and received his Ph.D. in zoology from Oxford University. He has worked in animal research, was a curator at the Zoological Society of London, and has been involved in many television programs on animal and human behavior. He is also a painter and has been a director of the Institute of Contemporary Arts in London. In America he is known mostly for his books, which popularize scientific observations and explanations of human and animal behavior: The Naked Ape *(1967),* The Human Zoo *(1969),* Manwatching *(1977), and* The Soccer Tribe *(1981). The following essay was published in* Manwatching. *One hallmark of Morris's style is an ease of explaining scientifically based concepts in simple language. Here he explains how a key human characteristic, the result of millions of years of tribal living, persists into modern life, though in a modern transformation.*

1 A territory is a defended space. In the broadest sense, there are three kinds of human territory: tribal, family and personal.

It is rare for people to be driven to physical fighting in defense of these "owned" spaces, but fight they will, if pushed to the limit. The invading army encroaching on national territory, the gang moving into a rival district, the trespasser climbing into an orchard, the burglar breaking into a house, the bully pushing to the front of a queue, the driver trying to steal a parking space, all of these intruders are liable to be met with resistance varying from the vigorous to the

From *Manwatching: A Field Guide to Human Behavior* by Desmond Morris. Published in 1977 by Harry N. Abrams, Inc. New York. Copyright © 1977 by Random House Group, Ltd .

savagely violent. Even if the law is on the side of the intruder, the urge to protect a territory may be so strong that otherwise peaceful citizens abandon all their usual controls and inhibitions. Attempts to evict families from their homes, no matter how socially valid the reasons, can lead to siege conditions reminiscent of the defense of a medieval fortress.

The fact that these upheavals are so rare is a measure of the success of Territorial Signals as a system of dispute prevention. It is sometimes cynically stated that "all property is theft," but in reality it is the opposite. Property, as owned space which is *displayed* as owned space, is a special kind of sharing system which reduces fighting much more than it causes it. Man is a cooperative species, but he is also competitive, and his struggle for dominance has to be structured in some way if chaos is to be avoided, The establishment of territorial rights is one such structure. It limits dominance geographically. I am dominant in my territory and you are dominant in yours. In other words, dominance is shared out spatially, and we all have some. Even if I am weak and unintelligent and you can dominate me when we meet on neutral ground, I can still enjoy a thoroughly dominant role as soon as I retreat to my private base. Be it ever so humble, there is no place like a home territory.

Of course, I can still be intimidated by a particularly dominant individual who enters my home base, but his encroachment will be dangerous for him and he will think twice about it, because he will know that here my urge to resist will be dramatically magnified and my usual subservience banished. Insulted at the heart of my own territory, I may easily explode into battle—either symbolic or real—with a result that may be damaging to both of us.

In order for this to work, each territory has to be plainly advertised as such. Just as a dog cocks its leg to deposit its personal scent on the trees in its locality, so the human animal cocks its leg symbolically all over his home base. But because we are predominantly visual animals we employ mostly visual signals, and it is worth asking how we do this at the three levels: tribal, family and personal.

First: the Tribal Territory. We evolved as tribal animals, living in comparatively small groups, probably of less than a hundred, and we existed like that for millions of years. It is our basic social unit, a group in which everyone knows everyone else. Essentially, the tribal territory consisted of a home base surrounded by extended hunting grounds.

Any neighbouring tribe intruding on our social space would be re-pelled and driven away. As these early tribes swelled into agricultural super-tribes, and eventually into industrial nations, their territorial de-fence systems became increasingly elaborate. The tiny, ancient home base of the hunting tribe became the great capital city, the primitive war-paint became the flags, emblems, uniforms and regalia of the spe-cialized military, and the war-chants became national anthems, marching songs and bugle calls. Territorial boundary-lines hardened into fixed borders, often conspicuously patrolled and punctuated with defensive structures—forts and lookout posts, check-points and great walls, and, today, customs barriers.

Today each nation flies its own flag, a symbolic embodiment of its territorial status. But patriotism is not enough. The ancient tribal hunter lurking inside each citizen finds himself unsatisfied by mem-bership of such a vast conglomeration of individuals, most of whom are totally unknown to him personally. He does his best to feel that he shares a common territorial defence with them all, but the scale of the operation has become inhuman. It is hard to feel a sense of belonging with a tribe of fifty million or more. His answer is to form sub-groups, nearer to his ancient pattern, smaller and more personally known to him—the local club, the teenage gang, the union, the specialist soci-ety, the sports association, the political party, the college fraternity, the social clique, the protest group, and the rest. Rare indeed is the indi-vidual who does not belong to at least one of these splinter groups, and take from it a sense of tribal allegiance and brotherhood. Typical of all these groups is the development of Territorial Signals–badges, costumes, headquarters, banners, slogans, and all the other displays of group identity. This is where the action is, in terms of tribal territori-alism, and only when a major war breaks out does the emphasis shift upwards to the higher group level of the nation.

Each of these modern pseudo-tribes sets up its own special kind of home base. In extreme cases non-members are totally excluded, in others they are allowed in as visitors with limited rights and under a control system of special rules. In many ways they are like miniature nations, with their own flags and emblems and their own border guards. The exclusive club has its own "customs barrier": the doorman who checks your "passport" (your membership card) and prevents strangers from passing in unchallenged. There is a government: the club committee; and often special displays of the tribal elders: the photographs or portraits of previous officials on the walls. At the heart of the specialized territories there is a powerful feeling of security and importance, a sense of shared defence against the outside world. Much of the club chatter, both serious and joking, directs itself against the rottenness of everything outside the club boundaries—in that "other world" beyond the protected portals.

In social organizations which embody a strong class system, such as military units and large business concerns, there are many territorial rules, often unspoken, which interfere with the official hierarchy. High-status individuals, such as officers or managers, could in theory enter any of the regions occupied by the lower levels in the peck order, but they limit this power in a striking way. An officer seldom enters a sergeant's mess or a barrack room unless it is for a formal inspection. He respects those regions as alien territories even though he has the power to go there by virtue of his dominant role. And in businesses, part of the appeal of unions, over and above their obvious functions, is that with their officials, headquarters and meetings they add a sense of territorial power for the staff workers. It is almost as if each military organization and business concern consists of two warring tribes: the officers versus the other ranks, and the management versus the workers. Each has its special home base within the system, and the territorial defence pattern thrusts itself into what, on the surface, is a pure social hierarchy. Negotiations between managements and unions are tribal battles fought out over the neutral ground of a boardroom table, and are as much concerned with territorial display as they are with resolving problems of wages and conditions. Indeed, if one side gives in too quickly and accepts the other's demands, the victors feel strangely cheated and deeply suspicious that it may be a trick. What they are missing is the protracted sequence of ritual and counter-ritual that keeps alive their group territorial identity.

Likewise, many of the hostile displays of sports fans and teenage gangs are primarily concerned with displaying their group image to rival fan-clubs and gangs. Except in rare cases, they do not attack one another's headquarters, drive out the occupants, and reduce them to a submissive, subordinate condition. It is enough to have scuffles on the borderlands between the two rival territories. This is particularly clear at football matches, where the fan-club headquarters becomes temporarily shifted from the clubhouse to a section of the stands, and where minor fighting breaks out at the unofficial boundary line between the massed groups of rival supporters. Newspaper reports play up the few accidents and injuries which do occur on such occasions, but when these are studied in relation to the total numbers of displaying fans involved it is clear that the serious incidents represent only a tiny fraction of the overall group behaviour. For every actual punch or kick there are a thousand war-cries, war-dances, chants and gestures.

Second: the Family Territory. Essentially, the family is a breeding unit and the family territory is a breeding ground, At the centre of this space, there is the nest—the bedroom—where, tucked up in bed, we feel at our most territorially secure. In a typical house the bedroom is upstairs, where a safe nest should be. This puts it farther away from the entrance hall, the area where contact is made, intermittently, with the outside world. The less private reception rooms, where intruders are allowed access, are the next line of defence. Beyond them, outside the walls of the building, there is often a symbolic remnant of the ancient feeding grounds—a garden. Its symbolism often extends to the plants and animals it contains, which cease to be nutritional and become merely decorative—flowers and pets. But like a true territorial space it has a conspicuously displayed boundary-line, the garden fence, wall, or railings. Often no more than a token barrier, this is the outer territorial demarcation, separating the private world of the family from the public world beyond. To cross it puts any visitor or intruder at an immediate disadvantage. As he crosses the threshold, his dominance wanes, slightly but unmistakably. He is entering an area where he senses that he must ask permission to do simple things that he would consider a right elsewhere. Without lifting a finger, the territorial owners exert their dominance. This is done by all the hundreds of small ownership "markers" they have deposited on their family territory: the ornaments, the "possessed" objects positioned in the rooms and on the walls; the furnishings, the furniture, the colours, the patterns, all owner-chosen and all making this particular home base unique to them.

It is one of the tragedies of modern architecture that there has been a standardization of these vital territorial living-units. One of the most important aspects of a home is that it should be similar to other homes only in a general way, and that in detail it should have many differences, making it a *particular* home. Unfortunately, it is cheaper to build a row of houses, or a block of flats, so that all the family living-units are identical, but the territorial urge rebels against this trend and house-owners struggle as best they can to make their mark on their mass-produced properties. They do this with garden-design, with front-door colours, with curtain patterns, with wallpaper and all the other decorative elements that together create a unique and different family environment. Only when they have completed this nest-building do they feel truly "at home" and secure.

When they venture forth as a family unit they repeat the process in a minor way. On a day-trip to the seaside, they load the car with personal belongings and it becomes their temporary, portable territory. Arriving at the beach they stake out a small territorial claim, marking it with rugs, towels, baskets and other belongings to which they can return from their seaboard wanderings. Even if they all leave it at once to bathe, it retains a characteristic territorial quality and other family groups arriving will recognize this by setting up their own "home" bases at a respectful distance. Only when the whole beach has filled up with these marked spaces will newcomers start to position themselves in such a way the inter-base distance becomes reduced. Forced to pitch between several existing beach territories they will feel a momentary sensation of intrusion, and the established "owners" will feel a similar sensation of invasion, even though they are not being directly inconvenienced.

The same territorial scene is being played out in parks and fields and on riverbanks, wherever family groups gather in their clustered units. But if rivalry for spaces creates mild feelings of hostility, it is true to say that, without the territorial system of sharing and space-limited dominance, there would be chaotic disorder.

15   Third: the Personal Space. If a man enters a waiting-room and sits 15 at one end of a long row of empty chairs, it is possible to predict where the next man to enter will seat himself. He will not sit next to the first man, nor will he sit at the far end, right away from him. He will choose a position about halfway between these two points. The next man to enter will take the largest gap left, and sit roughly in the middle of that, and so on, until eventually the latest newcomer will be forced to select a seat that places him right next to one of the already seated men. Similar patterns can be observed in cinemas, public urinals, aeroplanes, trains and buses. This is a reflection of the fact that we all carry with us, everywhere we go, a portable territory called a Personal Space. If people move inside this space, we feel threatened. If they keep too far

outside it, we feel rejected. The result is a subtle series of spatial adjustments, usually operating quite unconsciously and producing ideal compromises as far as this is possible. If a situation becomes too crowded, then we adjust our reactions accordingly and allow our personal space to shrink. Jammed into an elevator, a rush-hour compartment, or a packed room, we give up altogether and allow body-to-body contact, but when we relinquish our Personal Space in this way, we adopt certain special techniques. In essence, what we do is to convert these other bodies into "nonpersons." We studiously ignore them, and they us. We try not to face them if we can possibly avoid it. We wipe all expressiveness from our faces, letting them go blank. We may look up at the ceiling or down at the floor, and we reduce body movements to a minimum. Packed together like sardines in a tin, we stand dumbly still, sending out as few social signals as possible.

Even if the crowding is less severe, we still tend to cut down our social interactions in the presence of large numbers. Careful observations of children in play groups revealed that if they are high density groupings there is less social interaction between the individual children, even though there is theoretically more opportunity for such contacts. At the same time, the high-density groups show a higher frequency of aggressive and destructive behaviour patterns in their play. Personal Space—"elbow room"—is a vital commodity for the human animal, and one that cannot be ignored without risking serious trouble.

Of course, we all enjoy the excitement of being in a crowd, and this reaction cannot be ignored. But there are crowds and crowds. It is pleasant enough to be in a "spectator crowd," but not so appealing to find yourself in the middle of a rush-hour crush. The difference between the two is that the spectator crowd is all facing in the same direction and concentrating on a distant point of interest. Attending a theatre, there are twinges of rising hostility towards the stranger who sits down immediately in front of you or the one who squeezes into the seat next to you. The shared armrest can become a polite, but distinct, territorial boundary-dispute region. However, as soon as the show begins, these invasions of Personal Space are forgotten and the attention is focused beyond the small space where the crowding is taking place. Now, each member of the audience feels himself spatially related, not to his cramped neighbours, but to the actor on the stage, and this distance is, if anything, too great. In the rush-hour crowd, by contrast, each member of the pushing throng is competing with his neighbours all the time. There is no escape to a spacial relation with a distant actor, only the pushing, shoving bodies all around.

Those of us who have to spend a great deal of time in crowded conditions become gradually better able to adjust, but no one can ever become completely immune to invasions of Personal Space. This is because they remain forever associated with either powerful hostile or equally powerful loving feelings. All through our childhood we have been held to be loved and held to be hurt, and anyone who invades our Personal Space when we are adults is, in effect, threatening to extend his behaviour into one of these two highly charged areas of human interaction. Even if his motives are clearly neither hostile nor sexual, we still find it hard to suppress our reactions to his close approach. Unfortunately, different countries have different ideas about exactly how close is close. It is easy enough to test your own "space reaction": when you are talking to someone in the street or in any open space, reach out with your arm and see where the nearest point on his body comes. If you hail from western Europe, you will find that he is at roughly fingertip distance from you. In other words, as you reach out, your fingertips will just about make contact with his shoulder. If you come from eastern Europe you will find you are standing at "wrist distance." If you come from the Mediterranean region you will find that you are much closer to your companion, at little more than "elbow distance."

Trouble begins when a member of one of these cultures meets and talks to one from another. Say a British diplomat meets an Italian or an Arab diplomat at an embassy function. They start talking in a friendly way, but soon the fingertips man begins to feel uneasy. Without knowing quite why, he starts to back away gently from his companion. The companion edges forward again. Each tries in this way to set up a Personal Space relationship that suits his own background. But it is impossible to do. Every time the Mediterranean diplomat advances to a distance that feels comfortable for him, the British diplomat feels threatened. Every time the Briton moves back, the other feels rejected. Attempts to adjust this situation often lead to a talking pair shifting slowly across a room, and many an embassy reception is dotted with western-European fingertip-distance men pinned against the walls by eager elbow-distance men. Until such differences are fully understood, and allowances made, these minor differences in "body territories" will continue to act as an alienation factor which may interfere in a subtle way with diplomatic harmony and other forms of international transaction.

20   If there are distance problems when engaged in conversation, then there are clearly going to be even bigger difficulties where people must work privately in a shared space. Close proximity of others, pressing against the invisible boundaries of our personal body-territory, makes it difficult to concentrate on non-social matters. Flatmates, students sharing a study, sailors in the cramped quarters of a ship, and office staff in crowded workplaces, all have to face this problem. They solve it by "cocooning." They use a variety of devices to shut themselves off from the others present. The best possible cocoon, of course, is a small private room—a den, a private office, a study or a studio—which physically obscures the presence of other nearby territory-owners. This is the ideal situation for non-social work, but the space-sharers cannot enjoy this luxury. Their cocooning must be symbolic. They may, in certain cases, be able to erect small physical barriers, such as screens and partitions, which give substance to their invisible Personal Space boundaries, but when this cannot be done, other means must be sought. One of these is the "favoured object." Each space-sharer develops a preference, repeatedly expressed until it becomes a fixed pattern, for a particular chair, or table, or alcove. Others come to respect this, and friction is reduced. This system is often formally arranged (this is my desk, that is yours), but even where it is not, favoured places soon develop. Professor Smith has a favourite chair in the library. It is not formally his, but he always uses it and others avoid it. Seats around a mess-room table, or a board-room table, become almost personal property for specific individuals. Even in the home, father has his favourite chair for reading the newspaper or watching television. Another device is the blinkers-posture. Just as a horse that overreacts to other horses and the distractions of the noisy racecourse is given a pair of blinkers to shield its eyes, so people studying privately in a public place put on pseudo-blinkers in the form of shielding hands. Resting their elbows on the table, they sit with their hands screening their eyes from the scene on either side.

A third method of reinforcing the body-territory is to use personal markers. Books, papers and other personal belongings are scattered around the favoured site to render it more privately owned in the eyes of companions. Spreading out one's belongings is a well-known trick in public-transport situations, where a traveller tries to give the impression that seats next to him are taken. In many contexts carefully arranged personal markers can act as an effective territorial display, even in the absence of the territory owner. Experiments in a library revealed that placing a pile of magazines on the table in one seating position successfully reserved that place for an average of 77 minutes. If a sports-jacket was added, draped over the chair, then the "reservation effect" lasted for over two hours.

In these ways, we strengthen the defences of our Personal Spaces, keeping out intruders with the minimum of open hostility. As with all territorial behaviour, the object is to defend space with signals rather than with fists and at all three levels—the tribal, the family and the personal—it is a remarkably efficient system of space-sharing. It does not always seem so, because newspapers and newscasts inevitably magnify the exceptions and dwell on those cases where the signals have failed and wars have broken out, gangs have fought, neighbouring families have feuded, or colleagues have clashed, but for every territorial signal that has failed, there are millions of others that have not. They do not rate a mention in the news, but they nevertheless constitute a dominant feature of human society—the society of a remarkably territorial animal.

Shooting an Elephant

George Orwell

George Orwell is the pen name used by the British author Eric Blair (1903–1950). Orwell was born in the Indian village of Motihari, near Nepal, where his father was stationed in the Civil Service. India was then part of the British Empire; Orwell's grandfather too had served the Empire in the Indian Army. From 1907 to 1922 Orwell lived in England, returning to India and Burma and a position in the Imperial Police, which he held until 1927. This is the period about which he writes in "Shooting an Elephant." Thereafter he lived in England, Paris, Spain, and elsewhere, writing on a wide range of topics. He fought in the Spanish Civil War and was actively engaged in several political movements, always against totalitarianism of any kind. He is best known today for two novels of political satire: Animal Farm *(1945) and* 1984 *(1949). He was also a prolific journalist and essayist, with his essays collected in five volumes. "Shooting an Elephant" was first published in 1936 and later collected in a book of the same name in 1950. Note that Orwell is writing as an older, wiser man about events that took place when he was in his early twenties some two decades previously. This combined perspective of the young man experiencing the incident and the older man looking back on it is part of the rich reading experience.*

1   In Moulmein, in Lower Burma, I was hated by large numbers of   1
people—the only time in my life that I have been important
enough for this to happen to me. I was sub-divisional police officer
of the town, and in an aimless, petty, kind of way anti-European feel-

From *Shooting an Elephant and Other Essays* by George Orwell. Published by Harcourt Brace and Company. Harcourt Brace and Company and Heath & Co., Ltd.

ing was very bitter. No one had the guts to raise a riot, but if a European woman went through the bazaars alone somebody would probably spit betel juice over her dress. As a police officer I was an obvious target and was baited whenever it seemed safe to do so. When a nimble Burman tripped me up on the football field and the referee (another Burman) looked the other way, the crowd yelled with hideous laughter. This happened more than once. In the end the sneering yellow faces of young men that met me everywhere, the insults hooted after me when I was at a safe distance, got badly on my nerves. The young Buddhist priests were the worst of all. There were several thousand of them in the town and none of them seemed to have anything to do except stand on street corners and jeer at Europeans.

All this was perplexing and upsetting. For at that time I had already made up my mind that imperialism was an evil thing and the sooner I chucked up my job and got out of it the better. Theoretically—and secretly, of course—I was all for the Burmese and all against their oppressors, the British. As for the job I was doing, I hated it more bitterly than I can perhaps make clear. In a job like that you see the dirty work of Empire at close quarters. The wretched prisoners huddling in the stinking cages of the lock-ups, the grey, cowed faces of the long-term convicts, the scarred buttocks of the men who had been flogged with bamboos—all these oppressed me with an intolerable sense of guilt. But I could get nothing into perspective. I was young and ill-educated and I had had to think out my problems in the utter silence that is imposed on every Englishman in the East. I did not even know that the British Empire is dying, still less did I know that it is a great deal better than the younger empires that are going to supplant it. All I knew was that I was stuck between my hatred of the empire I served and my rage against the evil-spirited little beasts who tried to make my job impossible. With one part of my mind I thought of the British Raj as an unbreakable tyranny, as something clamped down, in *saecula saeculorum,* upon the will of prostrate peoples; with another part I thought that the greatest joy in the world would be to drive a bayonet into a Buddhist priest's guts. Feelings like these are the normal by-products of imperialism; ask any Anglo-Indian official, if you can catch him off duty.

One day something happened which in a roundabout way was enlightening. It was a tiny incident in itself, but it gave me a better glimpse than I had had before of the real nature of imperialism—the real motives for which despotic governments act. Early one morning the sub-inspector at a police station the other end of the town rang me up on the 'phone and said that an elephant was ravaging the bazaar. Would I please come and do something about it? I did not know what I could do, but I wanted to see what was happening and I got on to a pony and started out. I took my rifle, an old .44 Winchester and much too small to kill an elephant, but I thought the noise might be useful *in terrorem*. Various Burmans stopped me on the way and told me about the elephant's doings. It was not, of course, a wild elephant, but a tame one which had gone "must." It had been chained up, as tame elephants always are when their attack of "must" is due, but on the previous night it had broken its chain and escaped. Its mahout, the only person who could manage it when it was in that state, had set out in pursuit, but had taken the wrong direction and was now twelve hours' journey away, and in the morning the elephant had suddenly reappeared in the town. The Burmese population had no weapons and were quite helpless against it. It had already destroyed somebody's bamboo hut, killed a cow and raided some fruit-stalls and devoured the stock; also it had met the municipal rubbish van and, when the driver jumped out and took to his heels, had turned the van over and inflicted violence upon it.

The Burmese sub-inspector and some Indian constables were waiting for me in the quarter where the elephant had been seen. It was a very poor quarter, a labyrinth of squalid bamboo huts, thatched with palm-leaf, winding all over a steep hillside. I remember that it was a cloudy, stuffy, morning at the beginning of the rains. We began questioning the people as to where the elephant had gone and, as usual, failed to get any definite information. That is invariably the case in the East; a story always sounds clear enough at a distance, but the nearer you get to the scene of events the vaguer it becomes. Some of the people said that the elephant had gone in one direction, some said that he had gone in another, some professed not even to have heard of any elephant. I had almost made up my mind that the whole story was a pack of lies, when we heard yells a little distance away. There was a loud, scandalized cry of "Go away, child! Go away this instant!" and an old woman with a switch in her hand came round the corner of a hut, violently shooing away a crowd of naked children. Some more women followed, clicking their tongues and exclaiming; evidently there was something that the children ought not to have seen. I rounded the hut and saw a man's dead body sprawling in the mud. He was an Indian, a black Dravidian coolie, almost naked, and he could not have been dead many minutes. The people said that the elephant had come suddenly upon him round the corner of the hut, caught him with its trunk, put its foot on his back and ground him into the earth. This was the rainy season and the ground was soft, and his face had scored a trench a foot deep and a couple of yards long. He was lying on his belly with arms crucified and head sharply twisted to one side. His face was coated with mud, the eyes wide open, the teeth bared and grinning with an expression of unendurable agony. (Never tell me, by the way, that the dead look peaceful. Most of the corpses I have seen looked devilish.) The friction of the great beast's foot had stripped the skin from his back as neatly as one skins a rabbit. As soon as I saw the dead man I sent an orderly to a friend's house nearby to borrow an elephant rifle. I had already sent back the pony, not wanting it to go mad with fright and throw me if it smelt the elephant.

5   The orderly came back in a few minutes with a rifle and five cartridges, and meanwhile some Burmans had arrived and told us that the elephant was in the paddy fields below, only a few hundred yards away. As I started forward practically the whole population of the quarter flocked out of the houses and followed me. They had seen the rifle and were all shouting excitedly that I was going to shoot the elephant. They had not shown much interest in the elephant when he was merely ravaging their homes, but it was different now that he was going to be shot. It was a bit of fun to them, as it would be to an English crowd; besides they wanted the meat. It made me vaguely uneasy. I had no intention of shooting the elephant—I had merely sent for the rifle to defend myself if necessary—and it is always unnerving to have a crowd following you. I marched down the hill, looking and feeling a fool, with the rifle over my shoulder and an evergrowing army of people jostling at my heels. At the bottom, when you got away from the huts, there was a metalled road and beyond that a miry waste of paddy fields a thousand yards across, not yet ploughed but soggy from the first rains and dotted with coarse grass. The elephant was standing eight yards from the road, his left side towards us. He took not the slightest notice of the crowd's approach. He was tearing up bunches of grass, beating them against his knees to clean them and stuffing them into his mouth.

    I had halted on the road. As soon as I saw the elephant I knew with perfect certainty that I ought not to shoot him. It is a serious matter to shoot a working elephant—it is comparable to destroying a huge and costly piece of machinery—and obviously one ought not to do it if it can possibly be avoided. And at that distance, peacefully eating, the elephant looked no more dangerous than a cow. I thought then and I think now that his attack of "must" was already passing off; in which case he would merely wander harmlessly about until the mahout came back and caught him. Moreover, I did not in the least want to shoot him. I decided that I would watch him for a little while to make sure that he did not turn savage again, and then go home.

But at that moment I glanced round at the crowd that had followed me. It was an immense crowd, two thousand at the least and growing every minute. It blocked the road for a long distance on either side. I looked at the sea of yellow faces above the garish clothes—faces all happy and excited over this bit of fun, all certain that the elephant was going to be shot. They were watching me as they would watch a conjurer about to perform a trick. They did not like me, but with the magical rifle in my hands I was momentarily worth watching. And suddenly I realized that I should have to shoot the elephant after all. The people expected it of me and I had got to do it; I could feel their two thousand wills pressing me forward, irresistibly. And it was at this moment, as I stood there with the rifle in my hands, that I first grasped the hollowness, the futility of the white man's dominion in the East. Here was I, the white man with his gun, standing in front of the unarmed native crowd—seemingly the leading actor of the piece; but in reality I was only an absurd puppet pushed to and fro by the will of those yellow faces behind. I perceived in this moment that when the white man turns tyrant it is his own freedom that he destroys. He becomes a sort of hollow, posing dummy, the conventionalized figure of a sahib. For it is the condition of his rule that he shall spend his life in trying to impress the "natives," and so in every crisis he has got to do what the "natives" expect of him. He wears a mask, and his face grows to fit it. I had got to shoot the elephant. I had committed myself to doing it when I sent for the rifle. A sahib has got to act like a sahib; he has got to appear resolute, to know his own mind and do definite things. To come all that way, rifle in hand, with a thousand people marching at my heels, and then to trail feebly away, having done nothing—no, that was impossible. The crowd would laugh at me. And my whole life, every white man's life in the East, was one long struggle not to be laughed at.

But I did not want to shoot the elephant. I watched him beating his bunch of grass against his knees, with that preoccupied grandmotherly air that elephants have. It seemed to me that it would be murder to shoot him. At that age I was not squeamish about killing animals, but I had never shot an elephant and never wanted to. (Somehow it always seems worse to kill a *large* animal.) Besides, there was the beast's owner to be considered. Alive, the elephant was worth at least a hundred pounds; dead, he would only be worth the value of his tusks, five pounds, possibly. But I had got to act quickly. I turned to some experienced-looking Burmans who had been there when we arrived, and asked them how the elephant had been behaving. They all said the same thing: he took no notice of you if you left him alone, but he might charge if you went too close to him.

It was perfectly clear to me what I ought to do. I ought to walk up to within, say, twenty-five yards of the elephant and test his behavior. If he charged, I could shoot; if he took no notice of me, it would be safe to leave him until the mahout came back. But also I knew that I was going to do no such thing. I was a poor shot with a rifle and the ground was soft mud into which one would sink at every step. If the elephant charged and I missed him, I should have about as much chance as a toad under a steam-roller. But even then I was not thinking particularly of my own skin, only of the watchful yellow faces behind. For at that moment, with the crowd watching me, I was not afraid in the ordinary sense, as I would have been if I had been alone. A white man mustn't be frightened in front of "natives"; and so, in general, he isn't frightened. The sole thought in my mind was that if anything went wrong those two thousand Burmans would see me pursued, caught, trampled on and reduced to a grinning corpse like that Indian up the hill. And if that happened it was quite probable that some of them would laugh. That would never do. There was only one alternative. I shoved the cartridges into the magazine and lay down on the road to get a better aim.

10 The crowd grew very still, and a deep, low, happy sigh, as of people who see the theatre curtain go up at last, breathed from innumerable throats. They were going to have their bit of fun after all. The rifle was a beautiful German thing with cross-hair sights. I did not then know that in shooting an elephant one would shoot to cut an imaginary bar running from ear-hole to ear-hole. I ought, therefore, as the elephant was sideways on, to have aimed straight at his ear-hole; actually

I aimed several inches in front of this, thinking the brain would be further forward.

When I pulled the trigger I did not hear the bang or feel the kick—one never does when a shot goes home—but I heard the devilish roar of glee that went up from the crowd. In that instant, in too short a time, one would have thought, even for the bullet to get there, a mysterious, terrible change had come over the elephant. He neither stirred nor fell, but every line of his body had altered. He looked suddenly stricken, shrunken, immensely old, as though the frightful impact of the bullet had paralysed him without knocking him down. At last, after what seemed a long time—it might have been five seconds, I dare say—he sagged flabbily to his knees. His mouth slobbered. An enormous senility seemed to have settled upon him. One could have imagined him thousands of years old. I fired again into the same spot. At the second shot he did not collapse but climbed with desperate slowness to his feet and stood weakly upright, with legs sagging and head drooping. I fired a third time. That was the shot that did for him. You could see the agony of it jolt his whole body and knock the last remnant of strength from his legs. But in falling he seemed for a moment to rise, for as his hind legs collapsed beneath him he seemed to tower upward like a huge rock toppling, his trunk reaching skywards like a tree. He trumpeted, for the first and only time. And then down he came, his belly towards me, with a crash that seemed to shake the ground even where I lay.

I got up. The Burmans were already racing past me across the mud. It was obvious that the elephant would never rise again, but he was not dead. He was breathing very rhythmically with long rattling gasps, his great mound of a side painfully rising and falling. His mouth was wide open—I could see far down into caverns of pale pink throat. I waited a long time for him to die, but his breathing did not weaken. Finally I fired my two remaining shots into the spot where I thought his heart must be. The thick blood welled out of him like red velvet, but still he did not die. His body did not even jerk when the shots hit him, the tortured breathing continued without a pause. He was dying, very slowly and in great agony, but in some world remote from me where not even a bullet could damage him further. I felt that I had got to put an end to that dreadful noise. It seemed dreadful to see the great beast lying there, powerless to move and yet powerless to die, and not even to be able to finish him. I sent back for my small rifle and poured shot after shot into his heart and down his throat. They seemed to make no impression. The tortured gasps continued as steadily as the ticking of a clock.

In the end I could not stand it any longer and went away. I heard later that it took him half an hour to die. Burmans were bringing dahs and baskets even before I left, and I was told they had stripped his body almost to the bones by the afternoon.

Afterwards, of course, there were endless discussions about the shooting of the elephant. The owner was furious, but he was only an Indian and could do nothing. Besides, legally I had done the right thing, for a mad elephant has to be killed, like a mad dog, if its owner fails to control it. Among the Europeans opinion was divided. The older men said I was right, the younger men said it was a damn shame to shoot an elephant for killing a coolie, because an elephant was worth more than any damn Coringhee coolie. And afterwards I was very glad that the coolie had been killed; it put me legally in the right and it gave me a sufficient pretext for shooting the elephant. I often wondered whether any of the others grasped that I had done it solely to avoid looking a fool.

Why I Write

George Orwell

George Orwell is the pen name used by the British author Eric Blair (1903-1950). Orwell was born in the Indian village of Motihari, near Nepal where his father was stationed in the Civil Service. India was then part of the British Empire. From 1907 to 1922, Orwell lived in England returning to India and Burma and a position in the Imperial Police, which he held until 1927. Thereafter, he lived in England, Paris, Spain, and elsewhere, writing on a wide range of topics. He fought in the Spanish Civil War and was actively engaged in several political movements, always against totalitarianism of any kind. He is best known today for two novels of political satire: Animal Farm *(1945) and* 1984 *(1949). He was also a prolific journalist and essayist, with his essays collected in five volumes. Orwell wrote "Why I Write" near the end of his life, looking back and writing autobiographically about his own experiences and writing even as he generalizes about all writers. Though Orwell asserts that he, like all writers, is "vain, selfish and lazy," we take this with a grain of salt even as he gives us many insights into the writer's motivations.*

1 From a very early age, perhaps the age of five or six, I knew that when I grew up I should be a writer. Between the ages of about seventeen and twenty-four I tried to abandon this idea, but I did so with the consciousness that I was outraging my true nature and that sooner or later I should have to settle down and write books.

I was the middle child of three, but there was a gap of five years on either side, and I barely saw my father before I was eight. For this

From *Such, Such Were the Joys* by George Orwell. Published by Harcourt, Brace, & Co. Copyright © 1953 by Sonia Brownell Orwell, renewed 1981 by Mrs. George K. Perutz, Mrs. Miriam Gross, Dr. Michael Dickson, Executors of the Estate of Sonia Brownell Orwell.

and other reasons I was somewhat lonely, and I soon developed dis-agreeable mannerisms which made me unpopular throughout my schooldays. I had the lonely child's habit of making up stories and holding conversations with imaginary persons, and I think from the very start my literary ambitions were mixed up with the feeling of being isolated and undervalued. I knew that I had a facility with words and a power of facing unpleasant facts, and I felt that this created a sort of private world in which I could get my own back for my failure in everyday life. Nevertheless the volume of serious—i.e., seriously in-tended—writing which I produced all through my childhood and boyhood would not amount to half a dozen pages. I wrote my first poem at the age of four or five, my mother taking it down to dicta-tion. I cannot remember anything about it except that it was about a tiger and the tiger had "chair-like teeth"—a good enough phrase, but I fancy the poem was a plagiarism of Blake's "Tiger, Tiger." At eleven, when the war of 1914-18 broke out, I wrote a patriotic poem which was printed in the local newspaper, as was another, two years later, on the death of Kitchener. From time to time, when I was a bit older, I wrote bad and usually unfinished "nature poems" in the Georgian style. I also, about twice, attempted a short story which was a ghastly failure. That was the total of the would-be serious work that I actually set down on paper during all those years.

However, throughout this time I did in a sense engage in literary activities. To begin with there was the made-to-order stuff which I produced quickly, easily and without much pleasure to myself. Apart from school work, I wrote *vers d'occassion,* semi-comic poems which I could turn out at what now seems to me astonishing speed—at four-teen I wrote a whole rhyming play, in imitation of Aristophanes, in about a week—and helped to edit school magazines, both printed and in manuscript. These magazines were the most pitiful burlesque stuff that you could imagine, and I took far less trouble with them than I now would with the cheapest journalism. But side by side with all this, for fifteen years or more, I was carrying out a literary exercise of a quite different kind: this was the making up of a continuous "story" about myself, a sort of diary existing only in the mind. I believe this is a com-mon habit of children and adolescents. As a very small child I used to imagine that I was, say, Robin Hood, and picture myself as the hero of thrilling adventures, but quite soon my "story" ceased to be narcis-sistic in a crude way and became more and more a mere description of what I was doing and the things I saw. For minutes at a time this kind of thing would be running through my head: "He pushed the door open and entered the room. A yellow beam of sunlight, filtering through the muslin curtains, slanted on to the table, where a match-box, half open, lay beside the inkpot. With his right hand in his pocket he moved across to the window. Down in the street a tortoise-shell cat was chasing a dead leaf," etc. etc. This habit continued till I was about twenty-five, right through my non-literary years. Although I had to search, and did search, for the right words, I seemed to be making this descriptive effort almost against my will, under a kind of compulsion from outside. The "story" must, I suppose, have reflected the styles of the various writers I admired at different ages, but so far as I remember it always had the same meticulous descriptive quality.

When I was about sixteen I suddenly discovered the joy of mere words, i.e, the sounds and associations of words. The lines from *Paradise Lost,*

So hee with difficulty and labour hard
Moved on: with difficulty and labour hee.

which do not now seem to me so very wonderful, sent shivers down my backbone; and the spelling "hee" for "he" was an added pleasure. As for the need to describe things, I knew all about it already. So it is clear what kind of books I wanted to write, in so far as I could be said to want to write books at that time. I wanted to write enormous nat-uralistic novels with unhappy endings, full of detailed descriptions and arresting similes, and also full of purple passages in which words were used partly for the sake of their sound. And in fact my first com-pleted novel, *Burmese Days,* which I wrote when I was thirty but pro-jected much earlier, is rather that kind of book.

I give all this background information because I do not think one can assess a writer's motives without knowing something of his early development. His subject matter will be determined by the age he lives in—at least this is true in tumultuous, revolutionary ages like our own—but before he ever begins to write he will have acquired an emo-tional attitude from which he will never completely escape. It is his job, no doubt, to discipline his temperament and avoid getting stuck at some immature stage, or in some perverse mood: but if he escapes from his early influences altogether, he will have killed his impulse to write. Putting aside the need to earn a living, I think there are four great motives for writing, at any rate for writing prose. They exist in different degrees in every writer, and in any one writer the proportions will vary from time to time, according to the atmosphere in which he is living. They are:

1. Sheer egoism. Desire to seem clever, to be talked about, to be remembered after death, to get your own back on grown-ups who snubbed you in childhood, etc. etc. It is humbug to pretend that this is not a motive, and a strong one. Writers share this characteristic with scientists, artists, politicians, lawyers, soldiers, successful business-men—in short, with the whole top crust of humanity. The great mass of human beings are not acutely selfish. After the age of about thirty they abandon individual ambition—in many cases, indeed, they al-most abandon the sense of being individuals at all—and live chiefly for others, or are simply smothered under drudgery. But there is also the minority of gifted, wilful people who are determined to live their own lives to the end, and writers belong in this class. Serious writers, I should say, are on the whole more vain and self-centered than jour-nalists, though less interested in money.

2. Aesthetic enthusiasm. Perception of beauty in the external world, or, on the other hand, in words and their right arrangement. Pleasure in the impact of one sound on another, in the firmness of good prose or the rhythm of a good story. Desire to share an experi-ence which one feels is valuable and ought not to be missed. The aes-thetic motive is very feeble in a lot of writers, but even a pamphleteer or a writer of textbooks will have pet words and phrases which appeal to him for non-utilitarian reasons; or he may feel strongly about ty-pography, width of margins, etc. Above the level of a railway guide, no book is quite free from aesthetic considerations.

3. Historical impulse. Desire to see things as they are, to find out true facts and store them up for the use of posterity.

4. Political purpose—using the word "political" in the widest pos-sible sense. Desire to push the world in a certain direction, to alter other people's idea of the kind of society that they should strive after. Once again, no book is genuinely free from political bias. The opinion that art should have nothing to do with politics is itself a political attitude.

10 It can be seen how these various impulses must war against one 10 another, and how they must fluctuate from person to person and from time to time. By nature—taking your "nature" to be the state you have

attained when you are first adult—I am a person in whom the first three motives would outweigh the fourth. In a peaceful age I might have written ornate or merely descriptive books, and might have remained almost unaware of my political loyalties. As it is I have been forced into becoming a sort of pamphleteer. First I spent five years in an unsuitable profession (the Indian Imperial Police, in Burma), and then I underwent poverty and the sense of failure. This increased my natural hatred of authority and made me for the first time fully aware of the existence of the working classes, and the job in Burma had given me some understanding of the nature of imperialism: but these experiences were not enough to give me an accurate political orientation. Then came Hitler, the Spanish civil war, etc. By the end of 1935 I had still failed to reach a firm decision. I remember a little poem that I wrote at that date, expressing my dilemma:

A happy vicar I might have been
Two hundred years ago,
To preach upon eternal doom
And watch my walnuts grow;

But born, alas, in an evil time,
I missed that pleasant haven,
For the hair has grown on my upper lip
And the clergy are all clean-shaven.

And later still the times were good,
We were so easy to please,
We rocked our troubled thoughts to sleep
On the bosoms of the trees.

All ignorant we dared to own
The joys we now dissemble;
The greenfinch on the apple bough
Could make my enemies tremble.

But girls' bellies and apricots
Roach in a shaded stream,
Horses, ducks in flight at dawn,
All these are a dream.

It is forbidden to dream again;
We maim our joys or hide them;
Horses are made of chromium steel
And little fat men shall ride them.

I am the worm who never turned,
The eunuch without a harem;
Between the priest and the commissar
I walk like Eugene Aram,

And the commissar is telling my fortune
While the radio plays,
But the priest has promised an Austin Seven.
Far Duggie always pays.

I dreamed I dwelt in marble halls,
And woke to find it true;
I wasn't born for an age like this;
Was Smith? Was Jones? Were you?

The Spanish War and other events in 1936-37 turned the scale and thereafter I knew where I stood. Every line of serious work that I have written since 1936 has been written, directly or indirectly, *against* totalitarianism and *for* democratic Socialism, as I understand it. It seems to me nonsense, in a period like our own, to think that one can avoid writing of such subjects. Everyone writes of them in one guise or another. It is simply a question of which side one takes and what approach one follows. And the more one is conscious of one's political bias, the more chance one has of acting politically without sacrificing one's aesthetic and intellectual integrity.

What I have most wanted to do throughout the past ten years is to make political writing into an art. My starting point is always a feeling of partisanship, a sense of injustice. When I sit down to write a book, I do not say to myself, "I am going to produce a work of art." I write it because there is some lie that I want to expose, some fact to which I want to draw attention, and my initial concern is to get a hearing. But I could not do the work of writing a book, or even a long magazine article, if it were not also an aesthetic experience. Anyone who cares to examine my work will see that even when it is downright propaganda it contains much that a full-time politician would consider irrelevant. I am not able, and I do not want, completely to abandon the world-view that I acquired in childhood. So long as I remain alive and well I shall continue to feel strongly about prose style, to love the surface of the earth, and to take pleasure in solid objects and scraps of useless information. It is no use trying to suppress that side of myself. The job is to reconcile my ingrained likes and dislikes with the essentially public, non-individual activities that this age forces on all of us.

It is not easy. It raises problems of construction and language, and it raises in a new way the problem of truthfulness. Let me give just one example of the cruder kind of difficulty that arises. My book about the Spanish civil war, *Homage to Catalonia,* is, of course, a frankly political book, but in the main it is written with a certain detachment and regard for form. I did try very hard in it to tell the whole truth without violating my literary instincts. But among other things it contains a long chapter, full of newspaper quotations and the like, defending the Trotskyists who were accused of plotting with France. Clearly such a chapter, which after a year or two would lose its interest for any ordinary reader, must ruin the book. A critic whom I respect read me a lecture about it. "Why did you put in all that stuff?" he said. "You've turned what might have been a good book into journalism." What he said was true, but I could not have done otherwise. I happened to know, what very few people in England have been allowed to know, that innocent men were being falsely accused. If I had not been angry about that I should never have written the book.

In one form or another this problem comes up again. The problem of language is subtler and would take too long to discuss. I will only say that of late years I have tried to write less picturesquely and more exactly. In any case I find that by the time you have perfected any style of writing, you have always outgrown it. *Animal Farm* was the first book in which I tried, with full consciousness of what I was doing, to fuse political purpose and artistic purpose into one whole. I have not written a novel for seven years, but I hope to write another fairly soon. It is bound to be a failure, every book is a failure, but I know with some clarity what kind of book I want to write.

Looking back through the last page or two, I see that I have made it appear as though my motives in writing were wholly public-spirited. I don't want to leave that as the final impression. All writers are vain, selfish and lazy, and at the very bottom of their motives there lies a mystery. Writing a book is a horrible, exhausting struggle, like a long bout of some painful illness. One would never undertake such a thing if one were not driven on by some demon whom one can neither resist nor understand. For all one knows that demon is simply the same instinct that makes a baby squall for attention. And yet it is also true that one can write nothing readable unless one constantly struggles to efface one's own personality. Good prose is like a window pane. I cannot say with certainty which of my motives are the strongest, but I know which of them deserve to be followed. And looking back through my work, I see that it is invariably where I lacked a political purpose that I wrote lifeless books and was betrayed into purple passages, sentences without meaning, decorative adjectives and humbug generally.

Race Over

Orlando Patterson

Orlando Patterson (1940–) received his BS in economics from London University in England, and his PhD from the London School of Economics, in 1965. He served as a faculty member at the London School of Economics and the University of West Indies. He continued his career at Harvard in 1969 where he became the John Cowles Professor of Sociology in 2001. His early interest in Jamaican slavery led to research in the slavery system in world society. He served as special adviser to Jamaican Prime Minister Michael Manley, and the awards he has won include the Sorokin Prize, the Ralph Bunche Award of the American Political Science Association, and the National Book Award for nonfiction. He has written many books on sociology, including Freedom: Freedom in the Making of Western Culture *(1992),* Rituals of Blood: The Consequences of Slavery in the Two American Centuries *(1999); and three novels—*The Children of Sisyphus *(1987),* An Absence of Ruins *(1967), and* Die the Long Day *(1972).*

1 One can quibble with W. E. B. Du Bois's famous prediction for the twentieth century. This has been not simply the century of the color line but a century of Jim Crow and myriad other persecutions—many within color boundaries. But, if DuBois's epigraph was only half right, his modern-day disciples, who insist the color line will define the next one hundred years as well, are altogether wrong. The racial divide that has plagued America since its founding is fading fast—made obsolete by migratory, sociological, and biotechnological developments that are already under way. By the

middle of the twenty-first century, America will have problems aplenty. But no racial problem whatsoever.

For this we can thank four social patterns, each indigenous to a particular region of the country but which together will reshape the nation as a whole. The strongest and clearest might be called the California system. Cultural and somatic mixture will be its hallmark. A hybrid population, mainly Eurasian—but with a growing Latin element—will come to dominate the middle and upper classes, and will grow exponentially, especially after the 2020s. Lower-class Caucasians, middle-class racial purists, and most African Americans, under pressure from an endless stream of unskilled Mexican workers, will move away. Those African Americans who remain will be rapidly absorbed into the emerging mixed population. The California system will come to dominate the American and Canadian Pacific Rim.

The second major pattern might be called the Caribbean-American system. Increasingly, the countries of the Caribbean basin will be socially and economically integrated with the United States. As their fragile and already declining economies collapse (most dramatically in post-Castro Cuba), they will swarm the mainland by legal and illegal means. Florida will be the metropolitan center of this system, although Caribbean colonies will sprout all over the Northeast. Caribbean peoples will bring their distinctive concept of race and color to America, one in which people marry lighter and "white" as they move up the social ladder. This system will differ from the California one in that the dominant element will be Afro-Latin rather than Eurasian. Since the Caribbean is much closer than Asia, this system will also create a distinctive social type: genuinely transnational and post-national communities in which people feel equally at home in their native and American locations. Increasingly, people will spend their childhoods and retirements in the Caribbean and their productive years in America. The Caribbean-American system will compete with the African American community not only in the lower reaches of the labor force but as the nation's major source of popular culture, especially in music and sports. But, despite these differences, the Caribbean-American system, like the California one, will render the "one drop" rule obsolete.

The third and most problematic system will be the one now emerging in the Northeast and urban Midwest. Here, the economic situation for all classes of African Americans and native-born Latinos is likely to deteriorate—with the ending of affirmative action, a shrinking public sector, and competition from skilled and unskilled (mainly Caribbean basin) immigrant labor. The rise of workfare without compensating provision for child care, combined with the growing pattern of paternal abandonment of children, will further undermine traditional family norms among African American, Latino, and increasingly, the European American lower classes. Reversing the pattern that emerged after World War II, African Americans, Latinos, and the poorest Caucasians will move into the inner and secondary rings of what are now mainly European American middle-class sub-urbs. The middle classes will move to either gated ex-urbs or gentrified central cities—leaving a European American underclass that resembles other ethnic underclasses more and more.

But, although these developments will at first exacerbate racial conflict, they will ultimately transform racial frustrations into class ones. Indeed, for the first time in the nation's history, young, poor, and alienated Caucasians, African Americans, and Latinos will find common ground—based on social resentment and a common lumpen-proletarian, hip-hop culture. Even as these young people periodically engage in murderous racial gang fights, intermarriage and miscegena-tion will escalate as the young poor of all races break away from pres-ent gender and racial taboos. In contrast to the California and Florida systems, the growing hybrid population in the Northeast and indus-trial Midwest will be lower-class, alienated, and out of control. But it will be hybrid nonetheless.

The exception will be in the Southeast, in what may be called the Atlanta pattern. African Americans and European Americans will cling to notions of racial purity and will remain highly (and voluntar-ily) segregated from each other. Affirmative action will be the bulwark of this system, the price the European American elite willingly pays for "racial" stability and the reassuring presence of a culturally famil-iar but socially distant African American group and a pliant working class. The old Confederacy will remain a place where everyone knows who is white and who is black and need reckon with no in-between. But, as opposed to the nineteenth and twentieth centuries, when the South defined the terms of racial engagement on which the entire nation interacted (more or less brutally), in the twenty-first century the Southern model will become an increasingly odd and decreasingly relevant anachronism.

For the decline of race as a factor in American life will result not only from immigration, which can perhaps be halted, but also from biotechnology. More and more in the coming decades, Americans will gain the means to genetically manipulate human appearance. The foundations of genetic engineering are already in place. Given the interest of the affluent population in male-pattern baldness, the restoration of hair loss after cancer treatment, and cancer-free tanning, science is likely to create dramatic new methods of changing hair texture and skin color. Indeed, last November, scientists at Columbia University transplanted scalp cells from one person to another. I don't expect many African Americans to chose straight-haired whiteness for themselves or their progeny, but many will opt for varying degrees of hybridity. In a world dominated by mass culture, many will embrace changes that enhance their individuality. Once dramatically manipulable by human action, "race" will lose its social significance, and the myth of racial purity will be laid to rest.

By the middle of the next century, the social virus of race will have gone the way of smallpox. The twenty-first century, relieved of the obscuring blinkers of race, will be a century of class and class consciousness, forcing the nation to finally take seriously its creed that all are created equal. It should be interesting.

The Androgynous Man
Noel Perrin

*Noel Perrin (1927–), has pursued a wide variety of in-
terests. He has taught as a professor of English and environmental studies at Dartmouth, farmed in Vermont,
contributed articles and columns to high culture periodicals such as* The New Yorker *and* The Washington Post,
*and written a series of books in which he meditates on cul-
ture and art:* A Passport Secretly Green; *(1961);* First
Person Rural: More Essays of a Sometime Farmer
(1981); Last Person Rural *(1991); and* Solo: Life with
an Electric Cat *(1992). In the essay that follows, Perrin
criticizes the stereotypical role of the American male, suggesting an alternate, more feminized role that may be
healthier.*

1   The summer I was 16, I took a train from New York to Steam-   1
boat Springs, Colo., where I was going to be assistant horse
wrangler at a camp. The trip took three days, and since I was
much too shy to talk to strangers, I had quite a lot of time for reading. I read all of "Gone With the Wind." I read all the interesting articles in a couple of magazines I had, and then I went back and read
all the dull stuff. I also took all the quizzes, a thing of which magazines were even fuller then than now.

The one that held my undivided attention was called "How Mas-
culine/Feminine Are You?" It consisted of a large number of inkblots.
The reader was supposed to decide which of four objects each blot
most resembled. The choices might be a cloud, a steam engine, a caterpillar and a sofa.

When I finished the test, I was shocked to find that I was barely
masculine at all. On a scale of 1 to 10, I was about 1.2. Me, the horse

From *The New York Times Magazine* (February 5, 1984). Published by The New York
Times. Copyright © 1984 by The New York Times Company.

wrangler? (And not just wrangler, either. That summer, I had to skin a couple of horses that died—the camp owner wanted the hides.)

The results of that test were so terrifying to me that for the first time in my life I did a piece of original analysis. Having unlimited time on the train, I looked at the "masculine" answers over and over, trying to find what it was that distinguished real men from people like me—and eventually I discovered two very simple patterns. It was "masculine" to think the blots looked like man-made objects, and "feminine" to think they looked like natural objects. It was masculine to think they looked like things capable of causing harm, and feminine to think of innocent things.

Even at 16, I had the sense to see that the compilers of the test were using rather limited criteria—maleness and femaleness are both more complicated than *that*—and I breathed a huge sigh of relief. I wasn't necessarily a wimp, after all.

That the test did reveal something other than the superficiality of its makers I realized only many years later. What it revealed was that there is a large class of men and women both, to which I belong, who are essentially androgynous. That doesn't mean we're gay, or low in the appropriate hormones, or uncomfortable performing the jobs traditionally assigned our sexes. (A few years after that summer, I was leading troops in combat and, unfashionable as it now is to admit this, having a very good time. War is exciting. What a pity the 20th century went and spoiled it with high-tech weapons.)

What it does mean to be spiritually androgynous is a kind of freedom. Men who are all-male, or he-man, or 100 percent red-blooded Americans, have a little biological set that causes them to be attracted to physical power, and probably also to dominance. Maybe even to watching football. I don't say this to criticize them. Completely masculine men are quite often wonderful people: good husbands, good (though sometimes overwhelming) fathers, good members of society. Furthermore, they are often so unself-consciously at ease in the world that other men seek to imitate them. They just aren't as free as us androgynes. They pretty nearly have to be what they are; we have a range of choices open.

The sad part is that many of us never discover that. Men who are not 100 percent red-blooded Americans—say, those who are only 75 percent red-blooded—often fail to notice their freedom. They are too busy trying to copy the he-men ever to realize that men, like women, come in a wide variety of acceptable types. Why this frantic imitation? My answer is mere speculation, but not casual. I have speculated on this for a long time.

Partly they're just envious of the he-man's unconscious ease. Mostly they're terrified of finding that there may be something wrong with them deep down, some weakness at the heart. To avoid discovering that, they spend their lives acting out the role that the he-man naturally lives. Sad.

10 One thing that men owe to the women's movement is that this 10 kind of failure is less common than it used to be. In releasing themselves from the single ideal of the dependent woman, women have more or less incidentally released a lot of men from the single ideal of the dominant male. The one mistake the feminists have made, I think, is in supposing that *all* men need this release, or that the world would be a better place if all men achieved it. It wouldn't. It would just be duller.

So far I have been pretty vague about just what the freedom of the androgynous man is. Obviously it varies with the case. In the case I know best, my own, I can be quite specific. It has freed me most as a parent. I am, among other things, a fairly good natural mother. I like the nurturing role. It makes me feel good to see a child eat—and it turns me to mush to see a 4-year-old holding a glass with both small hands, in order to drink. I even enjoyed sewing patches on the knees of my daughter Amy's Dr. Dentons when she was at the crawling stage. All that pleasure I would have lost if I had made myself stick to the notion of the paternal role that I started with.

Or take a smaller and rather ridiculous example. I feel free to kiss cats. Until recently it never occurred to me that I would want to, though my daughters have been doing it all their lives. But my elder daughter is now 22, and in London. Of course, I get to look after her cat while she is gone. He's a big, handsome farm cat named Petrushka, very unsentimental, though used from kittenhood to being kissed on the top of the head by Elizabeth. I've gotten very fond of him (he's the adventurous kind of cat who likes to climb hills with you), and one night I simply felt like kissing him on the top of the head, and did. Why did no one tell me sooner how silky cat fur is?

Then there's my relation to cars. I am completely unembarrassed by my inability to diagnose even minor problems in whatever object

I happen to be driving, and don't have to make some insider's remark to mechanics to try to establish that I, too, am a "Man With His Machine."

The same ease extends to household maintenance. I do it, of course. Service people are expensive. But for the last decade my house has functioned better than it used to because I've had the aid of a volume called "Home Repairs Any Woman Can Do," which is pitched just right for people at my technical level. As a youth, I'd as soon have touched such a book as I would have become a transvestite. Even though common sense says there is really nothing sexual whatsoever about fixing sinks.

15   Or take public emotion. All my life I have easily been moved by 15 certain kinds of voices. The actress Siobhan McKenna's, to take a notable case. Give her an emotional scene in a play, and within 10 words my eyes are full of tears. In boyhood, my great dread was that someone might notice. I struggled manfully, you might say, to suppress this weakness. Now, of course, I don't see it as a weakness at all, but as a kind of fulfillment. I even suspect that the true he-men feel the same way, or one kind of them does, at least, and it's only the poor imitators who have to struggle to repress themselves.

Let me come back to the inkblots, with their assumption that masculine equates with machinery and science, and feminine with art and nature. I have no idea whether the right pronoun for God is He, She or It. But this I'm pretty sure of. If God could somehow be induced to take that test, God would not come out macho, and not feminismo, either, but right in the middle. Fellow androgynes, it's a nice thought.

Against Nature

Steven Pinker

Steven Pinker (1954–), formerly professor of Brain and Cognitive Sciences at Massachusetts Institute of Technology and now Johnstone Family Professor at Harvard, writes about the nature of the mind both as an extension of the brain and as a working mechanism. Pinker has written many books and essays about popular science and about scholarship in his fields of inquiry. His books include The Denial of Human Nature in Modern Life *(2002);* Visual Cognition *(1985); and* The Language Instinct *(1994). Pinker is able to express difficult concepts with clarity and even humor.*

Simple natural selection based on genetic combination and recombination cannot explain much of human nature. Pinker shows that human motives often contradict the strict rule of genetic selection for fitness and survival.

1   There is an old song by Tom Paxton in which an adult reminisces   1
about a wonderful childhood toy:

> It went ZIP! when it moved,
> And POP! when it stopped,
> And WHIRRR! when it stood still.
> I never knew just what it was
> And I guess I never will.

The whimsy of the song comes from the childlike pleasure in a complicated object with an inscrutable function. When we grow up, we demand to know what an artifact is designed to do. Coming across a

---

contraption in an antique store, we ask what it is, and when we are told that it is a cherry pitter, the springs, hinges, and levers all suddenly make sense in a satisfying rush of insight. This is called reverse engineering. In forward engineering, one designs a machine to do something; in reverse engineering, one figures out what a machine was designed to do.

The human body is a wonderfully complex assembly of struts, springs, pulleys, hinges, sockets, tanks, pipes, pumps, and filters, and since the seventeenth century, when William Harvey deduced that the valves in veins are there to make the blood circulate, we have understood the body by reverse engineering it. Even today we can be delighted to learn what mysterious parts are for. Why do we have wrinkled, asymmetrical ears? Because they filter sound waves coming from different directions in different ways. The sound shadow tells the brain whether the source of the sound is above or below, in front of or behind us.

The rationale for reverse engineering living things comes, of course, from Charles Darwin. He showed how "that perfection of structure and coadaptation which most justly excites our admiration" arises not from God's foresight but from natural selection operating over immense spans of time. Organisms vary, and in each generation the lucky variants that are better adapted to survival and reproduction take up a larger proportion of the population. The complicated machinery of plants and animals thus appears to have been engineered to allow them to survive and reproduce.

The human mind, which produces our behavior, is a product of the brain, another complex organ shaped by natural selection, and we should be able to reverse engineer it too. And so we have, for many parts of our psychology. Perception scientists have long realized that our sense of sight is not there to entertain us with pretty patterns but to grant us an awareness of the true forms and materials in the world. The selective advantage is obvious: Animals that know where the food, the predators, and the cliffs are can put the food in their stomachs, keep themselves out of the stomachs of others, and stay on the right side of the cliff tops. Many of our emotions are also products of natural engineering. Fear keeps us away from heights and dangerous animals; disgust deters us from eating bodily wastes and putrefying flesh.

5   But reverse engineering is possible only when you have an inkling   5
of what a device was designed to accomplish. We don't understand the cherry pitter until we catch on that it was designed as a machine

for removing pits from cherries rather than as a paperweight or wrist exerciser. The same is true in biological reverse engineering. Through the 1950s, many biologists worried about why organisms have body parts that seem to do them no good. Why do bees have a barbed stinger that pulls the bee's body apart when dislodged? Why do mammals have mammary glands, which skim nutrients from the mother's blood and package them as milk for the benefit of another animal?

Today we know that these are pseudo-problems, arising from the wrong idea of what the bodies of organisms are for. The ultimate goal of a body is not to benefit itself or its species or its ecosystem but to maximize the number of copies of the genes that made it in the first place. Natural selection is about replicators, entities that keep a stable identity across many generations of copying. Replicators that enhance the probability of their own replication come to predominate, regardless of whose body the replicated copies sit in. Genes for barbed stingers can predominate because copies of those genes sit in the body of the queen and are protected when the worker suicidally repels an invader. Genes for mammary glands can predominate because copies of those genes sit in the young bodies nourished by the milk.

So when we ask questions like "Who or what is supposed to benefit from an adaptation?" and "What is a design in living things a design for?," the theory of natural selection provides the answer: the long-term stable replicators, genes. This has become a commonplace in biology, summed up in Richard Dawkins's book title *The Selfish Gene* and in Samuel Butler's famous quip that a hen is an egg's way of making another egg.

What difference does all this make to reverse engineering the mind? For many parts of the mind, not much. Vision and fear seem clearly to benefit the perceiver and fearer. But when it comes to our social lives, where our actions often do not benefit ourselves, it makes a big difference who or what we take to be the ultimate beneficiary. Mammary glands were demystified when we realized that they benefit the genes for making the mammary glands—not the copies in the mother but the copies likely to be found in the milk drinker. In the same way, kind acts toward our children can be demystified when we realize that they can benefit copies of the genes that build a brain that inclines a person toward such kind acts—not the copies in the kind actor but the copies likely to be found in the beneficiaries. We nurture our children and favor our relatives because doing so has a good chance of helping copies of the genes for nurturance and nepotism inside the children and the relatives.

In the case of altruistic behavior toward nonrelatives, a different explanation is needed, but it still hinges on an ultimate benefit to the genes for the altruistic behavior. People tend to be nice to those who are nice to them. Genes for trading favors with other favor traders can prosper for the same reason that the partners in an economic trade can prosper: both parties are better off if what they gain is worth more to them than what they give up.

10   The theory that human social behavior is a product of natural   10 engineering for gene propagation came to be known in the 1970s as sociobiology and was summed up by saying that the brain is a fitness maximizer, or that people strive to spread their genes. It offered a realization of Darwin's famous prediction in *Origin of Species* that psychology would be based on a new foundation, fully integrated into our understanding of the natural world.

But there was one problem with the theory. When we look at human behavior around us, we discover that the brain-as-fitness-maximizer theory is obviously, crashingly, stunningly wrong. Much of human behavior is a recipe for genetic suicide, not propagation.

People use contraception. They adopt children who are unrelated to them. They take vows of celibacy. They watch pornography when they could be seeking a mate. They forgo food to buy heroin. In India some people sell their blood to buy movie tickets. In our culture people postpone childbearing to climb the corporate ladder, and eat themselves into an early grave.

What are we to make of this Darwinian madness? One response is to look for subtle ways in which behavior really might aid fitness. Perhaps celibate people have more time to raise large broods of nieces and nephews and thereby propagate more copies of their genes than they would if they had their own children. Perhaps priests and people in childless households make up for their lack of legitimate offspring by having many clandestine affairs. But these explanations feel strained, and less sympathetic observers have come to different conclusions: Human behavior has nothing to do with biology and follows arbitrary cultural norms instead.

To anyone with scientific curiosity, it would be disappointing if human behavior had to be permanently walled off from our understanding of the natural world. The founders of a new approach called evolutionary psychology—the anthropologists Donald Symons and John Tooby and the psychologist Leda Cosmides, all at the University of California at Santa Barbara—have shown that it needn't be. When you think it through, they argue, you find that the genecentered theory of evolution does not predict that people are fitness maximizers or gene propagators.

15   First, natural selection is not a puppet master that pulls the strings of behavior directly. The targets of selection, the genes buried in eggs and sperm, cannot control behavior either, because obviously they are in no position to see the world or to move the muscles. Naturally selected genes can only design the generator of behavior: the package of neural information—processing and goal-pursuing mechanisms called the mind.

That is why it is wrong to say that the point of human striving is to spread our genes. With the exception of the fertility doctor who artificially inseminated patients with his own semen, the donors to the sperm bank for Nobel Prize winners, and other weirdos, no human being (or animal) really strives to spread his or her genes. The metaphor of the selfish gene must be taken seriously: People don't selfishly spread their genes; genes selfishly spread themselves. They do it by the way they build our brains. By making us enjoy life, health, sex, friends, and children, the genes buy a lottery ticket for representation in the next generation, with odds that were favorable in the environment in which we evolved (because healthy, long-lived, loving parents did tend, on average, to send more genes into the next generation). Our goals are subgoals of the ultimate goal of the genes, replicating themselves. But the two are different. Resist the temptation to think of the goals of our genes as our deepest, truest, most hidden motives. Genes are a play within a play, not the interior monologue of the players. As far as we are concerned, our goals, conscious or unconscious, are not about genes at all but about health and lovers and children and friends.

Once you separate the goals of our minds from the metaphorical goals of our genes, many problems for a naturalistic understanding of human behavior evaporate. If altruism, according to biologists, is just helping kin or exchanging favors, both of which serve the interests of one's genes, wouldn't that make altruism merely a form of hypocrisy? Not at all. Just as blueprints don't necessarily specify blue buildings, selfish genes don't necessarily specify selfish organisms. Sometimes the most selfish thing a gene can do is to build a selfless brain—for example, one that gives rise to a loving parent or a loyal friend.

Take another example. In a review of three books on sexuality in the *New York Times Book Review,* the linguist Derek Bickerton wrote: "When a bird practices what zoologists call 'extra-pair copulation,' can we really call this adultery? . . . The intent of the two activities is completely different. Those who engage in extra-pair copulation usually aim to make babies; adulterers usually try to avoid them."

This is a perfect example of the confusion I am trying to cure—when birds fool around, they are most definitely not trying to "make babies," since birds have not had sex education and presumably do not engage in conscious family planning. They are trying to have sex, and building a desire for sex (including extra-pair copulation) into bird brains is the genes' way of making more genes.

But if a desire for sex serves the interests of the genes, are we condemned to an endless soap opera of marital treachery? Not if you remember that human behavior is the product of a complex brain with many components, which can be thought of as distinct circuits, modules, organs, or even "little agents," in the metaphor of the MIT computer scientist Marvin Minsky. Perhaps there is a component for sexual desire that serves the long-term interests of the genes by making more children, but there are, just as surely, other components that serve the interests of the genes in other ways. Among them are a desire for a trusting spouse (who will help bring up the copies of one's genes inside one's children), and a desire not to see one's own body—genes included—come to an early end at the hands of a jealous rival.

There is a second reason that behavior should not and does not maximize fitness. Natural selection operates over thousands of generations. For 99 percent of human existence, people lived as foragers in small nomadic bands. Our brains are adapted to that long-vanished way of life, not to brand-new agricultural and industrial civilizations. They are not wired to cope with anonymous crowds, written language, modern medicine, formal social institutions, high technology, and other newcomers to the human experience.

Since the modern mind is adapted to the Stone Age, not the computer age, there is no need to strain for adaptive explanations for everything we do, such as pornography, drugs, movies, contraception, careerism, and junk food. Before there was photography, it was adaptive to receive visual images of attractive members of the opposite sex because those images arose only from light reflecting off fertile bodies. Before opiates came in syringes, they were synthesized in the brain as natural analgesics. Before there were movies, it was adaptive to witness people's emotional struggles because the only struggles you could witness were among people you had to psych out every day. Before there was effective contraception, children were difficult to postpone, and status and wealth could be converted into more children and healthier ones. Before there was a sugar bowl, saltshaker, and butter dish on every table, and when lean years were never far away, you could never get too much sweet, salty, and fatty food.

And, to come full circle, right now you and I are co-opting yet another part of our minds for an evolutionarily novel activity. Our ancestors evolved faculties of intuitive engineering and intuitive science so that they could master tools and make sense of their immediate physical surroundings. We are using them today to make sense of the universe, life, and our own minds.

Reverse engineering our minds—figuring out what they are "designed" to accomplish—could be the fulfillment of the ancient injunction to know ourselves, but only if we keep track of who is designed to accomplish what. People don't have the goal of propagating genes; people have the goal of pursuing satisfying thoughts and feelings. Our genes have the metaphorical goal of building a complex brain in which the satisfying thoughts and feelings are linked to acts that tended to propagate those genes in the ancient environment in which we evolved. With that in mind, we might make better sense of the mysterious ways in which we humans pop, zip, and whir.

America: The Multinational Society

Ishmael Reed

Ishmael Reed (1938–), a poet, novelist, and essayist, was born in Chattanooga, Tennessee. Reed, who advocates that African-Americans must rediscover their identity with Africa, occasionally mixes black English and slang with standard English in his writing. His books include the po-etry collections Secretary to the Spirits *(1975) and* Poems: New and Collected Poems *(1988); the novels* Mumbo Jumbo *(1972),* The Last Days of Louisiana Red *(1974), and* Reckless Eyeballing *(1986); the essay collections* God Made Alaska for the Indians: Selected Essays *(1982),* Airing Dirty Laundry *(1993), and* Writin' is Fightin': Thirty-Seven Years of Boxing on Paper *(1988); and a play,* Hell Hath No Fury *(1960). Reed cofounded (with Victor Hernandez Cruz) the Before Columbus Foundation in 1976 to promote multiculturalism in American litera-ture. In 1981, he cofounded (with Al Young)* Quilt *maga-zine. In the following essay, published in* Writin' is Fightin', *Reed argues for a broader definition of culture for the United States, a definition that acknowledges the melange of cultures that influence life in North America.*

At the annual Lower East Side Jewish Festival yesterday, a Chinese woman ate a pizza slice in front of Ty Thuan Duc's Vietnamese gro-cery store. Beside her a Spanish-speaking family patronized a cart with two signs: "Italian Ices" and "Kosher by Rabbi Alper." And after the pastrami ran out, everybody ate knishes.
— *New York Times,* June 23, 1983

From *Writin' Is Fightin'* by Ishmael Reed. Published by Atheneum Publishers, an imprint of Macmillan Publishing Company. Copyright © 1983 by Ishmael Reed.

1   On the day before Memorial Day, 1983, a poet called me to describe a city he had just visited. He said that one section included mosques, built by the Islamic people who dwelled there. Attending his reading, he said, were large numbers of Hispanic people, forty thousand of whom lived in the same city. He was not talking about a fabled city located in some mysterious region of the world. The city he'd visited was Detroit.

     A few months before, as I was leaving Houston, Texas, I heard it announced on the radio that Texas's largest minority was Mexican-American, and though a foundation recently issued a report critical of bilingual education, the taped voice used to guide the passengers on the air trams connecting terminals in Dallas Airport is in both Spanish and English. If the trend continues, a day will come when it will be difficult to travel through some sections of the country without hearing commands in both English and Spanish; after all, for some Western states, Spanish was the first written language and the Spanish style lives on in the Western way of life.

     Shortly after my Texas trip, I sat in an auditorium located on the campus of the University of Wisconsin at Milwaukee as a Yale professor—whose original work on the influence of African cultures upon those of the Americas has led to his ostracism from some monocultural intellectual circles—walked up and down the aisle, like an old-time Southern evangelist, dancing and drumming the top of the lectern, illustrating his points before some serious Afro-American intellectuals and artists who cheered and applauded his performance and his mastery of information. The professor was "white." After his lecture, he joined a group of Milwaukeeans in a conversation. All of the participants spoke Yoruban, though only the professor had ever traveled to Africa.

     One of the artists told me that his paintings, which included African and Afro-American mythological symbols and imagery, were hanging in the local McDonald's restaurant. The next day I went to McDonald's and snapped pictures of smiling youngsters eating hamburgers below paintings that could grace the walls of any of the country's leading museums. The manager of the local McDonald's said, "I don't know what you boys are doing, but I like it," as he commissioned the local painters to exhibit in his restaurant.

5   Such blurring of cultural styles occurs in everyday life in the United States to a greater extent than anyone can imagine and is

probably more prevalent than the sensational conflict between people of different backgrounds that is played up and often encouraged by the media. The result is what the Yale professor, Robert Thompson, referred to as a cultural bouillabaisse, yet members of the nation's present educational and cultural Elect still cling to the notion that the United States belongs to some vaguely defined entity they refer to as "Western civilization," by which they mean, presumably, a civilization created by the people of Europe, as if Europe can be viewed in monolithic terms. Is Beethoven's Ninth Symphony, which includes Turkish marches, a part of Western civilization, or the late nineteenth and twentieth-century French paintings, whose creators were influenced by Japanese art? And what of the cubists, through whom the influence of African art changed modern painting, or the surrealists, who were so impressed with the art of the Pacific Northwest Indians that, in their map of North America, Alaska dwarfs the lower forty-eight in size?

Are the Russians, who are often criticized for their adoption of "Western" ways by Tsarist dissidents in exile, members of Western civilization? And what of the millions of Europeans who have black African and Asian ancestry, black Africans having occupied several countries for hundreds of years? Are these "Europeans" members of Western civilization, or the Hungarians, who originated across the Urals in a place called Greater Hungary, or the Irish, who came from the Iberian Peninsula?

Even the notion that North America is part of Western civilization because our "system of government" is derived from Europe is being challenged by Native American historians who say that the founding fathers, Benjamin Franklin especially, were actually influenced by the system of government that had been adopted by the Iroquois hundreds of years prior to the arrival of large numbers of Europeans.

Western civilization, then, becomes another confusing category like Third World, or Judeo-Christian culture, as man attempts to impose his small-screen view of political and cultural reality upon a complex world. Our most publicized novelist recently said that Western civilization was the greatest achievement of mankind, an attitude that flourishes on the street level as scribbles in public restrooms: "White Power," "Niggers and Spics Suck," or "Hitler was a prophet," the latter being the most telling, for wasn't Adolph Hitler the archetypal monoculturalist who, in his pigheaded arrogance, believed that one way and one blood was so pure that it had to be protected from alien strains at all costs? Where did such an attitude, which has caused so much misery and depression in our national life, which has tainted even our noblest achievements, begin? An attitude that caused the incarceration of Japanese-American citizens during World War II, the persecution of Chicanos and Chinese-Americans, the near-extermination of the Indians, and the murder and lynchings of thousands of Afro-Americans.

Virtuous, hardworking, pious, even though they occasionally would wander off after some fancy clothes, or rendezvous in the woods with the town prostitute, the Puritans are idealized in our schoolbooks as "a hardy band" of no-nonsense patriarchs whose discipline razed the forest and brought order to the New World (a term that annoys Native American historians). Industrious, responsible, it was their "Yankee ingenuity" and practicality that created the work ethic. They were simple folk who produced a number of good poets, and they set the tone for the American writing style, of lean and spare lines, long before Hemingway. They worshiped in churches whose colors blended in with the New England snow, churches with simple structures and ornate lecterns.

10   The Puritans were a daring lot, but they had a mean streak. They hated the theater and banned Christmas. They punished people in a cruel and inhuman manner. They killed children who disobeyed their parents. When they came in contact with those whom they considered heathens or aliens, they behaved in such a bizarre and irrational manner that this chapter in the American history comes down to us as a late-movie horror film. They exterminated the Indians, who taught them how to survive in a world unknown to them, and their encounter with the calypso culture of Barbados resulted in what the tourist guide in Salem's Witches' House refers to as the Witchcraft Hysteria.

The Puritan legacy of hard work and meticulous accounting led to the establishment of a great industrial society; it is no wonder that the American industrial revolution began in Lowell, Massachusetts, but there was the other side, the strange and paranoid attitudes toward those different from the Elect.

The cultural attitudes of that early Elect continue to be voiced in everyday life in the United States: the president of a distinguished university, writing a letter to the *Times,* belittling the study of African civilizations; the television network that promoted its show on the Vatican art with the boast that this art represented "the finest achievements of the human spirit." A modern up-tempo state of complex rhythms that depends upon contacts with an international community can no longer behave as if it dwelled in a "Zion Wilderness" surrounded by beasts and pagans.

When I heard a schoolteacher warn the other night about the invasion of the American educational system by foreign curriculums, I wanted to yell at the television set, "Lady, they're already here." It has already begun because the world is here. The world has been arriving at these shores for at least ten thousand years from Europe, Africa, and Asia. In the late nineteenth and early twentieth centuries, large numbers of Europeans arrived, adding their cultures to those of the European, African, and Asian settlers who were already here, and recently millions have been entering the country from South America and the Caribbean, making Yale Professor Bob Thompson's bouillabaisse richer and thicker.

One of our most visionary politicians said that he envisioned a time when the United States could become the brain of the world, by which he meant the repository of all of the latest advanced information systems. I thought of that remark when an enterprising poet friend of mine called to say that he had just sold a poem to a computer magazine and that the editors were delighted to get it because they didn't carry fiction or poetry. Is that the kind of world we desire? A humdrum homogeneous world of all brains and no heart, no fiction, no poetry; a world of robots with human attendants bereft of imagination, of culture? Or does North America deserve a more exciting destiny? To become a place where the cultures of the world crisscross. This is possible because the United States is unique in the world: The world is here.

How to Say Nothing in 500 Words

Paul Roberts

Paul Roberts (1917–1967) wrote clear and helpful writing textbooks, among them English Syntax *(1954),* Patterns of English *(1956),* Understanding English *(1958) and* English Sentences *(1962). He approached writing with the scientific discipline of a linguist. In the following excerpt from* Understanding English, *note his tendency to categorize and classify, to write descriptions and rules. In this way, the "art" of writing is transformed to the science (Latin for knowledge) of composition.*

Nothing About Something

1   It's Friday afternoon, and you have almost survived another week 1
of classes. You are just looking forward dreamily to the weekend when
the English instructor says: "For Monday you will turn in a five-
hundred-word composition on college football."

    Well, that puts a good big hole in the weekend. You don't have
any strong views on college football one way or the other. You get
rather excited during the season and go to all the home games and find
it rather more fun than not. On the other hand, the class has been
reading Robert Hutchins in the anthology and perhaps Shaw's
"Eighty-Yard Run," and from the class discussion you have got the
idea that the instructor thinks college football is for the birds. You are
no fool, you. You can figure out what side to take.

After dinner you get out the portable typewriter that you got for high school graduation. You might as well get it over with and enjoy Saturday and Sunday. Five hundred words is about two double-spaced pages with normal margins. You put in a sheet of paper, think up a title, and you're off:

Why College Football Should Be Abolished

College football should be abolished because it's bad for the school and also bad for the players. The players are so busy practicing that they don't have any time for their studies.

5   This, you feel, is a mighty good start. The only trouble is that it's   5 only thirty-two words. You still have four hundred and sixty-eight to go, and you've pretty well exhausted the subject. It comes to you that you do your best thinking in the morning, so you put away the typewriter and go to the movies. But the next morning you have to do your washing and some math problems, and in the afternoon you go to the game. The English instructor turns up too, and you wonder if you've taken the right side after all. Saturday night you have a date, and Sunday morning you have to go to church. (You shouldn't let English assignments interfere with your religion.) What with one thing and another, it's ten o'clock Sunday night before you get out the typewriter again. You make a pot of coffee and start to fill out your views on college football. Put a little meat on the bones.

Why College Football Should Be Abolished

In my opinion, it seems to me that college football should be abolished. The reason why I think this to be true is because I feel that football is bad for the colleges in nearly every respect. As Robert Hutchins says in his article in our anthology in which he discusses college football, it would be better if the colleges had race horses and had races with one another, because then the horses would not have to attend classes. I firmly agree with Mr. Hutchins on this point, and I am sure that many other students would agree too.

One reason why it seems to me that college football is bad is that it has become too commercial. In the olden times when people played football just for the fun of it, maybe college football was all right, but they do not play football just for the fun of it now as they used to in the old days. Nowadays college football is what you might call a big business. Maybe this is not true at all schools, and I don't think it is especially true here at State, but certainly this is the case at most colleges and universities in America nowadays, as Mr. Hutchins points out in his very interesting article. Actually the coaches and alumni go around to the high schools and offer the high school stars large salaries to come to their colleges and play football for them. There was one case where a high school star was offered a convertible if he would play football for a certain college.

Another reason for abolishing college football is that it is bad for the players. They do not have time to get a college education, because they are so busy playing football. A football player has to practice every afternoon from three to six, and then he is so tired that he can't concentrate on his studies. He just feels like dropping off to sleep after dinner, and then the next day he goes to his classes without having studied and maybe he fails the test.

(Good ripe stuff so far, but you're still a hundred and fifty-one words from home. One more push.)

Also I think college football is bad for the colleges and the universities because not very many students get to participate in it. Out of a college of ten thousand students only seventy-five or a hundred play football, if that many. Football is what you might call a spectator sport. That means that most people go to watch it but do not play it themselves.

(Four hundred and fifteen. Well, you still have the conclusion, and when you retype it, you can make the margins a little wider.)

10   These are the reasons why I agree with Mr. Hutchins   10
that college football should be abolished in American colleges and universities.

On Monday you turn it in, moderately hopeful, and on Friday it
comes back marked "weak in content" and sporting a big "D."

This essay is exaggerated a little, not much. The English instructor will recognize it as reasonably typical of what an assignment on
college football will bring in. He knows that nearly half of the class
will contrive in five hundred words to say that college football is too
commercial and bad for the players. Most of the other half will inform
him that college football builds character and prepares one for life and
brings prestige to the school. As he reads paper after paper all saying
the same thing in almost the same words, all bloodless, five hundred
words dripping out of nothing, he wonders how he allowed himself
to get trapped into teaching English when he might have had a happy
and interesting life as an electrician or a confidence man.

Well, you may ask, what can you do about it? The subject is one
on which you have few convictions and little information. Can you
be expected to make a dull subject interesting? As a matter of fact, this
is precisely what you are expected to do. This is the writer's essential
task. All subjects, except sex, are dull until somebody makes them interesting. The writer's job is to find the argument, the approach, the
angle, the wording that will take the reader with him. This is seldom
easy, and it is particularly hard in subjects that have been much discussed: College Football, Fraternities, Popular Music, Is Chivalry
Dead?, and the like. You will feel that there is nothing you can do with
such subjects except repeat the old bromides. But there are some
things you can do which will make your papers, if not throbbingly
alive, at least less insufferably tedious than they might otherwise be.

Avoid the Obvious Content

Say the assignment is college football. Say that you've decided to
be against it. Begin by putting down the arguments that come to your
mind: it is too commercial, it takes the students' minds off their studies, it is hard on the players, it makes the university a kind of circus
instead of an intellectual center, for most schools it is financially ru-
inous. Can you think of any more arguments just off hand! All right.

291

Now when you write your paper, *make sure that you don't use any of the material on this list.* If these are the points that leap to your mind, they will leap to everyone else's too, and whether you get a "C" or a "D" may depend on whether the instructor reads your paper early when he is fresh and tolerant or late, when the sentence "In my opinion, college football has become too commercial," inexorably repeated, has brought him to the brink of lunacy.

15   Be against college football for some reason or reasons of your own.   15
If they are keen and perceptive ones, that's splendid. But even if they are trivial or foolish or indefensible, you are still ahead so long as they are not everybody else's reasons too. Be against it because the colleges don't spend enough money on it to make it worth while, because it is bad for the characters of the spectators, because the players are forced to attend classes, because the football stars hog all the beautiful women, because it competes with baseball and is therefore un-American and possibly Communist inspired. There are lots of more or less unused reasons for being against college football.

Sometimes it is a good idea to sum up and dispose of the trite and conventional points before going on to your own. This has the advantage of indicating to the reader that you are going to be neither trite nor conventional. Something like this:

> We are often told that college football should be abolished because it has become too commercial or because it is bad for the players. These arguments are no doubt very cogent, but they don't really go to the heart of the matter. Then you go to the heart of the matter.

Take the Less Usual Side

One rather simple way of getting interest into your paper is to take the side of the argument that most of the citizens will want to avoid. If the assignment is an essay on dogs, you can, if you choose, explain that dogs are faithful and lovable companions, intelligent, useful as guardians of the house and protectors of children, indispensable in police work—in short, when all is said and done, man's best friends. Or you can suggest that those big brown eyes conceal, more often than not, a vacuity of mind and an inconstancy of purpose; that the dogs you have known most intimately have been mangy, ill-tempered

292

brutes, incapable of instruction; and that only your nobility of mind and fear of arrest prevent you from kicking the flea-ridden animals when you pass them on the street.

Naturally, personal convictions will sometimes dictate your approach. If the assigned subject is "Is Methodism Rewarding to the individual?" and you are a pious Methodist, you have really no choice. But few assigned subjects, if any, will fall in this category. Most of them will lie in broad areas of discussion with much to be said on both sides. They are intellectual exercises and it is legitimate to argue now one way and now another, as debaters do in similar circumstances. Always take the side that looks to you hardest, least defensible. It will almost always turn out to be easier to write interestingly on that side.

20 This general advice applies where you have a choice of subjects. If 20 you are to choose among "The Value of Fraternities" and "My Favorite High School Teacher" and "What I Think About Beetles," by all means plump for the beetles. By the time the instructor gets to your paper, he will be up to his ears in tedious tales about the French teacher at Bloombury High and assertions about how fraternities build character and prepare one for life. Your views on beetles, whatever they are, are bound to be a refreshing change.

Don't worry too much about figuring out what the instructor thinks about the subject so that you can cuddle up with him. Chances are his views are no stronger than yours. If he does have convictions and you oppose them, his problem is to keep from grading you higher than you deserve in order to show he is not biased. This doesn't mean that you should always cantankerously dissent from what the instructor says; that gets tiresome too. And if the subject assigned is "My Pet Peeve," do not begin, "My pet peeve is the English instructor who assigns papers on 'my pet peeve.'" This was still funny during the War of 1812, but it has sort of lost its edge since then. It is in general good manners to avoid personalities.

Slip out of Abstraction

If you will study the essay on college football . . . you will perceive that one reason for its appalling dullness is that it never gets down to particulars. It is just a series of not very glittering generalities: "football is bad for the colleges," "it has become too commercial," "football is a big business," "it is bad for the players," and so on. Such round phrases

293

thudding against the reader's brain are unlikely to convince him, though they may well render him unconscious.

If you want the reader to believe that college football is bad for the players, you have to do more than say so. You have to display the evil. Take your roommate, Alfred Simkins, the second-string center. Picture poor old Alfy coming home from football practice every evening, bruised and aching, agonizingly tired, scarcely able to shovel the mashed potatoes into his mouth. Let us see him staggering up to the room, getting out his econ textbook, peering desperately at it with his good eye, falling asleep and failing the test in the morning. Let us share his unbearable tension as Saturday draws near. Will he fail, be demoted, lose his monthly allowance, be forced to return to the coal mines? And if he succeeds, what will be his reward? Perhaps a slight ripple of applause when the third-string center replaces him, a moment of elation in the locker room if the team wins, of despair if it loses. What will he look back on when he graduates from college? Toil and torn ligaments. And what will be his future? He is not good enough for pro football, and he is too obscure and weak in econ to succeed in stocks and bonds. College football is tearing the heart from Alfred Simkins and, when it finishes with him, will callously toss aside the shattered hulk.

This is no doubt a weak enough argument for the abolition of college football, but it is a sight better than saying, in three or four variations, that college football (in your opinion) is bad for the players.

25 Look at the work of any professional writer and notice how consistently he is moving from the generality, the abstract statement, to the concrete example, the facts and figures, the illustration. If he is writing on juvenile delinquency, he does not just tell you that juveniles are (it seems to him) delinquent and that (in his opinion) something should be done about it. He shows you juveniles being delinquent, tearing up movie theatres in Buffalo, stabbing high school principals in Dallas, smoking marijuana in Palo Alto. And more than likely he is moving toward some specific remedy, not just a general wringing of the hands.

It is no doubt possible to be *too* concrete, too illustrative or anecdotal, but few inexperienced writers err this way. For most the soundest advice is to be seeking always for the picture, to be always turning general remarks into seeable examples. Don't say, "Sororities teach girls the social graces." Say "Sorority life teaches a girl how to carry on a conversation while pouring tea, without sloshing the tea into the saucer." Don't say, "I like certain kinds of popular music very much."

Say, "Whenever I hear Gerber Spinklittle play 'Mississippi Man' on the trombone, my socks creep up my ankles."

Get Rid of Obvious Padding

The student toiling away at his weekly English theme is too often tormented by a figure: five hundred words. How, he asks himself, is he to achieve this staggering total? Obviously by never using one word when he can somehow work in ten.

He is therefore seldom content with a plain statement like "Fast driving is dangerous." This has only four words in it. He takes thought, and the sentence becomes:

In my opinion, fast driving is dangerous.

30 Better, but he can do better still:

In my opinion, fast driving would seem to be rather dangerous.

If he is really adept, it may come out:
In my humble opinion, though I do not claim to be an expert on this complicated subject, fast driving, in most circumstances, would seem to be rather dangerous in many respects, or at least so it would seem to me.

Thus four words have been turned into forty, and not an iota of content has been added.

35 Now this is a way to go about reaching five hundred words, and if you are content with a "D" grade, it is as good a way as any. But if you aim higher, you must work differently. Instead of stuffing your sentences with straw, you must try steadily to get rid of the padding, to make your sentences lean and tough. If you are really working at it, your first draft will greatly exceed the required total, and then you will work it down, thus:

It is thought in some quarters that fraternities do not contribute as much as might be expected to campus life.

Some people think that fraternities contribute little to campus life.

The average doctor who practices in small towns or in the country must toil night and day to heal the sick.
Most country doctors work long hours.

40 When I was a little girl, I suffered from shyness and embarrassment in the presence of others. 40
I was a shy little girl.

It is absolutely necessary for the person employed as a marine fireman to give the matter of steam pressure his undivided attention at all times.
The fireman has to keep his eye on the steam gauge.

You may ask how you can arrive at five hundred words at this rate. Simply. You dig up more real content. Instead of taking a couple of obvious points off the surface of the topic and then circling warily around them for six paragraphs, you work in and explore, figure out the details. You illustrate. You say that fast driving is dangerous, and then you prove it. How long does it take to stop a car at forty and at eighty? How far can you see at night? What happens when a tire blows?! What happens in a head-on collision at fifty miles an hour! Pretty soon your paper will be full of broken glass and blood and headless torsos, and reaching five hundred words will not really be a problem.

Call a Fool a Fool

45 Some of the padding in freshman themes is to be blamed not on 45
anxiety about the word minimum but on excessive timidity. The student writes, "In my opinion, the principal of my high school acted in ways that I believe every unbiased person would have to call foolish." This isn't exactly what he means. What he means is, "My high school principal was a fool." If he was a fool, call him a fool. Hedging the thing about with "in-my-opinion's" and "it-seems-to-me's" and "as-I-see-it's" and "at-least-from-my-point-of-view's" gains you nothing. Delete these phrases whenever they creep into your paper.

The student's tendency to hedge stems from a modesty that in other circumstances would be commendable. He is, he realizes, young and inexperienced, and he half suspects that he is dopey and fuzzy-minded beyond the average. Probably only too true. But it doesn't help to announce your incompetence six times in every paragraph. Decide what you want to say and say it as vigorously as possible, without apology and in plain words.

Linguistic diffidence can take various forms. One is what we call *euphemism*. This is the tendency to call a spade "a certain garden implement" or women's underwear "unmentionables." It is stronger in some eras than others and in some people than others but it always operates more or less in subjects that are touchy or taboo: death, sex, madness, and so on. Thus we shrink from saying "He died last night" but say instead "passed away," "left us," "joined his Maker," "went to his reward." Or we try to take off the tension with a lighter cliché: "kicked the bucket," "cashed in his chips," "handed in his dinner pail." We have found all sorts of ways to avoid saying *mad*: "mentally ill," "touched," "not quite right upstairs," "feeble-minded," "innocent," "simple," "off his trolley," "not in his right mind. "Even such a now plain word as *insane* began as a euphemism with the meaning "not healthy."

Modern science, particularly psychology, contributes many poly-syllables in which we can wrap our thoughts and blunt their force. To many writers there is no such thing as a bad schoolboy. Schoolboys are maladjusted or unoriented or misunderstood or in need of guidance or lacking in continued success toward satisfactory integration of the personality as a social unit, but they are never bad. Psychology no doubt makes us better men or women, more sympathetic and tolerant, but it doesn't make writing any easier. Had Shakespeare been confronted with psychology, "To be or not to be" might have come out, "To continue as a social unit or not to do so. That is the personality problem. Whether 'tis a better sign of integration at the conscious level to display a psychic tolerance toward the maladjustments and repressions induced by one's lack of orientation in one's environment or—" But Hamlet would never have finished the soliloquy.

Writing in the modern world, you cannot altogether avoid modern jargon. Nor, in an effort to get away from euphemism, should you salt your paper with four-letter words. But you can do much if you will mount guard against those roundabout phrases, those echoing polysyllables that tend to slip into your writing to rob it of its crispness and force.

Beware of the Pat Expression

50 Other things being equal, avoid phrases like "other things being 50 equal." Those sentences that come to you whole, or in two or three doughy lumps, are sure to be bad sentences. They are no creation of yours but pieces of common thought floating in the community soup.

Pat expressions are hard, often impossible, to avoid, because they come too easily to be noticed and seem too necessary to be dispensed with. No writer avoids them altogether, but good writers avoid them more often than poor writers.

By "pat expressions" we mean such tags as "to all practical intents and purposes," "the pure and simple truth," "from where I sit," "the time of his life," "to the ends of the earth," "in the twinkling of an eye," "as sure as you're born," "over my dead body," "under cover of darkness," "took the easy way out," "when all is said and done," "told him time and time again," "parted the best of friends," "stand up and be counted," "gave him the best years of her life," "worked her fingers to the bone." Like other clichés, these expressions were once forceful. Now we should use them only when we cant possibly think of anything else.

Some pat expressions stand like a wall between the writer and thought. Such a one is "the American way of life." Many student writers feel that when they have said that something accords with the American way of life or does not they have exhausted the subject. Actually, they have stopped at the highest level of abstraction. The American way of life is the complicated set of bonds between a hundred and eighty million ways. All of us know this when we think about it, but the tag phrase too often keeps us from thinking about it.

So with many another phrase dear to the politician: "this great land of ours," "the man in the street," "our national heritage." These may prove our patriotism or give a clue to our political beliefs, but otherwise they add nothing to the paper except words.

Colorful Words

⁵⁵   The writer builds with words, and no builder uses a raw material ⁵⁵
more slippery and elusive and treacherous. A writer's work is a constant struggle to get the right word in the right place, to find that particular word that will convey his meaning exactly, that will persuade
the reader or soothe him or startle or amuse him. He never succeeds
altogether—sometimes he feels that he scarcely succeeds at all—but
such successes as he has are what make the thing worth doing.

There is no book of rules for this game. One progresses through
everlasting experiment on the basis of ever-widening experience.
There are few useful generalizations that one can make about words
as words, but there are perhaps a few.

Some words are what we call "colorful." By this we mean that they
are calculated to produce a picture or induce an emotion. They are
dressy instead of plain, specific instead of general, loud instead of soft.
Thus, in place of "Her heart beat," we write "Her heart *pounded,
throbbed, fluttered, danced.*" Instead of "He sat in his chair," we may
say, "He *lounged, sprawled, coiled.*" Instead of "It was hot," we may say,
"It was *blistering, sultry, muggy, suffocating, steamy, wilting.*"

However, it should not be supposed that the fancy word is always
better. Often it is as well to write "Her heart beat" or "It was hot" if
that is all it did or all it was. Ages differ in how they like their prose.
The nineteenth century liked it rich and smoky. The twentieth has
usually preferred it lean and cool. The twentieth-century writer, like
all writers, is forever seeking the exact word, but he is wary of sounding feverish. He tends to pitch it low, to understate it, to throw it away.
He knows that if he gets too colorful, the audience is likely to giggle.

See how this strikes you: "As the rich, golden glow of the sunset
died away along the eternal western hills, Angela's limpid blue eyes
looked softly and trustingly into Montague's flashing brown ones, and
her heart pounded like a drum in time with the joyous song surging
in her soul." Some people like that sort of thing, but most modern
readers would say, "Good grief," and turn on the television.

Colored Words

⁶⁰   Some words we would call not so much colorful as colored—that ⁶⁰
is, loaded with associations, good or bad. All words—except perhaps

structure words—have associations of some sort. We have said that the meaning of a word is the sum of the contexts in which it occurs. When we hear a word, we hear with it an echo of all the situations in which we have heard it before.

In some words, these echoes are obvious and discussable. The word *mother*, for example, has, for most people, agreeable associations. When you hear *mother* you probably think of home, safety, love, food, and various other pleasant things. If one writes, "She was like a *mother* to me," he gets an effect which he would not get in "She was like an aunt to me." The advertiser makes use of the associations of *mother* by working it in when he talks about his product. The politician works it in when he talks about himself.

So also with such words as *home, liberty, fireside, contentment, patriot, tenderness, sacrifice, childlike, manly, bluff, limpid.* All of these words are loaded with favorable associations that would be rather hard to indicate in a straightforward definition. There is more than a literal difference between "They sat around the fireside" and "They sat around the stove." They might have been equally warm and happy around the stove, but *fireside* suggests leisure, grace, quiet tradition, congenial company, and *stove* does not.

Conversely, some words have bad associations. *Mother* suggests pleasant things, but *mother-in-law* does not. Many mothers-in-law are heroically lovable and some mothers drink gin all day and beat their children insensible, but these facts of life are beside the point. The thing is that *mother* sounds good and *mother-in-law* does not.

Or consider the word *intellectual*. This would seem to be a complimentary term, but in point of fact it is not, for it has picked up associations of impracticality and ineffectuality and general dopiness. So also with such words as *liberal, reactionary, Communist, socialist, capitalist, radical, schoolteacher, truck driver, undertaker, operator, salesman, huckster, speculator.* These convey meanings on the literal level, but beyond that—sometimes, in some places—they convey contempt on the part of the speaker.

65 The question of whether to use loaded words or not depends on 65 what is being written. The scientist, the scholar, try to avoid them; for the poet, the advertising writer, the public speaker, they are standard equipment. But every writer should take care that they do not substitute for thought. If you write, "Anyone who thinks that is nothing but a Socialist (or Communist or capitalist)," you have said nothing ex-

cept that you don't like people who think that, and such remarks are effective only with the most naive readers. It is always a bad mistake to think your readers more naive than they really are.

Colorless Words

But probably most student writers come to grief not with words that are colorful or those that are colored but with those that have no color at all. A pet example is *nice*, a word we would find it hard to dispense with in casual conversation but which is no longer capable of adding much to a description. Colorless words are those of such general meaning that in a particular sentence they mean nothing. Slang adjectives, like *cool* ("That's real cool") tend to explode all over the language. They are applied to everything, lose their original force, and quickly die.

Beware also of nouns of very general meaning, like *circumstances, cases, instances, aspects, factors, relationships, attitudes, eventualities,* etc. In most circumstances you will find that those cases of writing which contain too many instances of words like these will in this and other aspects have factors leading to unsatisfactory relationships with the reader resulting in unfavorable attitudes on his part and perhaps other eventualities, like a grade of "D." Notice also what "etc." means. It means "I'd like to make this list longer, but I can't think of any more examples."

The Case for Curling Up with a Book

Carol Shields

Carol Shields (1935–2003) was born in Chicago and grew up in Oak Park, Illinois. She studied at Hanover College, the University of Exeter (England), and the University of Ottawa, and now lives in Winnipeg. Shields has won many prizes and awards for her fiction, including a Pulitzer Prize for The Stone Diaries *(1993) and both the National Book Critics Circle Award and the Prix de Lire in 1998 for* Larry's Party *(1997). In July of 2003, she died from complications of breast cancer. Her final novel,* Unless, *was published in 2002 and was nominated for, among others, the* Booker Prize. *In the following essay Shields writes eloquently on the experience of absorbing reading.*

1   Some years ago a Canadian politician, one of our more admirable figures, announced that he was cutting back on his public life because it interfered with his reading. *His reading*[—]notice the possessive pronoun, like saying his arm or his leg[—]and notice too, the assumption that human beings carry, like a kind of cerebral brief case, this built-in commitment to time and energy[:] *their reading.*

I'm told that people no longer know how to curl up with a book. The body has forgotten how to curl. Either we snack on paperbacks while waiting for the bus or we hunch over our books with a yellow underliner in hand. Or, more and more, we sit before a screen and "interact."

Curling up with a book can be accomplished in a variety of ways: in bed for instance, with a towel on a sunlit beach, or from an armchair parked next to a good reading lamp. What it absolutely requires

"The Case for Curling Up with a Book," by Carol Shields from *The Journal*, Spring 1997. Reprinted by permission of the Bella Pomer Agency, Canada.

is a block of uninterrupted time, solitary time and our society sometimes looks with pity on the solitary, that woman alone at the movies, that poor man sitting by himself at his restaurant table. Our hearts go out to them, but reading, by definition, can only be done alone. I would like to make the case today for solitary time, for a life with space enough to curl up with a book.

Reading, at least since human beings learned to read silently (and what a cognitive shift that was!) requires an extraordinary effort at paying attention, at remaining alert. The object of our attention matters less, in a sense, than the purity of our awareness. As the American writer Sven Birkerts says, it is better, better in terms of touching the self within us, that we move from a state of half-distraction to one of full attention. When we read with attention, an inner circuit of the brain is satisfyingly completed. We feel our perceptions sharpen and acquire edge. Reading, as many of you have discovered, is one of the very few things you can do only by shining your full awareness on the task. We can make love, cook, listen to music, shop for groceries, add up columns of figures all with our brain, our self that is, divided and distracted. But print on the page demands *all* of us. It is so complex, its cognitive circuitry so demanding; the black strokes on the white page must be apprehended and translated into ideas, and ideas fitted into patterns, the patterns then shifted and analyzed. The eye travels backward for a moment; this in itself is a technical marvel, rereading a sentence or a paragraph, extracting the sense, the intention, the essence of what is offered.

And ironically, this singleness of focus delivers a doubleness of perception. You are invited into a moment sheathed in nothing but itself. Reading a novel, *curled up* with a novel, you are simultaneously in your arm chair and in, for instance, the garden of Virginia Woolf in the year 1927, or a shabby Manitoba farmhouse conjured by Margaret Laurence, . . . participating fully in another world while remaining conscious of the core of your self, that self that may be hardwired into our bodies or else developed slowly, created over the long distance of our lives.

We are connected through our work, through our familial chain and, by way of the Internet, to virtually everyone in the world. So what of the private self which comes tantalizingly alive under the circle of the reading lamp, that self that we only occasionally touch and then with trepidation. We use the expression "being lost in a book," but we are really closer to a state of being found. Curled up with a novel about an

East Indian family for instance, we are not so much escaping our own splintered and decentred world as we are enlarging our sense of self, our multiplying possibilities and expanded experience. People are, after all, tragically limited: we can live in only so many places, work at a small number of jobs or professions; we can love only a finite number of people. Reading, and particularly the reading of fiction (perhaps I really do have a sales pitch here) lets us be other, to touch and taste the other, to sense the shock and satisfaction of otherness. A novel lets us be ourselves and yet enter another person's boundaried world, to share in a private gaze between reader and writer. *Your* reading, and here comes the possessive pronoun again, can be part of your life and there will be times when it may be the best part. . . .

[A] written text, as opposed to electronic information, has formal order, tone, voice, irony, persuasion. We can inhabit a book; we can possess it and be possessed by it. The critic and scholar Martha Nussbaum believes that attentive readers of serious fiction cannot help but be compassionate and ethical citizens. The rhythms of prose train the empathetic imagination and the rational emotions. . . .

Almost all of [us are] plugged into the electronic world in one way or another, reliant on it for its millions of bytes of information. But a factoid, a nugget of pure information, or even the ever-widening web of information, while enabling us to perform, does relatively little to nourish us. A computer connects facts but cannot reflect upon them. There is no depth, no embeddedness. It is, literally, software, plaintext, language prefabricated and sorted into byte sizes. It does not, in short, aspire; it rarely sings. Enemies of the book want to see information freed from the prison of the printed page, putting faith instead in free floating information and this would be fine if we weren't human beings, historical beings, thinking beings with a hunger for diversion, for narrative, for consolation, for exhortation.

We need literature on the page because it allows us to experience more fully, to imagine more deeply, enabling us to live more freely. Reading, [we] are in touch with [our best selves], and I think, too, that reading shortens the distance we must travel to discover that our most private perceptions are, in fact, universally felt. *Your* reading will intersect with the axis of *my* reading and of his reading and of her reading. Reading, then, offers us the ultimate website, where attention, awareness, reflection, understanding, clarity, and civility come together in a transformative experience.

Writing

William Stafford

William Stafford (1914–1993) grew up in Kansas and taught at Lewis and Clark College in Oregon. His books include Traveling Through the Dark *(1963), which received the National Book Award;* Stories That Could Be True *(1977), a collection of poems;* Writing the Australian Crawl *(1978), a collection of essays;* A Glass Face in the Rain *(1982);* You Must Revise Your Life *(1986), another collection of essays;* An Oregon Message *(1987); and* Passwords *(1991). Stafford describes a writing process that works for him—and might for you—in this timeless 1970 essay.*

1 A writer is not so much someone who has something to say as he is someone who has found a process that will bring about new things he would not have thought of if he had not started to say them. That is, he does not draw on a reservoir; instead, he engages in an activity that brings to him a whole succession of unforeseen stories, poems, essays, plays, laws, philosophies, religions, or—but wait!

Back in school, from the first when I began to try to write things, I felt this richness. One thing would lead to another; the world would give and give. Now, after twenty years or so of trying, I live by that certain richness, an idea hard to pin, difficult to say, and perhaps offensive to some. For there are strange implications in it.

One implication is the importance of just plain receptivity. When I write, I like to have an interval before me when I am not likely to be interrupted. For me, this means usually the early morning, before others are awake. I get pen and paper, take a glance out the window (often it is dark out there), and wait. It is like fishing. But I do not wait very long, for there is always a nibble—and this is where receptivity comes

Excerpted from "A Way of Writing.", *Field: Contemporary Poetry and Poetics,* no. 2. Published by Oberlin College Press.

in. To get started I will accept anything that occurs to me. Something always occurs, of course, to any of us. We can't keep from thinking. Maybe I have to settle for an immediate impression: it's cold, or hot, or dark, or bright, or in between! Or—well, the possibilities are endless. If I put down something, that thing will help the next thing come, and I'm off. If I let the process go on, things will occur to me that were not at all in my mind when I started. These things, odd and trivial as they may be, are somehow connected. And if I let them string out, surprising things will happen.

If I let them string out . . . Along with initial receptivity, then, there is another readiness: I must be willing to fail. If I am to keep on writing, I cannot bother to insist on high standards. I must get into action and not let anything stop me, or even slow me much. By "standards" I do not mean "correctness"—spelling, punctuation, and so on. These details become mechanical for anyone who writes for a while. I am thinking about what many people would consider "important" standards, such matters as social significance, positive values, consistency, etc. I resolutely disregard these. Something better, greater, is happening! I am following a process that leads so wildly and originally into new territory that no judgment can at the moment be made about values, significance, and so on. I am making something new, something that has not been judged before. Later others—and maybe I myself—will make judgments. Now, I am headlong to discover. Any distraction may harm the creating.

So, receptive, careless of failure, I spin out things on the page. And a wonderful freedom comes. If something occurs to me, it is all right to accept it. It has one justification: it occurs to me. No one else can guide me. I must follow my own weak, wandering, diffident impulses.

A strange bonus happens. At times, without my insisting on it, my writings become coherent; the successive elements that occur to me are clearly related. They lead by themselves to new connections. Sometimes the language, even the syllables that happen along, may start a trend. Sometimes the materials alert me to something waiting in my mind, ready for sustained attention. At such times, I allow myself to be eloquent, or intentional, or for great swoops (treacherous! not to be trusted!) reasonable. But I do not insist on any of that; for I know that back of my activity there will be the coherence of my self, and that indulgence of my impulses will bring recurrent patterns and meanings again.

This attitude toward the process of writing creatively suggests a problem for me, in terms of what others say. They talk about "skills" in writing. Without denying that I do have experience, wide reading, automatic orthodoxies and maneuvers of various kinds, I still must insist that I am often baffled about what "skill" has to do with the precious little area of confusion when I do not know what I am going to say and then I found out what I am going to say. That precious interval I am unable to bridge by skill. What can I witness about it? It remains mysterious, just as all of us must feel puzzled about how we are so inventive as to be able to talk along through complexities with our friends, not needing to plan what we are going to say, but never stalled for long in our confident forward progress. Skill? If so, it is the skill we all have, something we must have learned before the age of three or four.

A writer is one who has become accustomed to trusting that grace, or luck, or—skill.

Yet another attitude I find necessary: most of what I write, like most of what I say in casual conversation, will not amount to much. Even I will realize, and even at the time, that it is not negotiable. It will be like practice. In conversation, I allow myself random remarks—in fact, as I recall, that is the way I learned to talk—so in writing I launch many expendable efforts. A result of this free way of writing is that I am not writing for others, mostly; they will not see the product at all unless the activity eventuates in something that later appears to be worthy. My guide is the self, and its adventuring in the language brings about communication.

10   This process-rather-than-substance view of writing invites a final,   10 dual reflection:

1. Writers may not be special—sensitive or talented in any usual sense. They are simply engaged in sustained use of a language skill we all have. Their "creations" come about through confident reliance on stray impulses that will, with trust, find occasional patterns that are satisfying.

2. But writing itself is one of the great, free human activities. There is scope for individuality, and elation, and discovery, in writing. For the person who follows with trust and forgiveness what occurs to him, the world remains always ready and deep, an inexhaustible environment, with the combined vividness of an actuality and flexibility of a dream. Working back and forth between experience and thought, writers have more than space and time can offer. They have the whole unexplored realm of human vision.

A Modest Proposal

Jonathan Swift

*Born in Dublin, Ireland, Jonathan Swift (1667–1745)
entered the clergy after his education at Trinity College and
Oxford University. Through his long life he wrote in a wide
range of genres, including poetry, religious pamphlets, essays, and satires on various social and political themes. His
best-known work is* Gulliver's Travels, *a combination of
children's story and social satire. Swift was always a sup-
porter of Irish causes, as can be seen in "A Modest Proposal," which was published anonymously in 1729. In this
ironic essay, the speaker—the "I"—is not Swift himself but
a persona, a fictional voice who gives his proposal to cure
the ills of contemporary Ireland. It is true that Ireland at
this time had the problems described by this persona:
poverty, unemployment, a failing economy, exploitation by
the wealthy classes, conflict between the Anglican and
Catholic churches, and so on. This is the serious subject
Swift addresses through his satire. If you have not read or
heard of his "proposal" previously, read slowly and atten-
tively: you might be greatly surprised to learn the nature of
his proposition.*

It is a melancholy object to those who walk through this great town
or travel in the country, when they see the streets, the roads, and
cabin doors, crowded with beggars of the female sex, followed by
three, four, or six children, all in rags and importuning every passenger for an alms. These mothers, instead of being able to work for their
honest livelihood, are forced to employ all their time in strolling to
beg sustenance for their helpless infants, who, as they grow up, either
turn thieves for want of work, or leave their dear native country to
fight for the Pretender in Spain, or sell themselves to the Barbadoes.

I think it is agreed by all parties that this prodigious number of
children in the arms, or on the backs, or at the heels of their mothers,

and frequently of their fathers, is in the present deplorable state of the kingdom a very great additional grievance; and therefore whoever could find out a fair, cheap, and easy method of making these children sound, useful members of the commonwealth would deserve so well of the public as to have his statue set up for a preserver of the nation.

But my intention is very far from being confined to provide only for the children of professed beggars; it is of a much greater extent, and shall take in the whole number of infants at a certain age who are born of parents in effect as little able to support them as those who demand our charity in the streets.

As to my own part, having turned my thoughts for many years upon this important subject, and maturely weighed the several schemes of other projectors, I have always found them grossly mistaken in their computation. It is true, a child just dropped from its dam may be supported by her milk for a solar year, with little other nourishment; at most not above the value of two shillings, which the mother may certainly get, or the value in scraps, by her lawful occupation of begging; and it is exactly at one year old that I propose to provide for them in such a manner as instead of being a charge upon their parents or the parish, or wanting food and raiment for the rest of their lives, they shall on the contrary contribute to the feeding, and partly to the clothing, of many thousands.

5   There is likewise another great advantage in my scheme, that it   5 will prevent those voluntary abortions, and that horrid practice of women murdering their bastard children, alas, too frequent among us, sacrificing the poor innocent babes, I doubt, more to avoid the expense than the shame, which would move tears and pity in the most savage and inhuman breast.

The number of souls in this kingdom being usually reckoned one million and a half, of these I calculate there may be about two hundred thousand couples whose wives are breeders; from which number I subtract thirty thousand couples who are able to maintain their own children, although I apprehend there cannot be so many under the present distresses of the kingdom; but this being granted, there will remain an hundred and seventy thousand breeders. I again subtract fifty thousand for those women who miscarry, or whose children die by accident or disease within the year. There only remain an hundred and twenty thousand children of poor parents annually born. The question therefore is, how this number shall be reared and provided for, which, as I have already said, under the present situation of affairs, is utterly impossible by all the methods hitherto proposed. For we can neither employ them in handicraft nor agriculture; we neither build houses (I mean in the country) nor cultivate land. They can very seldom pick up livelihood by stealing till they arrive at six years old, except where they are of towardly parts; although I confess they learn the rudiments much earlier, during which time they can however be looked upon only as probationers, as I have been informed by a principal gentleman in the county of Cavan, who protested to me that he never knew above one or two instances under the age of six, even in a part of the kingdom so renowned for the quickest proficiency in that art.

I am assured by our merchants that a boy or a girl before twelve years old is no salable commodity; and even when they come to this age, they will not yield above three pounds, or three pounds and half a crown at most on the Exchange; which cannot turn to account either to the parents or the kingdom, the charge of nutriment and rags having been at least four times that value.

I shall now therefore humbly propose my own thoughts, which I hope will not be liable to the least objection.

I have been assured by a very knowing American of my acquaintance in London, that a young healthy child well nursed is at a year old a most delicious, nourishing, and wholesome food, whether stewed, roasted, baked, or boiled; and I make no doubt that it will equally serve in a fricassee or a ragout.

I do therefore humbly offer it to public consideration that of the hundred and twenty thousand children, already computed, twenty thousand may be reserved for breed, whereof only one fourth part to be males, which is more than we allow to sheep, black cattle, or swine; and my reason is that these children are seldom the fruits of marriage, a circumstance not much regarded by our savages, therefore one male will be sufficient to serve four females. That the remaining hundred thousand may at a year old be offered in sale to the persons of quality and fortune through the kingdom, always advising the mother to let them suck plentifully in the last month, so as to render them plump and fat for a good table. A child will make two dishes at an entertainment for friends; and when the family dines alone, the fore or hind quarter will make a reasonable dish, and seasoned with a little pepper or salt will be very good boiled on the fourth day, especially in winter.

I have reckoned upon a medium that a child just born will weigh twelve pounds, and in a solar year if tolerably nursed increaseth to twenty-eight pounds.

I grant this food will be somewhat dear, and therefore very proper for landlords, who, as they have already devoured most of the parents, seem to have the best title to the children.

Infant's flesh will be in season throughout the year, but more plentiful in March, and a little before and after. For we are told by a grave author, an eminent French physician, that fish being a prolific diet, there are more children born in Roman Catholic countries about nine months after Lent, than at any other season; therefore, reckoning a year after Lent, the markets will be more glutted than usual, because the number of popish infants is at least three to one in this kingdom; and therefore it will have one other collateral advantage, by lessening the number of Papists among us.

I have already computed the charge of nursing a beggar's child (in which list I reckon all cottagers, laborers, and four fifths of the farmers) to be about two shillings per annum, rags included; and I believe no gentleman would repine to give ten shillings for the carcass of a good fat child, which, as I have said, will make four dishes of excellent nutritive meat, when he hath only some particular friend or his own family to dine with him. Thus the squire will learn to be a good landlord, and grow popular among the tenants; the mother will have eight shillings net profit, and be fit for work till she produces another child.

Those who are more thrifty (as I must confess the times require) may flay the carcass; the skin of which artificially dressed will make admirable gloves for ladies, and summer boots for fine gentlemen.

As to our city of Dublin, shambles may be appointed for this purpose in the most convenient parts of it, and butchers we may be assured will not be wanting; although I rather recommend buying the children alive, and dressing them hot from the knife as we do roasting pigs.

A very worthy person, a true lover of his country, and whose virtues I highly esteem, was lately pleased in discoursing on this matter to offer a refinement upon my scheme. He said that many gentlemen of his kingdom, having of late destroyed their deer, he conceived that the want of venison might be well supplied by the bodies of young lads and maidens, not exceeding fourteen years of age nor under twelve, so great a number of both sexes in every county being now ready to starve for want of work and service; and these to be disposed of by their parents, if alive, or otherwise by their nearest relations. But with due deference to so excellent a friend and so deserving a patriot, I cannot be altogether in his sentiments; for as to the males, my American acquaintance assured me from frequent experience that their flesh was generally tough and lean, like that of our schoolboys, by continual exercise, and their taste disagreeable; and to fatten them would not answer the charge. Then as to the females, it would, I think with humble submission, be a loss to the public, because they soon would become breeders themselves; and besides, it is not improbable that some scrupulous people might be apt to censure such a practice (although indeed very unjustly) as a little bordering upon cruelty; which, I confess, hath always been with me the strongest objection against any project, how well soever intended.

But in order to justify my friend, he confessed that this expedient was put into his head by the famous Psalmanazar, a native of the island Formosa, who came from thence to London above twenty years ago, and in conversation told my friend that in his country when any young person happened to be put to death, the executioner sold the carcass to persons of quality as a prime dainty; and that in his time the body of a plump girl of fifteen, who was crucified for an attempt to poison the emperor, was sold to his Imperial Majesty's prime minister of state, and other great mandarins of the court, in joints from the gibbet, at four hundred crowns. Neither indeed can I deny that if the same use were made of several plump young girls in this town, who without one single groat to their fortunes cannot stir abroad without a chair, and appear at the playhouse and assemblies in foreign fineries which they never will pay for, the kingdom would not be the worse.

Some persons of a desponding spirit are in great concern about that vast number of poor people who are aged, diseased, or maimed, and I have been desired to employ my thoughts what course may be taken to ease the nation of so grievous an encumbrance. But I am not in the least pain upon that matter, because it is very well known that they are every day dying and rotting by cold and famine, and filth and vermin, as fast as can be reasonably expected. And as to the younger laborers, they are now in almost as hopeful a condition. They cannot get work, and consequently pine away for want of nourishment to a degree that if any time they are accidentally hired to common labor, they have not strength to perform it; and thus the country and themselves are happily delivered from the evils to come.

20   I have too long digressed, and therefore shall return to my subject. I think the advantages by the proposal which I have made are obvious and many, as well as of the highest importance.

For first, as I have already observed, it would greatly lessen the number of Papists, with whom we are yearly overrun, being the principal breeders of the nation as well as our most dangerous enemies; and who stay at home on purpose to deliver the kingdom to the Pretender, hoping to take their advantage by the absence of so many good Protestants, who have chosen rather to leave their country than to stay at home and pay tithes against their conscience to an Episcopal curate.

Secondly, the poorer tenants will have something valuable of their own, which by law may be made liable to distress, and help to pay their landlord's rent, their corn and cattle being already seized and money a thing unknown.

Thirdly, whereas the maintenance of an hundred thousand children, from two years old and upwards, cannot be computed at less than ten shillings a piece per annum, the nation's stock will be thereby increased fifty thousand pounds per annum, besides the profit of a new dish introduced to the tables of all gentlemen of fortune in the kingdom who have any refinement in taste. And the money will circulate among ourselves, the goods being entirely of our own growth and manufacture.

Fourthly, the constant breeders, besides the gain of eight shillings sterling per annum by the sale of their children, will be rid of the charge of maintaining them after the first year.

25   Fifthly, this food would likewise bring great custom to taverns, where the vintners will certainly be so prudent as to procure the best receipts for dressing it to perfection, and consequently have their houses frequented by all the fine gentlemen, who justly value themselves upon their knowledge in good eating; and a skillful cook, who understands how to oblige his guests, will contrive to make it as expensive as they please.

Sixthly, this would be a great inducement to marriage, which all wise nations have either encouraged by rewards or enforced by laws and penalties. It would increase the care and tenderness of mothers toward their children, when they were sure of a settlement for life to the poor babes, provided in some sort by the public, to their annual profit instead of expense. We should see an honest emulation among the married women, which of them could bring the fattest child to the market. Men would become as fond of their wives during the time of pregnancy as they are now of their mares in foal, their cows in calf, or sows when they are ready to farrow; nor offer to beat or kick them (as is too frequent a practice) for fear of a miscarriage.

Many other advantages might be enumerated. For instance, the addition of some thousand carcasses in our exportation of barreled beef, the propagation of swine's flesh, and improvement in the art of making good bacon, so much wanted among us by the great destruction of pigs, too frequent at our tables, which are no way comparable in taste or magnificence to a well-grown, fat, yearling child, which roasted whole will make a considerable figure at a lord mayor's feast or any other public entertainment. But this and many others I omit, being studious of brevity.

Supposing that one thousand families in this city would be constant customers for infants' flesh, besides others who might have it at merry meetings, particularly weddings and christenings, I compute that Dublin would take off annually about twenty thousand carcasses, and the rest of the kingdom (where probably they will be sold somewhat cheaper) the remaining eighty thousand.

I can think of no one objection that will possibly be raised against this proposal, unless it should be urged that the number of people will be thereby much lessened in the kingdom. This I freely own, and it was indeed one principal design in offering it to the world. I desire the reader will observe; that I calculate my remedy for this one individual kingdom of Ireland and for no other that ever was, is, or I think ever can be upon earth. Therefore, let no man talk to me of other expedients: of taxing our absentees at five shillings a pound: of using neither clothes nor household furniture except what is of our own growth and manufacture: of utterly rejecting the materials and instruments that promote foreign luxury: of curing the expensiveness of pride, vanity, idleness, and gaming in our women: of introducing a vein of parsimony, prudence, and temperance: of learning to love our country, in the want of which we differ even from Laplanders and the inhabitants of Topinamboo: of quitting our animosities and factions, nor acting any longer like the Jews, who were murdering one another at the very moment their city was taken: of being a little cautious not to sell our country and conscience for nothing: of teaching landlords to have at least one degree of mercy toward their tenants: lastly, of putting a spirit of honesty, industry, and skill into our shopkeepers; who, if a resolution could now be taken to buy only our native goods, would immediately unite to cheat and exact upon us in the price, the measure, and the goodness, nor could ever yet be brought to make one fair proposal of just dealing, though often and earnestly invited to it.

30 Therefore, I repeat, let no man talk to me of these and the like expedients, till he hath at least some glimpse of hope that there will ever be some hearty and sincere attempt to put them in practice. 30

But as to myself, having been wearied out for many years with offering vain, idle, visionary thoughts, and at length utterly despairing of success, I fortunately fell upon this proposal, which, as it is wholly new, so it hath something solid and real, of no expense and little trouble, full in our own power, and whereby we can incur no danger in disobliging England. For this kind of commodity will not bear exportation, the flesh being of too tender a consistence to admit a long continuance in salt, although perhaps I could name a country which would be glad to eat up our whole nation without it.

After all, I am not so violently bent upon my own opinion as to reject any offer proposed by wise men, which shall be found equally innocent, cheap, easy, and effectual. But before something of that kind shall be advanced in contradiction to my scheme, and offering a better, I desire the author or authors will be pleased maturely to consider two points. First, as things now stand, how they will be able to find food and raiment for an hundred thousand useless mouths and backs. And secondly, there being a round million of creatures in human figure throughout this kingdom, whose sole subsistence put into a common stock would leave them in debt two millions of pounds sterling, adding those who are beggars by profession to the bulk of farmers, cottagers, and laborers, with their wives and children who are beggars in effect; I desire those politicians who dislike my overture, and may perhaps be so bold to attempt an answer, that they will first ask the parents of these mortals whether they would not at this day think it a great happiness to have been sold for food at a year old in this manner I prescribe, and thereby have avoided such a perpetual scene of misfortunes as they have since gone through by the oppression of landlords, the impossibility of paying rent without money or trade, the want of common sustenance, with neither house nor clothes to cover them from the inclemencies of the weather, and the most inevitable prospect of entailing the like or greater miseries upon their breed forever.

I profess, in the sincerity of my heart, that I have not the least personal interest in endeavoring to promote this necessary work, having no other motive than the public good of my country, by advancing our trade, providing for infants, relieving the poor, and giving some pleasure to the rich. I have no children by which I can propose to get a single penny; the youngest being nine years old, and my wife past childbearing.

Decolonising the Mind
Ngũgĩ wa Thiong'o

Background

Ngũgĩ wa Thiong'o is regarded as one of the most important contemporary writers from the African continent. He wrote his first novels, *Weep, Not, Child* (1964) and *The River Between* (1965), in English, and *Caitaani Mutharava-Ini* (translated as *Devil on the Cross*, 1982) in his native language, Gĩkũyũ. He was chairman of the Department of Literature at the University of Nairobi until his detention, without trial, by the Kenyan authorities in 1976, an account of which appeared under the title *Detained: A Writer's Prison Diary* (1981). The international outcry over his imprisonment eventually brought about his release two years later, after which he left Kenya. The following selection comes from *Decolonising the Mind: The Politics of Language in African Literature* (1986), a work that constitutes, says Thiong'o, "my farewell to English as a vehicle for any of my writings." Subsequently, he has written novels and plays in Gĩkũyũ. Thiong'o currently is a Professor of Comparative Literature at New York University.

DECOLONISING THE MIND

I was born into a large peasant family: father, four wives and about twenty-eight children. I also belonged, as we all did in those days, to a wider extended family and to the community as a whole.

We spoke Gĩkũyũ as we worked in the fields. We spoke Gĩkũyũ in and outside the home. I can vividly recall those evenings of story-telling around the fireside. It was mostly the grown-ups telling the children

Reprinted from *Decolonising the Mind* (2003), by permission of the Copyright Clearance Center. Copyright © 2003 by James Currey Publishing, Ltd.

but everybody was interested and involved. We children would re-tell the stories the following day to other children who worked in the fields picking the pyrethrum flowers, tea-leaves or coffee beans of our European and African landlords.

The stories, with mostly animals as the main characters, were all told in Gĩkũyũ. Hare, being small, weak but full of innovative wit and cunning, was our hero. We identified with him as he struggled against the brutes of prey like lion, leopard, hyena. His victories were our victories and we learnt that the apparently weak can outwit the strong. We followed the animals in their struggle against hostile nature—drought, rain, sun, wind—a confrontation often forcing them to search for forms of co-operation. But we were also interested in their struggles amongst themselves, and particularly between the beasts and the victims of prey. These twin struggles, against nature and other animals, reflected real-life struggles in the human world.

5   Not that we neglected stories with human beings as the main characters. There were two types of characters in such human-centred narratives: the species of truly human beings with qualities of courage, kindness, mercy, hatred of evil, concern for others; and a man-eat-man two-mouthed species with qualities of greed, selfishness, individualism and hatred of what was good for the larger co-operative community. Co-operation as the ultimate good in a community was a constant theme. It could unite human beings with animals against ogres and beasts of prey, as in the story of how dove, after being fed with castor-oil seeds, was sent to fetch a smith working far away from home and whose pregnant wife was being threatened by these man-eating two-mouthed ogres.

There were good and bad story-tellers. A good one could tell the same story over and over again, and it would always be fresh to us, the listeners. He or she could tell a story told by someone else and make it more alive and dramatic. The differences really were in the use of words and images and the inflexion of voices to effect different tones.

We therefore learnt to value words for their meaning and nuances. Language was not a mere string of words. It had a suggestive power well beyond the immediate and lexical meaning. Our appreciation of the suggestive magical power of language was reinforced by the games we played with words through riddles, proverbs, transpositions of syllables, or through nonsensical but musically arranged words.[1] So we learnt the music of our language on top of the content. The language, through images and symbols, gave us a view of the world, but it had a beauty of its own. The home and the field were then our pre-primary school but what is important, for this discussion, is that the language of our evening teach-ins, and the language of our immediate and wider community, and the language of our work in the fields were one.

And then I went to school, a colonial school, and this harmony was broken. The language of my education was no longer the language of my culture. I first went to Kamaandura, missionary run, and then to another called Maanguuū run by nationalists grouped around the Gīkūyū Independent and Karinga Schools Association. Our language of education was still Gīkūyū. The very first time I was ever given an ovation for my writing was over a composition in Gīkūyū. So for my first four years there was still harmony between the language of my formal education and that of the Limuru peasant community.

It was after the declaration of a state of emergency over Kenya in 1952 that all the schools run by patriotic nationalists were taken over by the colonial regime and were placed under District Education Boards chaired by Englishmen. English became the language of my formal education. In Kenya, English became more than a language: it was *the* language, and all the others had to bow before it in deference.

Thus one of the most humiliating experiences was to be caught speaking Gīkūyū in the vicinity of the school. The culprit was given corporal punishment—three to five strokes of the cane on bare buttocks—or was made to carry a metal plate around the neck with inscriptions such as I AM STUPID or I AM A DONKEY. Sometimes the culprits were fined money they could hardly afford. And how did the teachers catch the culprits? A button was initially given to one pupil who was supposed to hand it over to whoever was caught speaking his mother tongue. Whoever had the button at the end of the day would

---

[1] Example from a tongue twister: 'Kaana ka Nikoora koona koora koora: na ko koora koona kaana ka Nikoora koora koora.' I'm indebted to Wangui wa Goro for this example. "Nichola's child saw a baby frog and ran away: and when the baby frog saw Nichola's child it also ran away.' A Gīkūyū speaking child has to get the correct tone and length of vowel and pauses to get it right. Otherwise it becomes a jumble of *k*'s and *r*'s and *na*'s [author's note].

sing who had given it to him and the ensuing process would bring out all the culprits of the day. Thus children were turned into witch-hunters and in the process were being taught the lucrative value of being a traitor to one's immediate community.

The attitude to English was the exact opposite: any achievement in spoken or written English was highly rewarded; prizes, prestige, applause; the ticket to higher realms. English became the measure of intelligence and ability in the arts, the sciences, and all the other branches of learning. English became *the* main determinant of a child's progress up the ladder of formal education.

As you may know, the colonial system of education in addition to its apartheid racial demarcation had the structure of a pyramid: a broad primary base, a narrowing secondary middle, and an even narrower university apex. Selections from primary into secondary were through an examination, in my time called Kenya African Preliminary Examination, in which one had to pass six subjects ranging from Maths to Nature Study and Kiswahili. All the papers were written in English. Nobody could pass the exam who failed the English language paper no matter how brilliantly he had done in the other subjects. I remember one boy in my class of 1954 who had distinctions in all subjects except English, which he had failed. He was made to fail the entire exam. He went on to become a turn boy in a bus company. I who had only passes but a credit in English got a place at the Alliance High School, one of the most elitist institutions for Africans in colonial Kenya. The requirements for a place at the University, Makerere University College, were broadly the same: nobody could go on to wear the undergraduate red gown, no matter how brilliantly they had performed in all the other subjects unless they had a credit—not even a simple pass!—in English. Thus the most coveted place in the pyramid and in the system was only available to the holder of an English language credit card. English was the official vehicle and the magic formula to colonial elitedom.

Literary education was now determined by the dominant language while also reinforcing that dominance. Orature (oral literature) in Kenyan languages stopped. In primary school I now read simplified Dickens and Stevenson alongside Rider Haggard. Jim Hawkins, Oliver Twist, Tom Brown—not Hare, Leopard and Lion—were now my daily companions in the world of imagination. In secondary school, Scott and G. B. Shaw vied with more Rider Haggard, John Buchan, Alan Paton, Captain W. E. Johns. At Makerere I read English: from Chaucer to T. S. Eliot with a touch of Graham Greene.

Thus language and literature were taking us further and further from ourselves to other selves, from our world to other worlds.

What was the colonial system doing to us Kenyan children? What were the consequences of, on the one hand, this systematic suppression of our languages and the literature they carried, and on the other the elevation of English and the literature it carried? To answer those questions, let me first examine the relationship of language to human experience, human culture, and the human perception of reality.

Language, any language, has a dual character: it is both a means of communication and a carrier of culture. Take English. It is spoken in Britain and in Sweden and Denmark. But for Swedish and Danish people English is only a means of communication with non-Scandinavians. It is not a carrier of their culture. For the British, and particularly the English, it is additionally, and inseparably from its use as a tool of communication, a carrier of their culture and history. Or take Swahili in East and Central Africa. It is widely used as a means of communication across many nationalities. But it is not the carrier of a culture and history of many of those nationalities. However in parts of Kenya and Tanzania, and particularly in Zanzibar, Swahili is inseparably both a means of communication and a carrier of the culture of those people to whom it is a mother-tongue.

Culture transmits or imparts those images of the world and reality through the spoken and the written language, that is through a specific language. In other words, the capacity to speak, the capacity to order sounds in a manner that makes for mutual comprehension between human beings is universal. This is the universality of language, a quality specific to human beings. It corresponds to the universality of the struggle against nature and that between human beings. But the particularity of the sounds, the words, the word order into phrases and sentences, and the specific manner, or laws, of their ordering is what distinguishes one language from another. Thus a specific culture is not transmitted through language in its universality but in its particularity as the language of a specific community with a specific history. Written literature and orature are the main means by which a particular language transmits the images of the world contained in the culture it carries.

Language as communication and as culture are then products of each other. Communication creates culture: culture is a means of communication. Language carries culture, and culture carries, particularly through orature and literature, the entire body of values by which we come to perceive ourselves and our place in the world. How people perceive themselves affects how they look at their culture, at their politics and at the social production of wealth, at their entire relationship to nature and to other beings. Language is thus inseparable from ourselves as a community of human beings with a specific form and character, a specific history, a specific relationship to the world.

So what was the colonialist imposition of a foreign language doing to us children?

20 The real aim of colonialism was to control the people's wealth: 20 what they produced, how they produced it, and how it was distributed; to control, in other words, the entire realm of the language of real life. Colonialism imposed its control of the social production of wealth through military conquest and subsequent political dictatorship. But its most important area of domination was the mental universe of the colonised, the control, through culture, of how people perceived themselves and their relationship to the world. Economic and political control can never be complete or effective without mental control. To control a people's culture is to control their tools of self-definition in relationship to others.

For colonialism this involved two aspects of the same process: the destruction or the deliberate undervaluing of a people's culture, their art, dances, religions, history, geography, education, orature and literature, and the conscious elevation of the language of the coloniser. The domination of a people's language by the languages of the colonising nations was crucial to the domination of the mental universe of the colonised.

Take language as communication. Imposing a foreign language, and suppressing the native languages as spoken and written, were already breaking the harmony previously existing between the African child and the three aspects of language. Since the new language as a means of communication was a product of and was reflecting the 'real language of life' elsewhere, it could never as spoken or written properly reflect or imitate the real life of that community. This may in part explain why technology always appears to us as slightly external, *their* product and not *ours*. The world 'missile' used to hold an alien far-away sound until I recently learnt its equivalent in Gĩkũyũ, *ngurukuhĩ*, and it made me apprehend it differently. Learning, for a colonial child, became a cerebral activity and not an emotionally felt experience.

But since the new, imposed languages could never completely break the native languages as spoken, their most effective area of domination was the third aspect of language as communication, the written. The language of an African child's formal education was foreign. The language of the books he read was foreign. The language of his conceptualisation was foreign. Thought, in him, took the visible form of a foreign language. So the written language of a child's upbringing in the school (even his spoken language within the school compound) became divorced from his spoken language at home. There was often not the slightest relationship between the child's written world, which was also the language of his schooling, and the world of his immediate environment in the family and the community. For a colonial child, the harmony existing between the three aspects of language as communication was irrevocably broken. This resulted in the disassociation of the sensibility of that child from his natural and social environment, what we might call colonial alienation. The alienation became reinforced in the teaching of history, geography, music, where bourgeois Europe was always the centre of the universe.

This disassociation, divorce, or alienation from the immediate environment becomes clearer when you look at colonial language as a carrier of culture.

Since culture is a product of the history of a people which it in turn reflects, the child was now being exposed exclusively to a culture that was a product of a world external to himself. He was being made to stand outside himself to look at himself. *Catching Them Young* is the title of a book on racism, class, sex, and politics in children's literature by Bob Dixon. 'Catching them young' as an aim was even more true of a colonial child. The images of this world and his place in it implanted in a child take years to eradicate, if they ever can be.

Since culture does not just reflect the world in images but actually, through those very images, conditions a child to see that world in a certain way, the colonial child was made to see the world and where he stands in it as seen and defined by or reflected in the culture of the language of imposition.

And since those images are mostly passed on through orature and literature it meant the child would now only see the world as seen in the literature of his language of adoption. From the point of view of alienation, that is of seeing oneself from outside oneself as if one was another self, it does not matter that the imported literature carried the great humanist tradition of the best in Shakespeare, Goethe, Balzac, Tolstoy, Gorky, Brecht, Sholokhov, Dickens. The location of this great mirror of imagination was necessarily Europe and its history and culture and the rest of the universe was seen from that centre.

But obviously it was worse when the colonial child was exposed to images of his world as mirrored in the written languages of his coloniser. Where his own native languages were associated in his impressionable mind with low status, humiliation, corporal punishment, slow-footed intelligence and ability or downright stupidity, non-intelligibility and barbarism, this was reinforced by the world he met in the works of such geniuses of racism as a Rider Haggard or a Nicholas Monsarrat; not to mention the pronouncement of some of the giants of western intellectual and political establishment, such as Hume ('. . . the negro is naturally inferior to the whites . . .')[2], Thomas Jefferson ('. . . the blacks . . . are inferior to the whites on the endowments of both body and mind . . . '),[3] or Hegal with his Africa comparable to a land of childhood still enveloped in the dark mantle of the night as far as the development of self-conscious history was concerned. Hegel's statement that there was nothing harmonious with humanity to be found in the African character is representative of the racist images of Africans and Africa such a colonial child was bound to encounter in the literature of the colonial languages.[4] The results could be disastrous.

---

[2]Quoted in Eric Williams, *A History of the People of Trinidad and Tobago*, London 1964, p. 32 [Author's note].

[3]Eric Williams, ibid, p. 31 [Author's note].

[4]In references to Africa in the introduction to his lectures in *The Philosophy of History*, Hegel gives historical, philosophical, rational expression and legitimacy to every conceivable European racist myth about Africa. Africa is even denied her own geography where it does not correspond to the myth. Thus Egypt is not part of Africa; and North Africa is part of Europe. Africa proper is the especial home of ravenous beasts, snakes of all kinds. The African is not part of humanity. Only slavery to Europe can raise him, possibly, to the lower ranks of humanity. Slavery is good for the African. 'Slavery is in and for itself *injustice*, for the essence of humanity is *freedom*; but for this man must be matured. The gradual abolition of slavery is therefore wiser and more equitable than its sudden removal.' (Hegel, *The Philosophy of History*, Dover edition, New York: 1956, pp. 91–9.) Hegel clearly reveals himself as the nineteenth-century Hitler of the intellect [Author's note].

In her paper read to the conference on the teaching of African literature in schools held in Nairobi in 1973, entitled 'Written Literature and Black Images'[5] the Kenyan writer and scholar Professor Mĩcere Mũgo related how a reading of the description of Gagool as an old African woman in Rider Haggard's *King Solomon's Mines* had for a long time made her feel mortal terror whenever she encountered old African women. In his autobiography *This Life* Sydney Poitier describes how, as a result of the literature he had read, he had come to associate Africa with snakes. So on arrival in Africa and being put up in a modern hotel in a modern city, he could not sleep because he kept on looking for snakes everywhere, even under the bed. These two have been able to pinpoint the origins of their fears. But for most others the negative image becomes internalised and it affects their cultural and even political choices in ordinary living.

---

[5]The paper is now in Akivaga and Gachukiah's *The Teaching of African Literature in Schools*, published by Kenya Literature Bureau [Author's note].

Notes on Punctuation

Lewis Thomas

Lewis Thomas (1913–1994), a physician, scientist, educator, and literary figure of some repute, was born in Flushing, New York. Educated at Princeton (B.S.), Harvard Medical School (M.D.), and Yale (M.A.), Lewis established a career in medical research, education, and administration. He was dean of the School of Medicine at New York University and Yale University and director of the Sloan-Kettering Cancer Center in New York City. Throughout his career in medicine, Thomas published extensively. Although much of his writing appeared in specialized scientific journals, his love of language and his ability to communicate complex topics to uninformed readers enabled him to gain an appreciative lay audience. Thomas's recognition as a skilled and enjoyable essayist began in the mid-1970s, when a series of columns written for the venerable New England Journal of Medicine *and collected in the book* Lives of a Cell, *won the National Book Award for Arts and Letters. Thomas assembled four additional collections of his essays, including* The Medusa and the Snail *(1979), from which this essay was taken. In this essay, Thomas's love of learning and good humor and optimism are evident, as they are in his scientific writing.*

1 There are no precise rules about punctuation (Fowler lays out some general advice (as best he can under the complex circumstances of English prose (he points out, for example, that we possess only four stops (the comma, the semicolon, the colon and the period (the question mark and exclamation point are not, strictly

speaking, stops; they are indicators of tone (oddly enough, the Greeks employed the semicolon for their question mark (it produces a strange sensation to read a Greek sentence which is a straightforward question: Why weepest thou; (instead of Why weepest thou? (and, of course, there are parentheses (which are surely a kind of punctuation making this whole matter much more complicated by having to count up the left-handed parentheses in order to be sure of closing with the right number (but if the parentheses were left out, with nothing to work with but the stops, we would have considerably more flexibility in the deploying of layers of meaning than if we tried to separate all the clauses by physical barriers (and in the latter case, while we might have more precision and exactitude for our meaning, we would lose the essential flavor of language, which is its wonderful ambiguity)))))))))))).

The commas are the most useful and usable of all the stops. It is highly important to put them in place as you go along. If you try to come back after doing a paragraph and stick them in the various spots that tempt you you will discover that they tend to swarm like minnows into all sorts of crevices whose existence you hadn't realized and before you know it the whole long sentence becomes immobilized and lashed up squirming in commas. Better to use them sparingly, and with affection, precisely when the need for each one arises, nicely, by itself.

I have grown fond of semicolons in recent years. The semicolon tells you that there is still some question about the preceding full sentence; something needs to be added; it reminds you sometimes of the Greek usage. It is almost always a greater pleasure to come across a semicolon than a period. The period tells you that that is that; if you didn't get all the meaning you wanted or expected, anyway you got all the writer intended to parcel out and now you have to move along. But with a semicolon there you get a pleasant little feeling of expectancy; there is more to come; read on; it will get clearer.

Colons are a lot less attractive, for several reasons: firstly, they give you the feeling of being rather ordered around, or at least having your nose pointed in a direction you might not be inclined to take if left to yourself, and, secondly, you suspect you're in for one of those sentences that will be labeling the points to be made: firstly, secondly and so forth, with the implication that you haven't sense enough to keep track of a sequence of notions without having them numbered. Also, many writers use this system loosely and incompletely, starting out with number one and number two as though counting off on their fingers but then going on and on without the succession of labels you've been led to expect, leaving you floundering about searching for the ninethly or seventeenthly that ought to be there but isn't.

Exclamation points are the most irritating of all. Look! they say, look at what I just said! How amazing is my thought! It is like being forced to watch someone else's small child jumping up and down crazily in the center of the living room shouting to attract attention. If a sentence really has something of importance to say, something quite remarkable, it doesn't need a mark to point it out. And if it is really, after all, a banal sentence needing more zing, the exclamation point simply emphasizes its banality!

Quotation marks should be used honestly and sparingly, when there is a genuine quotation at hand, and it is necessary to be very rigorous about the words enclosed by the marks. If something is to be quoted, the *exact* words must be used. If part of it must be left out because of space limitations, it is good manners to insert three dots to indicate the omission, but it is unethical to do this if it means connecting two thoughts which the original author did not intend to have tied together. Above all, quotation marks should not be used for ideas that you'd like to disown, things in the air so to speak. Nor should they be put in place around clichés; if you want to use a cliché you must take full responsibility for it yourself and not try to fob it off on anon., or on society. The most objectionable misuse of quotation marks, but one which illustrates the dangers of misuse in ordinary prose, is seen in advertising, especially in advertisements for small restaurants, for example "just around the corner," or "a good place to eat." No single, identifiable, citable person ever really said, for the record, "just around the corner," much less "a good place to eat," least likely of all for restaurants of the type that use this type of prose.

The dash is a handy device, informal and essentially playful, telling you that you're about to take off on a different tack but still in some way connected with the present course—only you have to remember that the dash is there, and either put a second dash at the end of the notion to let the reader know that he's back on course, or else end the sentence, as here, with a period.

The greatest danger in punctuation is for poetry. Here it is necessary to be as economical and parsimonious with commas and periods as with the words themselves, and any marks that seem to carry their own subtle meanings, like dashes and little rows of periods, even semi-colons and question marks, should be left out altogether rather than inserted to clog up the thing with ambiguity. A single exclamation point in a poem, no matter what else the poem has to say, is enough to destroy the whole work.

The things I like best in T. S. Eliot's poetry, especially in the *Four Quartets,* are the semicolons. You cannot hear them, but they are there, laying out the connections between the images and the ideas. Sometimes you get a glimpse of a semicolon coming, a few lines far-ther on, and it is like climbing a steep path through woods and seeing a wooden bench just at a bend in the road ahead, a place where you can expect to sit for a moment, catching your breath.

10 Commas can't do this sort of thing; they can only tell you how 10 the different parts of a complicated thought are to be fitted together, but you can't sit, not even take a breath, just because of a comma,

Challenge and Response
Arnold J. Toynbee

Background

1   Arnold J. Toynbee (1889–1975), perhaps the greatest modern   1
historian, was educated at Winchester and Balliol College, Oxford. He was professor of Byzantine and modern Greek language, literature, and history at King's College, London (1919–1924).
From 1925 to 1955, when he retired, Toynbee held the chair of research
professor of international history at the University of London and was
also the director of studies at the Royal Institute of International Affairs.
His monumental comparison of the historical patterns of twenty-six
civilizations, in *A Study of History*, was published in ten volumes between 1934 and 1954. Toynbee's research focused on questions of how
civilizations were created and why some flourished while others failed.
Toynbee discovered that challenges (such as those of climate and foreign
invasion) great enough to cause extinction of culture but not so severe
that the culture could not respond creatively was the ideal condition in
which great civilizations developed. In "Challenge and Response," from
A Study of History, Toynbee uses analogy as his main expository principle to synthesize conclusions he reached on the rise and decline of
civilizations.

CHALLENGE AND RESPONSE

The Problem Stated

What is the essential difference between the primitive and the higher
societies? It does not consist in the presence or absence of institutions
for institutions are the vehicles of the impersonal relations between

individuals in which all societies have their existence, because even the smallest of primitive societies is built on a wider basis than the narrow circle of an individual's direct personal ties. Institutions are attributes of the whole genus "societies" and therefore common properties of both its species. Primitive societies have their institutions—the religion of the annual agricultural cycle; totemism and exogamy; tabus, initiations and age-classes; segregations of the sexes, at certain stages of life, in separate communal establishments—and some of these institutions are certainly as elaborate and perhaps as subtle as those which are characteristic of civilizations.

Nor are civilizations distinguished from primitive societies by the division of labour, for we can discern at least the rudiments of the division of labour in the lives of primitive societies also. Kings, magicians, smiths and minstrels are all "specialists"—though the fact that Hephaestus,[1] the smith of Hellenic legend, is lame, and Homer, the poet of Hellenic legends, is blind, suggests that in primitive societies specialism is abnormal and apt to be confined to those who lack the capacity to be "all-round men" or jacks of all trades."

An essential difference between civilizations and primitive societies *as we know them* (the *caveat*[2] will be found to be important) is the direction taken by mimesis or imitation. Mimesis is a generic feature of all social life. Its operation can be observed both in primitive societies and in civilizations. In every social activity from the imitation of the style of film-stars by their humbler sisters upwards. It operates, however, in different directions in the two species of society. In primitive societies, as we know them, mimesis is directed towards the older generation and towards dead ancestors who stand, unseen but not unfelt, at the back of the living elders, reinforcing their prestige. In a society where mimesis is thus directed backward towards the past, custom rules and society remains static. On the other hand, in societies in process of civilization, mimesis is directed towards creative personalities who commanded a following because they are pioneers. In such societies, "the cake of custom," as Walter Bagehot[3] called it in his *Physics and Politics*, is broken and society is in dynamic motion along a course of change and growth.

---

[1] The Greek god of fire, metallurgy, and craftsmanship.
[2] Something important to remember, a significant reservation.
[3] Nineteenth-century economist.

331

5   But if we ask ourselves whether this difference between primitive   5
and higher societies is permanent and fundamental, we must answer
in the negative; for, if we only know primitive societies in a static condition, that is because we know them from direct observation only in
the last phases of their histories. Yet, though direct observation fails
us, a train of reasoning informs us that there must have earlier phases
in the histories of primitive societies in which these were moving
more dynamically than any 'civilized' society has moved yet. We have
said that primitive societies are as old as the human race, but we
should more properly have said that they are older. Social and institu-
tional life of a kind is found among some of the higher mammals
other than man, and it is clear that mankind could not have become
human except in a social environment. This mutation of subman into
man, which was accomplished, in circumstances of which we have no
record, under the aegis of primitive societies, was a more profound
change, a greater step in growth, than any progress which man has yet
achieved under the aegis of civilization.

  Primitive societies, as we know them by direct observation, may
be likened to people lying torpid upon a ledge on a mountain-side,
with a precipice below and a precipice above; civilizations may be
likened to companions of these sleepers who have just risen to their
feet and have started to climb up the face of the cliff above; while we
for our part may liken ourselves to observers whose field of vision is
limited to the ledge and to the lower slopes of the upper precipice and
who have come upon the scene at the moment when the different
members of the party happen to be in these respective postures and
positions. At first sight we may be inclined to draw an absolute distinction between the two groups, acclaiming the climbers as athletes
and dismissing the recumbent figures as paralytics; but on second
thoughts we shall find it more prudent to suspend judgement.

  After all the recumbent figures cannot be paralytics in reality; for
they cannot have been born on the ledge, and no human muscles
except their own can have hoisted them to this halting-place up the
face of the precipice below. On the other hand, their companions
who are climbing at the moment have only just left this same ledge
and started to climb the precipice above; and, since the next ledge is
out of sight, we do not know how high or how arduous the next pitch
may be. We only know that it is impossible to halt and rest before the
next ledge, wherever that may lie, is reached. Thus, even if we could
estimate each present climber's strength and skill and nerve, we could

not judge whether any of them have any prospect of gaining the ledge above, which is the goal of their present endeavours. We can, however, be sure that some of them will never attain it. And we can observe that, for every single one now strenuously climbing, twice that number (our extinct civilization) have fallen back onto the ledge, defeated. . . .

This alternating rhythm of static and dynamic, of movement and pause and movement, has been regarded by many observers in many different ages as something fundamental in the nature of the Universe. In their pregnant imagery the sages of the Sinic[4] Society described these alternations in terms of Yin and Yang—Yin the static and Yang the dynamic. The nucleus of the Sinic character which stands for Yin seems to represent dark coiling clouds overshadowing the Sun, while the nucleus of the character which stands for Yang seems to represent the unclouded sun-disk emitting its rays. In the Chinese formula Yin is always mentioned first, and within our field of vision, we can see that our breed, having reached the "ledge" of primitive human nature 300,000 years ago, has reposed there for ninety-eight per cent of that period before entering on the Yang-activity of civilization. We have now to seek for the positive factor, whatever it may be, which has set human life in motion again by its impetus. . . .

The Mythological Clue

An encounter between two superhuman personalities is the plot of some of the greatest dramas that the human imagination has conceived. An encounter between Yahweh[5] and the Serpent is the plot of the story of the Fall of Man in the Book of Genesis; a second encounter between the same antagonists, transfigured by a progressive enlightenment of Syriac souls, is the plot of the New Testament which tells the story of the Redemption; an encounter between the Lord and Satan is the plot of the book of Job; an encounter between the Lord and Mephistopheles is the plot of Goethe's *Faust*; an encounter between Gods and Demons is the plot of the Scandinavian Voluspa;[6] an en-

---

[4]"Sinic" refers to the Chinese.
[5]Jehovah.
[6]An ancient epic poem in Old Norse.

counter between Artemis and Aphrodite[7] is the plot of Euripides' *Hippolytus.*

10   We find another version of the same plot in that ubiquitous and   10
ever-recurring myth—a "primordial image" if ever there was one—of
the encounter between the Virgin and the Father of her Child. The characters in this myth have played their allotted parts on a thousand different stages under an infinite variety of names: Danae and the Shower of Gold; Europa and the Bull; Semele the Stricken Earth and Zeus the Sky that launches the thunderbolt; Creusa and Apollo in Euripides' *Ion*; Psyche and Cupid; Gretchen and Faust. The theme recurs, transfigured, in the Annuniciation. In our own day in the West this protean myth has re-expressed itself as the last word of our astronomers on the genesis of the planetary system, as witness the following *credo*:

> "We believe . . . that some two thousand million years ago . . . a second star, wandering blindly through space, happened to come within hailing distance of the Sun. Just as the Sun and Moon raise tides on the Earth, this second star must have raised tides on the surface of the Sun. But they would be very different from the puny tides which the small mass of the Moon raises in our oceans; a huge tidal wave must have travelled over the surface of the Sun, ultimately forming a mountain of prodigious height, which would rise ever higher and higher as the cause of the disturbance came nearer and nearer. And, before the second star began to recede, its tidal pull had become so powerful that this mountain was torn to pieces and threw off small fragments of itself, much as the crest of a wave throws off spray. These small fragments have been circulating round their parent sun ever since. They are the planets, great and small, of which our Earth is one."[8]

Thus out of the mouth of the mathematical astronomer, when all his complex calculations are done, there comes forth, once again, the myth of the encounter between the Sun Goddess and her ravisher that is so familiar a tale in the mouths of the untutored children of nature.

---

[7]The play by Euripides focuses on Aphrodite's (the goddess of love) revenge against Hippolytus, who was vowed to chastity as a follower of Artemis (Diana).

[8]Sir James Jeans, *The Mysterious Universe* (Cambridge: Cambridge University Press, 1930), pp. 1–2].

The presence and potency of this duality in the causation of the civilizations whose geneses we are studying is admitted by a Modern Western archaeologist whose studies begin with a concentration on environment and end with an intuition of the mystery of life:

> "Environment . . . is not the total causation in culture-shaping. . . . It is, beyond doubt, the most conspicuous single factor . . . But there is still an indefinable factor which may best be designated quite frankly as x, the unknown quantity, apparently psychological in kind . . . If x be not the most conspicuous factor in the matter, it certainly is the most important, the most fate-laden."[9]

In our present study of history this insistent theme of the super-human encounter has asserted itself already. At an early stage we observed that "a society . . . is confronted in the course of its life by a succession of problems" and that "the presentation of each problem is a challenge to undergo an ordeal."

Let us try to analyse the plot of this story or drama which repeats itself in such different contexts and in such various forms.

We may begin with two general features: the encounter is con-ceived of as a rare and sometimes as a unique event; and it has conse-quences which are vast in proportion to the vastness of the breach which it makes in the customary course of nature.

Even in the easy-going world of Hellenic mythology, where the gods saw the daughters of men that they were fair, and had their way with so many of them that their victims could be marshalled and pa-raded in poetic catalogues, such incidents never ceased to be sensa-tional affairs and invariably resulted in the births of heroes. In the versions of the plot in which both parties to the encounter are super-human, the rarity and momentousness of the event are thrown into stronger relief. In the Book of Job, "the day when the Sons of God came to present themselves before the Lord, and Satan came also among them," is evidently conceived of as an unusual occasion; and so is the encounter between the Lord and Mephistopheles in the "Pro-logue in Heaven" (suggested, of course, by the opening of the Book of Job) which starts the action of Goethe's *Faust*. In both these dra-

---

[9] P. A. Means, *Ancient Civilizations of the Andes* (New York and London: Scribners, 1931), pp. 25–26.

mas the consequences on Earth of the encounter in Heaven are tremendous. The personal ordeals of Job and Faust represent, in the intuitive language of fiction, the infinitely multiple ordeal of mankind; and, in the language of theology, the same vast consequence is represented as following from the superhuman encounters that are portrayed in the Book of Genesis and in the New Testament. The expulsion of Adam and Eve from the Garden of Eden, which follows the encounter between Yahweh and the Serpent, is nothing less than the Fall of Man; the passion of Christ in the New Testament is nothing less than Man's Redemption. Even the birth of our planetary system from the encounter of two suns, as pictured by our modern astronomer, is declared by the same authority to be "an event of almost unimaginable rarity."

In every case the story opens with a perfect state of Yin. Faust is perfect in knowledge; Job is perfect in goodness and prosperity; Adam and Eve are perfect in innocence and ease; the Virgins—Gretchen, Danae and the rest—are perfect in purity and beauty. In the astronomer's universe the Sun, a perfect orb, travels on its course intact and whole. When Yin is thus complete, it is ready to pass over into Yang. But what is to make it pass? A change in a state which, by definition, is perfect after its kind can only be started by an impulse or motive which comes from outside. If we think of the state as one of physical equilibrium, we must bring in another star. If we think of it as one of psychic beatitude or *nirvana*[10] we must bring another actor on to the stage: a critic to set the mind thinking again by suggesting doubts; and adversary to set the heart feeling again by instilling distress or discontent or fear or antipathy. This is the role of the Serpent in Genesis, of Satan in the Book of Job, or Mephistopheles in *Faust*, of Loki in the Scandinavian mythology, of the Divine Lovers in the Virgin myths.

In the language of science we may say that the function of the intruding factor is to supply that on which it intrudes with a stimulus of the kind best calculated to evoke the most potently creative variations. In the language of mythology and theology, the impulse or motive which makes a perfect Yin-state pass over into new Yang-activity comes from an intrusion of the Devil into the universe of

---

[10]Buddhism, a state of enlightenment free from passion and illusion.

God. The event can best be described in these mythological images because they are not embarrassed by the contradiction that arises when the statement is translated into logical terms. In logic, if God's universe is perfect, there cannot be a Devil outside it, while, if the Devil exists, the perfection which he comes to spoil must have been incomplete already through the very fact of his existence. This logical contradiction, which cannot be logically resolved, is intuitively transcended in the imagery of the poet and prophet, who give glory to an omnipotent God yet take it for granted that He is subject to two crucial limitations.

The first limitation is that, in the perfection of what He has created already, He cannot find an opportunity for further creative activity. If God is conceived of as transcendent, the works of creation are as glorious as ever they were but they cannot "be changed from glory into glory." The second limitation on God's power is that when the opportunity for fresh creation is offered to Him from outside He cannot but take it. When the Devil challenges Him He cannot refuse to take the challenge up. God is bound to accept the predicament because He can refuse only at the price of denying His own nature and ceasing to be God.

20 If God is thus not omnipotent in logical terms, is He still mythologically invincible? If He is bound to take up the Devil's challenge, is He also bound to win the ensuing battle? In Euripides' *Hippolytus*, where God's part is played by Artemis and the Devil's by Aphrodite, Artemis is not only unable to decline the combat but is foredoomed to defeat. The relations between the Olympians are anarchic and Artemis in the epilogue can console herself only by making up her mind that one day she will play the Devil's role herself at Aphrodite's expense. The result is not creation but destruction. In the Scandinavian version destruction is likewise the outcome in Ragnarök[11]— when "Gods and Demons slay and are slain"—though the unique genius of the author of *Voluspa* makes his Sibyl's vision pierce the gloom to behold the light of a new dawn beyond it. On the other hand, in another version of the plot, the combat which follows the

---

[11]In the *Volupsa*, a destructive battle between the gods and the powers of evil led by Loki, gives way to a vision (by the Sibyl, Voluspa) of a world resurrected through the efforts of the god Balder, where the sole surviving human beings, called "Life" and "Destring Life" repopulate the earth.

compulsory acceptance of the challenge takes the form, not of an exchange of fire in which the Devil has the first shot and cannot fail to kill his man, but of a wager which the Devil is apparently bound to lose. The classic works in which this wager *motif* is worked out are the Book of Job and Goethe's *Faust*.

It is in Goethe's drama that the point is most clearly made. After the Lord has accepted the wager with Mephistopheles in Heaven, the terms are agreed on Earth, between Mephistopheles and Faust, as follows:

> *Faust.* Comfort and quiet—no, no! none of these
> For me—I ask them not—I seek them not.
> If ever I upon the bed of sloth
> Lie down and rest, then be the hour in which
> I so lie down and rest my last of life.
> Canst thou by falsehood or by flattery
> Delude me into self-complacent smiles,
> Cheat me into tranquillity? Come then,
> And welcome, life's last day—be this our wager.
> *Meph.* Done.
> *Faust.* Done, say I: clench we at once the bargain.
> If ever time should flow so calmly on,
> Soothing my spirits in such oblivion
> That in the pleasant trance I would arrest
> And hail the happy moment in its course,
> Bidding it linger with me. . . .
> Then willingly do I consent to perish.[12]

The bearing of this mythical compact upon our problem of the geneses of civilizations can be brought out by identifying Faust, at the moment when he makes his bet, with one of those "awakened sleepers" who have risen from the ledge on which they had been lying torpid and have started to climb on up the face of the cliff. In the language of our simile, Faust is saying: "I have made up my mind to leave this ledge and climb this precipice in search of the next ledge above. In attempting this I am aware that I am leaving safety behind me. Yet, for the sake of the possibility of achievement, I will take the risk of a fall and destruction."

---

[12]Faust, 11. 1692–1706 (John Anster's translation).

In the story as told by Goethe the intrepid climber, after an ordeal of mortal dangers and desperate reverses, succeeds in the end in scaling the cliff triumphantly. In the New Testament the same ending is given, through the revelation of a second encounter between the same pair of antagonists, to the combat between Yahweh and the Serpent which, in the original version in Genesis, had ended rather in the manner of the combat between Artemis and Aphrodite in the *Hippolytus*.

In Job, *Faust* and the New Testament alike it is suggested, or even declared outright, that the wager cannot be won by the Devil; that the Devil, in meddling with God's work, cannot frustrate but can only serve the purpose of God, who remains master of the situation all the time and gives the Devil rope for the Devil to hang himself. Then has the Devil been created? Did God accept a wager which He knew He could not lose? That would be a hard saying; for if it were true the whole transaction would have been a sham. An encounter which was no encounter could not produce the consequences of an encounter—the vast cosmic consequence of causing Yin to pass over into Yang. Perhaps the explanation is that the wager which the Devil offers and which God accepts covers, and thereby puts in real jeopardy, a part of God's creation but not the whole of it. The part really is at stake; and, though the whole is not, the chances and changes to which the part is exposed cannot conceivably leave the whole unaffected. In the language of mythology, when one of God's creatures is tempted by the Devil, God Himself is thereby given the opportunity to re-create the World. The Devil's intervention, whether it succeeds or fails on the particular issue—and either result is possible—has accomplished that transition from Yin to Yang for which God has been yearning.

25   As for the human protagonist's part, suffering is the keynote of it   25 in every presentation of the drama, whether the player of the part is Jesus or Job or Faust or Adam and Eve. The picture of Adam and Eve in the Garden of Eden is a reminiscence of the Yin-state to which primitive man attained in the food-gathering phase of economy, after he had established his ascendancy over the rest of the flora and fauna of the Earth. The Fall, in response to the temptation to eat of the Tree of the Knowledge of Good and Evil, symbolizes the acceptance of a challenge to abandon this achieved integration and to venture upon a fresh differentiation out of which a fresh integration may—or may not—arise. The expulsion from the Garden into an unfriendly world

in which the Woman must bring forth children in sorrow and the Man must eat bread in the sweat of his face, is the ordeal which the acceptance of the Serpent's challenge has entailed. The sexual intercourse between Adam and Eve, which follows, is an act of social creation. It bears fruit in the birth of two sons who impersonate two nascent civilizations: Abel the keeper of sheep and Cain the tiller of the ground.

In our own generation, one of our most distinguished and original minded students of the physical environment of human life tells the same story in his own way:

"Ages ago a band of naked, houseless, fireless savages started from their warm home in the torrid zone and pushed steadily northward from the beginning of spring to the end of summer. They never guessed that they had left the land of constant warmth until in September they began to feel an uncomfortable chill at night. Day by day it grew worse. Now knowing its cause, they travelled this way or that to escape. Some went southward, but only a handful returned to their former home. There they resumed the old life, and their descendants are untutored savages to this day. Of those who wandered in other directions, all perished except one small band. Finding that they could not escape the nipping air, the members of this band used the loftiest of human faculties, the power of conscious invention. Some tried to find shelter by digging in the ground, some gathered branches and leaves to make huts and warm beds, and some wrapped themselves in the skins of the breasts that they had slain. Soon these savages had taken some of the greatest steps towards civilization. The naked were clothed; the houseless sheltered; the improvident learnt to dry meat and store it, with nuts, for the winter; and at last the art of preparing fire was discovered as a means of keeping warm. Thus they subsisted where at first they thought that they were doomed. And in the process of adjusting themselves to a hard environment they advanced by enormous strides, leaving the tropical part of mankind far in the rear."[13]

---

[13]Ellsworth Huntington, *Civilization and Climate,* 3rd edition (New Haven: Yale University Press. 1924), pp. 405–406.

A classical scholar likewise translates the story into the scientific terminology of our age:

"It is . . . a paradox of advancement that, if Necessity be the mother of Invention, the other parent is Obstinacy, the determination that you will go on living under adverse conditions rather than cut your losses and go where life is easier. It was no accident, that is, that civilization, as we know it, began in that ebb and flow of climate, flora and fauna which characterizes the fourfold Ice Age. Those primates who just 'got out' as arboreal conditions wilted retained their primacy among the servants of natural law, but they forewent the conquest of nature. Those others won through, and became men, who stood their ground when they were no more trees to sit in, who 'made do' with meat when fruit did not ripen, who made fires and clothes rather than follow the sunshine; who fortified their lairs and trained their young and vindicated the reasonableness of a world that seemed so reasonless."[14]

The first stage, then, of the human protagonist's ordeal is a transition from Yin to Yang through a dynamic act—performed by God's creature under temptation from the Adversary—which enables God Himself to resume His creative activity. But this progress has to be paid for; and it is not God but God's servant, the human sower, who pays the price. Finally, after many vicissitudes, the sufferer triumphant serves as the pioneer. The human protagonist in the divine drama not only serves God by enabling Him to renew His creation but also serves his fellow men by pointing the way for others to follow. . . .

The Myth Applied to the Problem

The Unpredictable Factor

By the light of mythology we have gained some insight into the nature of challenges and responses. We have come to see that creation is the outcome of an encounter, that genesis is a product of interaction.

---

[14]J. L. Myres, *Who Were the Greeks?* (Berkeley: University of California Press, 1930), pp. 277–278.

. . . We shall no longer be surprised if, in the production of civilizations, the same race or the same environment appears to be fruitful in one instance and sterile in another . . . We shall be prepared now to recognize that, even if we were exactly acquainted with all the racial, environmental, and other data that are capable of being formulated scientifically, we should not be able to predict the outcome of the interaction between the forces which these data represent, any more than a military expert can predict the outcome of a battle or campaign from an "inside knowledge" of the dispositions and resources of both the opposing general staffs, or a bridge expert the outcome of a game from a similar knowledge of all the cards in every hand.

30   In both these analogies "inside knowledge" is not sufficient to en- 30 able its possessor to predict results with any exactness or assurance because it is not the same thing as complete knowledge. There is one thing which must remain an unknown quantity to the best-informed onlooker because it is beyond the knowledge of the combatants, or players, themselves; and it is the most important term in the equation which the would-be calculator has to solve. This unknown quantity is the reaction of the actors to the ordeal when it actually comes. These psychological momenta, which are inherently impossible to weigh and measure and therefore to estimate scientifically in advance, are the very forces which actually decide the issue when the encounter takes place. And that is why the very greatest military geniuses have admitted an incalculable element in their successes. If religious, they have attributed their victories to God, like Cromwell; if merely superstitious, to the ascendancy of their "star," like Napoleon.

The Lowest Animal

Mark Twain

Background

1   Mark Twain (1835–1910), the pseudonym of Samuel Langhorn Clemens, was brought up in Hannibal, Missouri. After serving as a printer's apprentice, Twain became a steamboat pilot on the Mississippi (1857–1861), adopting his pen name from the leadsman's call ("mark twain" means "by the mark two fathoms") sounding the river in shallow places. After an unsuccessful attempt to mine gold in Nevada, Twain edited the *Virginia City Enterprise*. In 1865, in the *New York Saturday Press*, Twain published "Jim Smiley and his Jumping Frog," which then became the title story of *The Celebrated Jumping Frog of Calaveras County and Other Sketches* (1867). His reputation as a humorist was enhanced by *Innocents Abroad* (1869), a comic account of his travels through France, Italy, Palestine, and by *Roughing It* (1872), a delightful spoof of his mining adventures. His acknowledged masterpieces are *The Adventures of Tom Sawyer* (1876) and its sequel, *The Adventures of Huckleberry Finn* (1885), works of great comic power and social insight. Twain's later works, including *The Man that Corrupted Handleyburg* (1900), a fable about greed, and *The Mysterious Stranger* (1916), published six years after Twain's death, assail hypocrisy as endemic to the human condition. "The Lowest Animal" (1906) shows Twain at his most iconoclastic, formulating a scathing comparison between man and the so-called lower animals.

Reprinted from *Past to Present: Ideas That Changed Our World*, Stuart and Terry Hirschberg, eds. (2003), Prentice-Hall, Inc.

THE LOWEST ANIMAL

5   I have been studying the traits and dispositions of the "lower animals" 5
(so-called), and contrasting them with the traits and dispositions of
man. I find the result humiliating to me. For it obliges me to renounce
my allegiance to the Darwinian theory of the Ascent of Man from the
Lower Animals; since it now seems plain to me that that theory ought
to be vacated in favor of a new and truer one, this new and truer one
to be named the Descent of Man from the Higher Animals.

In proceeding toward this unpleasant conclusion I have not
guessed or speculated or conjectured, but have used what is commonly
called the scientific method. That is to say, I have subjected every pos-
tulate that presented itself to the crucial test of actual experiment, and
have adopted it or rejected it according to the result. Thus I verified
and established each step of my course in its turn before advancing to
the next. These experiments were made in London Zoological Gardens, and covered many months of painstaking and fatiguing work.

Before particularizing any of the experiments, I wish to state one
or two things which seem to more properly belong in this place than
further along. This in the interest of clearness. The massed experiments established to my satisfaction certain generalizations, to wit:

1. That the human race is of one distinct species. It exhibits slight
variations—in color, stature, mental caliber, and so on—due to climate, environment, and so forth; but it is a species by itself, and
not to be confounded with any other.
2. That the quadrupeds are a distinct family, also. This family exhibits variations—in color, size, food preferences and so on; but it
is a family by itself.
5 3. That the other families—the birds, the fishes, the insects, the reptiles, etc.—are more or less distinct, also. They are in the proces-
sion. They are links in the chain which stretches down from the
higher animals to man at the bottom.

Some of my experiments were quite curious. In the course of my
reading I had come across a case where, many years ago, some hunters
on our Great Plains organized a buffalo hunt for the entertainment of
an English earl—that, and to provide some fresh meat for his larder.
They had charming sport. They killed seventy-two of those great animals; and ate part of one of them and left the seventy-one to rot. In

order to determine the difference between an anaconda and an earl—if any—I caused seven young calves to be turned into the anaconda's cage. The grateful reptile immediately crushed one of them and swallowed it, then lay back satisfied. It showed no further interest in the calves, and no disposition to harm them. I tried this experiment with other anacondas; always with the same result. The fact stood proven that the difference between an earl and an anaconda is that the earl is cruel and the anaconda isn't; and that the earl wantonly destroys what he has no use for, but the anaconda doesn't. This seemed to suggest that the anaconda was not descended from the earl. It also seemed to suggest that the earl was descended from the anaconda, and had lost a good deal in the transition.

I was aware that many men who have accumulated more millions of money than they can ever use have shown a rabid hunger for more, and have not scrupled to cheat the ignorant and the helpless out of their poor servings in order to partially appease that appetite. I furnished a hundred different kinds of wild and tame animals the opportunity to accumulate vast stores of food, but none of them would do it. The squirrels and bees and certain birds made accumulations, but stopped when they had gathered a winter's supply, and could not be persuaded to add to it either honestly or by chicane. In order to bolster up a tottering reputation the ant pretended to store up supplies, but I was not deceived. I know the ant. These experiments convinced me that there is this difference between man and the higher animals: he is avaricious and miserly, they are not.

10 In the course of my experiments I convinced myself that among the animals man is the only one that harbors insults and injuries, broods over them, waits till a chance offers, then takes revenge. The passion of revenge is unknown to the higher animals.

Roosters keep harems, but it is by consent of their concubines; therefore no wrong is done. Men keep harems, but it is by brute force, privileged by atrocious laws which the other sex is allowed no hand in making. In this matter man occupies a far lower place than the rooster.

Cats are loose in their morals, but not consciously so. Man, in his descent from the cat, has brought the cat's looseness with him but has left the unconsciousness behind—the saving grace which excuses the cat. The cat is innocent, man is not.

Indecency, vulgarity, obscenity—these are strictly confined to man; he invented them. Among the higher animals there is no trace of them. They hide nothing; they are not ashamed. Man, with his soiled mind, covers himself. He will not even enter a drawing room with his breast and back naked, so alive are he and his mates to indecent suggestion. Man is "The Animal that Laughs." But so does the monkey, as Mr. Darwin pointed out; and so does the Australian bird that is called the laughing jackass. No—Man is the Animal that Blushes. He is the only one that does it—or has occasion to.

At the head of this article we see how "three monks were burnt to death" a few days ago, and a prior "put to death with atrocious cruelty." Do we inquire into the details? No; or we should find out that the prior was subjected to unprintable mutilations. Man—when he is a North American Indian—gouges out his prisoner's eyes; when he is King John, with a nephew to render untroublesome, he uses a red-hot iron; when he is a religious zealot dealing with heretics in the Middle Ages, he skins his captive alive and scatters salt on his back; in the first Richard's time he shuts up a multitude of Jew families in a tower and sets fire to it; in Columbus's time he captures a family of Spanish Jews and—but *that* is not printable; in our day in England a man is fined ten shillings for beating his mother nearly to death with a chair, and another man is fined forty shillings for having four pheasant eggs in his possession without being able to satisfactorily explain how he got them. Of all the animals, man is the only one that is cruel. He is the only one that inflicts pain for the pleasure of doing it. It is a trait that is not known to the higher animals. That cat plays with the frightened mouse; but she has this excuse, that she does not know that the mouse is suffering. The cat is moderate—unhumanly moderate: she only scares the mouse, she does not hurt it; she doesn't dig out its eyes, or tear off its skin, or drive splinters under its nails—man-fashion; when she is done playing with it she makes a sudden meal of it and puts it out of its trouble. Man is the Cruel Animal. He is along in that distinction.

15   The higher animals engage in individual fights, but never in organized masses. Man is the only animal that deals in that atrocity of atrocities, War. He is the only one that gathers his brethren about him and goes forth in cold blood and with calm pulse to exterminate his kind. He is the only animal that for sordid wages will march out, as the Hessians[1] did in our Revolution, and as the boyish Prince Napoleon did in the Zulu war, and help to slaughter strangers of his own species who have done him no harm and with whom he has no quarrel.

Man is the only animal that robs his helpless fellow of his country—takes possession of it and drives him out of it or destroys him. Man has done this in all the ages. There is not an acre of ground on the globe that is in possession of its rightful owner, or that has not been taken away from owner after owner, cycle after cycle, by force and bloodshed.

Man is the only Slave. And he is the only animal who enslaves. He has always been a slave in one form or another, and has always held other slaves in bondage under him in one way or another. In our day he is always some man's slave for wages, and does that man's work; and this slave has other slaves under him for minor wages, and they do *his* work. The higher animals are the only ones who exclusively do their own work and provide their own living.

Man is the only Patriot. He sets himself apart in his own country, under his own flag, and sneers at the other nations, and keeps multitudinous uniformed assassins on hand at heavy expense to grab slices of other people's countries, and keep *them* from grabbing slices of *his*. And in the intervals between campaigns he washes the blood off his hands and works for "the universal brotherhood of man"—with his mouth.

20 Man is the Religious Animal. He is the only Religious Animal.20 He is the only animal that has the True Religion—several of them. He is the only animal that loves his neighbor as himself, and cuts his throat if his theology isn't straight. He has made a graveyard of the globe in trying his honest best to smooth his brother's path to happiness and heaven. He was at it in the time of the Caesars, he was at it in Mahomet's time, he was at it in the time of the Inquistition, he was at it in France a couple of centuries, he was at it in England in Mary's day, he has been at it ever since he first saw the light, he is at it today in Crete—as per the telegrams quoted above—he will be at it somewhere else tomorrow. The higher animals have no religion. And we are told that they are going to be left out, in the Hereafter. I wonder why? It seems questionable taste.

Man is the Reasoning Animal. Such is the claim. I think it is open to dispute. Indeed, my experiments have proven to me that he is

---

[1]Hessians: the German auxillary soldiers brought over by the British to fight the Americans during the Revolutionary War.

the Unreasoning Animal. Note his history, as sketched above. It seems plain to me that whatever he is he is *not* a reasoning animal. His record is the fantastic record of a maniac. I consider that the strongest count against his intelligence is the fact that with that record back of him he blandly sets himself up as the head animal of the lot: whereas by his own standards he is the bottom one.

In truth, man is incurably foolish. Simple things which the other animals easily learn, he is incapable of learning. Among my experiments was this. In an hour I taught a cat and a dog to be friends. I put them in a cage. In another hour I taught them to be friends with a rabbit. In the course of two days I was able to add a fox, a goose, a squirrel and some doves. Finally a monkey. They lived together in peace; even affectionately.

Next, in another cage I confined an Irish Catholic from Tipperary, and as soon as he seemed tame I added a Scotch Presbyterian from Aberdeen. Next a Turk from Constantinople; a Greek Christian from Crete; an Armenian; a Methodist from the wilds of Arkansas; a Buddhist from China; a Brahman from Benares. Finally, a Salvation Army Colonel from Wapping. Then I stayed away two whole days. When I came back to note result, the cage of Higher Animals was all right, but in the other there was but a chaos of gory odds and ends of turbans and fezzes and plaids and bones and flesh—not a specimen left alive. These Reasoning Animals had disagreed on a theological detail and carried the matter to a Higher Court.

One is obliged to concede that in true loftiness of character, Man cannot claim to approach even the meanest of the Higher Animals. It is plain that he is constitutionally incapable of approaching that altitude; that he is constitutionally afflicted with a Defect which must make such approach forever impossible, for it is manifest, that this defect is permanent in him, indestructible, ineradicable.

I find this Defect to be *the Moral Sense.* He is the only animal that has it. It is the secret of his degradation. It is the quality *which enables him to do wrong.* It has no other office. It is incapable of performing any other function. It could never have been intended to perform any other. Without it, man could do no wrong. He would rise at once to the level of the Higher Animals.

Since the Moral Sense has but the one office, the one capacity—to enable man to do wrong—it is plainly without value to him. It is as valueless to him as is disease. In fact, it manifestly is a disease. *Rabies* is bad, but it is not so bad as this disease. Rabies enables a man to do a thing which he could no do when in a healthy state: kill his neighbor with a poisonous bite. No one is the better man for having rabies. The Moral Sense enables a man to do wrong. It enables him to do wrong in a thousand ways. Rabies is an innocent disease, compared to the Moral Sense. No one, then, can be the better man for having the Moral Sense. What, now, do we find the Primal Curse to have been? Plainly what it was in the beginning: the infliction upon man of the Moral Sense; the ability to distinguish good from evil; and with it, necessarily, the ability to *do* evil; for there can be no evil act without the presence of consciousness of it in the doer of it.

And so I find that we have descended and degenerated, from some far ancestor—some microscopic atom wandering at its pleasure between the mighty horizons of a drop of water perchance—insect by insect, animal by animal, reptile by reptile, down the long highway of smirchless innocence, till we have reached the bottom stage of development—namable as the Human Being. Below us—nothing. Nothing but the Frenchman.

The Civil Rights Movement: What Good Was It?

Alice Walker

Alice Walker (1944–) was born in Georgia to sharecrop-per parents. She attended Spelman College and Sarah Lawrence College and was active in the civil rights move-ment of the 1960s. Publishing her first novel, The Third Life of Grange Copeland, *at the age of 26, she has been a prolific writer since. In all, she has published five novels, two short story collections, two collections of essays, and sev-eral books of poems. Her novel* The Color Purple *(1982) is perhaps her best known, having won the American Book Award, the Pulitzer Prize, and the Candace Award of the National Coalition of 100 Black Women. The novel was also made into a prize-winning film by director Steven Spielberg. Walker's topics run the gamut of human experi-ence and include some harsh realities such as incest and racial violence as well as relationships within families and society. Walker wrote "The Civil Rights Movement: What Good Was It?" when she was only 23 years old; it was pub-lished in* In Search of Our Mothers' Gardens *(1967). Al-though it is not as colorful as most of her later writing, it is well crafted and powerful in its analysis of the impor-tance of the Civil Rights Movement.*

1   Someone said recently to an old black lady from Mississippi,   1
whose legs had been badly damaged by local police who arrested
her for "disturbing the peace," that the Civil Rights Movement
was dead, and asked, since it was dead, what she thought about it. The

old lady replied, hobbling out of his presence on her cane, that the Civil Rights Movement was like herself, "if it's dead, it shore ain't ready to lay down!"

This old lady is a legendary freedom fighter in her small town in the Delta. She has been severely mistreated for insisting on her rights as an American citizen. She has been beaten for singing Movement songs, placed in solitary confinement in prisons for talking about freedom, and placed on bread and water for praying aloud to God for her jailers' deliverance. For such a woman the Civil Rights Movement will never be over as long as her skin is black. It also will never be over for over twenty million others with the same "affliction," for whom the Movement can never "lay down," no matter how it is killed by the press and made dead and buried by the white American public. As long as one black American survives, the struggle for equality with other Americans must also survive. This is a debt we owe to those blameless hostages we leave to the future, our children.

Still, white liberals and deserting Civil Rights sponsors are quick to justify their disaffection from the Movement by claiming that it is all over. "And since it is over," they will ask, "would someone kindly tell me what has been gained by it?" They then list statistics supposedly showing how much more advanced segregation is now than ten years ago—in schools, housing, jobs. They point to a gain in conservative politicians during the last few years. They speak of ghetto riots and of the survey that shows that most policemen are admittedly too anti-Negro to do their jobs in ghetto areas fairly and effectively. They speak of every area that has been touched by the Civil Rights Movement as somehow or other going to pieces.

They rarely talk, however, about human attitudes among Negroes that have undergone terrific changes just during the past seven to ten years (not to mention all those years when there was a Movement and only the Negroes knew about it). They seldom speak of changes in personal lives because of the influence of people in the Movement. They see general failure and few, if any, individual gains.

5   They do not understand what it is that keeps the Movement from   5
"laying down" and Negroes from reverting to their former silent second-class status. They have apparently never stopped to wonder why it is always the white man—on his radio and in his newspaper and on his television—who says that the Movement is dead. If a Negro were audacious enough to make such a claim, his fellows might

hanker to see him shot. The Movement is dead to the white man because it no longer interests him. And it no longer interests him because he can afford to be uninterested: he does not have to live by it, with it, or for it, as Negroes must. He can take a rest from the news of beatings, killings, and arrests that reach him from North and South—if his skin is white. Negroes cannot now and will never be able to take a rest from the injustices that plague them, for they—not the white man—are the target.

Perhaps it is naive to be thankful that the Movement "saved" a large number of individuals and gave them something to live for, even if it did not provide them with everything they wanted. (Materially, it provided them with precious little that they wanted.) When a movement awakens people to the possibilities of life, it seems unfair to frustrate them by then denying what they had thought was offered. But what was offered? What was promised? What was it all about? What good did it do? Would it have been better, as some have suggested, to leave the Negro people as they were, unawakened, unallied with one another, unhopeful about what to expect for their children in some future world?

I do not think so. If knowledge of my condition is all the freedom I get from a "freedom movement," it is better than unawareness, forgottenness, and hopelessness, the existence that is like the existence of a beast. Man only truly lives by knowing; otherwise he simply performs, copying the daily habits of others, but conceiving nothing of his creative possibilities as a man, and accepting someone else's superiority and his own misery.

When we are children, growing up in our parents' care, we await the spark from the outside world. Sometimes our parents provide it—if we are lucky—sometimes it comes from another source far from home. We sit, paralyzed, surrounded by our anxiety and dread, hoping we will not have to grow up into the narrow world and ways we see about us. We are hungry for a life that turns us on; we yearn for a knowledge of living that will save us from our innocuous lives that resemble death. We look for signs in every strange event; we search for heroes in every unknown face.

It was just six years ago that I began to be alive. I had, of course, been living before—for I am now twenty-three—but I did not really know it. And I did not know it because nobody told me that I—a pensive, yearning, typical high-school senior, but Negro—existed in the minds of others as I existed in my own. Until that time my mind was locked apart from the outer contours and complexion of my body as if it and the body were strangers. The mind possessed both thought and spirit—I wanted to be an author or a scientist—which the color of the body denied. I had never seen myself and existed as a statistic exists, or as a phantom. In the white world I walked, less real to them than a shadow; and being young and well hidden among the slums, among people who also did not exist—either in books or in films or in the government of their own lives—I waited to be called to life. And, by a miracle, I was called.

10   There was a commotion in our house that night in 1960. We had 10 managed to buy our first television set. It was battered and overpriced, but my mother had gotten used to watching the afternoon soap operas at the house where she worked as a maid, and nothing could satisfy her on days when she did not work but a continuation of her "stories." So she pinched pennies and bought a set.

    I remained listless throughout her "stories," tales of pregnancy, abortion, hypocrisy, infidelity, and alcoholism. All these men and women were white and lived in houses with servants, long staircases that they floated down, patios where liquor was served four times a day to "relax" them. But my mother, with her swollen feet eased out of her shoes, her heavy body relaxed in our only comfortable chair, watched each movement of the smartly coiffed women, heard each word, pounced upon each innuendo and inflection, and for the duration of these "stories" she saw herself as one of them. She placed herself in every scene she saw, with her braided hair turned blond, her two hundred pounds compressed into a sleek size-seven dress, her rough dark skin smooth and *white*. Her husband became "dark and handsome," talented, witty, urbane, charming. And when she turned to look at my father sitting near her in his sweatshirt with his smelly feet raised on the bed to "air," there was always a tragic look of surprise on her face. Then she would sigh and go out to the kitchen looking lost and unsure of herself. My mother, a truly great woman who raised eight children of her own and half a dozen of the neighbors' without a single complaint, was convinced that she did not exist compared to "them." She subordinated her soul to theirs and became a faithful and timid supporter of the "Beautiful White People." Once she asked me, in a moment of vicarious pride and despair, if I didn't think that "they" were "jest naturally smarter, prettier, better." My mother asked this: a woman who never got rid of any of her children, never cheated on my father, was never a hypocrite if she could help it, and never even tasted liquor. She could not even bring herself to blame "them" for making her believe what they wanted her to believe: that if she did not look like them, think like them, be sophisticated and corrupt-for-comfort's-sake like them, she was a nobody. Black was not a color on my mother; it was a shield that made her invisible.

Of course, the people who wrote the soap-opera scripts always made the Negro maids in them steadfast, trusty, and wise in a home-remedial sort of way; but my mother, a maid for nearly forty years, never once identified herself with the scarcely glimpsed black servant's face beneath the ruffled cap. Like everyone else, in her daydreams at least, she thought she was free.

Six years ago, after halfheartedly watching my mother's soap operas and wondering whether there wasn't something more to be asked of life, the Civil Rights Movement came into my life. Like a good omen for the future, the face of Dr. Martin Luther King, Jr., was the first black face I saw on our new television screen. And, as in a fairy tale, my soul was stirred by the meaning for me of his mission—at the time he was being rather ignominiously dumped into a police van for having led a protest march in Alabama—and I fell in love with the sober and determined face of the Movement. The singing of "We Shall Overcome"—that song betrayed by nonbelievers in it—rang for the first time in my ears. The influence that my mother's soap operas might have had on me became impossible. The life of Dr. King, seeming bigger and more miraculous than the man himself, because of all he had done and suffered, offered a pattern of strength and sincerity I felt I could trust. He had suffered much because of his simple belief in nonviolence, love, and brotherhood. Perhaps the majority of men could not be reached through these beliefs, but because Dr. King kept trying to reach them in spite of danger to himself and his family, I saw in him the hero for whom I had waited so long.

What Dr. King promised was not a ranch-style house and an acre of manicured lawn for every black man, but jail and finally freedom. He did not promise two cars for every family, but the courage one day for all families everywhere to walk without shame and unafraid on their own feet. He did not say that one day it will be us chasing prospective buyers out of our prosperous well-kept neighborhoods, or in other ways exhibiting our snobbery and ignorance as all other ethnic groups before us have done; what he said was that we had a right to live anywhere in this country we chose, and a right to a meaningful well-paying job to provide us with the upkeep of our homes. He did not say we had to become carbon copies of the white American middle class; but he did say we had the right to become whatever we wanted to become.

15 Because of the Movement, because of an awakened faith in the newness and imagination of the human spirit, because of "black and white together"—for the first time in our history in some human relationship on and off TV—because of the beatings, the arrests, the hell of battle during the past years, I have fought harder for my life and for a chance to be myself, to be something more than a shadow or a number, than I had ever done before in my life. Before, there had seemed to be no real reason for struggling beyond the effort for daily bread. Now there was a chance at that other that Jesus meant when He said we could not live by bread alone.

I have fought and kicked and fasted and prayed and cursed and cried myself to the point of existing. It has been like being born again, literally. Just "knowing" has meant everything to me. Knowing has pushed me out into the world, into college, into places, into people.

Part of what existence means to me is knowing the difference between what I am now and what I was then. It is being capable of looking after myself intellectually as well as financially. It is being able to tell when I am being wronged and by whom. It means being awake to protect myself and the ones I love. It means being a part of the world community, and being *alert* to which part it is that I have joined, and knowing how to change to another part if that part does not suit me. To know is to exist: to exist is to be involved, to move about, to see the world with my own eyes. This, at least, the Movement has given me.

The hippies and other nihilists would have me believe that it is all the same whether the people in Mississippi have a movement behind them or not. Once they have their rights, they say, they will run all over themselves trying to be just like everybody else. They will be well fed, complacent about things of the spirit, emotionless, and without the marvelous humanity and "soul" that the Movement has seen them practice time and time again. "What has the Movement done," they ask, "with the few people it has supposedly helped?" "Got them white-collar jobs, moved them into standardized ranch houses in white neighborhoods, given them nondescript gray flannel suits?" "What are these people now?" they ask. And then they answer themselves, "Nothings!"

I would find this reasoning—which I have heard many, many times from hippies and nonhippies alike—amusing if I did not also consider it serious. For I think it is a delusion, a cop-out, an excuse to disassociate themselves from a world in which they feel too little has been changed or gained. The real question, however, it appears to me, is not whether poor people will adopt the middle-class mentality once they are well fed; rather, it is whether they will ever be well fed enough to be able to choose whatever mentality they think will suit them. The lack of a movement did not keep my mother from *wishing* herself bourgeois in her daydreams.

20   There is widespread starvation in Mississippi. In my own state of 20 Georgia there are more hungry families than Lester Maddox would like to admit—or even see fed. I went to school with children who ate red dirt. The Movement has prodded and pushed some liberal senators into pressuring the government for food so that the hungry may eat. Food stamps that were two dollars and out of the reach of many families not long ago have been reduced to fifty cents. The price is still out of the reach of some families, and the government, it seems to a lot of people, could spare enough free food to feed its own people. It angers people in the Movement that it does not; they point to the billions in wheat we send free each year to countries abroad. Their government's slowness while people are hungry, its unwillingness to believe that there are Americans starving, its stingy cutting of the price of food stamps, make many Civil Rights workers throw up their hands in disgust. But they do not give up. They do not withdraw into the world of psychedelia. They apply what pressure they can to make the government give away food to hungry people. They do not plan so far ahead in their disillusionment with society that they can see these starving families buying identical ranch-style houses and sending their snobbish children to Bryn Mawr and Yale. They take first things first and try to get them fed.

They do not consider it their business, in any case, to say what kind of life the people they help must lead. How one lives is, after all, one of the rights left to the individual—when and if he has opportunity to choose. It is not the prerogative of the middle class to determine what is worthy of aspiration. There is also every possibility that the middle-class people of tomorrow will turn out ever so much better than those of today. I even know some middle-class people of today who are not *all* bad.

I think there are so few Negro hippies because middle-class Negroes, although well fed, are not careless. They are required by the treacherous world they live in to be clearly aware of whoever or whatever might be trying to do them in. They are middle class in money and position, but they cannot afford to be middle class in complacency. They distrust the hippie movement because they know that it can do nothing for Negroes as a group but "love" them, which is what all paternalists claim to do. And since the only way Negroes can survive (which they cannot do, unfortunately, on love alone) is with the support of the group, they are wisely wary and stay away.

A white writer tried recently to explain that the reason for the relatively few Negro hippies is that Negroes have built up a "super cool" that cracks under LSD and makes them have a "bad trip." What this writer doesn't guess is that Negroes are needing drugs less than ever these days for any kind of trip. While the hippies are "tripping," Negroes are going after power, which is so much more important to their survival and their children's survival than LSD and pot.

Everyone would be surprised if the Israelis ignored the Arabs and took up "tripping" and pot smoking. In this country we are the Israelis. Everybody who can do so would like to forget this, of course. But for us to forget it for a minute would be fatal. "We Shall Overcome" is just a song to most Americans, *but we must do it.* Or die.

What good was the Civil Rights Movement? If it had just given this country Dr. King, a leader of conscience, for once in our lifetime, it would have been enough. If it had just taken black eyes off white television stories, it would have been enough. If it had fed one starving child, it would have been enough.

If the Civil Rights Movement is "dead," and if it gave us nothing else, it gave us each other forever. It gave some of us bread, some of us shelter, some of us knowledge and pride, all of us comfort. It gave us our children, our husbands, our brothers, our fathers, as men reborn and with a purpose for living. It broke the pattern of black servitude in this country. It shattered the phony "promise" of white soap operas that sucked away so many pitiful lives, It gave us history and men far greater than Presidents. It gave us heroes, selfless men of courage and strength, for our little boys and girls to follow. It gave us hope for tomorrow. It called us to life.

Because we live, it can never die.

The Perils of Indifference
Elie Wiesel

Elie Wiesel (1928–) was born in the village of Sighet in Romania to a religious Jewish family. In 1944 his life changed when his family was deported by the Nazis to Auschwitz, where his father died in 1945. After the camp was liberated by the Allied forces, Wiesel spent a few years in a French orphanage. In 1948 he entered the Sorbonne and began writing for the newspaper L'arche. *In 1954 he made the decision to write about the Holocaust, which led to the publication of his first book,* Night *(1958), followed by* Jews of Silence *(1966). In 1963 he became a U.S. citizen. In 1978 he was appointed chair of the Presidential Commission on the Holocaust, which led to the American memorial monument to the victims of Nazi oppression during World War II. In 1985 Wiesel received the Congressional Gold Medal of Achievement. The following year he received the Nobel Peace Prize. He has written numerous books dealing with the Holocaust, hatred, racism, genocide, and faith, including* Sages and Dreamers *(1991), and his memoir* All Rivers Run to the Sea *(1995). In the following speech he addresses Congress and the President about the need for vigilance in the face of evil.*

1   Mr. President, Mrs. Clinton, members of Congress, Ambassador Holbrooke, Excellencies, friends:
      Fifty-four years ago to the day, a young Jewish boy from a small town in the Carpathian Mountains woke up, not far from Goethe's

beloved Weimar, in a place of eternal infamy called Buchenwald. He was finally free, but there was no joy in his heart. He thought there never would be again. Liberated a day earlier by American soldiers, he remembers their rage at what they saw. And even if he lives to be a very old man, he will always be grateful to them for that rage, and also for their compassion. Though he did not understand their language, their eyes told him what he needed to know—that they, too, would remember, and bear witness.

And now, I stand before you, Mr. President—Commander-in-Chief of the army that freed me, and tens of thousands of others—and I am filled with a profound and abiding gratitude to the American people. Gratitude is a word that I cherish. Gratitude is what defines the humanity of the human being. And I am grateful to you, Hillary, or Mrs. Clinton, for what you said, and for what you are doing for children in the world, for the homeless, for the victims of injustice, the victims of destiny and society. And I thank all of you for being here.

We are on the threshold of a new century, a new millennium. What will the legacy of this vanishing century be? How will it be remembered in the new millennium? Surely it will be judged, and judged severely, in both moral and metaphysical terms. These failures have cast a dark shadow over humanity: two World Wars, countless civil wars, the senseless chain of assassinations (Gandhi, the Kennedys, Martin Luther King, Sadat, Rabin), bloodbaths in Cambodia and Nigeria, India and Pakistan, Ireland and Rwanda, Eritrea and Ethiopia, Sarajevo and Kosovo; the inhumanity in the gulag and the tragedy of Hiroshima. And, on a different level, of course, Auschwitz and Treblinka. So much violence; so much indifference.

5   What is indifference? Etymologically, the word means "no difference." A strange and unnatural state in which the lines blur between light and darkness, dusk and dawn, crime and punishment, cruelty and compassion, good and evil. What are its courses and inescapable consequences? Is it a philosophy? Is there a philosophy of indifference conceivable? Can one possibly view indifference as a virtue? Is it necessary at times to practice it simply to keep one's sanity, live normally, enjoy a fine meal and a glass of wine, as the world around us experiences harrowing upheavals?

Of course, indifference can be tempting—more than that, seductive. It is so much easier to look away from victims. It is so much easier to avoid such rude interruptions to our work, our dreams, our hopes.

It is, after all, awkward, troublesome, to be involved in another person's pain and despair. Yet, for the person who is indifferent, his or her neighbor are of no consequence. And, therefore, their lives are meaningless. Their hidden or even visible anguish is of no interest. Indifference reduces the Other to an abstraction.

Over there, behind the black gates of Auschwitz, the most tragic of all prisoners were the "Muselmanner," as they were called. Wrapped in their torn blankets, they would sit or lie on the ground, staring vacantly into space, unaware of who or where they were— strangers to their surroundings. They no longer felt pain, hunger, thirst. They feared nothing. They felt nothing. They were dead and did not know it.

Rooted in our tradition, some of us felt that to be abandoned by humanity then was not the ultimate. We felt that to be abandoned by God was worse than to be punished by Him. Better an unjust God than an indifferent one. For us to be ignored by God was a harsher punishment than to be a victim of His anger. Man can live far from God—not outside God. God is wherever we are. Even in suffering? Even in suffering.

In a way, to be indifferent to that suffering is what makes the human being inhuman. Indifference, after all, is more dangerous than anger and hatred. Anger can at times be creative. One writes a great poem, a great symphony. One does something special for the sake of humanity because one is angry at the injustice that one witnesses. But indifference is never creative. Even hatred at times may elicit a response. You fight it. You denounce it. You disarm it.

Indifference elicits no response. Indifference is not a response. In- difference is not a beginning; it is an end. And, therefore, indifference is always the friend of the enemy, for it benefits the aggressor—never his victim, whose pain is magnified when he or she feels forgotten. The political prisoner in his cell, the hungry children, the homeless refugees—not to respond to their plight, not to relieve their solitude by offering them a spark of hope is to exile them from human mem- ory. And in denying their humanity, we betray our own.

Indifference, then, is not only a sin, it is a punishment.

And this is one of the most important lessons of this outgoing century's wide-ranging experiments in good and evil.

In the place that I come from, society was composed of three simple categories: the killers, the victims, and the bystanders. During the darkest of times, inside the ghettoes and death camps—and I'm glad that Mrs. Clinton mentioned that we are now commemorating that event, that period, that we are now in the Days of Remembrance—but then, we felt abandoned, forgotten. All of us did.

And our only miserable consolation was that we believed that Auschwitz and Treblinka were closely guarded secrets; that the leaders of the free world did not know what was going on behind those black gates and barbed wire; that they had no knowledge of the war against the Jews that Hitler's armies and their accomplices waged as part of the war against the Allies. If they knew, we thought, surely those leaders would have moved heaven and earth to intervene. They would have spoken out with great outrage and conviction. They would have bombed the railways leading to Birkenau, just the railways, just once.

15   And now we knew, we learned, we discovered that the Pentagon   15
knew, the State Department knew. And the illustrious occupant of the White House then, who was a great leader—and I say it with some anguish and pain, because, today is exactly 54 years marking his death—Franklin Delano Roosevelt died on April the 12th, 1945. So he is very much present to me and to us. No doubt, he was a great leader. He mobilized the American people and the world, going into battle, bringing hundreds and thousands of valiant and brave soldiers in America to fight fascism, to fight dictatorship, to fight Hitler. And so many of the young people fell in battle. And, nevertheless, his image in Jewish history—I must say it—his image in Jewish history is flawed.

The depressing tale of the *St. Louis* is a case in point. Sixty years ago, its human cargo—nearly 1,000 Jews—was turned back to Nazi Germany. And that happened after the Kristallnacht, after the first state sponsored pogrom, with hundreds of Jewish shops destroyed, synagogues burned, thousands of people put in concentration camps. And that ship, which was already in the shores of the United States, was sent back. I don't understand. Roosevelt was a good man, with a heart. He understood those who needed help. Why didn't he allow these refugees to disembark? A thousand people—in America, the great country, the greatest democracy, the most generous of all new nations in modern history. What happened? I don't understand. Why the indifference, on the highest level, to the suffering of the victims?

But then, there were human beings who were sensitive to our tragedy. Those non-Jews, those Christians, that we call the "Righteous Gentiles," whose selfless acts of heroism saved the honor of their faith. Why were they so few? Why was there a greater effort to save SS murderers after the war than to save their victims during the war? Why did some of America's largest corporations continue to do business with Hitler's Germany until 1942? It has been suggested, and it was documented, that the Wehrmacht could not have conducted its invasion of France without oil obtained from American sources. How is one to explain their indifference?

And yet, my friends, good things have also happened in this traumatic century: the defeat of Nazism, the collapse of communism, the rebirth of Israel on its ancestral soil, the demise of apartheid, Israel's peace treaty with Egypt, the peace accord in Ireland. And let us remember the meeting, filled with drama and emotion, between Rabin and Arafat that you, Mr. President, convened in this very place. I was here and I will never forget it.

And then, of course, the joint decision of the United States and NATO to intervene in Kosovo and save those victims, those refugees, those who were uprooted by a man, whom I believe that because of his crimes, should be charged with crimes against humanity.

But this time, the world was not silent. This time, we do respond. This time, we intervene.

Does it mean that we have learned from the past? Does it mean that society has changed? Has the human being become less indifferent and more human? Have we really learned from our experiences? Are we less insensitive to the plight of victims of ethnic cleansing and other forms of injustices in places near and far? Is today's justified intervention in Kosovo, led by you, Mr. President, a lasting warning that never again will the deportation, the terrorization of children and their parents, be allowed anywhere in the world? Will it discourage other dictators in other lands to do the same?

What about the children? Oh, we see them on television, we read about them in the papers, and we do so with a broken heart. Their fate is always the most tragic, inevitably. When adults wage war, children perish. We see their faces, their eyes. Do we hear their pleas? Do we feel their pain, their agony? Every minute one of them dies of disease, violence, famine.

Some of them—so many of them—could be saved.

And so, once again, I think of the young Jewish boy from the Carpathian Mountains. He has accompanied the old man I have become throughout these years of quest and struggle. And together we walk towards the new millennium, carried by profound fear and extraordinary hope.

Cloning for Medicine

Ian Wilmut

Ian Wilmut (1944–) grew up in Coventry, England, the son of a mathematics teacher and housewife. He earned an honors degree in agricultural science at the University of Nottingham and a Ph.D. from Cambridge University, specializing in methods of deep-freeze preservation of boar semen. Wilmut completed other scientific work, on deep-freeze techniques with animal embryos and on the causes of prenatal death in sheep and pigs, before turning to his highly publicized work in cloning. He and his team of scientists at the Roslin Institute near Edinburgh, Scotland announced the birth of Dolly—the first cloned mammal—in 1997 and generated a controversy that continues to spark heated ethical debate. In this article, he presents a "popularized" discussion of work that is discussed in highly technical fashion elsewhere. Note that as he presents the technical information in a readable way, he includes musings on the ethical questions that scientists are sometimes assumed to ignore.

1   In the summer of 1995 the birth of two lambs at my institution, the Roslin Institute near Edinburgh in Midlothian, Scotland, heralded what many scientists believe will be a period of revolutionary opportunities in biology and medicine. Megan and Morag, both carried to term by a surrogate mother, were not produced from the union of a sperm and an egg. Rather their genetic material came from cultured cells originally derived from a nine-day-old embryo. That made Megan and Morag genetic copies, or clones, of the embryo.

"Cloning for Medicine" by Ian Wilmut, published in *Scientific American*, December 1998.

Before the arrival of the lambs, researchers had already learned how to produce sheep, cattle and other animals by genetically copying cells painstakingly isolated from early-stage embryos. Our work promised to make cloning vastly more practical, because cultured cells are relatively easy to work with. Megan and Morag proved that even though such cells are partially specialized, or differentiated, they can be genetically reprogrammed to function like those in an early embryo. Most biologists had believed that this would be impossible.

We went on to clone animals from cultured cells taken from a 26-day-old fetus and from a mature ewe. The ewe's cells gave rise to Dolly, the first mammal to be cloned from an adult. Our announcement of Dolly's birth in February 1997 attracted enormous press interest, perhaps because Dolly drew attention to the theoretical possibility of cloning humans. This is an outcome I hope never comes to pass. But the ability to make clones from cultured cells derived from easily obtained tissue should bring numerous practical benefits in animal husbandry and medical science, as well as answer critical biological questions.

How to Clone

Cloning is based on nuclear transfer, the same technique scientists have used for some years to copy animals from embryonic cells. Nuclear transfer involves the use of two cells. The recipient cell is normally an unfertilized egg taken from an animal soon after ovulation. Such eggs are poised to begin developing once they are appropriately stimulated. The donor cell is the one to be copied. A researcher working under a high-power microscope holds the recipient egg cell by suction on the end of a fine pipette and uses an extremely fine micropipette to suck out the chromosomes, sausage-shaped bodies that incorporate the cell's DNA. (At this stage, chromosomes are not enclosed in a distinct nucleus.) Then, typically, the donor cell, complete with its nucleus, is fused with the recipient egg. Some fused cells start to develop like a normal embryo and produce offspring if implanted into the uterus of a surrogate mother.

5   In our experiments with cultured cells, we took special measures   5
to make the donor and recipient cells compatible. In particular, we tried to coordinate the cycles of duplication of DNA and those of the production of messenger RNA, a molecule that is copied from DNA

and guides the manufacture of proteins. We chose to use donor cells whose DNA was not being duplicated at the time of the transfer. To arrange this, we worked with cells that we forced to become quiescent by reducing the concentration of nutrients in their culture medium. In addition, we delivered pulses of electric current to the egg after the transfer, to encourage the cells to fuse and to mimic the stimulation normally provided by a sperm.

After the birth of Megan and Morag demonstrated that we could produce viable offspring from embryo-derived cultures, we filed for patents and started experiments to see whether offspring could be produced from more completely differentiated cultured cells. Working in collaboration with PPL Therapeutics, also near Edinburgh, we tested fetal fibroblasts (common cells found in connective tissue) and cells taken from the udder of a ewe that was three and a half months pregnant. We selected a pregnant adult because mammary cells grow vigorously at this stage of pregnancy, indicating that they might do well in culture. Moreover, they have stable chromosomes, suggesting that they retain all their genetic information. The successful cloning of Dolly from the mammary-derived culture and of other lambs from the cultured fibroblasts showed that the Roslin protocol was robust and repeatable.

All the cloned offspring in our experiments looked, as expected, like the breed of sheep that donated the originating nucleus, rather than like their surrogate mothers or the egg donors. Genetic tests prove beyond doubt that Dolly is indeed a clone of an adult. It is most likely that she was derived from a fully differentiated mammary cell, although it is impossible to be certain because the culture also contained some less differentiated cells found in small numbers in the mammary gland. Other laboratories have since used an essentially similar technique to create healthy clones of cattle and mice from cultured cells, including ones from nonpregnant animals.

Although cloning by nuclear transfer is repeatable, it has limitations. Some cloned cattle and sheep are unusually large, but this effect has also been seen when embryos are simply cultured before gestation. Perhaps more important, nuclear transfer is not yet efficient. John B. Gurdon, now at the University of Cambridge, found in nuclear-transfer experiments with frogs almost 30 years ago that the number of embryos surviving to become tadpoles was smaller when donor cells were taken from animals at a more advanced developmental stage. Our first results with mammals showed a similar pattern. All the cloning studies described so far show a consistent pattern of deaths during embryonic and fetal development, with laboratories reporting only 1 to 2 percent of embryos surviving to become live offspring. Sadly, even some clones that survive through birth die shortly afterward.

Clones with a Difference

The cause of these losses remains unknown, but it may reflect the complexity of the genetic reprogramming needed if a healthy offspring is to be born. If even one gene inappropriately expresses or fails to express a crucial protein at a sensitive point, the result might be fatal. Yet reprogramming might involve regulating thousands of genes in a process that could involve some randomness. Technical improvements, such as the use of different donor cells, might reduce the toll.

The ability to produce offspring from cultured cells opens up relatively easy ways to make genetically modified, or transgenic, animals. Such animals are important for research and can produce medically valuable human proteins.

The standard technique for making transgenic animals is painfully slow and inefficient. It entails microinjecting a genetic construct—a DNA sequence incorporating a desired gene—into a large number of fertilized eggs. A few of them take up the introduced DNA so that the resulting offspring express it. These animals are then bred to pass on the construct [see "Transgenic Livestock as Drug Factories," by William H. Velander, Henryk Lubon and William N. Drohan; SCIENTIFIC AMERICAN, January 1997].

In contrast, a simple chemical treatment can persuade cultured cells to take up a DNA construct. If these cells are then used as donors for nuclear transfer, the resulting cloned offspring will all carry the construct. The Roslin Institute and PPL Therapeutics have already used this approach to produce transgenic animals more efficiently than is possible with microinjection.

We have incorporated into sheep the gene for human factor IX, a blood-clotting protein used to treat hemophilia B. In this experiment we transferred an antibiotic-resistance gene to the donor cells along with the factor IX gene, so that by adding a toxic dose of the antibiotic neomycin to the culture, we could kill cells that had failed to take up the added DNA. Yet despite this genetic disruption, the proportion of embryos that developed to term after nuclear transfer was in line with our previous results.

The first transgenic sheep produced this way, Polly, was born in the summer of 1997. Polly and other transgenic clones secrete the human protein in their milk. These observations suggest that once techniques for the retrieval of egg cells in different species have been perfected, cloning will make it possible to introduce precise genetic changes into any mammal and to create multiple individuals bearing the alteration.

15 Cultures of mammary gland cells might have a particular advantage as donor material. Until recently, the only practical way to assess whether a DNA construct would cause a protein to be secreted in milk was to transfer it into female mice, then test their milk. It should be possible, however, to test mammary cells in culture directly. That will speed up the process of finding good constructs and cells that have incorporated them so as to give efficient secretion of the protein.

Cloning offers many other possibilities. One is the generation of genetically modified animal organs that are suitable for transplantation into humans. At present, thousand of patients die every year before a replacement heart, liver or kidney becomes available. A normal pig organ would be rapidly destroyed by a "hyperacute" immune reaction if transplanted into a human. This reaction is triggered by proteins on the pig cells that have been modified by an enzyme called alpha-galactosyl transferase. It stands to reason, then, that an organ from a pig that has been genetically altered so that it lacks this enzyme might be well tolerated if doctors gave the recipient drugs to suppress other, less extreme immune reactions.

Another promising area is the rapid production of large animals carrying genetic defects that mimic human illnesses, such as cystic fibrosis. Although mice have provided some information, mice and humans have different genes for cystic fibrosis. Sheep are expected to be more valuable for research into this condition, because their lungs resemble those of humans. Moreover, because sheep live for years, scientists can evaluate their long-term responses to treatments.

Creating animals with genetic defects raises challenging ethical questions. But it seems clear that society does in the main support research on animals, provided that the illnesses being studied are serious ones and that efforts are made to avoid unnecessary suffering.

The power to make animals with a precisely engineered genetic constitution could also be employed more directly in cell-based therapies for important illnesses, including Parkinson's disease, diabetes and muscular dystrophy. None of these conditions currently has any fully effective treatment. In each, some pathological process damages specific cell populations, which are unable to repair or replace themselves. Several novel approaches are now being explored that would provide new cells—ones taken from the patient and cultured, donated by other humans or taken from animals.

To be useful, transferred cells must be incapable of transmitting new disease and must match the patient's physiological need closely. Any immune response they produce must be manageable. Cloned animals with precise genetic modifications that minimize the human immune response might constitute a plentiful supply of suitable cells. Animals might even produce cells with special properties, although any modifications would risk a stronger immune reaction.

Cloning could also be a way to produce herds of cattle that lack the prion protein gene. This gene makes cattle susceptible to infection with prions, agents that cause bovine spongiform encephalitis (BSE), or mad cow disease. Because many medicines contain gelatin or other products derived from cattle, health officials are concerned that prions from infected animals could infect patients. Cloning could create herds that, lacking the prion protein gene, would be a source of ingredients for certifiable prion-free medicines.

The technique might in addition curtail the transmission of genetic disease. Many scientists are now working on therapies that would supplement or replace defective genes in cells, but even successfully treated patients will still pass on defective genes to their offspring. If a couple was willing to produce an embryo that could be treated by advanced forms of gene therapy, nuclei from modified embryonic cells could be transferred to eggs to create children who would be entirely free of a given disease.

Some of the most ambitious medical projects now being considered envision the production of universal human donor cells. Scientists know how to isolate from very early mouse embryos undifferentiated stem cells, which can contribute to all the different tissues of the adult. Equivalent cells can be obtained for some other species, and humans are probably no exception. Scientists are learning how to differentiate stem cells in culture, so it may be possible to manufacture cells to repair or replace tissue damaged by illness.

Making Human Stem Cells

Stem cells matched to an individual patient could be made by creating an embryo by nuclear transfer just for that purpose, using one of the patient's cells as the donor and a human egg as the recipient. The embryo would be allowed to develop only to the stage needed to separate and culture stem cells from it. At that point, an embryo has only a few hundred cells, and they have not started to differentiate. In particular, the nervous system has not begun to develop, so the embryo has no means of feeling pain or sensing the environment. Embryo-derived cells might be used to treat a variety of serious diseases caused by damage to cells, perhaps including AIDS as well as Parkinson's, muscular dystrophy and diabetes.

25 Scenarios that involve growing human embryos for their cells are 25 deeply disturbing to some people, because embryos have the potential to become people. The views of those who consider life sacred from conception should be respected, but I suggest a contrasting view. The embryo is a cluster of cells that does not become a sentient being until much later in development, so it is not yet a person. In the U.K., the Human Genetics Advisory Commission has initiated a major public consultation to assess attitudes toward this use of cloning.

Creating an embryo to treat a specific patient is likely to be an expensive proposition, so it might be more practical to establish permanent, stable human embryonic stem-cell lines from cloned embryos. Cells could then be differentiated as needed. Implanted cells derived this way would not be genetically perfect matches, but the immune reaction would probably be controllable. In the longer term, scientists might be able to develop methods for manufacturing genetically matched stem cells for a patient by "dedifferentiating" them directly, without having to utilize an embryo to do it.

Several commentators and scientists have suggested that it might in some cases be ethically acceptable to clone existing people. One scenario envisages generating a replacement for a dying relative. All such possibilities, however, raise the concern that the clone would be treated as less than a complete individual, because he or she would likely be subjected to limitations and expectations based on the family's knowledge of the genetic "twin." Those expectations might be false, because human personality is only partly determined by genes. The clone of an extrovert could have a quite different demeanor. Clones of athletes, movie stars, entrepreneurs or scientists might well choose different careers because of chance events in early life.

Some pontificators have also put forward the notion that couples in which one member is infertile might choose to make a copy of one or the other partner. But society ought to be concerned that a couple might not treat naturally a child who is a copy of just one of them. Because other methods are available for the treatment of all known types of infertility, conventional therapeutic avenues seem more appropriate. None of the suggested uses of cloning for making copies of existing people is ethically acceptable to my way of thinking, because they are not in the interests of the resulting child. It should go without saying that I strongly oppose allowing cloned human embryos to develop so that they can be tissue donors.

It nonetheless seems clear that cloning from cultured cells will offer important medical opportunities. Predictions about new technologies are often wrong: societal attitudes change; unexpected developments occur. Time will tell. But biomedical researchers probing the potential of cloning now have a full agenda.

When We Were Very Young: Archaeologists Uncover Traces of Childhood

Samuel M. Wilson

Samuel Wilson (1956–) teaches in the Anthropology De-partment at the University of Texas at Austin. An archae-ologist and historical anthropologist, he studies the prehistory of the Caribbean where he has carried out re-search on the small island of Nevis for several years. His books include The Emperor's Giraffe and Other Stories of Culture Contact *(1999) and* The Aboriginal People of the Caribbean *(1997). He publishes widely in acade-mic journals and also writes frequent columns for* Natural History *magazine, of which the following is a recent rep-resentative. This essay illustrates his interest in what arti-facts from former inhabitants can tell us about the world we live in today.*

1   Among the artifacts left behind by the Iroquois people who lived   1
in southern Ontario in late prehistoric times was a miniature
pot made from a lump of clay. A tiny thumb or finger, too
small to be a grown-up's, had shaped the inside of the pot, leaving the
impression of a tiny fingernail. Archaeologists have also recovered
small clay versions of smoking pipes, impractical because they lack
holes. These were children's toys—small and ephemeral, easily overlooked in the refuse of the past. Just as male scholars were typically

"When We Were Very Young: Archaeologists Uncover Traces of Childhood," by
Samuel M. Wilson, reprinted from *Natural History*, November 1999, pp. 58–61.

once blind to the presence of women in the archaeological record, grown-up archaeologists often don't look for children in the past.

The inhabitants of Cerén, a Mayan site in western El Salvador, fled in A.D. 595, leaving everything in place—crops in the field, pots of food, their most cherished goods. A nearby volcanic eruption covered the whole settlement with ash. Carefully excavated by archaeologist Payson Sheets and his colleagues, this site gives us a remarkable glimpse of life in the Mayan Classic period. One of the houses at Cerén contained a complete inventory of the artifacts of everyday life. Next to an interior doorway, just (in my view) where a kid would sit, was a diminutive pot and a scattering of twenty small shards of pottery. Reporting on these finds, Christian J. Zier remarks (with due scholarly caution) that they "may be the playthings of a child and could indicate that this is a child's room. This statement is tentative at best and will remain so."

In my own excavations in North America and the Caribbean, I have found odds and ends that did not fall into any obvious category: a collection of colored rocks, a few fossilized casts of the inside of shellfish, a half-burned lump of clay with a hole in it, poorly made little arrowheads. Not until I had children and saw their piles of treasure did the finds start to make sense. At times I have come close to throwing away something my children prized, thinking it was a piece of junk, and as an archaeologist I may have done just that with the artifacts of children who lived long ago.

Various unusual things are relegated to the category of "enigmatic finds" and get stuck at the end of archaeological reports. Going over the artifacts from the Israeli site of Tell Jemmeh, Smithsonian archaeologist Gus Van Beek noticed some rounded disks an inch or two across. They were made from pieces of broken pottery and had two holes drilled through them. Earlier archaeologists had taken them for buttons or had simply described them as "perforated disks." But Van Beek saw in them a "buzz," a simple toy he recalled from childhood. To play, you loop string through the two holes and hold one end of the loop in each hand. When the string is wound up and you pull the two ends of the loop apart, the disk in the middle will spin and make a buzzing sound. Van Beek identified archaeological examples of this toy at other sites in the Near East, as well as in Pakistan, India, China, Japan, and Korea. Buzzes have been found in the sites of Native American peoples in North and South America, and even in the remains of British army camps from the Revolutionary War.

5   Children's toys today include many low-tech items that are com-   5
mon around the world. Rattles, whistles, bull-roarers (a slat of wood
tied to the end of a thong and whirled around the head), balls, tops,
and buzzes are fun to play with by themselves. There are also the
pieces and markers that go along with games. The most common
kinds of toys, however, allow children to do things that grownups do,
but on a miniature scale: small versions of hunting and fishing gear,
model boats, baskets, dolls, pots, and plates.

In his *Laws*, Plato argued that "the man who is to make a good
builder must play at building toy houses, and to make a good farmer
he must play at tilling land; and those who are rearing them must provide each child with toy tools modeled on real ones" (translation by
R. G. Bury). I wonder whether Plato ever gave a boy or girl an "educational" toy and then watched as the child made a temple to Diony-
sus out of the box it came in.

In the dry shelters of the Lower Pecos region on the Texas-Mex-
ico border, normally perishable artifacts made of wood, fiber, and
leather have been well preserved. Archaeologist Ken Brown studied
more than a hundred such artifacts, identifying child-size versions of
digging sticks, wood and fiber snares, and netted backpack frames. He
sees these as tools for teaching children how to behave and survive in
the world and, perhaps, even make a small contribution to the group's
quest for food.

In 1879 a famine wiped out the village of Kukulik on Saint
Lawrence Island, south of the Bering Strait between Alaska and
Siberia. Excavation of the site in the 1930s brought to light an extraordinary range of artifacts made of wood, bone, and other materials.
Among the objects were dolls, miniature kayaks, and small carved
bears and seals. Similarly, the prehistoric Thule of Canada and Green-
land left behind numerous dolls and miniatures of adult artifacts. In
a recent study, archaeologist Robert W. Park, of the University of Wa-
terloo, Ontario, compared these to the traditional toys of the Inuit,
the Thule's descendants.

A great many archaeologists are justifiably wary of viewing any
given miniature artifact as a plaything. Miniature versions of everyday objects can have potent ritual significance. An exhibit at the
Idaho State Historical Museum in Boise ("Backtracking: Ancient Art
of Southern Idaho") included a number of human figurines identified
as possible dolls. Some Shoshone people who visited the exhibit, de-

scendants of makers of the artifacts, saw them as the powerful representations of the supernatural character Nu'-numbi and perhaps taken from a shaman's paraphernalia.

Probably the most famous of prehistoric artifacts that are thought to be toys are the wheeled dogs and other animals from pre-Conquest tombs in Mexico. They have attracted a lot of attention because they show that ancient Mesoamericans understood the principle of the wheel—even though they put it to no practical application, perhaps because they lacked draft animals and lived in mountainous terrain. Archaeologist Francisco Javier Hernandez argued in an extensive study that these were ritual objects (of now unknown meaning) made to be used in burials. This is probably also the case with the elaborate dioramas buried with Egyptian royalty in the third and fourth millennia B.C., in which miniature figures carried the things people would need in the next world.

The idea that artifacts we identify as toys might once have had deeper meanings connects with the influential argument put forward by French historian Philippe Ariès in his 1960 classic, *Centuries of Childhood*. He contended that the Western conception of childhood as a distinct stage of human development and as a protected time of make-believe and play has emerged only in the past few centuries.

A child's early years would indeed have been different in the past, if only because mortality rates and demographics were generally different. In Roman society, for instance, infant mortality may have been as high as one-third of live births, and half the population was under the age of twenty. Some have argued that in prehistory, and even in recent centuries, parents showed relative indifference toward younger children precisely because so few survived. But burials of children with grave goods show that children were cherished as early as Upper Paleolithic times. At the Russian site of Sungir, for example, a man, a girl, and a boy were buried together with ivory spears, stone tools, small animal carvings, and thousands of beads carved from the tusks of mammoths. The grave dates to about 23,000 years ago. Such deliberate burials became more common during the Upper Paleolithic, and through them, children become more visible in the archaeological record.

Although Upper Paleolithic people may not have considered childhood to be a carefree and innocent stage of life, they apparently did distinguish it from adulthood and marked the transition through ritual. Some of the painted caves of northern Spain and southwestern France, including the recently discovered caves of the Ardèche in France, preserve footprints of young people. And the cavern called Gargas, in the Pyrenees, has hundreds of handprints stenciled onto the walls—some, judging by their size, the hands of adolescents or children. These traces may have been left by young people at the time of their initiation into adulthood.

An awareness of childhood can contribute to the more general effort, current in archaeology, to look for individuals in prehistory, to trace families and lineages through time and discover what motivated people to behave the way they did. Formerly, archaeologists tended to view past societies as a composite of integrated subsystems—economy, demography, politics, social organization, and so on. By focusing more on individuals and the choices they confronted, we come face to face with the concrete agents of change in human prehistory. In doing so, perhaps we shall even discover that children were among their societies' most important innovators.

A Vindication of the Rights of Woman

Mary Wollstonecraft

Mary Wollstonecraft (1759–1797) was born in London, England. Wollstonecraft worked as a teacher, governess, translator, and literary advisor. A very early feminist, she wrote Thoughts on the Education of Daughters *(1787) and* A Vindication of the Rights of Women *(1792). In this essay, Wollstonecraft argues that providing women with the opportunity to improve their minds is in the best interests of both men and women.*

1

M y own sex, I hope, will excuse me, if I treat them like rational creatures, instead of flattering their *fascinating* graces, and viewing them as if they were in a state of perpetual childhood, unable to stand alone. I earnestly wish to point out in what true dignity and human happiness consists—I wish to persuade women to endeavor to acquire strength, both of mind and body, and to convince them that the soft phrases, susceptibility of heart, delicacy of sentiment, and refinement of taste, are almost synonymous with epithets of weakness, and that those beings who are only the objects of pity and that kind of love, which has been termed its sister, will soon become objects of contempt.

Dismissing, then, those pretty feminine phrases, which the men condescendingly use to soften our slavish dependence, and despising that weak elegance of mind, exquisite sensibility, and sweet docility of manners, supposed to be the sexual characteristics of the weaker vessel, I wish to show that elegance is inferior to virtue, that the first object of laudable ambition is to obtain a character as a human being, regardless of the distinction of sex; and that secondary views should be brought to this simple touchstone.

This is a rough sketch of my plan; and should I express my conviction with the energetic emotions that I feel whenever I think of the subject, the dictates of experience and reflection will be felt by some of my readers. Animated by this important object, I shall disdain to cull my phrases or polish my style; I aim at being useful, and sincerity will render me unaffected; for, wishing rather to persuade by the force of my arguments, than dazzle by the elegance of my language, I shall not waste my time in rounding periods, or in fabricating the turgid bombast of artificial feelings, which, coming from the head, never reach the heart. I shall be employed about things, not words! and, anxious to render my sex more respectable members of society, I shall try to avoid that flowery diction which has slided from essays into novels, and from novels into familiar letters and conversation.

These pretty superlatives, dropping glibly from the tongue, vitiate the taste, and create a kind of sickly delicacy that runs away from simple unadorned truth; and a deluge of false sentiments and overstretched feelings, stifling the natural emotions of the heart, render the domestic pleasures insipid, that ought to sweeten the exercise of those severe duties, which educate a rational and immortal being for a nobler field of action.

5 The education of women has, of late, been more attended to than 5 formerly; yet they are still reckoned a frivolous sex, and ridiculed or pitied by the writers who endeavor by satire or instruction to improve them. It is acknowledged that they spend many of the first years of their lives in acquiring a smattering of accomplishments; meanwhile strength of body and mind are sacrificed to libertine notions of beauty, to the desire of establishing themselves—the only way women can rise in the world—by marriage. And this desire making mere animals of them, when they marry they act as such children may be expected to act—they dress; they paint, and nickname God's creatures. Surely these weak beings are only fit for a seraglio!—Can they be expected to govern a family with judgment, or take care of the poor babes whom they bring into the world?

If then it can be fairly deduced from the present conduct of the sex, from the prevalent fondness for pleasure which takes place of ambition, and those nobler passions that open and enlarge the soul; that the instruction which women have hitherto received has only tended, with the constitution of civil society, to render them insignificant objects of desire—mere propagators of fools!—if it can be proved that in aiming to accomplish them, without cultivating their understandings, they are taken out of their sphere of duties, and made ridiculous and useless when the short-lived bloom of beauty is over, I presume that *rational* men will excuse me for endeavoring to persuade them to become more masculine and respectable.

Indeed the word masculine is only a bugbear: there is little reason to fear that women will acquire too much courage or fortitude; for their apparent inferiority with respect to bodily strength, must render them, in some degree, dependent on men in the various relations of life; but why should it be increased by prejudices that give a sex to virtue, and confound simple truths with sensual reveries?

Women are, in fact, so much degraded by mistaken notions of female excellence, that I do not mean to add a paradox when I assert, that this artificial weakness produces a propensity to tyrannize, and gives birth to cunning, the natural opponent of strength, which leads them to play off those contemptible infantine airs that undermine esteem even whilst they excite desire. Let men become more chaste and modest, and if women do not grow wiser in the same ratio, it will be clear that they have weaker understandings. It seems scarcely necessary to say, that I now speak of the sex in general. Many individuals have more sense than their male relatives; and, as nothing preponderates where there is a constant struggle for an equilibrium, without it has naturally more gravity, some women govern their husbands without degrading themselves, because intellect will always govern.

The Act of Writing: One Man's Method

William Zinsser

William Zinsser (1922–) was born in New York City. A graduate of Princeton University (1944), Zinsser has worked as a feature and editorial writer, drama editor, and film critic for the New York Herald Tribune; *a columnist for* Life, Look, *and the* New York Times; *an editor for the Book-of-the-Month Club; and an English instructor at Yale University. Zinsser's books include* Pop Goes America *(1963),* On Writing Well: An Informal Guide to Writing Nonfiction *(1976),* Writing With a Word Processor *(1983),* Writing to Learn *(1988),* Willie and Dwike *(1984), and* Spring Training *(1989). In the following excerpt from* Writing With a Word Processor, *Zinsser explains why a word processor helps him do what he already does well even better: write clearly.*

1 Writing is a deeply personal process, full of mystery and surprise. No two people go about it in exactly the same way. We all have little devices to get us started, or to keep us going, or to remind us of what we think we want to say, and what works for one person may not work for anyone else. The main thing is to get something written—to get the words out of our heads. There is no "right" method. Any method that will do the job is the right method for you.

It helps to remember that writing is hard. Most nonwriters don't know this; they think that writing is a natural function, like breathing, that ought to come easy, and they're puzzled when it doesn't. If you find that writing is hard, it's because it is hard. It's one of the hardest things that people do. Among other reasons, it's hard because it requires thinking. You won't write clearly unless you keep forcing yourself to think clearly. There's no escaping the question that has to be constantly asked: What do I want to say next?

So painful is this task that writers go to remarkable lengths to postpone their daily labor. They sharpen their pencils and change their typewriter ribbon and go out to the store to buy more paper. Now these sacred rituals, as [the computer manuals] would say, have been obsoleted.

When I began writing this book on my word processor I didn't have any idea what would happen. Would I be able to write anything at all? Would it be any good? I was bringing to the machine what I assumed were wholly different ways of thinking about writing. The units massed in front of me looked cold and sterile. Their steady hum reminded me that they were waiting. They seemed to be waiting for information, not for writing. Maybe what I wrote would also be cold and sterile.

5   I was particularly worried about the absence of paper. I knew that 5 I would only be able to see as many lines as the screen would hold—twenty lines. How could I review what I had already written? How could I get a sense of continuity and flow? With paper it was always possible to flick through the preceding pages to see where I was coming from—and where I ought to be going. Without paper I would have no such periodic fix. Would this be a major hardship?

The only way to find out was to find out. I took a last look at my unsharpened pencils and went to work.

My particular hang-up as a writer is that I have to get every paragraph as nearly right as possible before I go on to the next paragraph. I'm somewhat like a bricklayer: I build very slowly, not adding a new row until I feel that the foundation is solid enough to hold up the house. I'm the exact opposite of the writer who dashes off his entire first draft, not caring how sloppy it looks or how badly it's written. His only objective at this early stage is to let his creative motor run the full course at full speed; repairs can always be made later. I envy this writer and would like to have his metabolism. But I'm stuck with the one I've got.

I also care how my writing looks while I'm writing it. The visual arrangement is important to me: the shape of the words, of the sentences, of the paragraphs, of the page. I don't like sentences that are dense with long words, or paragraphs that never end. As I write I want to see the design that my piece will have when the reader sees it in type, and I want that design to have a rhythm and a pace that will invite the reader to keep reading. O.K., so I'm a nut. But I'm not alone; the visual component is important to a large number of people who write.

One hang-up we visual people share is that our copy must be neat. My lifelong writing method, for instance, has gone like this. I put a piece of paper in the typewriter and write the first paragraph. Then I take the paper out and edit what I've written. I mark it up horribly, crossing words out and scribbling new ones in the space between the lines. By this time the paragraph has lost its nature and shape for me as a piece of writing. It's a mishmash of typing and handwriting and arrows and balloons and other directional symbols. So I type a clean copy, incorporating the changes, and then I take that piece of paper out of the typewriter and edit it. It's better, but not much better. I go over it with my pencil again, making more changes, which again make it too messy for me to read critically, so I go back to the typewriter for round three. And round four. Not until I'm reasonably satisfied do I proceed to the next paragraph.

10 This can get pretty tedious, and I have often thought that there 10 must be a better way. Now there is. The word processor is God's gift, or at least science's gift, to the tinkerers and the refiners and the neatness freaks. For me it was obviously the perfect new toy. I began playing on page 1—editing, cutting and revising—and have been on a rewriting high ever since. The burden of the years has been lifted.

Mostly I've been cutting. I would guess that I've cut at least as many words out of this book as the number that remain. Probably half of those words were eliminated because I saw that they were unnecessary— the sentence worked fine without them. This is where the word processor can improve your writing to an extent that you will hardly believe. Learn to recognize what is clutter and to use the DELETE key to prune it out.

How will you know clutter when you see it? Here's a device I used when I was teaching writing at Yale that my students found helpful; it may be a help here. I would put brackets around every component in a student's paper that I didn't think was doing some kind of work. Often it was only one word—for example, the useless preposition that gets appended to so many verbs (order up, free up), or the adverb whose meaning is already in the verb (blare loudly, clench tightly), or the adjective that tells us what we already know (smooth marble, green grass). The brackets might surround the little qualifiers that dilute a writer's authority (a bit, sort of, in a sense), or the countless phrases in which the writer explains what he is about to explain (it might be pointed out, I'm tempted to say). Often my brackets would surround an entire sentence—the sentence that essentially repeats what the previous sentence has said, or tells the reader something that is implicit, or adds a detail that is irrelevant. Most people's writing is littered with phrases that do no new work whatever. Most first drafts, in fact, can be cut by fifty percent without losing anything organic. (Try it; it's a good exercise.)

By bracketing these extra words, instead of crossing them out, I was saying to the student: "I may be wrong, but I think this can go and the meaning of the sentence won't be affected in any way. But *you* decide: read the sentence without the bracketed material and see if it works." In the first half of the term, the students' papers were festooned with my brackets. Whole paragraphs got bracketed. But gradually the students learned to put mental brackets around their many different kinds of clutter, and by the end of the term I was returning papers to them that had hardly any brackets, or none. It was always a satisfying moment. Today many of those students are professional writers. "I still see your brackets," they tell me. "They're following me through life."

You can develop the same eye. Writing is clear and strong to the extent that it has no superfluous parts. (So is art and music and dance and typography and design.) You will really enjoy writing on a word processor when you see your sentences growing in strength, literally before your eyes, as you get rid of the fat. Be thankful for everything that you can throw away.

15   I was struck by how many phrases and sentences I wrote in this 15
book that I later found I didn't need. Many of them hammered home a point that didn't need hammering because it had already been made. This kind of overwriting happens in almost everybody's first draft, and it's perfectly natural—the act of putting down our thoughts makes us garrulous. Luckily, the act of editing follows the act of writing, and this is where the word processor will bail you out. It intercedes at the point where the game can be won or lost. With its help I cut hundreds of unnecessary words and didn't replace them.

Hundreds of others were discarded because I later thought of a better word—one that caught more precisely or more vividly what I was trying to express. Here, again, a word processor encourages you to play. The English language is rich in words that convey an exact shade of meaning. Don't get stuck with a word that's merely good if you can find one that takes the reader by surprise with its color or aptness or quirkiness. Root around in your dictionary of synonyms and find words that are fresh. Throw them up on the screen and see how they look.

Also learn to play with whole sentences. If a sentence strikes you as awkward or ponderous, move your cursor to the space after the period and write a new sentence that you think is better. Maybe you can make it shorter. Or clearer. Maybe you can make it livelier by turning it into a question or otherwise altering its rhythm. Change the passive verbs into active verbs. (Passive verbs are the death of clarity and vigor.) Try writing two or three new versions of the awkward sentence and then compare them, or write a fourth version that combines the best elements of all three. Sentences come in an infinite variety of shapes and sizes. Find one that pleases you. If it's clear, and if it pleases you and expresses who you are, trust it to please other people. Then delete all the versions that aren't as good. Your shiny new sentence will jump into position and the rest of the paragraph will rearrange itself as quickly and neatly as if you had never pulled it apart.

Another goal that the word processor will help you to achieve is unity. No matter how carefully you write each sentence as you assemble a piece of writing, the final product is bound to have some ragged edges. Is the tone consistent throughout? And the point of view? And the pronoun? And the tense? How about the transitions? Do they pull the reader along, or is the piece jerky and disjointed? A good piece of writing should be harmonious from beginning to end in the voice of the writer and the flow of its logic. But the harmony usually requires some last-minute patching.

I've been writing this book by the bricklayer method, slowly and carefully. That's all very well as far as it goes—at the end of every chapter the individual bricks may look fine. But what about the wall? The only way to check your piece for unity is to go over it one more time from start to finish, preferably reading it aloud. See if you have executed all the decisions that you made before you started writing. . . .

20   I mention this [in part] because word processors are going to be   20
widely used by people who need to impart technical information: matters of operating procedure in business and banking, science and

technology, medicine and health, education and government and dozens of other specialized fields. The information will only be helpful if readers can grasp it quickly and easily. If it's muddy they will get discouraged or angry, or both, and will stop reading.

You can avoid this dreaded fate for your message, whatever it is, by making sure that every sentence is a logical sequel to the one that preceded it. One way to approach this goal is to keep your sentences short. A major reason why technical prose becomes so tangled is that the writer tries to make one sentence do too many jobs. It's a natural hazard of the first draft. But the solution is simple: see that every sentence contains only one thought. The reader can accommodate only one idea at a time. Help him by giving him only one idea at a time. Let him understand A before you proceed to B.

In writing this book I was eager to explain the procedures that I had learned about how word processors work, and I would frequently lump several points together in one sentence. Later, editing what I had written, I asked myself if the procedure would be clear to someone who was puzzling through it for the first time—someone who hadn't struggled to figure the procedure out. Often I felt that it wouldn't be clear. I was giving the reader too much. He was being asked to picture himself taking various steps that were single and sequential, and that's how he deserved to get them.

I therefore divided all troublesome long sentences into two short sentences, or even three. It always gave me great pleasure. Not only is it the fastest way for a writer to get out of a quagmire that there seems to be no getting out of; I also like short sentences for their own sake. There's almost no more beautiful sight than a simple declarative sentence. This book is full of simple declarative sentences that have no punctuation and that carry one simple thought. Without a word processor I wouldn't have chopped as many of them down to their proper size, or done it with so little effort. This is one of the main clarifying jobs that your machine can help you to perform, especially if your writing requires you to guide the reader into territory that is new and bewildering.

Not all my experiences, of course, were rosy. The machine had disadvantages as well as blessings. Often, for instance, I missed not being able to see more than twenty lines at a time—to review what I had written earlier. If I wanted to see more lines I had to "scroll" them back into view.

25   But even this wasn't as painful as I had thought it would be. I 25
found that I could hold in my head the gist of what I had written and
didn't need to keep looking at it. Was this need, in fact, still another
writer's hang-up that I could shed? To some extent it was. I discovered,
as I had at so many other points in this journey, that various crutches
I had always assumed I needed were really not necessary. I made a decision to just throw them away and found that I could still function.
The only real hardship occurred when a paragraph broke at the bottom of the screen. This meant that the first lines of the paragraph were
on one page and the rest were on the next page, and I had to keep
flicking the two pages back and forth to read what I was writing. But
again, it wasn't fatal. I learned to live with it and soon took it for
granted as an occupational hazard.

   The story that I've told in this chapter is personal and idiosyn-
cratic: how the word processor helped one writer to write one book.
In many of its details it's everybody's story. All writers have different
methods and psychological needs. . . .